EVIL IN MODERN THOUGHT

AN ALTERNATIVE

HISTORY

OF PHILOSOPHY

EVIL IN MODERN THOUGHT

AN ALTERNATIVE

HISTORY

OF PHILOSOPHY

WITH A NEW PREFACE
BY THE AUTHOR

SUSAN NEIMAN

PRINCETON UNIVERSITY PRESS
PRINCETON AND OXFORD

COPYRIGHT © 2002 BY PRINCETON UNIVERSITY PRESS

Published by
Princeton University Press
41 William Street
Princeton, New Jersey 08540

In the United Kingdom:
Princeton University Press
3 Market Place
Woodstock, Oxfordshire OX20 1SY

All Rights Reserved

Seventh printing, and first paperback printing, with a new
preface, 2004

Paperback ISBN 0-691-11792-6

The cloth edition of this book has been cataloged as follows

Library of Congress Control Number 2002070374

ISBN 0-691-09608-2

British Library Cataloging-in-Publication Data is available

This book has been composed in ITC Garamond Light

Printed on acid-free paper. ∞

pup.princeton.edu

Printed in the United States of America

15   14

ISBN-13: 978-0-691-11792-8 (pbk.)

ISBN-10: 0-691-11792-6 (pbk.)

FOR

BENJAMIN

SHIRAH

LEILA

The great assumption that what has taken place in the world has also done so in conformity with reason—which is what first gives the history of philosophy its true interest—is nothing else than trust in Providence, only in another form.

—Hegel, *Introduction to the Lectures on the History of Philosophy*

CONTENTS

PREFACE TO THE PAPERBACK EDITION

Can a history of thought about evil provide a framework for thinking about the present?

The question posed itself with particular force as I opened one short sharp message after another in mid-September 2001. Friends and colleagues who knew I was finishing a book on this subject wrote to ask: is it another Lisbon earthquake, or not? No less stunned or shaken than any other honest mortal at that moment, I rued whatever I'd done to suggest I had answers others didn't. If Hegel were right that philosophy's wisdom comes with hindsight, the owl of Minerva should take more time before taking wing.

Yet it soon became clear that September 11 was indeed a historical turning point that would change our discussion of evil. As in the central cases discussed in *Evil in Modern Thought*, what shook us to the core was only partly the result of the magnitude of evil that took place in them. Many people yearn for measures of absolute weight. But would we be helped by putting the genocide at Auschwitz at 1.0 on a scale that left the genocide in Cambodia at 0.87—or the other way around? It doesn't take much more than naming such yearnings to point out their hollowness. Comparing genocides, or natural disasters, makes sense only with regard to particular goals: preferably, preventing future ones. Once we are facing evils, trying to measure them is a matter of abstraction at best, political calculation at worst. It makes little sense to call September 11 the most horrible case of terrorism in history, but it was the most spectacular. Al Qaeda's instinct for symbol ensured this much success: a nearly global perception that our ability to navigate the world was infinitely more precarious than it had been the day before. The perception was so wide and swift that for the first time in history not space but time became shorthand. If naming a city—Lisbon or Auschwitz—was enough for earlier ages to record deepest shock and horror, the twenty-first century began by naming a date.

The breathless sense that the ground we depend on has suddenly vanished cannot be predicted. Some earthquakes create it, and some do not. When certain disasters strike, a mixture of reaction and reflection leads us to question our sense of ourselves, of evil, and our vulnerability in the face of it. History arises from a confluence of contingencies—a fact that would occupy many thinkers discussed in this book. It's a fact that means that events which are truly evil are just as truly open to manipulation and distortion. It would be foolish to think that philosophical work could directly affect either terrorism or the worst reactions to it. Political problems demand political solutions. But in creating clarity, philosophy can offer moral orientation that helps sort our reactions to them. It can begin by showing that though September 11 transformed all sorts of political realities, it shaped no new moral reality. On the contrary: most disturbing was the way it combined modern technological structures with old-fashioned moral ones. On the one side there was massive and well-coordinated destruction, and massive and well-coordinated perception of it—at a scale earlier ages couldn't imagine. On the other, there was the sheer and deliberate wish to cause as much death and fear as possible—an image of evil so old-fashioned we couldn't expect it.

Most of us who thought about the nature of evil had come to view it differently. Though few books are apt to draw more fire than Hannah Arendt's *Eichmann in Jerusalem*, few conclusions are in fact more widely accepted. For what Arendt meant in saying that evil may be banal was simply that it need not be demonic. After Auschwitz, at the latest, we learned that the greatest crimes can be committed by people less likely to arouse terror and awe than contempt and disgust. Thoughtlessness can be more dangerous than malice; we are more often threatened by self-serving refusal to see the consequences of conventional actions than by defiant desires for destruction. For whether they're restrained by cowardice or by something nobler, most people refrain from acting those desires out.

What happened on September 11 was hardly the product of mindless agents whose self-serving and self-pitying actions led to evils they never quite intended. On the contrary: the Al Qaeda terrorists knew exactly what they did. Their clear intentions, and thoughtfulness in realizing them, were evident at every turn—down to the pilots who sought lessons in flying planes without learning to land them. Their goals were as perfectly calculated as they were perfectly malicious.

That they were underwritten by an ideology is unimportant; most actions are. The crimes occurred without warning or recourse: no targeting of particular agents, no raising of demands, which arguably mitigate the sheer will to destruction in other acts of terrorism. There was no way but chance to escape these terrorists. Only timing prevented the deaths of the far greater numbers that were originally expected. But the massive fear and havoc that were just as surely intended will be with us for years to come.

Does the presence of this sort of old-fashioned evil cast doubt on the analysis of its more banal and subtle forms? Only for those who believe that evil has an essence which stays constant through its appearances. This book argues that it does not. Our understanding of evil has changed sharply over time. Attempts to capture the forms of evil within a single formula risk becoming one-sided or trivial. Neither Osama bin Laden nor Adolf Eichmann is uniquely paradigmatic, and an account of evil cut solely to fit one or the other will leave out something we ignore at our peril. While both men represent forms that evil can take, neither man exhausts them.

If evil can't be defined in a way that ensures we will recognize it, what's the point of using the concept at all? One answer to this question is a general one. Not knowing what is common to a New England meadow and a Bach cantata doesn't stop you from finding both of them beautiful. This is not to locate beauty in the beholder's eye, but to claim that locating it will be a matter of sharp and careful analysis— not of general concepts but of particular instances. Judging something to be beautiful, and persuading others to share your judgment, requires the ability to describe *that* object with *those* details, with enough discrimination and passion to be singularly moved, and moving. In moral as in aesthetic judgments, what counts is less the way you frame general ideas than the way you connect them with particular experience.

All this may be true and still be unsatisfying. For moral judgments have consequences that aesthetic judgments do not. In recent days, what makes thoughtful people consider abandoning talk about evil aren't metaphysical concerns about relativism but political concerns about distortion. The fact that we have no absolute means to determine when one act is evil, and another merely awful, leaves this very powerful term wide open to manipulation. If we take evil seriously, we have to take it seriously—and consider that some ways of abusing the word can lead to evil themselves. As I write, the Bush administration is busy making use of events that were undeniably evil to further partisan ends judged by much of the world to be a greater threat to a peaceful and just world order than any we have seen in decades. It's not the first time that "evil" has been part of a war cry, but whether or not the administration achieves all its goals in doing so, it will remain a classic example of the politicization of evil for many years.

What may be even worse is the focus on one form of evil so single-minded as to suggest that no other kind matters at all. And the form we witnessed on September 11 is the easiest kind to pick out: easier to recognize than less visible forms of violence, easier to confront than the slower and subtler forms of destruction to which we are slowly and subtly becoming inured. Single-mindedness, however, is not confined to the Bush administration. Many of its critics were so thoroughly persuaded by more banal paradigms of evil that they were slow to acknowledge the terrorist attack as the evil it was. In that delay they missed the moment of collective horror that gripped most people, whatever their political convictions, around the globe. It's a simple horror beyond consensus expressed in the thought Arendt described on learning of the death camps: many things are possible, but *this* ought not to have happened. The impossible became true, and what is true quickly becomes routine. These moments of horror are frighteningly short-lived. The genocide that was unthinkable before Auschwitz became a regrettable piece of reality after it. And if, as experts tell us, we were slow to see the threat of global terrorism before September 11, we have made up for it since by imagining future scenarios that compete to outdo each other in scope and scale.

Kant thought we could understand much about humanity by focusing not on the French Revolution, but on international reaction to it. His point concerned hope, but it's equally fruitful to focus on moments of horror. Even though such visceral, collective moments may be vulnerable to media manipulation, they also provide an index of the deepest judgments we share in common. It's this kind of moment, and its background, that I have tried to examine historically. What's decisive is the reaction rather than the event itself, be it reaction to reports of a death camp in Poland, or a lynching in Mississippi, or terrorist attack in New York. Strain as we will, our efforts to discover an essence in each of these are unlikely to be fruitful, and focusing on features common to some of them is liable to blind us to others. Some blindness is cultivated deliberately. When powerful forces practice bureaucratic forms of evil, many of those without power will see no other response than simple, self-conscious actions with evil ends. My claim is not merely that violence breeds violence, but that a more sinister sort of symbiosis is at work here. Each party to such conflicts insists with great conviction that its opponents' actions are truly evil, while its own are merely expedient. It's a simple failure, but one that can cause no end of misery as long as each side is certain that the other embodies evil at its core. Perhaps the very worst legacy of the Nazis was to leave everything else in the shadow of the death camps; Auschwitz was so extreme that next to it, too much can look benign. But focusing on its singularity is no less dangerous than any other such focus. Evils come in too many forms to confine.

Given the difficulties of using the word responsibly, it's easy to understand the urge to give up talk of evil altogether—were it not for the fact that we have moral needs, and one of them is calling things by their proper names. It isn't *false* to call a mass murder bad, but if nothing more occurs to you when faced with a pile of corpses you have seen as much, and as little, as a man who calls a Vermeer portrait pretty. Of course muting our language would avoid some mistakes. But if these are all the words we can find by way of reaction, our perception and our judgment have failed. It is as shortsighted as it is condescending to explain the international rise in religious fundamentalism by suggesting that people want easy answers to the problems of a complex world. No doubt, sometimes, they do. But they just as surely want worldviews that express moral standpoints: that human dignity is a good which cannot be bartered, that some actions are so vile they cannot be redeemed. Clarity should never be confused with simplicity, moral clarity least of all. But a view that has no means to express legitimate needs for moral clarity will leave people to seek it elsewhere, and to settle for moral simplicity instead. Scruples about using moral language responsibly should lead us to use it responsibly, not to abandon it entirely—leaving the moral ammunition in unscrupulous hands.

The examples in *Evil in Modern Thought* are offered in the hope that genuine moral clarity can arise through the philosophical analysis of particular events as they are reflected and understood in the network of assumptions in which they occur. None of the analyses are meant to be exhaustive, and none of the events are meant to be exclusive. I focus on the Lisbon earthquake and the mass murder at Auschwitz because these, respectively, have a claim to be viewed as the beginning and end of the modern. A thorough study of moral watersheds in modern thought would include a number of other cases, especially those which must be more ambivalently understood. Here the French Revolution and Hiroshima leap to mind, and no discussion of twentieth-century evils can be complete without a far more thorough discussion of Stalinism than the few remarks scattered in these pages. In writing *Evil in Modern Thought* I sought to be exemplary; to provide instances of the kinds of analysis of evils that could serve as models for further ones, as well as a historical and conceptual framework in which to place them. The historical framework shows that the changes in our conceptions of evil were not arbitrary. Through understanding the intellectual developments surrounding particular events we come to see why, for example, the Lisbon earthquake was seen as an evil in one moment, a misfortune in the next. At the same time, it would be mistaken to think historical changes are stable. Freud's view of providence as the projection of infantile wishes is blisteringly modern, but in muddying the distinction between natural and moral evils it takes us back to the Book of Job. And when one contemporary French philosopher compares Auschwitz to an earthquake, while another calls terrorism a virus, we must wonder how clear was our understanding of evil and intention after all. Historical understanding helps us to reflect on further developments in the concept of evil—and to use it wisely in the future.

Historical investigation is one axis on the map offered here, while conceptual reflection forms the other. Rather than telling a strictly chronological story, I divide thinkers into rough groups that crossed other differences. In place of the familiar distinction between rationalists and empiricists I argue that philosophy is better understood as a struggle between those who seek an order to explain the appearances that overwhelm us, and those who insist on taking reality on its face. Those views were developed into metaphysical ones of differing weight and complexity, but they reflect conflicting intuitions most of us share: that behind all its forms there must be a better and truer reality than the one we know; or, on the contrary, that this belief is a piece of wishful thinking we should have outgrown. The map sketched in *Evil in Modern Thought* is far from complete; several critics claimed that one essential author or another had been ignored. Indeed, many were. I hope that others will expand on the framework offered here.

A history of the changes in our understanding of evil is especially incomplete without a history of the changes in our efforts to overcome it. Here is room for crucial work. *Evil in Modern Thought* asks readers to wonder about things we pass by unnoticed: for example, that the 1755 earthquake at Lisbon was experienced with moral aftershocks of a force and intensity that thinkers two centuries later would reserve for genocide. It's at least as important that we pause to wonder at other developments: how little time has passed since public execution by torture, and the sale of men and women on auction blocks, were ordinary sights in ordinary cities throughout the civilized world. To stop at these signposts of moral development is not to forget how far we have to go. But these examples remind us that historical analysis needn't be a vehicle for skepticism or an argument for relativism. It also reminds us that humankind, on occasion, makes moral progress—and sustains our attempts to make more.

Does the focus on history leave philosophy more parochial? Isn't philosophy meant to concern itself with timeless matters? Goodness, truth, and beauty may be sublime, but they are apt to appear sublimely dull outside of Plato's heaven—unless brought to life in real time and space. Seeing how earlier thinkers developed their views in response to real, historical problems makes it easier to see how contemporary thinkers might do the same. The response to *Evil in Modern Thought* suggests that the timeless subjects have lost some of their appeal in abstraction. The interest the book aroused—among those who are professional philosophers as well as those who are not—reflects the strength of desire to return to the place, closer to home, where philosophy arises. I have argued that the great philosophers of the canon were concerned with nothing more or less gripping than the questions that move bright seventeen-year-olds to wonder, and worry, about sense and meaning. These are questions that unite moral and metaphysical concerns and show why each of them matters. Rather than allowing us to put such questions behind us, growing up, I suspect, makes us more aware of the role of contingency and fortune in human life, and concerned about whether it should be celebrated or mourned. We wonder whether explaining things comes too close to justifying them, and if so where we should stop. We worry about how to maintain a commitment to fairness when the world as a whole does not. We ask about the point of making theoretical sense of the world when we cannot make sense of misery and terror. Growing up makes us think more and not less often about whether history presents anything but grounds for despair, or whether hopes for progress are based on anything but wishful thinking. We may do it with irony, with dryness or passion, but we find one way or another to engage with some piece of the problem misprized as the meaning of life. Focusing on such questions is not a matter of exchanging sloppy good intentions for critical thinking. All to the contrary: the texts discussed in what follows should reveal that few things give rise to thought of comparably breathtaking rigor and depth, and above all to dialogue, the way philosophy begins.

ACKNOWLEDGMENTS

Several institutions provided crucial support that gave me time to write this book. The Shalom Hartman Institute offered the most congenial place to work in the State of Israel, as well as a fellowship enabling me to devote time to research. An ACLS senior fellowship allowed me to complete much of the writing during 1999–2000; good fortune, and the Rockefeller Foundation, allowed me to draft the final chapter at the Villa Serboni in Bellagio.

Earlier versions of some passages appeared in the following essays: "Metaphysics to Philosophy: Rousseau and the Problem of Evil," in *Reclaiming the History of Ethics: Essays for John Rawls*, ed. B. Herman, C. Korsgaard, and A. Reath (Cambridge University Press, 1997); "Theodicy in Jerusalem," in *Hannah Arendt in Jerusalem*, ed. S. Ascheim (University of California Press, 2001); and "What Is the Problem of Evil?" in *Rethinking Evil: Contemporary Perspectives*, ed. M. P. Lara (University of California Press, 2001).

This book was long in the making, and provides occasion for acknowledging debts incurred before work on it began. Though none of them would entirely agree with the way I've done it, I would like to thank the people who taught me how to do philosophy. In chronological order, I am indebted to Burton Dreben for using the resources of analytic philosophy to illuminate what he called the big picture; to Stanley Cavell for making space for culture within English-speaking philosophy; to John Rawls for showing how the history of philosophy is not merely an archive for philosophy but a part of it; to Margherita von Brentano for maintaining the Enlightenment's strengths in full awareness of its weaknesses; to Jacob Taubes for making theological questions kosher for philosophical discourse. A number of friends and colleagues read the manuscript and offered vital criticism and encouragement. I am deeply if differently indebted to Richard Bernstein, Sander Gilman, Moshe Halbertal, Eva Illouz, Jeremy Bendik Keymer, Claudio Lange, Jonathan Lear, Iris Nachum, and James Ponet. Among the friends from whom I have learned, I must single out Irad Kimhi, who from the earliest stages spent countless hours helping me to think more clearly about the issues discussed here. Finally, Ian Malcolm was a superb editor, whose insight and engagement contributed much to improving the final shape of the book. Gabriele Karl provided expert and warmhearted secretarial support; Andreas Schulz's assistance was invaluable in the preparation of the bibliography.

My children had more than the usual share of burdens to shoulder during the writing of this book; they did it with more than the usual grace. A dedication is but small thanks for the patience and love with which they accompany my work.

EVIL IN MODERN THOUGHT

AN ALTERNATIVE

HISTORY

OF PHILOSOPHY

Introduction

> The aspects of things that are most important for us are hidden because of their simplicity and familiarity. (One is unable to notice something—because it is always before one's eyes.) The real foundations of his inquiry do not strike a person at all.—And this means: we fail to be struck by what, once seen, is most striking and most powerful.
>
> —Wittgenstein, *Philosophical Investigations*, #129

The eighteenth century used the word *Lisbon* much as we use the word *Auschwitz* today. How much weight can a brute reference carry? It takes no more than the name of a place to mean: the collapse of the most basic trust in the world, the grounds that make civilization possible. Learning this, modern readers may feel wistful: lucky the age to which an earthquake can do so much damage. The 1755 earthquake that destroyed the city of Lisbon, and several thousand of its inhabitants, shook the Enlightenment all the way to East Prussia, where an unknown minor scholar named Immanuel Kant wrote three essays on the nature of earthquakes for the Königsberg newspaper. He was not alone. The reaction to the earthquake was as broad as it was swift. Voltaire and Rousseau found another occasion to quarrel over it, academies across Europe devoted prize essay contests to it, and the six-year-old Goethe, according to several sources, was brought to doubt and consciousness for the first time. The earthquake affected the best minds in Europe, but it wasn't confined to them. Popular reactions ranged from sermons to eyewitness sketches to very bad poetry. Their number was so great as to cause sighs in the contemporary press and sardonic remarks from Frederick the Great, who thought the cancellation of carnival preparations months after the disaster to be overdone.

Auschwitz, by contrast, evoked relative reticence. Philosophers were stunned, and on the view most famously formulated by Adorno, silence is the only civilized response. In 1945 Arendt wrote that the problem of evil would be the fundamental problem of postwar intellectual life in Europe, but even there her prediction was not quite right. No major philosophical work but Arendt's own appeared on the subject in English, and German and French texts were remarkably oblique. Historical reports and eyewitness testimony appeared in unprecedented volume, but conceptual reflection has been slow in coming.

It cannot be the case that philosophers failed to notice an event of this magnitude. On the contrary, one reason given for the absence of philosophical reflection is the magnitude of the task. What occurred in Nazi death camps was so absolutely evil that, like no other event in human history, it defies human capacities for understanding. But the question of the uniqueness and magnitude of Auschwitz is itself a philosophical one; thinking about it could take us to Kant and Hegel, Dostoevsky and Job. One need not settle questions about the relationship of Auschwitz to other crimes and suffering to take it as paradigmatic of the sort of evil that contemporary philosophy rarely examines. The differences in intellectual responses to the earthquake at Lisbon and the mass murder at Auschwitz are differences not only in the nature of the events but also in our intellectual constellations. What counts as a philosophical problem and what counts as a philosophical reaction, what is urgent and what is academic, what is a matter of memory and what is a matter of meaning—all these are open to change.

This book traces changes that have occurred in our understanding of the self and its place in the world from the early Enlightenment to the late twentieth century. Taking intellectual reactions to Lisbon and Auschwitz as central poles of inquiry is a way of locating the beginning and end of the modern. Focusing on points of doubt and crisis allows us to examine our guiding assumptions by examining what challenges them at points where they break down: what threatens our sense of the sense of the world? That focus also underlies one of this book's central claims: the problem of evil is the guiding force of modern thought. Most contemporary versions of the history of philosophy will view this claim to be less false than incomprehensible. For the problem of evil is thought to be a theological one. Classically, it's formulated as the question: How could a good God create a world full of innocent suffering? Such questions have been off-limits to philosophy since Immanuel Kant argued that God, along with many other subjects of classical metaphysics, exceeded the limits of human knowledge. If one thing might seem to unite philosophers on both sides of the Atlantic, it's the conviction that Kant's work proscribes not just future philosophical references to God but most other sorts of foundation as well. From this perspective, comparing Lisbon to Auschwitz is merely mistaken. The mistake seems to lie in accepting the eighteenth century's use of the word *evil* to refer to both acts of human cruelty and instances of human suffering. That mistake might come naturally to a group of theists, who were willing to give God the responsibility for both, but it shouldn't confuse the rest of us. On this view Lisbon and Auschwitz are two completely different kinds of events. *Lisbon* denotes the sort of thing insurance companies call natural disasters, to remove them from the sphere of human action. Thus human beings are absolved of responsibility not only for causing or compensating them but even for thinking about them, except in pragmatic and technological terms. Earthquakes and volcanoes, famines and floods inhabit the borders of human meaning. We want to understand just so much about them as might help us gain control. Only traditional—that is, premodern—theists will seek in them significance. *Auschwitz*, by contrast, stands for all that is meant when we use the word *evil* today: absolute wrongdoing that leaves no room for account or expiation.

Initially, then, no two events will strike us as more different. If there's a problem of evil engendered by Lisbon, it can occur only for the orthodox: how can God allow a natural order that causes innocent suffering? The problem of evil posed by Auschwitz looks like another entirely: how can human beings behave in ways that so thoroughly violate both reasonable and rational norms? It is just this sense that the problems are utterly different which marks modern consciousness. The sharp distinction between natural and moral evil that now seems self-evident was born around the Lisbon earthquake and nourished by

Rousseau. Tracing the history of that distinction, and the ways in which the problems refused to stay separate, is one aim of this book.

A central reason for locating the modern as beginning at Lisbon is precisely for its attempt to divide responsibility clearly. Close look at that attempt will reveal all its irony. Though the *philosophes* perpetually accused Rousseau of nostalgia, Voltaire's discussion of the earthquake left far more in God's hands than did Rousseau's. And when Rousseau invented the modern sciences of history and psychology to cope with questions the earthquake brought to the surface, it was in defense of God's order. Ironies notwithstanding, the consciousness that emerged after Lisbon was an attempt at maturity. If Enlightenment is the courage to think for oneself, it's also the courage to assume responsibility for the world into which one is thrown. Radically separating what earlier ages called natural from moral evils was thus part of the meaning of modernity. If Auschwitz can be said to mark its ending, it is for the way it marks our terror. Modern conceptions of evil were developed in the attempt to stop blaming God for the state of the world, and to take responsibility for it on our own. The more responsibility for evil was left to the human, the less worthy the species seemed to take it on. We are left without direction. Returning to intellectual tutelage isn't an option for many, but hopes for growing up now seem void.

The history of philosophy, like that of nations or individuals, should teach us not to take for granted the intersection of assumptions where we find ourselves standing at particular moments in time. Learning this is a crucial part of the self-knowledge that was always philosophy's goal. But history of philosophy achieves such knowledge only when it is sufficiently historical. More often, the history of philosophy is approached as if our constellations and categories were self-evident. In broadest terms, we probably agree with Comte's view of intellectual history as progressing from theological to metaphysical to scientific ages. On such a view, thinkers whose world was shattered by the Lisbon earthquake would confirm all conviction in Enlightenment naïveté. At best, their reaction seems quaint, a sign of intellectual immaturity befitting an era that found itself on the border between theology and metaphysics. If one believes the world is ruled by a good and powerful father figure, it's natural to expect his order to be comprehensibly just. Jettison that belief, and whatever expectations remain are unresolved residues of childish fantasy. Thus the intellectual shock waves generated by Lisbon, when noticed at all, are seen as the birth pangs of a sadder but wiser era that has learned to live on its own.

This view, I will argue, is itself a historical one, for nothing is easier than stating the problem of evil in nontheist terms. One can state it, for example, as an argument with Hegel: not only is the real not identical with the rational; they aren't even related. To make this observation, you need no theory. Any observation of the world that continues for more than a couple of minutes should do. Every time we make the judgment *this ought not to have happened*, we are stepping onto a path that leads straight to the problem of evil. Note that it is as little a moral problem, strictly speaking, as it is a theological one. One can call it the point at which ethics and metaphysics, epistemology and aesthetics meet, collide, and throw up their hands. At issue are questions about what the structure of the world must be like for us to think and act within it. Those questions will quickly become historical. For what most demands explanation is not how moral judgments are justified, but why those that are so clearly justified were disregarded in the past. When one begins to seek explanation, one can end in anything from myth, like the Fall, to metaphysics, like Hegel's *Phenomenology*. What's important is that the place one begins is perfectly ordinary.

I believe it is the place where philosophy begins, and threatens to stop. For it involves questions more natural, urgent, and pervasive than the skeptical epistemological quandaries conventionally said to drive modern philosophy. It's *possible* to begin to worry about the difference between appearance and reality because you notice that a stick looks refracted in a pool of water, or because a dream is so vivid that you want to grasp one of its objects for a moment or two of sleepy half-consciousness. But you wake in your bed, slap your face if you have to, pull the stick out of the water if you're really in doubt. Were the problem of evil that easy to dispel, the massive effort spent in hundreds of years of philosophy would be in need of explanation.

The picture of modern philosophy as centered in epistemology and driven by the desire to ground our representations is so tenacious that some philosophers are prepared to bite the bullet and declare the effort simply wasted. Rorty, for example, finds it easier to reject modern philosophy altogether than to reject the standard accounts of its history. His narrative is more polemical than most, but it's a polemical version of the story told in most philosophy departments in the second half of the twentieth century. The story is one of tortuously decreasing interest. Philosophy, like some people, was prepared to accept boredom in exchange for certainty as it grew to middle age. What began as metaphysics—the description of the basic structures of reality—ended as epistemology: the attempt to track if not to ground the foundations of our knowledge.

On literary grounds alone, the narrative is flawed, for it lacks what is central to dramatic movement anywhere: a compelling motive. Except for the anachronistic desire to distinguish themselves from natural scientists, it's a narrative of philosophers who act without intention. The ground for earlier metaphysical inquiries is nearly as opaque as the motives for their successor. In both cases, great thinkers simply got stuck out of sheer curiosity investigating very general questions about the way things are. There is no good reason for the history of philosophy to have consisted in this story: as Descartes himself knew, none but madmen ever really think all our representations might be dreams. Throughout the *Critique of Pure Reason* Kant wrote that something must account for the inexhaustible effort that philosophers devote to a subject that brings no results. He thought the labors could not be guided by pure speculation alone. They are too hard and too frustrating to be driven by purposes and problems that are not urgent.

Kant's conclusion that speculative labors are moved by practical ends should not be read narrowly. For the last thing I wish to argue is that in addition to epistemology, the history of philosophy was *also* concerned with ethics. It was, of course, as contemporary work on the history of ethics has shown well. But the problem of evil shows the hopelessness of twentieth-century attempts to divide philosophy into areas that may or may not be connected. To see this, we needn't consider explicitly holist authors like Spinoza or Hegel. The most skeptical of empiricists himself should give pause. Which miracles did Hume want us to question? Which customs did he want us to keep? Is he more concerned with sympathy or with substance?—Is *Anna Kare-nina* about love more than justice?—Twentieth-century philosophy is not unique in its ability to confuse puzzles with problems. Even Socrates did it sometimes; it's an ability that may be part of the impulse to question opinion with which philosophy begins. Medieval philosophy revealed how questions not merely of life and death, but of *eternal* life and death, could turn into quandaries about substance. The dangers of sophistry and scholasticism are present in the possibility of philosophy itself. What is new is not these dangers but a fragmentation of the subject that would have been foreign to philosophers from Plato to Nietzsche. This very fragmentation may prevent us from seeing the problem of evil for what it is. The fact that the world contains neither justice nor meaning threatens our ability both to act in the world and to understand it. The demand that the world be intelligible is a demand of practical and of theoretical reason, the ground of thought that philosophy is called to provide. The question of whether this is an ethical or a metaphysical problem is as unimportant as it is undecidable, for in some moments it's hard to view as a philosophical problem at all. Stated with the right degree of generality, it is but unhappy description: this is our world. If that isn't even a question, no wonder philosophy has been unable to give it an answer. Yet for most of its history, philosophy has been moved to try, and its repeated attempts to formulate the problem of evil are as important as its attempts to respond to it.

Let me summarize the claims for which I will argue.

1. Eighteenth- and nineteenth-century philosophy was guided by the problem of evil. Like most short statements, this one is too simple. Nevertheless, I intend to show that as an organizing principle for understanding the history of philosophy, the problem of evil is better than alternatives. It is more inclusive, comprehending a far greater number of texts; more faithful to their authors' stated intentions; and more interesting. Here interest is not merely an aesthetic category, important as that is, but also an explanatory one, which answers Kant's question: What drives pure reason to efforts that seem to have neither end nor result?

2. The problem of evil can be expressed in theological or secular terms, but it is fundamentally a problem about the intelligibility of the

world as a whole. Thus it belongs neither to ethics nor to metaphysics but forms a link between the two.

3. The distinction between natural and moral evils is itself a historical one that developed in the course of the debate.

4. Two kinds of standpoint can be traced from the early Enlightenment to the present day, regardless of what sort of evil is in question, and each is guided more by ethical than by epistemological concerns. The one, from Rousseau to Arendt, insists that morality demands that we make evil intelligible. The other, from Voltaire to Jean Améry, insists that morality demands that we don't.

My own sympathies tend toward the former line of views, while acknowledging the force of the latter. This allows me, I hope, to answer the objection that is most troubling: the problem of evil facing the eighteenth century was so different from our own that comparing them involves not just conceptual but moral confusion. Comparing Lisbon to Auschwitz can seem not mistaken but monstrous, for it risks either viewing the latter as one more or less natural disaster, thus excusing the architects; or comparing the Creator to criminals of the worst sort. It is hard to say which is worse: contemplating the redemption of the commandant of Auschwitz or the violation of images of God even atheists want to retain. For this reason, apart from isolated remarks, the two events have been left to stand as symbols for the breakdown of the worldviews of their eras, and the question of how we got from one to the other has not been addressed. If some uneasiness about understanding seems right to preserve, I trust it will shape inquiry rather than preclude it.

Among the many things this book will not offer is a definition of evil or criteria for distinguishing evil actions from those that are simply very bad. This might be a task for a book of ethics, but the problem of evil concerns something else. To describe that problem, one might ask: what's the difference between calling one action evil, and another, a crime against humanity? They can often be interchanged. But a crime is something for which we have procedures—at least for punishing, if not for preventing. To say this is to say that a crime can be ordered, fit in some manner into the rest of our experience. To call an action evil is to suggest that it cannot—and that it thereby threatens the trust in the world that we need to orient ourselves within it. I will argue that evils cannot be compared, but they should be distinguished. What happened on September 11 was one kind of evil; what happened at Auschwitz was another. Getting clear about the differences will not put an end to evil, but it may help prevent our worst reactions to it.

To lament the loss of absolute standards for judging right and wrong ought to be superfluous a century after Nietzsche, but someone seems to do it every day. Nearly anyone who ever taught a humanities course will have met students who discovered that words like *good* and *evil* are out of date, since used by different cultures in different ways. What may have gone unnoticed is that while few today will claim certainty about general ethical principles, most are quite certain about particular ethical paradigms. Loss of certainty about the general foundations of value has not affected certainty about particular instances of it; perhaps quite the contrary. Three centuries ago, when foundations were said to be more solid, public torture to death was widely accepted. Today it is pretty universally condemned regardless of differences over principle. As Rwanda or Bosnia can show us, universal condemnation may be worth next to nothing. My point is about the relation not of theory to practice, but of general principle to particular paradigm. There may be no general principle that proves torture or genocide wrong, but this does not prevent us from taking them to be paradigmatic of evil.

I therefore assume that we have such examples, and that they change over time, without any interest in giving justification, or even criteria, for them. Even if we lack general principles of the kind we imagine other ages to have cherished, this is enough for my purposes. Since I do not think an intrinsic property of evil can be defined, I am, rather, concerned with tracing what evil does to us. If designating something as evil is a way of marking the fact that it shatters our trust in the world, it's that effect, more than the cause, which I want to examine. It should follow that I have even less intention of solving the problem of evil than I do of defining evil itself. My interest is, rather, to explore what changes in our understanding of the problem of evil reveal about changes in our understanding of ourselves, and of our place in the world. I proceed on the increasingly shared assumption that examining the history of philosophy can be a way of engaging in philosophy itself. Traditional intellectual history might proceed by chroni-cling successive thinkers' accounts of evil, and tracing sources and pat-terns of influence. Traditional philosophical studies might evaluate the success of competing accounts and try to offer a better one. My goal is another entirely: to use different responses to the problem of evil as a means of understanding who we have become in the three centuries that separate us from the early Enlightenment.

This book began as the study of an interesting topic oddly ignored in the historiography of philosophy. It soon threatened to explode all confines. If I am even close to correct, the problem of evil is so perva-sive that an exhaustive and systematic treatment of it would require an exhaustive and systematic treatment of most of the history of philoso-phy. Merely listing the right names can seem hopeless. Instead of at-tempting such a project, I've made several choices that eschew it. First, I've limited my discussion to the period beginning with the Enlighten-ment, and dated the Enlightenment as beginning in 1697, with the pub-lication of Bayle's *Dictionary*. There are good reasons for dating it ear-lier. One would be to explore gnostic imagery in the person credited with fathering modern philosophy, René Descartes. Descartes's evil demon is not a thought experiment but a threat. Unlike its pale heir, the brain in the vat, the devil was a real concern. What if the world were created by a Being whose whole purpose was to cause us torment and illusion? God knows it sometimes looks that way. If the absence of Descartes may seem troubling, that of Spinoza may be worse. Both are clearly crucial for understanding later discussion of these problems, but then, so is Plato. One could easily spend a lifetime studying the problem of evil and be no better for it. Instead, I have chosen to restrict discussion to its development from the beginning of the period in which we began to be most recognizably who we are. If history, as Bayle wrote, is the history of crimes and misfortunes, attempts to make sense of it are doomed not just to falsehood but to ridicule. It's a choice, but not an arbitrary one, to view the Enlightenment as beginning under pressure to prove Bayle wrong.

Even within these confines, this study cannot be exhaustive, and to mark this I have chosen nonchronological form. Though my interest is in the development of ideas such as those that link Rousseau's second

Discourse to Arendt's *Eichmann in Jerusalem,* I have explored such development thematically. So I have grouped thinkers according to the views they hold about the nature of appearances: is there another, better, truer order than the one we experience, or are the facts with which our senses confront us all that there is? Is reality exhausted by what is, or does it leave room for all that could be? Dividing philosophers according to their stance on one large question is rough division, and produces odd alliances. Among philosophers who insisted on finding order in addition to the miserable one presented by experience, I include Leibniz, Pope, Rousseau, Kant, Hegel, and Marx. Among those who denied the reality of anything beyond brute appearances, I discuss Bayle, Voltaire, Hume, Sade, and Schopenhauer. Nietzsche and Freud cannot be fit into either division, however broadly construed, but raise sufficiently similar questions to deserve their own chapter. As I argue in the final chapter, the twentieth century presents particular philosophical problems. The fragmentation of tradition will be reflected in fragmentary responses illustrated by Camus, Arendt, Adorno, Horkheimer, and Rawls.

Grouping philosophers this way overlooks many crucial differences between them. But it's no cruder than the division of thinkers into rationalists and empiricists, a schema with which it is partly coextensive. The latter will seem more natural to those who believe that the guiding questions of modern philosophy are questions about the theory of knowledge. If these are your main concern, you will group philosophers according to whether they believe the main source of knowledge to be reason or experience, and will view other differences between them as incidental. Yet this division was not obvious to Kant, who is credited with overcoming it, or to Hegel, the modern philosopher who devoted most thought to the history of philosophy itself. For the *Critique of Pure Reason,* the first controversy in the history of philosophy concerns appearance and reality: are ideas or experience the final court of appeal? This question takes us through the history of philosophy all the way back to Plato. The worry that fueled debates about the difference between appearance and reality was *not* the fear that the world might not turn out to be the way it seems to us—but rather the fear that it would.

Many of the thinkers discussed in chapter 1 would reject each other's company. But despite occasional elements of melancholy, all are united by some form of hope for a better order than the one we experience. Those in chapter 2, by contrast, share a brilliant, cheerful bleakness that concluded with Schopenhauer's stupendous pessimism. Nietzsche and Freud maintain a sort of heroic scorn toward discussions of the subject that preceded their own, and any straws we might be tempted to clutch thereafter. The thinkers chosen to illustrate twentieth-century thought about evil display humility born of a sense of fragility and awe. Thinkers can be grouped in terms that belong to metaphysics (how do they view the reality of appearances?) as well as terms that come from psychology (do they make room for a fundamentally hopeful stance toward the world?). I will argue that the problem of evil requires thought about both. The way we organize philosophical discourse is not the most important thing challenged by the problem of evil, but it is surely the easiest to change.

In general, I focus on major figures in the canon. This underlines the fact that the problems discussed are not peripheral to the tradition but basic to the work of its most central thinkers. Were this an ordinary history of philosophy, it would be irresponsible to describe the transition from Kant to Hegel without discussing Fichte and Schelling, or to move from Hegel to Marx without addressing Feuerbach. I have done both, and probably things that are worse. My interest is less in tracing causal connections between authors than in showing how certain general developments make sense. For this, it should be enough to choose samples of work that were particularly exciting and important, in the hope that they will illuminate the rest. But hundreds of rich and influential texts will thereby be ignored, and choices could have been made differently. The only consolation for the resulting inadequacy is the way in which it confirms my initial claim: the history of philosophy is so steeped in the problem of evil that the question is not where to begin but where to stop. An attempt to be complete would be doomed to failure from the start. Should this book open lines of inquiry, rather than exhaust them, it will have achieved its goal.

I have called this an alternative history of philosophy because its aims are as different as its style and methods. One aim, in the felicitous expression of an anonymous reader, is to reorient the discipline to the real roots of philosophical questioning. I am grateful for the metaphor, which allows me to argue that, in some form or other, the problem of evil is the root from which modern philosophy springs. Once brought to life, philosophical discourse can grow on its own, and its branches may extend or tangle in all directions. Thus entire schools of thought could develop that have little to do with the questions raised here. Kant and Hume and Hegel all raised questions that would lead philosophers reading them centuries later to think about relationships between language and world, or the foundations of knowledge. But if, as I argue, those questions are less central to the heart of their thought than was previously assumed, we must come to view our own philosophical landscape differently.

This book is not merely intended to be of interest both to those who are professional philosophers and those who are not, but to show that throughout most of its history, philosophy itself was of interest both to those who were professional philosophers and those who were not. Like many others, I came to philosophy to study matters of life and death, and was taught that professionalization required forgetting them. The more I learned, the more I grew convinced of the opposite: the history of philosophy was indeed animated by the questions that drew us there. Thus I have written in a manner that should be open to those without formal philosophical training, keeping notes and other scholarly apparatus to a minimum. In the spirit of that Enlightenment, then, in which Lessing and Mendelssohn coauthored essays for international prize contests on the relations between poetry and metaphysics, Kant wrote for the eighteenth-century version of the *New York Review*, and Sade begged to have volumes of Rousseau sent to him in the Bastille, this book is written in tentative hope.

Chapter One
FIRE FROM HEAVEN

Philosophy makes no secret of it. The confession of

Prometheus: "In one word, I hate all the gods," is its very own

confession, its own sentence against all heavenly and earthly

gods who refuse to recognize human self-consciousness as

the supreme divinity—by the side of which none other

shall be held.

—Marx, *Dissertation*

He may be the first Enlightenment hero. Alfonso X became king of Castile in 1252, and his reign was full of trouble from the start. He repudiated his wife, on the ground that she was barren, then sent to Denmark for another. By the time the princess of Denmark arrived in Spain, the queen was pregnant with the first of nine children she would bring into the world. Neither woman ever forgave Alfonso, though his brother, archbishop of Seville, gave up his seat to marry the Danish princess. The learning and eloquence that gave Alfonso a splendid reputation in other countries did not impress his Castilian contemporaries, who seemed to resent him. Though he was the first king of Castile who caused public acts to be written in the Spanish tongue, and commissioned a Spanish translation of the Bible, it didn't lead to the flowering of local culture that translations into the vernacular produced in neighboring France. Rather, many later historians held the works he sponsored to be responsible for the ignorance and barbarity that they claimed spread over Spain. The children he had longed for turned out to be ingrates. One of them, Sancho, tired of waiting to inherit the throne and conspired with the king of Granada to over-throw his father. Alfonso's death in 1284 put an end to the ensuing civil war but not to his misfortune, for his will was entirely ignored: the rebel Sancho remained on the throne, and his own heart, which he had ordered buried on Mount Calvary, was left to molder with his other remains in Seville.

Medieval and early modern thinkers viewed this saga as a confirmation of Providence. All Alfonso's troubles were punishment for one nearly unspeakable sin, and hence were confirmation of God's presence, justice, and even capacity for irony. For Sancho's rebellion, in particular, was the fitting response to the rebellion his own father instigated against the Heavenly Father Himself. Alfonso's revolt began as an act of scholarship. He sent to Toledo for learned Jews to instruct him in astronomy and commissioned one Rabbi Isaac Hazan to draw up astronomical tables, known thereafter as *Tablas Alfonsinas*, at considerable expense. After several years of intensive study, Alfonso remarked, "If I had been of God's counsel at the Creation, many things would have been ordered better."[1]

This little sentence, or some variation of it, expressed the essence of blasphemy for close to half a millennium. Bayle said no one was ignorant of Alfonso's astronomical studies and their consequences, and was scrupulous in footnoting numerous variants of the story. In several of them, even the rebellion of his son wasn't considered sufficient punishment. One who presumed to judge the heavens should be answered more directly, so a number of commentators had Alfonso or his family hit by lightning. A certain Rodericus Sanctius wrote that an angel appeared in a dream to convey a message from the celestial council warning Alfonso to repent.

> But Alphonsus laughed, and repeated his blasphemy. . . . The Night following there were such horrible storms, accompanied with Thunder and Lightning, as if Heaven was falling. The Fire from Heaven burned, in Alphonsus' chamber, the King and Queen's Cloaths; then the Prince in Distress sent for the Hermit, confessed his Sins to him, cried, humbled himself, and retracted

his Blasphemy. The more he wept, the more the Storm diminished, and at last quite ceased. (Bayle 2, 380)[2]

Bayle contested this account and other versions involving lightning. Such a wonderful accident, he argued, would be confirmed by more sources, particularly if it took place in Spain, whose inhabitants were always delighted to find evidence of miracles. Bayle wished to naturalize the story and may thereby be Alfonso's first defender. The king, in Bayle's account, committed prosaic sins: he neglected domestic political interests in favor of astronomical learning, preferring to "make a Noise" in foreign countries by cultivating his knowledge rather than attending to relations with his family and other subjects. Here we see ordinary, not criminal, narcissism. Though the former might render his subsequent downfall more comprehensible, Bayle still did not think he deserved it. On the contrary. Bayle devoted several footnotes to the infamous sentence and gave it a modern and more charitable reading. Alfonso's belief that the heavens look remarkably disordered may be a comment not on God's workmanship but on the defects of Ptolemaic astronomy, which were all too apparent by 1697. It all depends where the emphasis falls. Had Alfonso asserted "If *I* had been of God's counsel at Creation . . . ," it would indeed sound like scandalous conceit. But, Bayle proposes, the claim could be read as follows: "If I had been of *God's* counsel at Creation. . . ." In that case the object of derision is not the Creator but the sorry medieval astronomers, whose ridiculous system did no honor to Him.

Whether or not we sympathize with such nascent deconstruction, we are likely to support Bayle, and to go several steps further. Alfonso's remark will strike modern readers as so harmless that the wrath it provoked for centuries, much less the possible judgment of heaven, will be hard to understand. Even those who take patience and humility to be primary virtues can view Alfonso as manifesting them. He might, after all, have left the cosmic order to divine jurisdiction and devoted his attention to the business of earthly kings, like falconry and wenching. It would have been simpler, and brought simpler rewards: all Alfonso got for the years spent learning to calculate epicycles was the dubious blessing of posthumous notoriety. Since it wasn't even good science, not even a glimpse of the truth crowned his efforts. His life, by all counts, looks a model of failure. Yet apart from the vanity that might afflict anyone, his motives were perfectly good ones. Alfonso sought to learn the secrets of the science that was viewed as the very highest so as better to understand and revere the Creation. And in uttering the remark that made him famous, there was no wish to blaspheme, just to point out the truth: an ordinary, hardworking Spanish king could design a better world than the one received wisdom ascribed to an omnipotent Creator.

His fate, therefore, will seem hardly more just than Job's, whose story of endless suffering was also paradigmatic for writers concerned with the problem of evil. It is important to note that, like Alfonso's misfortunes, Job's were not viewed as unfair until a very late date. Sometime during the Enlightenment, commentators stopped looking for ways in which Job's torments could be justified. According to Kant, who wrote a wonderful essay on the subject, they had previously done so in the hope that God would be eavesdropping. Having lost that hope, they had less motivation to try out variations on possible theodicies, which showed either that Job was secretly guilty of something after all, so that loss of all he had was *justified* punishment, or that he was being tried today to be rewarded the more surely tomorrow. Earlier writers identified with Job's friends, the theodicy-makers who found justification. Later ones identified with Job, who found none. Tracing this development might be an interesting way of spending a lifetime, which wouldn't be long enough to examine the vast literature the Book of Job inspired. But let us return to Alfonso, whose remark hardly reached the presumption of his biblical predecessor. Job did not go so far as to follow his wife's suggestion that he curse God and die, but he did curse the day he was born, close enough to cursing Creation itself. Alfonso only suggested that it could be improved.

I will argue that Alfonso was less harmless than we think. Medieval observers were not entirely mistaken in reading his wish to advise God as the first step in a process that led to something they could not have imagined: not only the nineteenth century's wish to displace God but Nietzsche's announcement that the deed had been done and was no longer even shocking. Let's begin by considering the functions Alfonso performed in the Enlightenment.

GOD'S ADVOCATES: LEIBNIZ AND POPE

Leibniz wrote that everyone condemns Alfonso's opinion that the world could be better.[3] He joined in the general condemnation and wondered why, despite it, the world of philosophers and theologians contained so many latter-day Alfonsos. For anyone who thinks God could have made the world better and chose not to do so thinks that God is not as good as He could be. Leibniz put the point gently. His *Theodicy* is one long response to the work of Bayle, who minced fewer words. History, said Bayle, is the history of the crimes and misfortunes of the human race. A God who could have created a world that contained fewer crimes and misfortunes, and chose not to do so, seems nothing but a giant criminal Himself.

Leibniz invented the word *theodicy* to describe the defense of God in categories taken from legal discourse. Before we examine his defense, let us look at the attack that provoked it. Bayle's work will be examined on its own terms in chapter 2. Here I wish simply to mark what was exceptional in the charges he laid at God's door. God had been on trial since the Book of Job, at the latest, and if the framers of that text pressed any point with clarity, it's that He had it coming. For we, the readers, can see that things are even worse than Job suspects. He begs for understanding. Suppose he had known that the death of his ten children was the result of a bet God made with Satan, like two thuggish schoolboys contesting for power? One who undertakes to try the righteous in such ways will be called to account sooner or later Himself. Job, who cannot read the prologue to his story, might be satisfied by God's mere appearance as a witness, but later ages would demand more in the way of defense. As the crimes He was charged with looked graver and graver, and He seemed unwilling even to appear to address the accusations, modern writers felt bound to condemn him, in absentia, to something like death.

Bayle argued that Christianity made the problem worse. Before Bayle it was easier to view Christianity as a sensible solution to the problem of evil. As one believer put it, "Job is the question, and Jesus is the answer." The details of the solution are as various as the differences in Christian doctrine, but the statement marks the belief in messianic redemption, and the hope for eternal life, at the core of any Christian view. God Himself, in those views, took on as cruel a set of punishments as any human ever suffered. Indeed, they were made all the crueler by the fact of his utter innocence. His miraculous resurrection, which would make the agony on the cross seem a fleeting nightmare, is a prototype of that open to anyone who chooses to believe in the miracle.

Belief in miracles, for Bayle, was not a problem. He regarded the world as generally mysterious. One more break in a rather incomprehensible natural order would pose no great difficulty (Bayle 1, 194). The problem lies, rather, in the internal structure of the Christian solution itself. The torments of the damned, even without the doctrine of predestination, are the block on which reason stumbles. For however bad a sin may be, it has to be finite. An infinite amount of hellfire is therefore simply unjust.[4] To imagine a God who judges many of the forms of life He created to be sinful, then tortures us eternally for our brief participation in them, is hardly to imagine a solution to the problem of evil. Positing a God who may permit infinite and eternal suffering is of little help in stilling doubt about a God who clearly permits finite and temporal suffering.

Matters were far worse for those who accept the doctrine of predestination. Though neither Bayle nor Leibniz did so, both took it very seriously. Manichaean heresies viewed the world as ruled by good and evil principles forever engaged in conflict. Bayle thought Manichaeism would be far more prevalent had it developed in an age that took predestination as seriously as did his own. Anyone who believes that our worldviews have become *less* heartening over time should recall the basic elements of that doctrine. According to Calvinism, the number of those who will be eternally damned is much larger than the number of those who will be eventually saved. Who shall be redeemed is decided by God at, or before, the moment of birth. Any action you perform may reflect your prospects of burning forever, but nothing you can do will affect them. Sade himself made an effort, but was unable to invent something worse, and no modern tyrant even tried. Death is a mercy here entirely lacking. Torture without limit falls on unbaptized babies, noble princes, and brutal gangsters alike—and its author is the Creator we are bound to revere.

The doctrine is the logic of omnipotence gone mad. Is the Creator all-powerful? *But of course.* Then He can do what He wants? *Just the meaning of* power. Can He break all the laws? *Well, He made them.* Laws of reason? *We should judge Him?* Laws of justice? *Ditto, likewise.* Any justice? *If He chooses.* Every step is unexceptionable, till we are led to a system choked with evil so inscrutable that we turn to modern worldviews for relief. Sheer randomness will be a respite.

It is just the randomness of guilt and punishment, along with the presence of good as well as evil, that creates philosophical problems. For even Bayle knew that life contains something besides vice and pain. The fact that we sometimes meet up with virtue and happiness is just what's confusing. If all of humankind were wicked and miserable, we could conclude it to be the creation of a wicked and miserable deity, who created in his own image and for his own perverse pleasure. If the justice of such a world weren't obviously apparent, it would be hard to find anyone who might care. But this is not the world we live in. Bayle says it's the mixture of happiness and suffering, wickedness and virtue, that leads us to reflection and makes Manichaeism seem the most reasonable of views. The picture of a world ruled by good and evil principles locked in perpetual struggle preserves belief in God's benevolence. Far from being the Author of sin and misery, God is always attempting to prevent it. He is simply hindered by the strength of His opponent. If this view makes God into a large and long-living parent, well-meaning but bounded, it does less violence to our intuitions than do other options. It may be hard to acknowledge God's limits, but it's less frightening than denying His goodwill. Manichaeism may not explain experience, but it certainly seems to reflect it, by underlining the bewildering alternation between good and evil that structures human life. Alfonso would have been unlikely to mutter if the natural world presented *nothing* but flawed machinery. It is just the presence of some matchless order, along with the existence of other parts without rhyme and reason, that caused his complaint. Some experience of understanding creates expectations of more. To be sure, the belief in such order long preceded modern science. Kant thought it was manifest in the change of the seasons. The fact that delicate flowers are preserved through winter storms should suffice to convince any skeptic that the world was designed by an awesome Creator. And if the coming of spring may seem more of a miracle in East Prussia than in the south of Spain, it's an event that can evoke wonder anywhere.

Ordinary wonder at the world's bits of order makes ordinary experience fractured. Discontinuity between understanding and blind groping, decency and horror, frames the texture of our lives. Thus, Bayle concludes, Manichaeism is the most reasonable response to experience. Let us take his conclusion at face value. Reason's response to experience is a demand for Manichaeism. Faith's response is affirmation of Christianity. In 1697, even in the progressive Holland where Bayle was writing, it is not hard to guess which of the two will be condemned.

No wonder Bayle was happy to take up Alfonso's defense. For the king's mild-mannered suggestion put a foot in the door. Alfonso stood for any claim that human reason contains in itself more sense and order than the world it faces. Bayle's belief in the general incomprehensibility of all things used Alfonso as champion. Leibniz had to rebut him in the effort to show the world to be in principle transparent. So he took up Alfonso thirteen years later. Bayle had argued that reason, and all the evidence of experience, leave God condemned. Any attempt to retain faith will not only lack rational foundation; it must positively defy it.

The *Theodicy* thus set out to prove the conformity of faith with reason, though for later readers like Voltaire it served to prove the absurdity of faith in reason. Leibniz undertook to defend a Creator accused of unparalleled crime. His defense rests on two points. The first is that the accused could not have done otherwise. Like any other agent, He was constrained by the possibilities available to Him. The other line of defense invokes the claim that all the Creator's actions in fact happen for the best. One part of the defense is an inquiry into the grounds of the accused's actions, while the other concerns the true nature of their consequences in the world. It is there that Leibniz's claims look not only prior to experience but positively immune to it. For he makes quite clear that any fact, however awful, is compatible with the claim that this world is the best of all possible ones. Leibniz's assertion is no claim about the goodness of this world; it simply tells us that any other world would have been worse. Those who want to reject it will be told that they don't know enough to do so, and this is surely true. The statement is just as impossible to disprove as it is to confirm. Take Leibniz's attempt to speculate about how the balance of good and evil might cohere. It's possible, he says, that all crimes and misfortunes are concentrated on this planet. In that case, it would be the lot of human beings to bear the burden of the universe, while inhabitants of other planets are much more blessed and happy than we are. This *is* possible, of course, but it's no less possible that the denizens of other galaxies exceed us in wickedness and misery. That didn't deter Leibniz from trying the same sort of speculation on the hardest of theological claims for his account, the claim that the number of the damned is greater than the number of the saved. Perhaps, he considers, there is incomparably more good in the glory of all the saved, few as they are in number, than there is evil in the misery of the damned.—Perhaps there is. On the face of it, one possibility is just as likely as any other. In the latter case, it is hard to know how to state the alternatives coherently. In the realm of sheer possibility, not much is excluded.

Leibniz's defense of God's justice depends on his division of all our misery into metaphysical, natural, and moral evil. It's this division, together with his assumption of a causal link between them, that will strike us as sorely in need of defense. For Leibniz, metaphysical evil is the degeneration inherent in the limits of the substance(s) of which the world is made. Natural evil is the pain and suffering we experience in it. Moral evil is the crime for which natural evil is the certain and inevitable punishment. The assumption that moral and natural evils are causally linked is an assumption Leibniz never subjected to scrutiny. Modern readers may turn every page of the *Theodicy* with the hope that its author will address the point most in need of argument, but Leibniz held the connection between moral and natural evils to be too self-evident to warrant serious question. The complexity of his accounts of freedom does not make up for the simplicity of his account of the relations between sin and suffering. That account rests on an understanding of the Fall considered, most generally, as an explanation of why life is not what it should be. Long ago, it was. The earth was a garden in which everything was good. Hunger was stilled without effort; children were born without pain. We knew neither death nor shame nor confusion. If you had to design a world, wouldn't you design it like that?

If this is the way things ought to be, something must explain the way they are. The idea that the problem was caused by our ancestors' sins does not depend on what they did. To complain that a taste of the wrong kind of fruit shouldn't be enough to bring a death sentence on the heads of all their descendants is to miss the philosophical point, and Christian attempts to make the deed look worse than it was are wasted effort. Something trivial is precisely appropriate. What counts in the first instance is not the justice of the connection between what they did and what they suffered, but that there be a connection at all. Why do bad things happen? Because bad things were done. Better to have some causal explanation than to remain in the dark. To connect sin and suffering is to separate the world into moral and natural evils, and to create thereby a framework for understanding human misery.

For contemporary readers, the distinction between suffering and sin is so fundamental that eighteenth-century discussion will seem simply confused. The fact that one word *evil* was able to designate both testifies to the closeness of the link conceived between them. For rationalists, the link was straightforwardly causal. Natural evils could be nothing but punishment; to leave room for a neutral conception of suffering, and ask about its relation to moral evil, was to ask more than faith could bear. Note that the connection between natural and moral evils could be made without reason by any voluntarist: this would be just to say that God makes no concessions to our understanding but sends what He chooses according to His will. If the rationalist tends to collapse the distinction by making all evils moral ones, the voluntarist's rejection of a comprehensible notion of God's morality tends to make all evils natural. Sin and suffering both come from the Creator, who relates them as He will. For Leibniz, such a view makes God a worse tyrant than the emperor Caligula, who had his laws written in so small a print, and posted in so high a place, that no one could read them. A

Creator who gives us no clear directions about the links between sin and suffering is nothing but a monster; more monstrous still would be a Creator who didn't link them at all.

All this is traditional enough, though remembering its context makes Leibniz's efforts on God's behalf more poignant. In a world where Bayle evoked the nightmares suggested by Calvinism, Manichaeism was a real possibility. Descartes's evil demon was not science fiction but theology. Leibniz's God may not be a hero, but other options were infinitely worse. What is modern in Leibniz's account is the conviction that the causal links between sin and suffering will become clearer with time, as will the ways in which, despite appearances to the contrary, God has ordered all those links for the best. Leibniz puts his trust in explanation still to come. We have no evidence that good will come from evil, and quite a lot of reason to doubt it. What makes Leibniz's faith in the future something better than Panglossian?

Few thinkers in history were more persuaded of the scope and possibilities created by the early scientific revolutions, and the *Theodicy* is happy to use them as part of its argument for acknowledging Providence. One thing they have taught is a matter of size. Leibniz says ancient beliefs that the universe was "puny" prevented Augustine from giving an adequate explanation of evil. As long as only one planet was thought to be inhabited, the apparent prevalence of evils over goods could not be explained. Now that we know that the universe is vast, Leibniz argued, we can better place our own troubles in perspective. Today the thought of an infinite number of galaxies may give us pause, but only for a moment. For the charge that the problem of evil arises from shortsighted egotism doesn't need modern science for support. It can be found even in the Bible, where the Voice from the Whirlwind accuses Job of selfishly focusing on his own case. God has ostriches and antelopes to care for, as well as human beings; how can Job demand all His attention? Discoveries about the size of the universe cannot support an argument either way, for we were told all along that God's Creation was not confined to human being. Either, as the author of Job would thunder, God's hands were quite full with the variety of forms of life on this planet, without looking for creatures on others. Alternatively, the skeptic can reply that, unlike an overworked parent, the unspoken metaphor that carries the burden of this argument, God was supposed to be omnipotent.

Thus the discovery that the universe is larger than supposed cannot be among the discoveries of science that will prove much help with the problem of evil. Among the other sources of his confidence is Leibniz's invention of the calculus, which made him not only one of the greatest admirers of the early scientific revolutions but also an agent of them. But the leap Leibniz imagined, from the calculus he and Newton simultaneously invented to the universal calculus that would be the basis of the science of the future, seems almost as vast today as the universe that then impressed him. Indeed, what's hard to understand is the tenacity of Leibniz's belief in the discovery of a method that would solve every problem. His most famous vision of the future is one in which two people warring over politics or religion would exchange their swords for pencils. With a cheerful "Come, let us calculate," they would solve every disagreement as easily as we solve equations. The universal calculus would not only resolve old problems but would function as a logic of discovery. It would work so well that even a scientist who wished to go astray would fail to do so: his hand, said Leibniz, would refuse to write an error. For the calculus would reveal the rational order in language as ordinary language does not. Sometimes Leibniz thought of it as the language spoken by Adam before the tower of Babel; elsewhere he holds it to have a form only mathematics can capture. Once he tried to work it out in hieroglyphics. Though none of these attempts came close to fruition, he was so convinced that the next would be successful that he bade his readers give thought to the greatest problem future science would face: gratifying vanity. For once the universal calculus was discovered, all the sciences, from metaphysics to history, would be completed so effortlessly and automatically that any fool could do it. What challenge would be left for ambitious young talent?

Leibniz did not expect all his readers to share his own confidence in the inevitability of scientific triumph. The distinctions between early rationalists and empiricists were less fixed than post-Kantian polemics often suggest. Still, Leibniz's exchanges with leading empiricists like Locke, Clarke, and Bayle taught him to expect the charge that he placed too much trust in reason. Here Alfonso could help, for he signified all the follies of empiricism. The appeal to experience is, in the end, always appeal to experience limited by particular place and time. Poring over Ptolemaic tables by torchlight, Alfonso concluded that the universe was deficient. Within the boundaries of his own experience, his conclusion made sense. Recall that it was not only Ptolemaic astronomy but also ordinary experience and common sense that put the earth in the center of the universe. Which of our senses tells us that the earth moves? Had Alfonso but lived to see the discoveries of Copernicus and Kepler, he would have marveled at the system and harmony with which the universe is run. The fault lay not in the universe but in the poverty of Alfonso's experience, and this should give us pause. It's a mark of the modern that Leibniz no longer found the king appalling but subjected him to ridicule, in a message that was perfectly clear. Anyone inclined to challenge the fact that Leibniz's defense of God was utterly a priori should consider the alternative. In another few centuries understanding of the universe, and God's purposes in it, should progress unimaginably. Today's scoffers will look as silly as a Spanish king shaking his head over antiquated astronomy and complaining that the world makes no sense. Alfonso makes the appeal to experience itself look ridiculous, while Leibniz buys time for science to prove this world to be best.

> If we hold the same opinion as King Alfonso, we shall, I say, receive this answer: You have known the world only since the day before yesterday, you see scarce farther than your nose, and you carp at the world. Wait until you know more of the world . . . and you will find there a contrivance and a beauty transcending all imagination. Let us thence draw conclusions as to the wisdom and goodness of the author of things, even in the things that we know not. (Leibniz 248)

In passages such as this, and other parts of the *Theodicy*, Leibniz offered himself as a defender of the faith, in contrast to those "ridiculous critics of God's works" who use the awfulness of experience to claim that God might have done better. His defense of God argued that God could *not* have done any better than He did. But every lawyer has his price. In the process of defending God, Leibniz disempowered Him. More exactly, Leibniz went so far in meeting our needs for understanding the Creator in terms with which we make sense that he gave us a God created in *our* image. Hegel compared him to a vendor in an open market: Leibniz's God can offer only what's available. We should not grumble if the produce isn't perfect but should be content when we know it's the best that can be had (Hegel 5, 3:341). Hegel's metaphor may seem unfair. Neoplatonists could explain evil by defects in the nature of matter. As a Christian, Leibniz was bound by the view that God is also Creator of matter itself. His God is no greengrocer but the Maker of seeds and weather, markets and buyers alike.

How then to explain the defects in all of them? Leibniz's solution was to move all problems back. God created matter but not form. The truth of everything, including the essence of every possible object, is contained in the eternal forms, which function in ways similar to a simple reading of Plato's. Before God decided which of all possible worlds He should choose to make real, He looked at all the forms, calculated which ones would fit together, and chose the best of all possible combinations. The forms are just the rules of reason. Imagining God to *want* to be free of them is to imagine a God who is mad. Yet in defending God against voluntarism, Leibniz did just that of which rationalism is traditionally accused: he put reason above God Himself. Reading Leibniz together with Hegel, one begins to think in pictures: God comparing essences in a ghostly supermarket. If reason itself is more powerful than God, since it prescribes laws that presume to limit Him, it is no wonder that God could come to seem superfluous. The late idealist choice to ignore the middleman and enthrone reason itself might seem just a matter of good sense dictated by Ockham's razor as well as burgeoning market economics. Thus the orthodox charge against every form of rationalism could come to seem comprehensible. To demand or give reasons for God's behavior is to demand to judge Him. Even if the judgment comes out in His favor, it involves an element of presumption that religious views will find unacceptable. In vain will the rationalist protest that reason too is God's creation, and we shouldn't despise His gifts. The traditionalist must answer: did He give it because He thought He would require our help?

The process by which the wish to defend God with reasons would become the wish to displace God with reason was a long one. If the wisdom of hindsight lets us understand traditional fears, the early Enlightenment did not. All to the contrary. Much has been made of the ways in which the scientific revolutions led to skepticism about religious tradition by challenging accepted worldviews. Far less has been said about the ways in which, at the time, they seemed to support faith. Eventually, it may be true that faith in science replaced faith in God; for a very long time, it only strengthened it. The idea goes back to the Renaissance and reached its peak in the middle of the eighteenth century. Pope's couplet, cut as the great man's epitaph, likened the birth of Newton to a second Creation:

Nature and Nature's laws lay hid in Night
God said: Let Newton be! And all was Light.

But it wasn't only Newton. Every new discovery seemed to prove the argument from design. Indeed, for the eighteenth century the argument from design was less an argument than a piece of hard data. Its central claim was just this: the evidence for God's existence is nothing less than the whole of Creation. For the latter is so shot through with order and design that it could not have originated by accident. We needn't point to something as grand or distant as the heavens; the structure of our own hands or eyes will do as well. Designs of that intricacy require a Designer. As Newton's expositor Samuel Clarke summarized:

Yet the notices that God has been pleased to give us of himself are so many and so obvious in the constitution, order, beauty and harmony of the several parts of the world, in the form and structure of our own bodies and the wonderful powers and faculties of our souls, in the unavoidable apprehensions of our own minds and the common consent of all other men, in everything within us and everything without us, that no man of the meanest capacity and greatest disadvantages whatsoever, with the slightest and most superficial observation of the works of God and the lowest and most obvious attendance to the reason of things, can be ignorant of Him; but he must be utterly without excuse. (Clarke, 91)

Science was viewed not as rival but as servant of faith, since every new discovery was a discovery of law. Any advance of science was proof of more order in the universe. Even further, our ability to make discoveries was evidence of our own powers, and of the fit between those powers and the natural world. Wonder upon wonder, God had created human minds and a natural world that were exactly and perfectly balanced to respond to each other. Each new discovery could confirm the glory of each. In his *Religion within the Limits of Reason Alone*, written at the close of the eighteenth century, Kant wrote that King David could never have adored the Creator as we can, for he knew too little of the wonders of Creation. Thus his psalms must pass as empty sound, for the emotion we feel on contemplating the work of God's hand, now manifest in modern science, is too great to express. Such views were as present in literature as in philosophy, in French as in German. The eighteenth-century best-seller *L'An 2440* was a utopian tract depicting Enlightenment fantasies of a future without the injustice and misery of the old regime. Despite all his radicalism, its Rousseau-inspired author imagined religious education that required future generations to look through the telescope and microscope in order to reveal God's presence and glory through this "communion of two infinities. If, by some aberration, an atheist were to appear among them, the Parisians would bring him around with an assiduous course of experimental physics" (quoted in Darnton, 130).

Contemplating such texts makes it is easier to understand Leibniz's confidence that, somehow or other, science would find the hidden connections between happiness and virtue that current experience fails to show. Bayle, says Leibniz, asks "a little too much: he wishes for a detailed explanation of how evil is connected with the best possible scheme for the universe. That would be a complete explanation of the phenomena" (Leibniz, 214). A complete explanation *is* an unreasonable demand—particularly in an era exploding with excitement over partial ones. The example of Alfonso was hope and warning at once: not itself a discovery, or a method for making one, but the sort of thing that could keep one going in the absence of either. Didn't the world get more intelligible all the time?

An unhappy traveler, uncertain of reaching his goal, draws comfort from looking backward to recall how far he's come. The early Enlightenment took Alfonso as consolation. He made clear how great was our progress in grasping the world. Inexplicable death and pain, of course, did not diminish in the wake of eighteenth-century science's discoveries, but neither did expectations of coming to understand them. For hopes were high to behold—or preferably to be—the Newton of the mind. The nearly universal confidence that there would be one may seem amusing for those used to deep conflict between science and the soul—through religion or the categories of ordinary psychology. But we should not read our own distinctions between what the eighteenth century called natural and moral sciences into earlier eras any more than we should our distinctions between natural and moral evils. For an age that had yet to distinguish between hard and soft sciences, the expectation that someone would do for mind what Newton had done for matter was almost trivial. Each was just a piece of universe waiting to be explained. Much less obvious was the kind of explanation that was expected. To wish to be the Newton of the mind was *not* to wish to explain mental experience in physical terms. The search for naturalistic explanation was not yet, or not universally, a search for mechanistic explanation. Natural was opposed to supernatural, and meant something like "lawlike," but the type of law that would turn out to be explanatory was hardly fixed.

Two things that the eighteenth century expected of a second Newton will surprise contemporary readers, but they are clear from the most important text we have on the subject, an early note Kant left unpublished. The Newton of the mind, it indicates, would answer King Alfonso's objection that God's design is flawed. It is for this reason that Leibniz had promised that the causal connections between moral and physical evils now hidden would be made manifest with the progress of science. Suffering that seems entirely random, hence liable to make us doubt God's goodness, would be shown to be the effect of some sin we had secretly committed. Moreover, suffering would be shown to be itself the cause of some greater good, so that the network of causality now partly traceable throughout the physical universe would be seamlessly extended to the moral one. If this seems far-fetched, imagine how implausible a connection between the phases of the moon and the motion of the tides must have seemed. After these had been placed in causal relation, what other kinds of connection might not be soon to come?

The second service expected of the coming Newton follows from the first one. A Newton of the mind would not remove God's presence from the universe (by reducing spirit to soulless mechanism, as is often suggested) but would eloquently testify to it. Newton viewed his work as testimony to the glory of God, and no eighteenth-century admirer would have disagreed. Alfonso's doubts about the cosmos had been laid to rest forever by the English scientist, who was rewarded for his labor in defense of the Creator by the repeated epithet "immortal" along with the earthly title "Sir Isaac." While most of early science was viewed as a series of proofs for the argument from design, Newton's was paradigmatic. Not only had he seen connections where others saw chaos, found the most elegant and far-reaching formulas, joined heaven and earth by relating their movements. Even more precisely, Newton had shown that given a description of the initial conditions and properties of all its parts, one could derive the state of the system of the universe at any given time. Once the system is set in motion, it runs more or less on its own. Later it would seem clear that a God whose only task was to create a perfect world might be in danger of disappearing from it, but at the time Newton's vision was a vision of God's greatness. For most seventeenth- and eighteenth-century thinkers, God's presence was such a given that consequences which now seem obvious will not have occurred to them. People feared an incompetent God, like Alfonso's, or a malevolent God, like Descartes's. As the following chapter will argue, the Enlightenment offered possibilities that seem more frightening than any we now imagine; but an entirely absent God was rarely among them.

The *Theodicy* is often credited with inspiring Pope's *Essay on Man*. Published in 1734, the *Essay* was probably the eighteenth century's favorite poem. Kant was wont to quote Pope in university lectures, Voltaire was happy to translate him, and when Hume addressed the question whether politics can be scientific, his starting point wasn't

Montesquieu but the English poet. The meaning of Pope's views was debated from one end of Europe to the other. Part of such debate was a contest sponsored by the Prussian Academy. The questions proposed by the Academy tell us much about the framework of eighteenth-century intellectual culture:

> The Academy requests an investigation into the Popean system which contains the sentence "everything is good". In particular, each contestant should (first) determine what the true sense of this sentence is, according to its author; (second) exactly compare it to the system of optimism, or choice of the best; (thirdly) state the reasons for or against accepting the Popean system.

The exactness of analysis of the questions at issue is only apparent, as the most famous entry to the contest was at pains to show. "Pope a Metaphysician!" is its title, and Lessing and Mendelssohn clearly enjoyed coauthoring it. It's hard to imagine another motive for writing, since the scorn they heaped on the Academy for posing the question virtually ensured that the prize would go to someone else. Their discussion is occasionally funny, but more often reminiscent of the pedantic swagger with which some philosophers discuss literary texts in private. Their main point, argued at greater length than it need be, is that Pope is a poet concerned to clothe philosophical ideas in attractive dress, but unable to develop them with any depth or consistency. Hence, they conclude, he's unworthy of serious philosophical engagement. For this reason alone he differs from Leibniz. Perhaps they share certain moral claims, but their principles are entirely different. Lessing and Mendelssohn were right to stress Pope's distance from Leibniz. Pope may seem to simply mold the well-meant orthodoxies that Leibniz defended, but in fact he undermines them, as many of his contemporaries recognized. In so doing, he takes crucial steps toward the world we will see in Rousseau. That world is not apparent from many of the *Essay*'s most famous verses:

> All Nature is but Art, unknown to thee;
> All Chance, Direction, which thou canst not see;
> All Discord, Harmony not understood;

All partial Evil, universal Good:
And in spite of Pride, in erring Reason's spite,
One truth is clear, WHATEVER IS, IS RIGHT.
(Pope, 289–95)

This certainly sounds like Leibniz—except that it is written as a poem and not a legal brief, thus making enjoyable a message in which modern readers will find little else to enjoy. Pope seems to assert the unbroken goodness of Creation as it stands; the existence of an order behind appearances which assures that unbroken goodness; and the presumption and ignorance of anyone who dares to suggest the world could be improved. Pope's very art may seem to lend fervor to his defense of the established order that makes it even more alien than Leibniz's. ("All this dread ORDER break—for whom? For thee? / Vile worm! Oh madness! Pride! Impiety!" (Pope, 257–8). But Pope knew that his contemporaries would regard the *Essay* differently, and he took care to publish anonymously. For even this seemingly conservative claim could be read as seditious. As Voltaire pointed out, if whatever is, is right, there is no room for original sin—or Providence itself. Progressive intellectuals may have loved it, but traditional readers described it as a nursery of heretical opinions, and the chief cause of vice among Christians. One critic compared Pope to Eve seducing Adam in the Garden of Eden; for like her he pandered to his readers' lower faculties with the beauty of his verse, and befuddled their minds by overheating their bodies.

The quarrel between philosophy and poetry is an old one, as is the philosopher's suspicion of good writing as merely seductive. Relatively generous critics like Lessing and Mendelssohn saw the work as simply confused, but hostile critics called it intentionally confusing. They charged that Pope manipulated readers with sensual pleasure to mask corrupt, impious views. Pope cannot have been unaware of the tension between the genres when he decided to write philosophical poetry. Presumably he chose it because neither medium alone was fit to express what he wanted. Poetry itself never seeks the kinds of judgments of meaning and morals that Pope often intended. But philosophy alone is too straightforward, too unambiguous to do justice to the complexity

Pope saw in the human condition. Poetry has a wider range of responses than those open to philosophy, mixing tones, changing mood and mode, shifting from the somber to the ironic without looking for grounds. The unclarity of which Pope was accused is, I believe, entirely intentional; he sought to reflect, not to resolve, the complexity of the questions at issue.

The *Essay* has been called an exercise in which a very troubled writer struggled to convince himself of a system of ideas he could not wholly accept. This is probably true. Poetry can record that struggle without settling it, and this alone may give it an advantage over philosophy, which seeks conclusive solution. Pope's *Essay* records the struggle between hope and despair that can take place daily in anyone who thinks about the questions he raised. By using poetry, he could use resources of irony, metaphor, and paradox to hold that struggle in tension without seeking to resolve it. For resolving it would require him to reduce the very many perspectives one can take on the matter into one final and decisive one. Since the poem itself is about the multiplicity of perspective, such finality would be false to the reality of human experience.

One of Pope's first critics complained, "Have poets so extensive a Privilege that they may boldly assert the wildest Paradoxes, provided they utter them in sounding Language?" The question is meant to be rhetorical, but the answer, I think, is: yes, they do. Part of the work of poetry is just to express paradox without absurdity, to give form to contradiction without stilling it, to give voice to tension without dissolving it. Poets can leave things open that philosophers cannot.[5] Pope uses question almost as often as he uses assertion, makes hypothetical as often as categorical statements. In so doing, he not only states our ignorance of the great metaphysical questions he seeks to resolve—one major theme of the *Essay*—but shows it in the very form of the text. If Pope loved to remind us of how little we understand, the paradoxes and shifts in the poem allow us to feel it. When we cannot even determine Pope's position on the problem of evil, how can we hope to find a solution to the problem itself?

To emphasize the skepticism eighteenth-century readers felt in the poem, rather than the affirmation of order now apparent to us, seems to put Pope closer to Bayle than to Leibniz. Like Bayle, Pope denied that we can understand the order of the universe, and thought it foolish and arrogant to try. This amounts to the claim that only faith can resolve the problem of evil with which Leibniz and other metaphysicians had wrestled. But unlike Bayle, who was content to regard most things as beyond our understanding, Pope's poem began to suggest that there is *some* problem of evil that might be within our reach. With this he unlocked a door to the modern that Rousseau would open. For the *Essay* that began and ended with a defense of Providence is, after all, the *Essay on Man*.

Modern readers may be surprised by how little interest Leibniz showed in the human. The *Theodicy* devoted a great deal more attention to divine than to human freedom, and makes reference to human choice and passion more by way of example than anything else. Eighteenth-century readers analyzed fine differences between Pope's "Whatever is, is right" and Leibniz's "Everything happens for the best," but perhaps the greatest difference is that it is impossible to imagine Leibniz's claim followed by the great couplet with which Pope followed his.

> Know then thyself, presume not God to scan
> The proper study of mankind is Man.
> (Pope, 1–2)

Traditional readers lambasted the poem for focusing on "man" rather than "immortal man"—the latter being the only object thought proper for pious and serious contemplation. With his very title, Pope signaled a shift of focus from God's nature and responsibilities to our own. In so doing, he began to push the problem of evil out of the realm of metaphysics and theology into the world of ethics and psychology, and therewith to a set of questions we can recognize as our own. Pope directs us to understand ourselves, our passions, and our possibilities, for only these have bearing on any problem of evil we may hope to affect.

The absence of a notion of original sin, and the cheerful description of the initial state of nature, foreshadowed Rousseau's. So did the moral psychology Pope drew from them. His attempt to give a naturalistic account of the passions was not as deep or complex as Rousseau's. Nor was his claim that ordinary self-love can be cultivated to aim at the general good. Still they point in the same direction, and the consequences were plain. For those committed to belief in original sin, salvation could come only by grace (or, depending on how much freedom one ascribed to individuals, by repeated threats of eternal damnation). But if, as Pope thought, our own self-love is inherently social, then acting virtuously is natural. It may even be pleasant. If that's the case, what's needed to eradicate most evils is not prayers and threats, but self-knowledge and social arrangements. This is anything but the Cosmic Toryism of which Pope was later accused.

A poet with Pope's eye for irony would have been amused to learn that the naturalist impulse which was born in service of religion came to seem antithetical to it. But the original intention is evident not only in Pope's claim that God's wise design links self-love and sociability, but in his far-reaching attack on the appeal to final causes. The rejection of final causes was not undertaken simply in service of mechanical ones. Rather, Pope believed that thinking in terms of final causes leads to rebellion and despair. Assuming the world is made to suit our purposes, we are outraged and miserable when it doesn't. To recognize that the universe is not created for our needs is not to assert that it's indifferent to them. The line between patience and resignation is one Pope wished to preserve. His insistence that the final causes of things cannot be known, and should therefore drop out of view, is meant to keep the balance. His examples can be chilling: a man who thinks that all the world exists for his benefit is no better than a pampered goose who believes that the farmer who fattens him exists for his. Removing teleology from the world began as an attempt to preserve significance, not to destroy it. The ultimate meaning of Creation may be forever out of our reach. But this, for Pope, was no ground for despair. We need not fear that its resistance to our purposes means it has none at all.

NEWTON OF THE MIND: JEAN-JACQUES ROUSSEAU

Suggestions are not science, however well expressed. As much as Kant loved to quote Pope, he never called him a second Newton. That was an honor he reserved for Rousseau. This choice is anything but obvious. In an age when it was common to work in multiple genres, Rous-

seau was extravagant: he wrote opera and literature as well as tracts
declaiming against them, moved from political theory to theology with
ease and erudition, and in the *Emile* and the *Confessions*, invented
genres of his own. The one thing he did not engage in, unlike most of
his contemporaries, was anything they would have classified as science—with the exception of a small treatise on botany that he wrote
toward the end of his life. Yet Kant believed that only Rousseau was
comparable to Newton. This meant, he wrote, that Rousseau had justified God and proved Pope's thesis true. We must assume that the thesis
of Pope which Kant has in mind is the one the eighteenth century
quoted most often: whatever is, is right. Rousseau will have proved it
if he has refuted the objections of Alfonso and the Manichaeans. But
why did Kant write that, before Rousseau, those objections were valid?
Leibniz used Alfonso to counsel patience. As rhetoric, it was probably
more effective than the maledictions preferred by others. Instead of
calling those who complain about the quality of Creation "vile worms,"
Leibniz made them targets of ridicule. After being a fool, how did Alfonso become again a threat?

How does a straw become the last one? The metaphor underscores
just the thinness of causal explanation. Burdens grow until the beast
collapses under the accumulated weight of contradiction, disappointment, and exhaustion. The eighteenth-century faith in scientific discoveries that would reinforce traditional faith in Providence was not destroyed by any single event. Lisbon focused the problem, but it didn't
invent it. For one thing, natural disaster was part of the literature. Pope
had no trouble mentioning plagues, earthquakes, and volcanoes. All
these were events that no serious thinker took to undermine belief in
the greatness of Creation. Significantly, he attacks those who hold
moral evils to be a greater threat than natural ones.

> If plagues or earthquakes break not Heaven's design,
> Why then a Borgia, or a Catiline?
> (Pope, 32)

At least two reasons were offered for the suggestion that moral evils
threaten faith in Providence more surely than do natural ones. The first
was that natural evils display something sublime, even beautiful, that

cannot be found in moral ones. No decent Enlightenment thinker regarded moral evils as anything but vile. Even more important was the persistent assumption that natural evils exist as punishment for moral ones. The former therefore required no justification. Far from breaking Heaven's design, they were a crucial part of it, for they were evidence of a moral order in which every sin had consequences. More puzzling was a world whose Creator allowed crimes that would require such punishment. This was a Leibnizian problem, the reason he devoted the bulk of the *Theodicy* to developing a notion of divine freedom that could function in the limits of necessity. Pope clearly found it less troubling. This was partly because he was beginning to develop notions of moral psychology that would allow for explanations of moral evil. But more important, he held any other, more traditional problem of evil to be inexplicable. Earthquakes, like other catastrophes, could be incorporated into natural law—depending on how interested one was in geology. They could also be worked into a system in which sin and suffering were self-evidently connected—depending on how sanguine one was about our ability to discover such connections. Pope himself was not. He mentions that "several of the ancients, and many of the Orientals" regard those who are struck by lightning as special favorites of Heaven. Pope sees such views as more reason to be skeptical about ever understanding the ways of Providence rather than as a clue to them. If there are signs, we cannot read them.

Thus enlightened theists like Leibniz and Pope had standard ways of coping with catastrophe. They argued that a world which works according to general natural law is far better than a world requiring God's intervention in special cases. The latter would be ad hoc and chaotic, unbefitting the dignity of a majestic and omnicompetent sovereign. Physical accidents that sometimes occur are the unfortunate side effects of those general laws which give the world order and allow us to orient ourselves in it. To rail against their Author because of occasional negative consequences would be as stupid, and ungrateful, as to rail against a monarch whose great system of law contains an occasional weakness. For it's far better to have sporadic injustice in a society governed by law than to live in a state of permanent anarchy.

These claims may show where analogies between divine and earthly rulers break down, and turn us into democrats on both fronts. Not the least among problems with this sort of argument was Leibniz's choice of example to illustrate it. We can't expect the weather system to change its nature, he wrote, because the rain that produces a harvest in one field prevents a picnic in another. It did not take all the resources of French pathos available to Voltaire to point out that the Lisbon earthquake was hardly a spoiled outing. Initially, however, the century's deepest thinkers tried to treat it with the traditional resources available for discussing disaster. Both Kant's and Rousseau's initial reactions to Lisbon were highly unimpressive, revealing them as nothing more than good students of Leibniz and Pope. Kant argued with more conviction than consistency both that earthquakes sometimes have beneficial consequences, and that they are in any case only natural events. Rousseau attacked Voltaire for depriving him of hope for a better world, and the citizens of Lisbon for living in cities, where earthquakes do maximum damage.

It was a curious phenomenon. Here Rousseau began to demarcate a sphere of natural accident that is neutral: disaster has no moral worth whatsoever and need have no negative effects. The latter were the result solely of human failure. On the one hand, this was the beginning of a modern distinction between natural and moral evil. It is crucial to such a distinction that natural evils have no inherent significance. They are neither punishment nor sign but part of an order that is, literally, meaningless. On the other hand, the distinction was fed by archaic appeals to guilt that end in making even those evils caused by natural disaster somehow or other our fault—and hence having meaning after all. The traditional assumption that there must be a connection between sin and suffering was thereby both canceled and preserved. It should come as no surprise that Rousseau's characteristic focus on human contributions to our own suffering appeared in orthodox religious contexts. Hence his remarks about Lisbon remained more traditional than Voltaire's. While Rousseau underlined the modern separation between natural and moral evil, he did so in a way that seemed to blame us for both. And the only positive suggestion he offered for alleviating either form of evil was a return to a society with more primitive architecture.

Traditional features of Rousseau's discussion of evil were even more evident in the one explicit reference he made to Alfonso himself. It occurred in a reply to objections made to his own first publication. The *Discourse on the Arts and Sciences* argued that the study of philosophy leads to little but vanity. There Rousseau considered the difference between the philosopher and the farmer. The philosopher imagines he can understand God's ways and has the right to judge them. By contrast, the farmer

> does not censure God's works, and does not attack his master to show off his own adequacy. The blasphemous statement of Alfonse X will never enter the mind of the common man.
> (Rousseau 1, 36)

Though Rousseau claimed to admire Leibniz's optimism, the difference between them was profound. Leibniz was optimistic not only about God's goodness but about our capacities for understanding it. Unlike Leibniz, Rousseau never suggested that Alfonso would have done better to study modern science. On the contrary: he would have done better not to study at all.

Rousseau's most sustained discussion of Providence occurred in the "Creed of the Savoyard Vicar," that part of *Emile* which managed to offend almost everyone. This section caused the book to be collected and burned by the public executioner in Paris. Its author was spared a similar fate, but he was saved from imprisonment only by a warning from the prince de Conti, who urged him to leave France at dawn before the warrant for his arrest could be served. The authorities read the book as a severe attack on religion, since Rousseau denied both original sin and the need for religious instruction, and preached an unacceptable degree of religious tolerance. While the book was banned by the establishment for undermining religion, it was loathed by the *philosophes* for the opposite offense. For though the "Creed" argued against traditional forms of religious authority, it clearly defended traditional faith in Providence. Rousseau's grounds for that faith were unembellished: there must be reward and punishment in another world, or the miseries of this one would be too much to bear. The straightforward pathos with which the "Creed" voiced Rousseau's declaration of faith can seem so traditional that contemporary readers may find it insipid. They will surely miss, on first reading, what was once experienced as critical.

No wonder Rousseau's Parisian patrons held him to have returned to views of which educated people should be ashamed—and no wonder Kant's description of Rousseau as a second Newton is usually ignored.[6] And yet, I will argue, Kant did not exaggerate. Despite its initial appearance, Rousseau's discussion is so new and profound that it radically changed our construction of the problem of evil. Although the eighteenth century was dominated by discussions of the question, it's fair to say that Rousseau was the first to treat the problem of evil as a *philosophical* problem—as well as to offer the first thing approaching a solution to it.

Before Rousseau, thinkers were forced into one of two positions. To claim that this world is the best is to view all evils as ultimately apparent: anything we take to be evil is in fact a necessary part of a greater plan. Leibniz thought we would someday understand it, and Pope thought we wouldn't. They agreed, however, that there *is* an order in which everything that looks like evil leads to the good of the larger whole. The result is that no particular evil is genuine. Everything we experience as evil works more or less like radical medical treatment by a competent doctor: as awful as it seems to the patient, all the alternatives are worse. This was called the doctrine of optimism, and many felt it gave optimists a bad name. For it seems to amount to straightforward denial. So Rousseau viewed it in answering a Leibnizian named Charles Bonnet:

> To deny the existence of evil is a most convenient way of excusing the author of that evil; the Stoics formerly made themselves a laughing-stock for less. (Rousseau 1, 233–34)

Rousseau also pointed out that such doctrines lead to quietism. If evils are merely apparent, and everything is the best that it could be, there's no need to do anything about them. Indeed, any action might count as impious—as many authorities used traditional theodicy to argue.

Optimism could preclude not only practical action but theoretical undertaking as well. All that's left is the orthodox theory that dissolves certain questions by fiat. If there is no genuine evil, how could there be a problem of it?

As we will see in the following chapter, critics of optimism were forced into the opposite role. Those who acknowledged that evils are genuine found that they literally defy explanation. Not only do all the resources of reasoning fail to explain them; the persistence of evil makes us doubt all the resources of reasoning itself. Taking evil seriously seemed to demand that we deny philosophy: it is hopeless to analyze evil, and probably wrong to try. The most we can do is describe it. Denying philosophy, for some, amounted to denying God as well. Rousseau's novel *La Nouvelle Héloïse* contains one character representing the voice of good common sense. He is noble, and virtuous, but committed to atheism. For

> Wolmar contented himself with observing that we must recognize that, little or great, evil indeed exists, and from this existence alone he inferred the absence of power, intelligence or goodness in the First Cause. (Rousseau 2, 352)

Whether or not Wolmar is actually modeled on Hume, with whom Rousseau eventually quarreled, he expresses the view that Hume voiced best: admitting the reality of evil precludes providing an account of it. Occasionally thinkers countered by proposing Manichaeism as the most reasonable response to the problem of evil. But even Bayle was aware that this was less a solution to the problem than a reflection of it: *There are two forces in the universe, one of good, one of evil.*—This is just the world we see, not an explanation of it. No wonder Bayle thought faith to be the deeper response. Before Rousseau, in short, there were just two options: either there is no problem of evil, or there is no answer to it.

Tradition seemed to offer another, and just as he was partly influenced by Seneca, Rousseau built on Augustine's account. For Augustine, the connection between moral and natural evil was clear: infinite punishment for infinite guilt. He thus had no need to deny the reality of either sort of evil; in fact, he insisted on it, at considerable length. The original sin of ungrateful disobedience was just as bad as the punishment that followed it: expulsion from Eden, and the loss of the eternal life we could have had there. But neither of these horrors can be laid at God's door. God's benevolence wasn't called into question by the presence of evil, for we are its authors. God loved us enough to make us in His image, and allowed us a share in Creation by giving us free will. Our abuse of that gift was so thorough that only a miracle, the Passion of Jesus, can save us.

This sketch should reveal all the distance between Rousseau and traditional solutions before him. Like Augustine, Rousseau held human freedom to be God's greatest gift; like Augustine, he was tireless in describing the ways we abuse it. Unlike Augustine, Rousseau held the Fall, and any possible redemption from it, to be explicable in terms that are completely natural. Here *natural* meant scientific, as opposed to religious. Rousseau replaced theology with history, grace with educational psychology. In so doing, he took the responsibility for evil out of God's hands and put it squarely in ours. Augustine is sometimes said to have given humankind responsibility for evil. It seems more accurate to say he gave humankind the *blame* for evil, but this is not the same. On Augustine's account, perhaps Adam and Eve, but only Adam and Eve, could have done otherwise. Without massive supernatural intervention, we surely cannot. Augustine's discussion of free will left him open to Bayle's charge: generous donors don't offer gifts that will destroy their recipients.

Rousseau's account vindicated God all the more surely as it did so without damning humankind. Evil is our own doing, but we are not inherently perverse. The entire catalog of crimes and misfortunes can be seen as not fully intentional but mistaken. Thus knowledge, not penance, is needed. Once we have it, we are free to undo the damage any time. Rousseau's notion of freedom left metaphysics aside. The little discussion he devoted to traditional questions of free will was fairly conventional. New in his account was the recognition that freedom has real conditions. If we care about freedom, we must care about history and politics, education and psychology. Metaphysics is as little required for redemption as is grace and will just as surely be taken care of—or not—without our intervention.

For Rousseau, both the problem of evil and its solution depend on the idea that evil developed over time. This assumes, in turn, that human beings develop over time, both as species and individual beings. *Human nature has been altered.* Thus begins the second *Discourse,* and its force becomes clear only when we recall how earlier thinkers saw human nature as much the same through time and space. Classical Greek thought viewed the cosmos as eternal, and the relation of human beings within it as eternally fixed. In arguing that God, or apocalypse, could turn the course of the cosmos, Jewish and Christian thought broke with static conceptions that prevailed before them. But the doctrine of original sin depends on the idea that human nature could change at most once: at the time of the Fall. And many Enlightenment thinkers used the new discoveries provided by commerce and travel to argue not for the variety of human nature but for its depressing unity.[7] If human nature is fixed, any evils we cause or suffer will be fixed within it. The one is as immutable as the other. This leads to a view as comfortable as it is depressing. If human nature was corrupted through one wrong choice in Eden, our particular choices can make little difference. For Rousseau, by contrast, human nature itself has a history. Our choices affect it.

History is the right kind of category to introduce because it enables us to understand the world and gives us hope for changing it. History leaves space between necessity and accident, making actions intelligible without being determined. If the introduction of evil was necessary, we can be saved only by a miracle. If it was an accident, then the world, where it matters, makes no sense. History, by contrast, is dynamic. If evil was introduced into the world, then it might also be eradicated—as long as its development is not fundamentally mysterious. After Rousseau, we need not deny the reality of evil. We can, rather, incorporate it into a world whose intelligibility is expanding. Exploring evil as historical phenomenon becomes part of our efforts to make the world more comprehensible in theory, and more acceptable in practice.

Kant saw Rousseau's view as revolutionary as much because it allowed us to state the problem of evil as because it offered solutions. The task was to determine a relation between moral and natural evils, or risk acknowledging that the world has no justice or meaning. Rousseau was the first to assert a relation without calling it punishment, hence the first to see a solution that doesn't depend on miracle. He thus could avoid bad faith—a notion he more or less invented—and still affirm the glory of God. Rousseau never denied the depth of evil, and he enraged most of his contemporaries by showing that they were both more corrupt and more miserable than they'd noticed. Yet his claim that such misery was a result of clear historical processes, and could be undone by others, made his work one long witness to Providence.

If the particular details of his solution to the problem of evil are unimportant, the fact that there *are* details is not. It was crucial that there be some. Details were evidence that Leibniz's promises were not empty. Would-be optimists waited decades for someone to make evil intelligible, to show that, all murky appearances to the contrary, the world was the best it could be. Rousseau's account was designed to do that: revealing a world that was good at the core, awaiting only human action to make it better. His account is found in the second *Discourse* and the *Emile*, books related to each other as diagnosis and prescription. The second *Discourse* offered an alternative to the story of the Fall. It explained how the noble savage, though free of evil and suffering in the state of nature, came to spawn the wretched creatures who pass for civilized humanity. Rousseau's alternative incorporated elements of the new science. Like Newton, Rousseau began from a minimalist description of the bodies to be explained and showed how the present state of affairs followed naturally from a few initial properties. All the vices that currently plague us could be explained through a few developmental principles. A little vanity, and the alienation from our own natures that accompanies it, can take us all the way to the systems of artifice and injustice now organizing our world. Rousseau's account of evil was naturalistic because it required no reference to supernatural forces or sin. Not only divine but human intention began to disappear from view in the very moment evil emerged. Evil arose as collective process, not as act of individual will. This was no appeal to necessity: his emphasis on history was meant to show that evil arose through a process that was thoroughly understandable but contingent. We became wicked without willing it, through a series of particular events. There are tendencies to weakness within human nature, but their course is not inevitable. The second *Discourse* showed how certain processes, once begun, gain compelling momentum. But momentum is not inevitability: the world could, at each point, have been otherwise.

The story doesn't matter. (But neither, I suggested, does the story Rousseau wished to replace. *You can eat all the fruit in the garden but that one.* Why not?) Rousseau stressed the unimportance of the content of his story in the outrageous statement that opens the book: "Let us begin by setting aside the facts, for they do not affect the matter at hand" (Rousseau 1, 139). This is the realm of myth, not quite history, but any other narrative of origins will be mythic too. Rousseau described one particular descent from primeval innocence to civilized misery, but we might have gone down in a number of ways. Evil came into the world through a long slow development during which human beings alienated themselves from their own true nature. Evil is thus external, not intrinsic to who we are, and it involves precisely a focus on the external rather than the essential. The noble savage knows who he is and what he needs without considering the views and needs of others. Civilized people never even see themselves when they're not reflected in others' eyes.

Downfall wasn't present in the social process itself. History began in isolation. Savages gathered food, met occasionally to copulate, and scattered again without emotion other than the capacity for pity, which takes the place of active benevolence. Pity ensured that mothers cared for their infants until the age of two, when they could disappear into the forest to fend for themselves. The radical isolation Rousseau imagined was broken by one natural accident or another. A harsh winter, a dry summer forced these solitary nomads to band together into tribes, sharing labor and land. While they lived in simple villages, property was held in common, and division of labor was kept to a minimum. As in the biblical Fall, the original dissonance in this paradise was erotic. The moment people gathered in groups, the human shape of sexuality was formed. Desire for the other's body is easy to feel, and not hard to gratify; desire for the other's desire is complex. As soon as it's present, public esteem acquires value. Each wants to appear better than the others to arouse the attention of the opposite sex. This initial regard for the way we appear, and the competition in which it puts us with others, is a part of our nature that is perfectly neutral. From it can develop that alienation from our nature which is the source of evil.

So long as confined to donning paint and feathers, trying to excel in song or dance around a fire before a hut, alienation needn't be fatal. What's the decisive point in the catastrophe that became civilization? Readers of the second *Discourse* can easily feel bewildered. At several points in his retelling of history, Rousseau interrupts his narrative to assert that a particular event was the key to humankind's downfall. Each event is introduced with authority and passion—until he discovers the next one. After human sexuality he named the discoveries of iron and wheat, the division of labor, and private ownership of land, with increasingly emphatic rhetoric each time. Possibly, Rousseau was confused, or didn't notice the contradictions. I think it more likely that he held no one moment for decisive. No point was the turning point in civilization, and it's a mistake to try to seek one. He intended, rather, to show that once certain processes begin, the move to the next stage of civilization—and misery—is almost, but not quite, inevitable. At several points in time, we might have turned the course of history. Since we didn't, the process by which we passed from self-sufficient decency to the web of dependence and betrayal that makes up the social world is a process we must understand.

Rousseau was the first to propose a natural connection between sin and suffering. Our misery isn't groundless but results from our sins. The relation between the two is all the more direct for the fact that it requires no intervention from God. We suffer because of our actions, but not through direct divine punishment. Every sin contains its own penalty as a natural consequence, every virtue its own reward. We are the authors of our own suffering and could be the source of our happiness—not because God is keeping score and meting out justice, but because He has so arranged the world that such justice is part of a natural order.

Evil brings its own misery in big things and small. Rousseau discussed how to punish children, should they need it, in book 2 of *Emile*. He insisted that punishment should follow intrinsically from wrongdoing and should not be experienced as a product of the authority's will. For children, he argues, accept natural evils as necessary. What they reject are attempts by other human beings to impose things on them. These will always be experienced as arbitrary, hence resented as evils—even if carried out for the child's own good. The child who cheerfully accepts the statement that the sweets are all gone will rebel against the statement that she can't have any before dinner. So a child who breaks a window should suffer a night in the cold; a child who tells a lie should experience a world in which no one believes him. Rousseau wanted education to mirror the natural world, in which misdeed and misery are internally related.

This conviction could be the source of what sounds like sympathy. More than other radical thinkers, particularly those born at the bottom of the social world, Rousseau noticed rich people's pain. Indeed, he insisted on it. This may be partly an attempt at seduction, but Rousseau was more likely to confront than persuade. When he repeatedly argued that aristocracy suffers from its own false needs, it's doubtful that he was trying to tempt them. It wasn't his style, and he was too shrewd to expect many converts. His point was systematic. Like other evils, gathering wealth has immediate costs. The rich man must deny others' claims to his riches, isolating himself in boredom and fear. The luxuries he enjoys are more painful to lose than they are pleasurable to discover. Each object creates new sources of discontent faster than it satisfies old ones. Rousseau's analysis of false needs and consumerism is very prescient, but his point is as theological as it is political. Understood rightly, evil is not even tempting, for the universe is so constructed that suffering follows evil as the night the day.

The opposite, of course, is just as true: most of the time, virtue leads straight to happiness. This is entirely different from the Stoic claim that virtue is the same thing as happiness. Rousseau scorned Stoics as simple deniers. Contemplating your own virtue may be good advice in a Roman prison, where there's nothing else to console you, but calling this the highest form of pleasure is sheer self-deception. If this is all the consolation philosophy can offer, no wonder most people prefer faith. Rousseau's claim was another entirely: those actions which are good are also the most pleasant and have the most pleasant consequences—not in moral, but in sensual terms. Toward the end of *Emile*, he slipped into reverie, imagining life as a man of vast wealth. Rousseau was sure that if he had it, he'd continue to live much the same simple life he enjoyed without it. Rousseau may have been tortured, but he was no ascetic. The *Confessions* reveals that he understood pleasure, if he seldom knew quite what to do with it. His fantasy was not about heavenly but about earthly rewards: "I would be temperate out of sensuality" (Rousseau 3, 345). Rustic cottages are more cheerful; simple dress is more comfortable; country dinners taste better than sumptuous Parisian fare. One need not share his taste to understand his meaning: virtue and happiness are *causally* connected.

With this in mind, we can understand features of Rousseau's writing that look simply odd. For readers of the view sketched thus far should find it overly cheerful. Just to grant a great deal for the sake of argument, suppose that moral evils do lead to natural ones in the social and political realm. What about death and disease, which are out of our hands? Rousseau's remarks about both should be seen systematically. He often asserted that death itself is not an evil. The noble savage doesn't fear it; the Spartan mother doesn't mourn it (Rousseau 3, 40). Healthy people, he argued, find loss of freedom a greater horror than loss of life. Health itself is also part of nature, and civilization brings diseases for which it has no cure. Rousseau's oft-repeated insistence on the illnesses caused by the medical profession and practices of his day are partly the complaints of a chronically ill man in the hands of eighteenth-century quacks. They were no less an expression of philosophical conviction: most of the evils called natural are part of a world we have ruined, and could come to control. *Emile*'s first sentence could sum up all of Rousseau's thought:

> Everything is good as it leaves the hands of the Author of nature; everything degenerates in the hands of men.

This must apply to bodies as well as minds. Hence the discussion, in *Emile* and elsewhere, of diet and posture, exercise and sleep. Rousseau's treatment of them was always part prescription, part theodicy. If we follow nature's instructions, we can see how well she works. Death itself is a part of nature. The fact that we do not live forever is no more of an evil than the fact that we do not have wings or live on air. Only a humanity estranged from its own nature, hence unable to accept natural necessity, will view death itself as an evil.

Thus everything in Rousseau's world testified to Creation. Whatever God made was good. But ruin, once begun, occurs with great speed. Disaster in Genesis seems a matter of minutes. Though centuries elapsed between the eating of forbidden fruit and sins so great that they provoked the Flood, their description takes a couple of pages. In Rousseau's Fall too, the debacle is swift, the damage possibly irreparable. The second *Discourse* was perceived as unremittingly dark. Voltaire called it Rousseau's "new work against mankind," while others demanded a prescription for the illness called civilization that Rousseau had diagnosed. His answer was bleak: you don't call the doctor once the patient is dead. When he wrote the diagnosis, he couldn't see a cure. Though his work displayed clear nostalgia for the state of nature, he saw a return to it as no more likely than a return to Eden. Lost innocence cannot be found. But by 1762, Rousseau saw a chance for salvation. In the *Emile*, the isolated savage of the second *Discourse* was given another chance. This time, Rousseau took care that he wouldn't be left on his own. He designed an education meant to undo the processes the *Discourse* had described. Raised as nature intended, the child would not be vulnerable to the evils of civilization, and could play a role in constructing a better one.

Rousseau called *Emile* his brightest work, and reading it was the one event, besides the French Revolution, that ever broke Kant's routine. We should now be able to understand why. Providence was no longer an extraordinary occurrence but a matter of natural law. *Emile* argued that the same natural processes which caused moral evil could be used to cure it. It's important to note that the goal was not to return us to the state of nature but to produce something better. Emile should be raised in the country, with so little formal education that civilized society will find him savage. But at eighteen, the age of reason, he will not only be a young man whose freedom and self-respect are second to none; he will also have become a philosopher (Rousseau 3, 315, 458). *Emile* is the proof that any ordinary boy can realize the Enlightenment dream. Freedom, reason, and sexuality were the source of the errors that brought evil into Creation. Properly managed, just those capacities can be molded to form human beings far more noble than anything possible in the state of nature.

Especially important was the idea that redemption would take place through the very processes that led us to ruin. For a God who allowed our natural faculties to lead us to catastrophe that only a miracle can get us out of isn't as good as one who gave us the means to repair our own damage. Indeed, Rousseau went one step further. He wished to prove the goodness of Creation by proving the goodness of its toughest cases. What Christianity had blamed for disaster—desires for sex and knowledge—could be used to overcome it. Thus God is not to be blamed but all the more to be praised for giving us tools that can overcome corruption just as naturally as they can cause it. They thereby lead to firmer and deeper virtue than we would have without them.

Only self-knowledge can save us, but it's just as hard to get as it is crucial. This may be the single clearest statement running through Rousseau's work. Self-knowledge is rare because we're masters of self-deception; it's crucial because viewing ourselves through others' opinions perpetuates alienation and vanity. Knowledge of humankind as a species teaches us to distinguish what's essential to human nature from what's been altered. Knowledge of ourselves as individuals teaches us to distinguish our own true needs from the false ones that cloud all our efforts at virtue. Rousseau didn't aim to counter the Enlightenment but to give it solid foundation. As Kant saw, Rousseau's goal was to produce not a modern savage but a man who can think for himself. Most education proceeds by creating desires to display one's accomplishments or meet others' expectations. But the knowledge that will lead to self-knowledge must come from true needs the child gradually develops. Emile should not read until his twelfth year. His slow introduction to culture was based in part on Rousseau's observation of child development. At least as important as empirical observation was the theory of humankind's evolution as a species laid out in the second *Discourse*. Culture and sexuality were born at the same moment, and each draws much of its power from the other. Human beings invest bodies with souls, biology with ideas, which creates the potential for redemption as well as danger. From the moment we invented song and dance to attract other savages' attention, culture and sexuality combined to create cycles of vanity and alienation from which we have yet to recover. By handling both of them carefully, the educator can turn a natural drive into a search for the ideal erotic object. This creates a love for the ideal itself—the source of any human striving we may value.

Rousseau went even further. If properly managed, sexual desire could be the link between self-interest and morality that other thinkers sought in vain. What links members of civil society? Hobbes's instrumentalist social contract provided too little; Enlightenment claims that we're naturally social presume too much. We are neither so brutish nor so benevolent as each would imagine. There is one act, however, in which your own interest is identical with the interest of the other. This is erotic love. If done as it should be, conflict between human desires is dissolved just then.

Thus love between men and women is the cornerstone on which Rousseau would found a society to overcome all the evils civilization produced. In seeking that love, Emile must learn all the arts and sciences can teach us about the human heart and soul. In finding that love, all the destructive force of art and science is overcome. These themes are introduced just after the "Creed of the Savoyard Vicar," which denied that the church is needed to save us. Instead of grace, Emile is offered love, and not just any love at that: he finds salvation in the love of *Sophia*, and he will not settle for less. In case you might have missed it, Rousseau drew attention to the fact that the name of Emile's beloved was not accidental. Small wonder church authorities took exception.[8]

There may be a moment of kitsch in every vision of salvation. What saves Rousseau's from being overwhelmed by it are the elements Kant saw as Newtonian. *Emile* conflated genres, for it isn't only a novel. It's also a manual of instruction. It offered directions for the right use of our faculties, as well as description of a long, controlled experiment. (When we consider that eighteenth-century chemistry relied on what it called rational analysis rather than experiments in laboratories, the fact that *Emile* was a thought experiment appears less important.) Rousseau insisted that Emile be an average boy, with nothing but ordinary intelligence and talent. He may be an invention, but he's not an invention of anything special. Whatever works in this case will work, mutatis mutandis, in others. Without the *Emile*, the Fall in the second *Discourse* would be just as mythic, and just as irrevocable, as that in Genesis. With the *Emile*, we enter the world of organization. Conditions for redemption may be hard to arrange, but they're entirely prosaic. The overcoming of evil is almost banal.

Another feature of the work that must have seemed Newtonian was its causal relation of processes hitherto kept separate. As Newton united apparently diverse phenomena into one single order, Rousseau linked behaviors no one had connected. The child who must listen to his nurse's senseless prattle is prepared to swallow all the nonsense with which tyrants fool their peoples. The fables she reads him form his soul to be flattered, guaranteeing his future manipulation. Two centuries of social psychology ensure that we're no longer surprised by this kind of connection, and we may dispute any of the ones Rousseau drew. In its time, *Emile* was without precedent. The relations drawn there between details of child raising and political life-worlds were no less surprising than Newton's discovery that earthly and celestial motion could be explained by the same laws.

Here's the 1765 note that contains Kant's analogy:

> Newton was the first to see order and regularity combined with great simplicity, where disorder and ill-matched variety had reigned before. Since then comets have been moving in geometric orbits. Rousseau was the first to discover in the variety of shapes that men assume the deeply concealed nature of man and to observe the hidden law that justifies Providence. Before them, the objections of Alfonso and the Manichaeans were valid. After Newton and Rousseau, God is justified, and Pope's thesis is henceforth true. (Kant 2, 58.12)

How did Rousseau's account answer the objections of Alfonso? Early in the century Leibniz used Alfonso to counsel patience, but patience was wearing thin. Newton had showed the natural order to be the best, but what about the moral one? When Leibniz wrote the *Theodicy*, the two seemed so clearly connected that evidence of progress in the one could sustain hope of progress in the other. Science had provided causal connections medieval learning could not dream. This gave strong reason to hope it would come to explain the relations between moral and natural evil. By midcentury, people felt need for more evidence. It no longer sufficed just to say that the moral order was in principle as intelligible as the physical one. Somebody had to show it, in no little detail. Rousseau defended Providence by showing that it works. Evil arose in a good world through a series of natural, comprehensible, but avoidable (thus free) processes. By adapting the same natural, comprehensible, but avoidable (thus free) processes, evil could be overcome.

Rousseau's psychology appeared to Kant a gift from heaven. For since the great scientific revolutions, progressive thinkers increasingly abandoned classical conceptions of particular Providence, which required God's frequent intervention in human affairs. Most turned to a conception which praised the wonder of a universe so governed by law and order that it required no interference from the power that created it. General Providence was viewed as more appropriate to notions of God's majesty and more consistent with increasing revelations of science. As a program, it was commonly accepted, but Rousseau proposed an account of how general Providence might actually work. His moral psychology did not abolish distinctions between moral and natural evils but wrote them into nature. Where every sin carries its own punishment naturally, punishment may be viewed not as an evil but as a warning. Thus Rousseau could view his account as an advance upon Leibniz's rather than an alternative to it. In Rousseau's system too, the evil in natural evil virtually disappears, since its benefits are as clear as they're just. Cold air teaches wild boys not to break windows without submitting them to human coercion. Indigestion shows Parisian decadents the folly of their banquets without subjecting them to sermons. Pain is as providential as any earlier theodicy could wish. Indeed, it may be more so. Rousseau's account asserts suffering to be part of a natural order finer and vaster than earlier theologians had dreamed.

It's a striking moment in the history of philosophy. What would come to seem two completely different problems of evil were bound together. The question of why free rational beings make immoral choices still occupies ethics and moral psychology today, devoid of all connection to the question it was developed to solve. Rousseau needed a solution to the question left open by Augustine: *how* can free will lead to the moral evil that causes natural suffering? Without some such answer, the appeal to human freedom on which theodicy is based must falter. Rousseau's answer inaugurated work in several directions, theoretical and practical, and spawned lines of development in ethics and political theory, pedagogy and psychology. Progress in philosophy took place through elements of a very old tradition. It's less clear that Rousseau's account answered the questions with which it began.

While there were hints in similar directions before him, Rousseau's work created the modern shape of the problem of evil. In focusing attention on the question of moral evil, and its historical and psychological causes, it offered little to those concerned with the traditional problem. It had virtually nothing to say about earthquakes. Rousseau's discussion of Lisbon is almost feeble. His explicit discussions of Providence let us draw two messages: we should worry about the evils for which we're responsible, and God will take care of the rest. The first half of the message is modern. Rousseau made it more so by increasing the number of evils for which we're responsible. In so doing, he would make traditional theists uneasy. For his Creation is so perfect that its Creator is liable to become superfluous. God is benevolent, but we do not need Him. Here too Rousseau was close to Newton. Both wanted to demonstrate God's greatness by showing the flawlessness of His order. Both ended by describing an order so flawless it could almost run on its own.

Voltaire, as we'll see, was still angry at God. This creates more connection to Him than Rousseau seemed to have. The noble savage has as little need of the Lord as does Emile. Both need, instead, the perfect tutor—whom *Emile*'s author, with pardonable confusion, often confounds with Jean-Jacques. The tutor's function is not to teach Emile about the world but to control it for him. As pedagogy, *Emile* is sometimes attacked on moral grounds. The child should be raised naturally, but his environment is entirely artificial. He should be educated for freedom, but his tutor manipulates his every experience. Such attacks miss the point of the unnatural elements of Emile's environment. Rousseau cannot be faulted on grounds of bad faith. *Emile* is not *Summerhill*. Emile's world is not controlled for the reasons of safety or comfort that give liberal educators scruples. There Rousseau is remarkably blithe. *His concern is to create not a world that will never harm the child, but one that will always make sense to him.* In it, the connections between action and reward, moral evil and its natural consequences, are always manifest. The tutor must manipulate the world so that all constraints have the appearance of natural necessity. Bad consequences will never be missing, nor will they appear as arbitrary punishment. They are simply as they should be—the natural effects of ordinary causes.

The tutor's job is to correct the oversights of Providence. Emile should always learn from experience. He studies geometry not by proving theorems but by calculating at what angle the ladder must be placed to reach cherries on the tree. He learns astronomy not by hearing lectures but by getting lost in the forest and finding his way home by the stars. The most important lesson he must learn is that virtue and happiness are intrinsically connected. Some such lessons are easy. Rousseau will give the child no speeches about the corruption of luxury. It's enough, he thinks, to appeal to his senses: any healthy child will like country food better than a cramped Paris banquet. What to do when the connections are murkier; where the link between happiness and virtue, suffering and wickedness seems out of reach? There the tutor steps in—not with words, but with actions. His job is not to describe those connections, just to underscore the operations of Providence. And if necessary, he can always make a contribution to them. Like Newton's God, he need not intervene very often. But nature is never designed well enough to do without him entirely.

Rousseau is often accused of incoherence, and the number of conflicting interpretations of his work can seem to support the accusation. Some readers, from Voltaire to Judith Shklar, have emphasized the dark and somber tone found in many of his works instead of the hopeful notes emphasized here. Rousseau's *moods* about whether his solutions were viable surely wavered. Even a more steadfast person could be torn in two directions when faced with the problems he saw so clearly, and Rousseau may have been the most tormented soul in the history of philosophy. But his texts make available the more hopeful line that readers like Kant and Cassirer drew. The idea that the problem of evil might be formulated in a way that gives a key to its solution is not only supported by the relationships between species and individual development sketched above. It is also underlined by Rousseau's tireless search for political solutions. These ranged from the general theory of the *Social Contract* to the particular attempts to help Poland and Corsica formulate new political orders. Through education and politics, Rousseau thought we could reshape most things that now look natural. The true nature thereby exposed mostly works as it should. Surely the need for an occasional pedagogically guiding hand isn't enough to threaten your faith in it?

Divided Wisdom: Immanuel Kant

All the elements for explosion were assembled. Did Kant try to prevent it, or did he provide the match? To see how his work fuels both impulses, we must elaborate its background. Leibniz used Alfonso to defuse a danger, transforming him from a threat against faith in God's perfection to a rash if good-natured fool. In Kant's hands he once again became a challenge. All science aimed at making the world intelligible. Philosophy, insofar as it was separate from other sciences, perhaps even the queen of them, had to safeguard the possibility of intelligibility itself. Rousseau tried to do it, but the costs were significant.

We've already seen the first: God's role in the world decreases. God wasn't entirely absent in Rousseau's version of Providence, but He was more of a shadow than anything else. The more responsibility for evil accrues to the human, the less belongs to the divine. Empowering humanity was precisely Rousseau's intention. Even more than Leibniz's, Rousseau's success was greater than he'd planned. Leibniz vindicated God by restricting His choices through eternal forms. The result, as Hegel put it, was too much of a fairy tale to really disturb anyone (Hegel 7, 3:340). Rousseau vindicated God by shifting our focus to moral evil and arguing that He'd given us resources to control it. Once the most rational response to Alfonso became the vision of a world for which God is not responsible, Alfonso himself receded from view. His questions were too modest, his challenge to God too polite. The icon of the late Enlightenment is another figure entirely.

Prometheus didn't ask the gods to hear his advice. He defied them completely, stole their fire, and brought light to humankind. They weren't about to offer it, and he wasn't about to wait for them. The discussion of Prometheus in eighteenth- and nineteenth-century thought in Hans Blumenberg's *Work on Myth* is so good that I will not try to add to it, except to draw one conclusion implicit in his work. Goethe's poem "Prometheus" ignited the Pantheism Controversy, the eighteenth-century debate that invented the word *nihilism*.[9] These are the crucial lines:

> When I was a child,
> Not knowing my way
> I turned my erring eyes
> Sunward, as if above there were
> An ear to hear my lamentation,
> A heart like mine
> To care for the distressed.

> Who helped me
> Against the Titans' wanton insolence
> Who rescued me from death, from slavery?
> Have you not done all this yourself,
> Holy glowing heart?
> And young and good, you glowed
> Betrayed, with thanks for rescue
> To him who slept above?

> I honor you? For what?
> Have you ever eased the suffering
> Of the oppressed?
> Have you ever stilled the tears of the frightened?
> Was I not wielded to manhood
> By almighty Time
> And eternal fate,
> My masters and yours?

Did you fancy perchance
That I should hate life
And fly to the desert
Because not all
My blossom dreams ripened?

Here I sit, forming men
In my own image
A race to be like me
To suffer, to weep
To delight and to rejoice
And to defy you,
As I do.
(Goethe, in Kaufmann)

The *Pantheismusstreit* began when Lessing heard the poem and avowed that it fit his own Spinozistic views. But Spinoza was a pantheist, not a pagan. What in this poem could be common to both views? It must be the denial of Providence. In the worlds of Spinoza and Prometheus, God's intentions are not hidden from us; as far as we're concerned, there are none. For Blumenberg, who stressed Goethe's impact on the course of German philosophy, his "fundamental idea is that God would have had to arrange the world differently if he had been concerned about man" (Blumenberg 3, 556).

Rousseau, of course, had argued otherwise. But the extent of the tutor's role in *Emile* displayed the flaw in his system that would prove to undo it. If the natural world routinely connected happiness and virtue, we just might overlook an occasional earthquake. But if the natural education that is supposed to reveal the goodness of human nature requires *constant* intervention, how good can the connections be? Rousseau could protest that in the original state of nature, connections were more direct. The tutor must engage in myriad forms of manipulation because we live in a world that's been spoiled. Emile's isolation from it can never be total. He was born into a society which destroyed the natural order that the tutor must work to rebuild. But if the work is as extensive as all that, the hopes for redemption of even one child look precarious, and all the old questions return in new form. Perhaps God did create a world whose moral order is transparent, and the world's defects are our own making. But why is the order so fragile? Either we or the world should have been made less vulnerable: we to moral corruption, or the world to being damaged by it. Arranged as they are, human beings and the natural world hardly seem to have been made for each other.

It's easy to conclude that they're not. Purpose then drops out of Creation entirely, to become located in human beings. The universe is not only indifferent to human purposes, but positively resistant to them. One can try to be a Spinozist and do without purpose altogether. Spinozism was resisted, however, not only because it was anathema to orthodoxy, but because Prometheus better captures the intuitions of ordinary experience. We seek light and warmth and everything that follows from them. To get them, we're compelled to work by stratagem or force, and we pay, often dearly, for every advance we're lucky enough to succeed in wresting from the natural world. If few of us find our lives reflected in Spinoza's vision of a world in which our own purposes are merely apparent, even fewer will resort to real paganism. So modern dualism becomes compelling. The resistance of nature that we experience daily, in matters great and small, is not the work of angry anthropomorphic deities but simply part of the arbitrary stuff of the universe. Natural evils are neither just punishment for something despicable nor unjust punishment for something heroic, but framework of the human condition. That condition is structured by mortality and, even more generally, by finitude. Being limited is being who we are. If finitude isn't punishment, it's no evidence of sin. It isn't exactly a *lack*; it may not even be a property. We have purposes; the world does not. Both of these constitute something essential to the nature of each, and neither has any meaning at all.

Thus the problem of evil became *structurally* irresolvable. These are assumptions worked out clearly by Kant. As he described it, the problem of evil presupposes a systematic connection between happiness and virtue, or, conversely, between natural and moral evil. But the world seems to show no such connection at all. Virtue is the domain of human reason, which Kant defined as the faculty of purposes. Happiness depends on events in the natural world. The difference between reason and nature is, for Kant, the difference on which the world turns. The one is a matter of what ought to be; the other is a matter of what is. Each makes its own claims, and nothing is more important than learning to distinguish them. Recognizing reality and demanding to change it are fundamentally different activities. Both wisdom and virtue depend on keeping them separate, but all our hopes are directed to joining them. Whether we're trying to make sense of the world by understanding or by altering it, we are guided by an idea of the Unconditioned—a world that would be, as a whole, transparent to human reason. If it were transparent, it would be as it should be. If it were as it should be, we would have no more demands, theoretical or practical. The world, made for our purposes, would be the best of all possible ones. We could not even formulate a question about it.

For Kant this set of assumptions was neither foolish nor trivial. Nor does it express a psychological need of our species that might have been different. It embodies what he called a need of reason that is presupposed in any attempt to make sense of the world. And yet it's a need that can never be met: the gap between *is* and *ought* is not accidental but systematic. It's a gap that will leave us permanently torn.

Immanuel Kant has already appeared in this book, and will accompany it to the end. Any narrative of the history of modern philosophy will assign him a central place. Mine must begin by showing, first, that he was concerned with the problem of evil at all. For it seems paradigmatic of those questions which may indeed, as he wrote, be prescribed by the very nature of reason itself, but which transcend all reason's powers to answer. Kant's enthusiastic notes about Rousseau and his essays on earthquakes belong to his early, pre-Critical work. His intellectual life began with the Leibnizian views his mature, Critical work undermined. Traces of his early views inhabit the later texts. Those with an open eye can find them in surprising places. The example of the relation of ground to consequent that he gives in the "Metaphysical Deduction"—hardly a soft spot in the Critical Philosophy—comes straight from classic discussions of the problem of evil. *If there is perfect justice, the obstinately wicked are punished* (A73/B99). This is the example used to illustrate the principle that became, in Kant's system, the principle of sufficient reason. But Kant's examples are often problematic; scholars could view this as a relic of early obsessions that the later work condemned to irrelevance. For such hints notwithstanding, Kant's most central discovery was the discovery that we are, necessarily, ignorant. Questions about God and His purposes, the nature and sense of Creation, thus the materials for thinking about the problem of evil, are all out of bounds. The wish to answer them is the wish to transcend the limits of human reason. And the wish to transcend those limits is uncomfortably close to the wish to be God.

Appearances are seldom completely deceptive. The warning not to seek to displace God is exactly one-half of the message of Kant's Critical Philosophy. His thought about these questions developed, of course, from the enthusiastic note of 1765 to the virtual despair of his last essay in 1800. Tracing that development could be the task of one long book. Here I will attempt something much more schematic. I begin by sketching that line of Kant's thought which condemns the wish to be God. I conclude by sketching the line that suggests it's a wish we can never extinguish. In trying to resolve that conflict, thinkers like Schelling and Hegel took the road to Absolute Idealism. Kant himself remained simply torn.

Dissatisfaction comes from the wish to be God. If any one claim is the message of Kant's epistemology, it is this. Traditional metaphysics could not solve the questions it posed because those questions transcend the limits of human knowledge. To answer them, we would need access to the absolute reality of the world as a whole. Kant's questions are so deep that once they are posed, they virtually answer themselves. Everyone else simply failed to ask them. *Can we know things as they are in themselves, independent of whatever conditions we need to know them?* The fact that we cannot is nearly tautological. *Does human knowledge have conditions?* Doubtless. *What might they be?* This requires work, and the first half of the *Critique of Pure Reason* is devoted to it. *Do we create what we perceive, or are objects of perception given to us?* Of course they are given—to anyone but God. *What structures must exist to create the possibilities in which they can be given?* Frameworks of space, time, and very general concepts lie ready to structure the unordered data of perception. *Can't we get beyond them?* Beyond space? Beyond time? *I don't want to be God.* Of course not. *Just to know things as they really are.* Without the conditions that make it possible for human beings to know things? *Without any mediation that is external to things in themselves.*

> If by the complaints—*that we have no insight whatsoever into the inner nature of things*—it be meant that we cannot conceive by pure understanding what the things which appear to us may be in themselves, they are entirely illegitimate and unreasonable. For what is demanded is that we should be able to know things, and therefore intuit them, without senses, and therefore that we should have a faculty of knowledge altogether different from the human, and this not only in degree but as regards intuition likewise in kind—in other words, that we should be not men but beings of whom we are unable to say whether they are even possible, much less how they are constituted. (A277/B333)

To know objects independently of the conditions under which they can be given to us would be to know them through what Kant calls intellectual intuition—a capacity that would allow us to perceive in and through the moment of creation. Don't bother trying to understand this; Kant's point is that you can't. The concept of intellectual intuition isn't an attempt to describe a different kind of intuition, but to make us wonder about our own. God, presumably, perceives through the act of creation—a perception not even to be compared with our mediated perception of things like soup or books or tables, which we create from material that is given to us. Our wish to perceive things differently is a wish that makes no sense. We cannot even express it.[10]

Nevertheless it's the wish that underlies all the epistemology and metaphysics that took place before Kant's Copernican Revolution. Some philosophers were explicit in viewing the search for knowledge as *imitatio Dei.* Plato was so certain that approaching wisdom entails despising the sensual conditions which limit human knowledge that his Socrates is happy to die in order to transcend them. Leibniz views God's knowledge to be less finite than ours only because He lives longer than we do. This gives Him time to unfold all the truths contained in complete concepts, hence to know why what seemed contingent was actually necessary. Had we the same amount of time at our disposal, we too could know the same. Empiricists, who stressed the sensual component of knowledge, thought there were principled differences between God's knowledge and our own. Locke, for example, believed that only God knows essences, while we know accidents. But even those empiricists for whom God disappears entirely tacitly relied on a model of knowledge that would be appropriate to Him alone. Hume's ontology contains neither God nor soul, nor even causes or objects in ordinary senses. But despite the radical skepticism of his metaphysics, he neglected to pose the question put by Kant. In failing to ask whether there are conditions on perception of those bundles of impressions that do make up his world, Hume failed to note the fundamental fact about human knowledge: whatever the stuff we perceive turns out to be, it is not created by us. The Scottish atheist underestimated the magnitude of the fact that we aren't God.

Kant called his own view transcendental idealism, and juxtaposed it with transcendental realism. However they sought it, he held that earlier philosophers sought a route straight to the heart of reality, shunning any form of mediation as a restriction on knowledge. They all thereby presupposed a model of unmediated knowledge that made everything else look deficient. Kant thought every attempt to overcome those deficiencies was an attempt to overcome the limits imposed by the nature of the human. Such attempts are senseless railing against what is so far beyond possibility that we cannot even imagine it. So essential are the limitations on our knowledge that we should not perceive them as failings. For even to imagine another way of knowing that would be successful must surpass all our powers of thought. Earlier philosophy viewed the finitude of human knowledge as a problem; Kant viewed it as a fact. More precisely, it is *the* fact about knowledge, defining every epistemological relation we have to the world. Kant had no tendencies toward quietism. His awareness of our limits, and the threats of contingency, never led him to give up in the face of them; this was the man who introduced the first lightning rods to the city of Königsberg. Nor did he urge us to be content with our lot. As was clear when he discussed Job, he found plenty of grounds for complaint about the human condition. The finitude of knowledge was just not among them. This may be the biggest difference between Kant and Leibniz. Since, for Leibniz, human knowledge was like God's knowledge, but smaller, a grievance about its limits is built into the structure of his epistemology. Without his high hopes for overcoming those limits by some form of progress in science, Leibniz's view would succumb to the pessimism enshrined in its structure. The philosopher renowned for the claim that this world is the best of all possible ones built dissatisfaction into his theory of knowledge—while being content to leave the world as it is.

Kant recognized the power of the wish to be God, and offered the deepest of epistemological reasons for letting it go. If it's the nature of human knowledge to be limited in ways he described, many traditional questions of metaphysics must be out of bounds. Whether the world as a whole is intelligible is a question without sense. But as deep as are the epistemological grounds for rejecting it, Kant offered even deeper, moral ones in the second *Critique*.

A child was killed through violence or neglect. A criminal betrayed his way into power he enjoys without penalty or regret. Fill in examples as you choose. What do you mean when you say: *that should not have happened?* Kant says you mean that happiness and virtue should be systematically connected, and the connection should be causal. Those who are righteous for the sake of righteousness itself should be blessed because of it. They deserve all the goods nature can bestow on humanity—not merely satisfaction with their own righteousness. Those who are wicked ought to suffer—not merely through the pains of tormented conscience, which they show little evidence of feeling anyway, but through something imposed by the world itself. Innocent people should not be harmed. (Our intuitions about those who are neither righteous nor wicked are more complex. On the one hand, harming them is paradigmatic of evil action. On the other, they do not quite fit into the reward-and-punishment thinking that affects this problem.) The assumption that happiness and virtue should be systematically connected is so deep that it is seldom even stated, but Kant holds it to be at the bottom of every moral critique. Every moment of despair in the face of others' suffering, every expression of outrage at the sight of others' cruelty, is based on conviction that the world should work on principle. The use of the adjective *innocent* to modify the noun *suffering* testifies to the automatic way in which the principle is accepted. Before you dismiss it as a relic of naive wishful thinking, ask yourself whether the principle can be coherently negated. *Happiness and virtue should not be systematically connected.* Can normative claims contain contradiction? Try thinking a consequence that could follow from this one. *Those who help others should be slowly tortured.* You can say words like these, but they make as much sense as saying *A is not A*. But a world in which happiness and virtue were systematically *dis*connected would express more order than is evident in the world. What about sheer random relation, something like the disorder we often seem to experience? *Generosity should sometimes be noticed, sometimes disregarded. People who show it should be met with blank indifference.* You can imagine such a world, but can you imagine wanting it? Here the random may be still bleaker than the willfully perverse.

Chapter 4 will discuss Kant's reasons for thinking that the idea of this world as the best one is not a childish wish. It is rather, he believes, a requirement of human reason. Here the question is not why it's reasonable to have such a wish, but why we ought never to know whether that wish is fulfilled. Kant thought all moral action has one goal: to realize a world in which happiness and virtue are systematically connected. Every time we act rightly, we are acting to bring the world closer to this ideal. The knowledge that we often fail, and that the world fails to work with us, may lead to despair only faith can heal. In Kant's view we must believe that all our efforts to be virtuous will be completed by a Being who controls the natural world in ways we do not. We have no evidence that such a Being exists. But only such a Being could provide the systematic links between happiness and virtue that reason demands. Reason needs such belief in order to maintain its commitments: to waking up ever again, through half-success and failure, to continue the struggle to create another world. Kant argued for this kind of faith throughout his work. He was sure that without some such faith, we would succumb to resignation at best, and cynicism at worst. How else can we face a life that increasingly shows us how rarely the world reveals the connections between happiness and virtue that reason demands?

The crucial difference between this view and the traditional one is Kant's conviction that we should not know those connections. Leibniz hoped the progress of science would make all connections between natural and moral evils manifest. Once we could see them, we would know in detail what we now know merely as a general principle: this world is the best of all possible ones. Others doubted we would ever succeed in knowing those connections, but no one ever doubted that we *should*. For it seemed unquestionable that knowledge of the connections between happiness and virtue would strengthen both of them. We'd be less liable to despair, and less prone to decadence, were we certain the world works as it should.

Kant was nowhere more stunning than when denying all that. He argued just the opposite. Knowledge of the connections between happiness and virtue is not only metaphysically impossible but morally disastrous. Consider your relations with people in power. You may want to compliment without meaning to flatter. You may try to smile from sheer graciousness, try to give just from fullness of heart. Perhaps you enjoy and respect them, and seek ways to express it. How often can you forget the hope of goods they can bestow? Jobs or money? On occasion. What about that vaguer advancement which results from general esteem? For how long? Where the connections between good behavior and its reward are obvious, only saints can act without instrumentalizing. The rest of us will calculate, in terms of varying subtlety.

Now imagine a world where you knew what God knows: how *every* right action will be rewarded, every wrong one avenged. Could you engage in moral action? Act out of pure goodwill? Kant says that you could not, at least not consistently. Your relationship to God would be that which you have toward your employer, writ very, very large. If you are lucky, he has all the virtues, and you may want to please him for the sake of being pleasant. But while he controls the means to your existence, you can never know that you will meet him without instrumental considerations in the background. The analogy is imperfect only because the constellations are so different in size. In the world we're imagining, we're imagining a relation between a Being whose power is so absolute that He can right any wrong and reward any right—and everybody else. This is the fantasy that's expressed in many a standard prayer. Were it to be realized, we would be undone. A morally transparent world would preclude the possibility of morality.

The best of all possible worlds is not a world we could live in, for the very notion of human freedom depends on limitation. To act freely is to act *without* enough knowledge or power—that is, without omniscience or omnipotence. Not knowing whether our good intentions will be rewarded is essential to our having them. If we knew the world was the world that we long for, human nature would change beyond recognition. Kant thinks our behavior would improve. Who would dare commit a crime if he were certain that the cosmic order actually worked? Some version of eternal damnation would suffice to deter almost anyone from almost anything. But good behavior is not the same as moral behavior, and the struggle to achieve the latter, which makes up human decency, would simply disappear. Like puppets pulled by a master, we would do nothing but move for carrots and sticks.

"Our faith is not scientific knowledge, and thank Heaven it is not!" (Kant 11, 2.2). This claim is central to Kant's thought as a whole. It was widely and early criticized. Heinrich Heine found it cheap, and the rest of the nineteenth century couldn't stand it. Yet thanking Heaven for remaining inscrutable can make perfect sense. Providence itself requires that we cannot know it. Our very uncertainty about whether Providence works as it should is one more testimony to the awesome wisdom that orders Creation. For, Kant continued,

> suppose we could attain to scientific knowledge of God's existence . . . all our morality would break down. In his every action, man would represent God to himself as rewarder or avenger. This image would force itself on his soul, and his hope for reward and fear of punishment would take the place of moral motives. (Kant 11, 2.2)

This is deeper than the charge that theodicy leads to quietism posed in the question: If you know God will always take care of the world, why should you bother to do so yourself? Kant was also concerned with that problem. It led him to insist that faith in a world which coordinates happiness and virtue can't be faith in another world to come but in a transformation of the world that we live in. Temporal suffering is not advance payment for eternal bliss. But the problem of quietism could be handled by traditional means: if the systematic connections between virtue and happiness are causal ones, we first have to act well in order to see them. The more radical point is another. Solving the problem of evil is not only impossible but immoral. For knowing the connections between moral and natural evils would undermine the possibility of morality.

If this weren't enough, Kant's last works add more dramatic reproaches. Theodicy is not merely impossible and immoral; it also tends toward blasphemy. Here Kant was less concerned with logical than with psychological relations. His analysis of the motives that led thinkers to create theodicies is brilliant. Traditional metaphysicians expatiated on the glory and justice of God in the hope that He would be listening and would reward them accordingly. This is very wishful thinking. What else could drive them to deny the brute force of pain? Kant thought they could not possibly believe in the connections between natural and moral evils they asserted without evidence. The claim that all suffering is just payment for some crime or another is belied by ordinary experience every day. To repeat it to Job as he cries on the ash-heap is to sin against the friend whose righteousness his friends should know and whose pain they should acknowledge. It is also to sin against truth itself, as only a scoundrel could do.

So Kant denounced the standard position one might call the theodicy of ignorance. *God's standpoint is not our standpoint; His wisdom is incomparable; what may seem to be against our interests may be in fact the best means of realizing them; unlike God, we cannot judge what is best for the whole.* It's a view one might think Kant would find congenial, but he attacked it with vehemence, calling it an apology that requires no refutation but the abomination of anyone with the least feeling for morality (Kant 8, A202). What's wrong with saying that God has ways we cannot understand?

For Kant, even this much knowledge is too much knowledge. To say that God has purposes, though we don't know them, is to say that God has purposes. That's precisely what was in doubt. To assert it a priori is to trade recognition of the reality of suffering for a consolation so abstract it cannot really comfort. It must be meant to work like a charm: if I assert God's justice and wisdom often enough and loudly enough, perhaps He'll bestow it on me. It's an infantile form of Pascal's wager. This way, at least, I run no risks. (Think of the trouble Alfonso got into for simply questioning.)

Superstition may strike you as silly but harmless. For Kant it is blasphemy. The problem with superstition is less what it does to us—turning what should be autonomous adults into self-made, foolish children—than what it does to God. Every superstition is an act of idolatry, the attempt to appease or flatter a powerful being in the hope that he'll reward us, on earth or elsewhere. Kant's God hates sacrifices in every form. Kant saw little difference between burning an entrail, doing a rain-dance, or saying a prayer for eternal salvation, except that the latter is likely to contain more hypocrisy. This theme runs throughout Kant's *Religion within the Limits of Reason Alone*, the book that was banned by the Prussian censor. It fueled his conviction in the *impiety* of theodicy. To defend God by insisting a priori that He always rewards happiness with virtue is to fly so directly in the face of experience that one who does it can only have one of two base motives. If he isn't hoping that God is eavesdropping and will reward his flattery—a hope that debases the Creator no less than the created—he must be out to convert or console. But to win friends for God by pointing out the fruits of His friendship is to give instrumental reasons for being holy— a clear contradiction, and a vile one at that. No wonder Kant held the biblical prohibition on God's image to be central and sublime. To break our tendency toward idolatry, our idea of God must be so exalted that we cannot even represent it.

Kant's discussion of idolatry occurred in his discussion of the moral law. Rewards should never be dangled to make us moral, any more than images of God's likeness should ever be offered to make us pious. Rather than encouraging morality or holiness with incentives, such processes dilute and debase them. Goodness is genuine only if done for goodness' sake. Attempts to give extrinsic reasons for virtue do not merely weaken virtue; they destroy its very essence. To illustrate, Kant began with examples on which all will agree. There is a fundamental difference between the shopkeeper who never cheats because cheating is wrong, and one who never cheats because a reputation for honesty will bring him more customers. Their behavior may never be different, but one is moral and the other is not. This is the root intuition that led Kant to the position others would call deontological: action is moral action only if done from regard for the moral law itself, regardless of consequences. Kant's insistence on this view acknowledges the depth to which thinking about Providence lies behind our thought about ethics and action, as it attempts to undo that thinking. For maintaining this view, he was accused of everything from a masochism that demands we get no pleasure from good actions, to a mad passion for justice which, like that of Kleist's Michael Kohlhaas, lays waste to every other good in its path. Yet Kant's ethical writings, if read as a whole, make clear that he neither scorned happiness nor despised human desire for the goods of the world. Over and over, he insisted on them. He also insisted on what he took to be simple honesty: virtue is one thing, and happiness another.

This is a claim that ought to be trivial. But its implications are so difficult that we'd prefer to deny it, in any one of a number of ways. If we acknowledge the gap between virtue and happiness, we seem bound to acknowledge that though virtue may lie in our hands, happiness most certainly does not. Kant was even more merciless than Rousseau in attacking those Stoics who tried to collapse happiness into virtue. They thereby wished to give us an illusion of power. For any but gods, this is simply bad faith. Consciousness of one's own virtue may be the noblest source of happiness, but it's very far from being the only one. In Job's case it was a particular source of bitterness, when he lost all other conditions required for happiness: knowing he'd done nothing to deserve his fate made his fate all the harder to bear. Should a righteous man be comforted by the thought that his suffering is not merely suffering, but evidence that the world as a whole is unjust?

But look at the choices. We cannot be virtuous in order to be happy, for virtue as means is not really virtue. The shopkeeper who knows that fraudulent scales prevent potential customers from sending small children or blind aunts to his store cares not about honesty but about investment. Virtuous actions undertaken in the service of happiness may not be evil, but they are not examples of virtue. It's this idea that led Schiller and others to think Kant held only unhappy people to be good ones. Yet Kant insisted that the desire for happiness is a desire of human reason, which the Stoics were dishonest to deny. If we should neither be virtuous in order to be happy nor persuade ourselves that being virtuous is all we need to be happy, how should we view their relation?

Kant said we should be virtuous for the sake of virtue alone. But doing our duty makes us worthy to be happy—which is not the same thing as making us happy. The relation we're imagining is not quite a causal one. It means going through the world like Orpheus through hell. If we do not turn, eyes focused straight toward what's right, we may hope to have it all: virtue and reward. If we falter for a moment, the object is gone. To look for reward is to lose the virtue that is its rightful condition. Yet Kant would be the last to say to Orpheus that his songs should be enough.

Heine attacked Kant for several forms of bad faith, but the attitude Kant demanded is anything but dishonest. It is certainly tortured— more bluntly, hellish. He knew it demanded extraordinary faith in a world that gives us few grounds for trust. In a universe of earthquakes, can you count on contingency to work in your favor? Why should Hades keep a promise?

Rousseau gave the young Kant something like grounds. The *Emile* can be read much as Newton's *Principia* can be: both were background texts Kant used in describing general laws that structure our world. The argument he gave for rational faith is faith in a world that works roughly as those works described. *Emile* depicted a natural order in which virtue is the cause of happiness—not because God intervenes to reward us, nor because people raised virtuously are good at calculating, but because the natural order is so good that this is roughly how things work. As Kant grew older, the order seems less certain to him. For the problem is worse than it initially seemed. It may be right to separate the rightness of an action from the goodness of its consequences, but both clearly matter. And like everything else in the natural world, the consequences are not up to us. Perhaps you can give up your own claims to happiness and are willing to settle for virtue. You will want all the more to know that your right actions had the consequences you intended, that your virtue itself was successful. This knowledge too is fundamentally out of reach.

Kant's last essay addressed this subject, but most readers dismiss it entirely. "On the Supposed Right to Lie from Altruistic Motives" considers the following case. Your innocent friend took refuge in your cellar from a murderer pursuing him. When the murderer arrives at your doorstep demanding to know his whereabouts, should you tell a lie? Kant says you should not, and his reason will puzzle. It is possible that if you lie and tell the murderer your friend is elsewhere, he will leave the house to continue his pursuit, thereby running straight into your friend, who just managed to slip out the basement window to what he thought was safety. This argument has seemed so awful that it's been used to maintain that the elderly Kant suffered from Alzheimer's disease. Kant's attackers have been delighted with what they view as an instance of rigorism that ends in absurdity. If other passages in Kant seem blindly rule-bound and formalistic, none seems to give better reason for rejecting his moral philosophy than one suggesting that betraying your friend to a murderer is preferable to telling a lie. Most Kantians agree this is the thrust of the essay. But arguing that it's the wrong consequence to draw from Kant's ethics as a whole, they opt to save the latter by dismissing this short work.

At first glance, the essay does seem ridiculous: its central argument looks less appropriate to philosophy than to slapstick. The vision of murderer and victim crashing into one another is enough to raise guffaws or eyebrows—if it weren't also a vision of the tragic. For just as surely as comedy, tragedy lives on wrong identifications, opportunities missed and grabbed in the split of a second, paths crossed at the least expected moments, intentions that hit marks their agents never aimed at. It is, in short, about the power of the contingent, and the importance of the fact that we don't control the natural world. Kant's discussion of the murderer underlined all that. His point was not that it's *better* to betray your friend than to lie about his whereabouts, still less that telling lies is a fate worse than death. Though many readers overlook it, Kant was willing to consider lying to protect the fragile ego of an author. This shows a healthy skepticism about truth telling that belies his

reputation and suggests he might allow lying—if successful—to protect other things as well.[11] His point was, rather, one we have no wish
to hear: our power over the consequences of our actions is really very
small. What lies in our hands is good intention itself.

It's easier to dismiss Kant than to dismiss the implications of his
essay, once taken seriously. The absurdity in this example underscores
both the depth and the scope of contingency. Maturity is a theme and
a goal of all Kant's philosophy; accepting one's limits is always a part
of it, as well as of commoner demands for growing up. The last essay
hints that not even maturity is an option, for there seem to be no limits
to the limits of our power. We can give up dreams of revolution, settle
down to plant a garden with our friends. What's to stop a mad assassin
from breaking into it? What ensures safe access to the escape route
devised to avoid him? As there is no limit to our lack of power, so there
is no limit to the number of things that can go wrong. Meditating on
them can be a recipe for comedy, or for paralyzing sorts of neurosis,
but they are no less numerous for the fact that living successfully requires us to forget them.

Successful lives, like maturity, seemed to depend on moderation.
This was urged by Greek thinkers, like Socrates, whom Nietzsche
blamed for the death of tragedy and the birth of a world that eschews
both tragedy and fairy tale. It's a world where Oedipus and Jocasta
turn out to be first cousins once removed, and are free to grow fat and
bored together. Instead of the plague that ravished Thebes, their reign
heralds nothing worse than a rise in unemployment and a decline in
the GNP. The point is not that such a world is unimaginable. Nothing
could be easier to imagine. The problem is that even should Oedipus
choose to seek it, its realization is not in his hands. Small dreams are no
surer to come true than great ones, and either can become nightmare in
the blink of an eye. Recognizing one's limits seems a form of fair trade:
if we withdraw some of our claims on the world, surely those remaining will be met. Yet the wish to determine the world can't be
coherently limited, for you cannot know which event will turn out to
be not just another event, but one that will change your life. Romance
is one exposition of this fact, tragedy another.

Tragedy is about the ways that virtue and happiness fail to rhyme, for the want, or the excess, of some inconsiderable piece of the world which happens to be the only thing that mattered. Kant's work was written in increasing awareness of it. If the older Nietzsche made the sage of Königsberg a figure of fun, the younger Nietzsche paid his work the compliment of calling it tragic. The tragedy is real. Kant's understanding of the ways that the wish to be God fuels most of our mistakes is as deep as his understanding of the ways that only being God would really help. The wish to be God isn't simply pathological; its alternative is blind trust in the world to work as it should. What leads you to it?

Nothing shows the dilemma so clearly as Kant's attacks on Stoic thought. Stoics sought to secure satisfaction in exchange for renouncing happiness. Perhaps you are tempted to follow them. Suppose you don't care about happiness, but only about the realization of that virtue for which you've renounced everything else. Kant wouldn't believe you, but let that be his problem. Yours is another. Being satisfied that you've acted rightly is just as little in your control as any other kind of reward. You may keep heart and soul trained on the Highest Good before you, let no sideways glance distract your way. Still the question is not whether Eurydice will follow, but whether *anything* will. You may opt for sainthood, and it's still up for grabs. Your friend in the cellar could slip out the door.

The gap between our purposes and a nature that is indifferent to them leaves the world with an almost unacceptable structure. For it's easy to resign oneself to finitude—as long as it stays within limits. If we cannot even guarantee our own effective virtue, we may incline to a rage no Stoicism can still. Of the many distinctions Kant took wisdom and sanity to depend upon drawing, none was deeper than the difference between God and all the rest of us. Kant reminds us as often as possible of all that God can do and we cannot. Nobody in the history of philosophy was more aware of the number of ways we can forget it. He was equally conscious of the temptation to idolatry, the alternative route to confusing God with other beings. Kant's relentless determination to trace the ways we forget our finitude was matched only by his awareness that such forgetting is natural. Here forgetting is prescribed by the nature of reason and virtue themselves. If the desire to reject human finitude is the desire to control the world just enough to achieve our rightly chosen ends, it's a desire that morality itself should make sense. What desire could be more worthy?

The legitimacy of the wish to overcome human limit shapes the expression of the categorical imperative: *Act as though the principle of your action were to become by your will a **universal law of nature**.* In the original German of his *Groundwork of the Metaphysics of Morals*, the words "universal law of nature" are printed in boldface. The formulation begs for explanation, and much has been written about it. One aspect has not been sufficiently emphasized. Universal laws can be imagined by anyone; universal laws of nature are given by one Being alone. In giving us this formula, Kant gave us a chance to pretend to be God. Every time we face a moral dilemma, we are to imagine reenacting the Creation. What choices would we make if given a chance to create the best of all possible worlds?

Kant's examples move from logic to preference: some kinds of world would break down entirely; others would just not be the best they could be. So he sometimes discusses cases that lead to worlds we cannot coherently imagine, and sometimes those that lead to worlds we cannot really want. Consider his first example of moral dilemma. The *Groundwork* introduces a man who, "reduced to despair by a series of evils, feels a weariness with life but is still in possession of his reason sufficiently to ask whether it would not be contrary to his duty to himself to take his own life" (Kant 5, 422). How is he to decide the question? Kant suggested he formulate the principle he would act on if he killed himself, then challenged him to imagine a world where that principle worked as smoothly and effortlessly as the law of gravity. Here is his principle: "For love of myself, I make it my principle to shorten my life when by a longer duration it threatens more evil than satisfaction" (ibid.). Could we imagine the world running according to such a law? In such a world, every threat that life would bring more evil than satisfaction would lead, inevitably, to suicide. Kant thinks this a world we cannot imagine.

Note that when we use this fantasy to test our own principles, we are meant to use all we know about how the world works. It's often been noted that the fact that people have memories, and record acts of deception, is crucial for the *Groundwork*'s more famous example of lying: deception would have little consequence if we forgot when we were deceived. For Kant, it seemed clear that life's evils outweigh its satisfactions. Indeed, he held that on hedonistic grounds, no rational being would continue to be alive. This wasn't an unusual opinion, as we'll see in chapter 3. Current conceptions of eighteenth-century optimism notwithstanding, the belief that human life contains less good than evil seemed sheer common sense. Kant presupposed it in arguing that a world in which everyone shortened a life that threatened more evil than goodness would simply self-destruct. As a competent God, you could not allow such a law to be enacted. If it worked as well as your other laws of nature, your creatures would shortly disappear.

It's an interesting offer. The perspective Kant provided was both challenge and consolation. The categorical imperative can be viewed as a constraint on our self-interested and sensual drives, but it's also a chance to escape our own limits anytime we feel brought low by them. If the blows of bad fortune have left you in despair, you can leave them, for a moment, as lawgiving sovereign. If sharp or petty needs make meanness seem tempting, there's a device to create nobility of character that is second to none. The *Groundwork of the Metaphysics of Morals* states that everyone should regard himself as lawgiver of the world at all times (Kant 5, 438). *Imitatio Dei* was proscribed as a principle for guiding acts of knowledge, but it was all the more present in everything else.

While rejecting every comparison between ourselves and God in the theoretical realm, Kant was determined to shape us in each other's image in the practical one. He was explicit in repeating that God's will, like ours, must be determined by criteria of pure practical reason. Nothing about being God makes His decisions authoritative—except the fact, which is almost accidental, that His decisions always turn out to be right ones. God operates according to the same moral laws as we do; He just never neglects to obey them. And if God is a more perfect version of an ordinary human agent, for practical reason we are just a less perfect version of God. When following the categorical imperative, human agents are to imagine themselves writ large. Like Leibniz's God examining the essences of all things and deciding which combination to actualize, we should test our maxims according to the laws of nature we know. Like Leibniz's God, when we're not creating according to the law of noncontradiction, we are to create according to the principle of the best. Some laws would not actually lead to sheer breakdown, but are they the best a good legislator could devise? Kant considered a world made to run on the principle that nobody should ever help another. Such a world is not impossible, unlike that of Hobbes: were humankind really inclined to perpetual war as a universal law of nature, its demise would be swift and assured. By contrast, a world ruled by mutual indifference would be able to function. Yet it's hardly the best one a creative God could discover. Far better to produce one where generous sympathy had the status of law.

Kant's emphasis that moral laws must be universal ones has been ascribed to everything from particularly Prussian rigidity to general Enlightenment Eurocentrism. It is not my present interest to defend him from such reproaches. I wish only to underline that part of Kant's universalism which stems from concerns about consequence and control. Kant asked us to consider our actions from the perspective of universal lawmaking not only because doing so expressed the core of any demand for fairness. As Kant himself knew, the categorical imperative also expresses folk wisdom and religious precept. Putting yourself in the other fellow's shoes, or refusing to do to him what you don't want done to you, is not a new suggestion.

The demand that we consider moral principles as universal laws formulates a fantasy of power as well as a sense of justice. If moral laws were universal laws of nature, they would actually work. Lying continues to work because not everybody does it—at least not all the time. People can live indifferent to the welfare of others because they can regularly depend on finding someone who cares about their own. Universal laws have no exceptions. Knowing this, you couldn't hope to get away with the things you hope others will refrain from trying. Were moral laws transformed into laws of nature, they would always have consequences as predictable and reliable as physics itself. As things now stand, any particular moral action may have any consequence whatsoever. This makes the finitude we can accept in the realm of knowledge hardly endurable in the realm of action. If we were God, we could change moral principles into sovereign law. Were God Himself to enact such a law, moral principles would lose all connection with freedom. The problem is one of the worth of morality, and each alternative seems unacceptable. Good intentions without consequence are empty; lawlike behavior without intention blind.

It is one of the extraordinary moments in the Critical Philosophy. We do not actually want God to create the world we long for, but we want to be able to imagine it often. The only autonomous way to imagine it is to imagine ourselves as creators. By 1784, you need not be a monarch to challenge Creation. Kant wanted each of us to engage in fantasies that Alfonso dared not dream. Rather than sitting at God's elbow offering suggestions, you can redesign Creation every time you decide something significant. This time, there's no fear of getting punished; quite the contrary. The fantasy of replacing God is the test by which morality itself is decided.

> Two things fill the mind with awe and wonder the more often and more steadily we reflect upon them: the starry heavens above me and the moral law within me. I do not merely conjecture them and seek them as though obscured in darkness or in the transcendent region beyond my horizon: I see them before me, and I associate them directly with the consciousness of my own existence. . . . The former view of a countless multitude of worlds annihilates, as it were, my importance as an animal creature, which must give back to the planet (a mere speck in the universe) the matter from which it came, the matter which is for a little time provided with vital force, we know not how. The latter, on the contrary, infinitely raises my worth as that of an intelligence by my personality, in which the moral law reveals a life independent of all animality and even of the whole world of sense—at least so far as it may be inferred from the purposive existence assigned to my existence by this law, a destination which is not restricted to the conditions and limits of this life but reaches into the infinite. (Kant 6, 162)

This may be the most quoted passage in Kant's entire work, for it expresses the tension that animates his thought as a whole. Kant offered a metaphysic of permanent rupture. The gap between nature and freedom, *is* and *ought*, conditions all human existence. For Walter Benjamin, it was this gap that made Kant's work so modern: later philosophy, he wrote, was an eleventh-hour flight from the honesty of Kant's dualism (Benjamin 1, 2:32). Integrity requires affirming the dissonance and conflict at the heart of experience. It means recognizing that we are never, metaphysically, at home in the world. This affirmation requires us to live with the mixture of longing and outrage that few will want to bear. Kant never let us forget either the extent of our limits or the legitimacy of our wish to transcend them. Neither is less important than the other, though one way to distinguish analytic from continental readings of Kant's work is through the ways each tried to forget. Analytic philosophy emphasized Kant's recognition of the senselessness of our desire for transcendence; continental philosophy, Kant's recognition of our longing for it. The difference is easy to state: is our urge to move beyond experience a piece of obsolete psychology, or of the logic of the human condition? Kant thought it was the latter, for in fact he was perfectly split. The desire to surpass our limits is as essential to the structure of the human as the recognition that we cannot. Hence it's no surprise that he was the last figure both traditions took in common.

The stance he recommended is not one either tradition—nor perhaps any other—could maintain over time. Along with the constant reminder that we are not God, Kant gives us permission to pretend that we are. A very cheerful reader could view this as a way of having his cake and eating it too, but not for very long. Kant's later work, the *Critique of Judgment*, suggested that not even he could stand so much tension, or tragedy. Why else devote a book to showing that we and the world were made for each other, and that all art and science combine to prove it? Again the problem is not finitude but futility. We may be able to accept the former, but it's positively wrong to accept the latter. Where it's only a matter of knowledge, the fact that what affects us is not created by us causes little problem. It would be easy to acknowledge that not controlling the natural world is part of being human, were it not for the fact that *things go wrong*. The thought that the rift between reason and nature is neither error nor punishment but the fault line along which the universe is structured can be a source of perfect terror.

In the *Critique of Judgment* Kant viewed that rift as a source of wonder. Both knowledge and ignorance combined to make room for faith. Kant called our attention to a miracle: reason and nature were made for each other; the world is a place where we feel at home. Consider the fact of induction. From the infinite number of possible connections between objects and events in the world, human beings regularly pick out some that turn out to be laws of nature. In the vast array of data and possible explanations of data that the given world offers our senses, the frequency with which we get it right is utterly fortuitous. The pleasure that scientists and small children feel at discovery is tinged with surprise: what a marvel that the world and my cognitive powers fit together! Cassirer said the average person doesn't see this problem of induction and thus overlooks the pleasure he feels at its solution. One might add that the average person doesn't make the problem quite as hard as Kant did by emphasizing continually the sheer and basic difference between mind and world. If his transcendental self feels pleasure on discovering itself reflected in nature, it's against a background of fear that it will be found nowhere at all.

That was, in the end, the vision of Hume, whose world without self *or* transcendence seemed to Kant a nightmare. Reading Hume, Kant wrote, awoke him from the dogmatic slumber into which he'd been rocked by Leibnizian metaphysics. For Hume, induction was a myth. Since we cannot know whether the causal connections we pick out are genuine, our decision to call some of them laws is a matter of convenience and habit. (Perhaps deep convenience, and good habits, but no more than that.) What for Hume was a myth was for Kant a miracle, and a key to understanding the world as a whole. In insisting on the split between reason and nature, Kant began by denying that purpose was a feature of nature. Purpose was, rather, the feature that defined reason. Both in science and in morality, reason's task is to propose ends that are not present in experience but direct us to something beyond experience. Kant inherited the classical definition of the human as the rational animal. But reason, for him, was a matter not of knowledge but of creating and pursuing purposes.[12] By the time we've finished reading his first two critiques, we should be persuaded that purposiveness is the fundamental feature of the human.

The third *Critique* surprises readers by claiming that purposiveness is a fundamental feature of nature too—or rather, of the way we must approach nature. Its two halves describe how beauty and knowledge bear witness to purpose. Beauty, for Kant, is sheer purposiveness alone, the experience of perfect line and balance, harmony and form— the experience, in short, of design. Where we find purposiveness existing for its own sake, we feel aesthetic pleasure. Purposiveness without purpose gives us pleasure by showing our own defining quality reflected in the world itself. Science requires the assumption that the world was built not just for some purposes but for our purposes. Nothing else could explain the wonder that it's a place we come to know.

The *Critique of Judgment* gives a definition of purposiveness: the lawfulness of contingency. If the miracle of fit between our faculties of knowledge and all the laws of nature is explained by the fact that both share the category of purposiveness, there is law instead of chaos. Nature must be viewed as a work of art. This means we must view it as the product of a conscious Creator who is just as free as we are. Art itself is the emblem of freedom, in nature and outside of it. Thus we not only trade dissonance for harmony; we seem to get a foolproof version of the argument from design. Though he had argued that it was invalid, Kant couldn't refrain from calling it the only proof of God's existence that impresses the man on the street as well as the scholar, and it's clear he was always drawn to it. A world that constantly evokes pleasure at the discovery of design within it, that can be understood only by our assuming our own essential feature running through its heart—such a world could only be the product of a benevolent Designer. For He gave us a world where metaphysical conflict is minimal, since its pieces so perfectly mirror each other.

Kant was at pains to deny that these are claims to knowledge of all that his earlier work had argued can never be known. Rather, he repeated, they are claims about our own capacities. They reveal nothing about the structure of the world as it is. Whether investigating its laws in the course of doing science, or enjoying its properties as art, we cannot help viewing the world to be purposive—but this may be just a statement about human inadequacy. The world itself remains unknown. Kant repeated such lines often enough to be boring, and his repetition suggests a guilty conscience. Though no one worked harder to show that the question of whether the world is made for us cannot even be properly formulated, no one seems more tempted to give it a positive answer.

To undercut his own temptation, Kant introduced a counterpart to miracle: certain forms of disaster. Nature gives us the beautiful but also the sublime, and the latter is shot through with violence. In an instant of lightning, or a volcano's explosion, we experience something close to beauty—but for its revelation that the world is *not* made for us after all. To judge nature to be beautiful is to feel satisfaction: if I had made the world, I would have done it just like that. To judge nature to be sublime is to be aware of something surpassing any capacities I ever dreamed: however much greater I imagine my creative powers, they would never suffice to do *that*. The sublime is not merely chaotic; it is overwhelming. Primitive peoples experience it in horror and fear. The awe that accompanies the sublime comes not just from the feeling that I could not have created something as crazy as lightning, but from the thought that on balance, I would not have done so. Practical reason cannot forget that the sublime is always dangerous—a threat to our purposes—however glorious it may sometimes appear. The best of all possible worlds is not only a world without earthquakes; it doesn't contain as much as a storm.

Kant's notion of the sublime, and its function as a sign of contrapurposiveness, is deep and important. Its difference from Romantic notions, which saw the sublime as a heightened form of the beautiful, deserves far more exploration than is possible here. Yet Kant's reminder that the world sometimes runs counter to our purposes is relatively brief; the sublime takes up twenty-six pages of his attention. The rest of the *Critique of Judgment* is a meditation on harmony. That the harmony is not part of the world, but part of our ability to approach it, is a point Kant repeated endlessly. But his oscillation between expressions of wonder at the design radiating through the world's features, and expressions of bad conscience at his own wonder, is too constant and swift. In the course of it Kant takes back with one hand what he gives with the other so often that one cannot blame Romantics for getting dizzy. And while Kant's titanic vision of the human would strike them as appealing, "unhappy consciousness" barely begins to describe someone who could steal fire in one moment, and construct his own punishment in the next. It's a talent that could come to wear thin.— *God creates as we do, and we create as He* (said in a whisper, and said very fast). *The world was made for our purposes, and we for the world's.*—But we can't ever know this. We also can't ever know anything without assuming it. (Some cultures avoid positive forms of assertion to avoid the evil eye. Is Kant's hesitation merely the result of theoretical worries?) *The world is my world, and then of course it isn't.* In the face of all this torment, why not quit and call it home?

REAL AND RATIONAL: HEGEL AND MARX

Hegel never said that he was God. He left that to Kojeve, and even the latter admitted it was madness (Kojeve, 120). But long before Nietzsche, Hegel said that God was dead. And the logic of the process that led him to the claim seems to force the conclusion that *someone* must replace the Creator. If logic did compel such a claim, most people would be tempted to reject logic and philosophy itself. Hegel took himself to have completed them. Kierkegaard thought that anyone who overlooks the infinite difference between God and man must be crazy, or committed to blasphemy (Kierkegaard, 207). I want to show why Hegel was neither. It may remain hard to grasp exactly what it means to identify self, God, and world without madness or sacrilege. But the process that led Hegel to try it makes sense.

First we must acknowledge that he really does identify them. Neither the difficulty of his language nor the demands of common sense should let us overlook it.[13] In Hegel's philosophy, the knowing self becomes God. His *Phenomenology of Spirit*, usually considered his central work, has been described as the autobiography of God (Tucker, 45). Even atheists are often wary of this much sacrilege. But two considerations should prevent us from rejecting his identification of self and God out of hand. The first is that how much space exists between human and divine nature is an open question. Kant, and most forms of Judaism, held the space to be infinite, and much twentieth-century theology followed them. But the answer isn't self-evident, and both paganism and Christianity leave it open. Centuries of Christian attempts to articulate the Incarnation make this clear. Christianity itself can be viewed as a meditation on the relation between man and God, an attempt to understand the possibilities and perils of each becoming the other. Hegel wrote that Christianity betrayed its Jewish origins by separating divine and human nature too radically.[14] His work can be seen as continuing Christian tradition rather than rejecting it—not despite its identification of the self with God but because of it.[15] Hegel's work explored better ways for human nature to become divine and for God's presence to be realized in the being He created. Not for nothing did He create in His own image. Hegel's explorations in these directions may lead to heresy. But it's heresy similar to Pelagianism or Albigensianism: doctrines a church may decide to condemn, but not because they are entirely foreign intrusions.

Nor does the heretical impulse usually begin as an impulse to blasphemy. Far from expressing a wish to attack God, it's usually moved by a wish to defend Him.[16] Hegel's wish to take God's place developed naturally from Rousseau's desire to vindicate God by taking evil on ourselves. God's subsequent disappearance could be predicted from the *Emile*, which is why authorities were quick to burn it. But the more seriously we take responsibility for evil, the larger we must become. What ended as a way of displacing God began as a means of unburdening Him. If the outcome looks like madness, there is nothing in it but method.

Hegel's identification of self and God is thus neither as foreign to Western tradition nor as blasphemous as it may appear. But isn't it at least anachronistic? Taking his claims about God, or the World Spirit, seriously is hard because they seem completely obsolete. Kant offered metaphysical, moral, and religious grounds for driving God out of philosophy altogether. Those grounds were convincing enough to lead Moses Mendelssohn, Germany's greatest Leibnizian, to complain that Kant had dashed everything to pieces. The late eighteenth and early nineteenth centuries saw the permanent separation of philosophy and theology as the most important consequence of Kant's Copernican Revolution. If any theological questions remained to be treated philosophically, they were to be treated with a sense of embarrassment. Yet Hegel would write that

> God plays a far greater role in modern philosophy than in the ancient, because the comprehension of the absolute opposition of thought and being is now the main demand. (Hegel 7, 3:347)

Hegel was hardly unaware of the conclusions others drew from Kant's reflections. He understood them superbly. If Hegel could nevertheless reject Kantian proscriptions and return God to philosophical discourse, it's because, paradoxically, he was the first to give a secular formulation of the problem of evil. What's at stake in the problem of evil, as Hegel reformulated it, is the absolute opposition of thought and being, rational and real. Kant came close to Hegel's formulation in describing the need for systematic connection between happiness and virtue, but his language was still directly theological. Hegel circumvented Kantian prohibitions on philosophical theology by recasting the problem of evil in metaphysical terms.

His claim that his philosophy is theodicy is often ignored out of embarrassment. For what shall we do with *self-conscious* anachronism? The *Introduction to the Lectures on the Philosophy of World History* is unabashed.

> Our investigation can be seen as a theodicy, a justification of the ways of God (such as Leibniz attempted in his own metaphysical manner, but using categories which were as yet abstract and indeterminate). It should enable us to comprehend all the ills of the world, including the existence of evil, so that the thinking spirit may yet be reconciled with the negative aspects of existence; and it is in world history that we encounter the sum total of evil . . . we must first of all know what the ultimate design of the world really is, and secondly, we must see that this design has been realized and that evil has not been able to maintain a position of equality beside it. (Hegel 5, 43)

A few pages later, Hegel makes clear that he is not only prepared to return to Leibniz but anxious to outdo him. The task of philosophy is to make us understand that the real world is as it ought to be, and to show that nothing can thwart God's purposes. Philosophy reveals

> that God's will must always prevail in the end, and that world history is nothing more than the plan of providence. The world is governed by God, and world history is the content of his government and the execution of his plans. To comprehend this is the task of the philosophy of world history, and its initial assumption is that the ideal is fulfilled and that only that which corresponds to the ideal possesses reality . . . *the aim of philosophy is to defend reality against its detractors.* (Hegel 5, 67; my emphasis)

Students of Kant will find Hegel's return to Leibniz breathtakingly blithe. His claim that the actual world is as it should be equals the claim that this world is the best. Heine called Hegel the German Pangloss. But not even Pangloss claimed that *only* the ideal possesses reality. If empirical evidence provided by events like Lisbon didn't dispatch such claims, Kant's metaphysics should have finished them off.

But Hegel's return to obsolescence is based on an idea of the modern. Kant viewed the world as structurally flawed, built along a gap between the *is* and the *ought* that admits but the shakiest of bridges. He accused earlier philosophers of bad faith in denying the gap, and insisted on giving each side equal weight. For Kant, the claims of reason are no less legitimate than those of nature. There is no reason to suppose that they will coincide, and evidence enough to show how often they don't. For Hegel, Kant's insistence on a principled infinite distance between *is* and *ought* is just as unnecessary as the distance between human and God. Neither distinction is in the nature of things; each one is created. The gap is not metaphysical but a product of history. Kant's misery was self-imposed, for the dualism he located in the structure of reality could be overcome. Hegel thought Kant expressed modern alienation. The dualism between self and nature that Kant emphasized reflects one between individual and community, which in turn reflects the split between virtue and happiness itself. All these divisions are indeed part of our present experience of the world, but they're not written into it. For Hegel these disjunctions presented problems to be overcome, not reasons for accepting Kant's unhappy solutions. In his readiness to accept as final what was the result of historical process, Hegel believed Kant was giving up too soon.

The eighteenth century saw the birth of modern consciousness of alienation. Hegel opened the nineteenth by locating alienation in modernity itself. Kant and Hegel differed over whether the alienation itself was new, or only the consciousness of it. If Hegel was right, alienation is a modern product. The unhappiness it produces is self-imposed. Thus the remaining question is which modern tool can overcome it. For Hegel, the answer is history—both as diagnosis and cure. His idea that history is both cause and redemption of our suffering owes much to Rousseau. After Hegel, modern inventions from economics to biology were proposed to overcome the misery Kant thought was produced by irrevocable metaphysical split. Nineteenth-century thinkers inherited Hegel's absolute confidence that the alienation which cuts through our lives was a product of modern culture and could therefore be overcome by it. Their confidence can give the nineteenth century an air of smug self-satisfaction. Against them, Nietzsche spoke of a metaphysical wound that can never be healed. When he wrote, in *Schopenhauer as Educator*, that anyone who thinks political events are enough to provide remedies deserves to become a professor of philosophy at a German university, he was probably thinking of Hegel. Nietzsche thought his contemporaries' confidence in progress unbearably vulgar. But it's easy to reply that his talk of metaphysical wounds just projects private growing pains—which threatens to be self-indulgent, even decadent, if nourished past a certain age. Why should the heart of the world be irreparably broken?

For Hegel, the flaw Kant thought to be structural was an expression of Kant's own weakness, a failure of the courage to think independently that Kant saw as the key to Enlightenment. Hadn't Kant divided the world into reason and nature, then given reason sovereignty? Hadn't Kant told us that reason is the faculty we share with God? We should have the courage to draw consequences. "There cannot be two kinds of reason and two kinds of spirit, a divine reason and a human one that were completely different. Human reason, the consciousness of its Being is reason, the divine in humankind" (Hegel 6, 40). Hegel's logic dictated conclusions that Kant's provincial Pietist nerves could not quite face. If reason rules the world, let reason rule the world. This should not remain a matter of wishful thinking, or hopeful imperatives, but of determining force. Kant's refusal to overcome the gap between reason and nature was worse than a refusal to think to the end. For what's outside us, it meant renouncing hopes of affecting the world. The *ought* is utterly ineffective. It remains a pathetic expression of empty desire that only marks a guilty conscience. For what's inside us, it exists as reproach. Since the split between reason and nature runs inside the soul as outside it, the *ought* becomes merely a means of self-punishment. Kant defined freedom as obedience to laws one gives to oneself. For Hegel, this substitutes self-imposed bonds for external ones. What slave glorified his own chains with more conviction? No wonder Kant could not do without the hope of heaven.

Hegel wished to bring it back to earth. "The sole aim of philosophical inquiry is **to eliminate the contingent**" (Hegel 5, 28; the original is printed in bold). For Kant, whether the contingent was reasonable is a matter of faith. This leaves us utterly dependent on divine goodwill. The third *Critique* recalled the miracle that contingency works as it ought to, but Kant's last essay recalls how often it does not. He had celebrated the success of induction by reminding us of the serendipity of science. How lucky that from all the wild array of data we so often pick out what coalesces to confirm laws of nature! But Kant knew how many accidents are less happy. Insisting that moral action depends on determining your will, not the world, even if this entails telling truth to assassins, he insisted on how many consequences of our actions are determined by chance. Hegel's demand to eliminate contingency was moved by the horror of cases like these. Necessity may be bleak, but contingency is tragic. What Hegel described as "mental torture" is entirely impersonal. It arises for the spectator of history as well as its agent.

> Without rhetorical exaggeration, we need only compile an accurate account of the misfortunes which have overtaken the finest manifestations of national and political life, and of personal vir-

tues or innocence, to see a most terrifying picture take shape before our eyes. Its effect is to intensify our feelings to an extreme pitch of hopeless sorrow with no redeeming circumstances, to counterbalance it. We can only harden ourselves against it or escape from it by telling ourselves that it was ordained by fate and could not have been otherwise. (Hegel 5, 68)

Why does Hegel think that showing suffering to be necessary is a way to escape it? To tell an individual that an awful event could not have been different offers consolation's barest bones. At most, it spares her the anguish of self-torment about what she might have changed. Perhaps removing some anguish is better than removing none at all. Hegel captures our sense that tragic events are most tragic when they could have been prevented by trivial changes. (After all his efforts to circumvent the prophecy, how could Oedipus have arrived at just that crossroads? At just that moment?) But Hegel is notoriously less concerned with individual misery than with what he called disinterested sorrow. Such sorrow arises through awareness of our finitude (Hegel 3, 1:143). In fact it isn't finitude itself but the futility which results from it that causes the pain. Recall the unhappiness that arose from contemplating your choices when you meet an assassin. For Kant you are entirely free: to lie or meander, to strike him, block the door. You run through any number of options, make a quick decision, and act upon it. This is the commonsense assertion of self-determination. But common sense, and Kant himself, quickly find that this is not enough. What you wanted was to determine not yourself but the world; to preserve your friend's life, not your good conscience. Kant's appeal to the latter was an appeal from despair. So Hegel saw the categorical imperative—on charitable days. He wanted to be happy, not merely free.

Those who find Hegel's notion of necessity problematic should return to Kant's notion of freedom. For Hegel reached it in the attempt to avoid problems that Kant's system could not avoid. The examples Kant chose to illustrate our freedom reveal, among other things, his own sense of desolation. He thought a proof of human freedom to be impossible; instead he offered a thought experiment. The *Critique of Practical Reason* considers a man who claims that his desire is uncontrollable whenever he passes a brothel. Kant begs to differ: were the man to be shown the gallows on which he would be hanged the moment after gratifying his desire, he would find himself quite able to resist. We're then asked to consider the same man, the same gallows, another occasion. Our hero (for so he has potentially become) must decide whether to refuse not the charms of a woman of easy virtue, but the threats of an unjust sovereign who orders him to write a letter condemning an innocent man to death. Kant held that though none of us knows what we would do in such a moment, each of us knows what's possible: to refuse to cause another's death even at the price of our own. In ordinary cases, all other desire is second to desire for life itself. When we're faced with moral choices of this sort, the desire to be decent may overcome even that.

Kant thought such examples immensely important. As he put it, even businessmen, women, and ten-year-old boys can understand their message: our mastery over our own goodwill is so absolute that it matches the power of the most absolute sovereign. Kant thought this showed the reality of freedom. For a Hegelian, it just as surely shows its limits. What we want, of course, is not that the sovereign should send us to our death, but that he should not send an innocent man to his. The fact that we can choose not to aid the sovereign is little comfort. For the alternative is not the determination of the self but the annihilation of it. If your self can affect nothing in the world but its own disappearance, its freedom is empty indeed. Kant's attachment to cases that pit life against death demonstrates the depth of our freedom while underscoring its limit. The momentary feeling of power that accompanies the realization that life and death are in your hands must yield to despair at the realization that, very often, nothing else is. If these are the fruits of freedom, no wonder Hegel has so little fear of necessity.

The problems of our relative helplessness in the face of contingency arise whether we're thinking of moral evils or natural ones. For the former are also an instance of the latter: we are one of the things that go wrong in the world. Freedom, if it's universal freedom, must allow for the failure of others. Later philosophers often forget that the greatest enemies of human freedom were not metaphysical but political. Even the Enlightenment's greatest metaphysician was more concerned with removing unjust sovereigns than with providing proofs about substance. But for Hegel, political self-determination could never be enough. This is not a matter of his particular political views but of his estimation of the power of contingency. Here he was gripped by the sort of case Kant's assassin reveals. The murderer at your doorstep has you just as surely in his power as does the unjust sovereign, and it's hard to imagine which political action could change that. Call him mad, and view outbreaks of madness as natural events. You are back in the realm of earthquakes. Carry out fantasies of controlling crime or madness through some yet-to-be-discovered science of human behavior, and you will have eliminated freedom.

There's no particular reason to retain Kant's example; the reader may choose another. But we should not forget that its very improbability is completely modern. The randomness of life and death is the feature most emphasized in accounts of survival in totalitarian regimes. Survival depended on events so accidental that they undercut rational behavior itself. Contingency blurs the lines between moral and natural evil the eighteenth century tried to draw, for it is both microscopic and all-pervasive. Chance can turn our best efforts to be moral into quixotic last stands. The will to be *effectively* moral is therefore the will to remove it. Contingency must be eliminated entirely. This can be done with a logic that doesn't stop at guaranteeing that contingent events are simply necessary. Rather, it should show that what's essential is morally necessary. Every *is* and every *ought* must be identical.

Hegel was one of philosophy's most acute readers of its own history, with a wonderful eye. He was right to see himself as Leibniz's heir. Recall that Leibniz insisted on three sorts of evil: natural and moral evil were distinct from metaphysical evil, which he saw as the ultimate source of the others. The eighteenth century abandoned the notion of metaphysical evil and called it finitude. Rousseau viewed it as a natural necessity we find easy to accept. We are born and we die, and in between our powers to control nature are severely limited. These are aspects of any condition we could call human. Distinguishing them from those features which are changeable is what wisdom is, presumably, about. By the mid–eighteenth century, discussion was largely confined to the possibility of eliminating natural evils (suffering), moral evils (sin), and the uneven connection between them. Medicine and technology were to combat the first, pedagogy and better economic relations the second, and political justice would address the third. These Enlightenment hopes set agendas well into the nineteenth century. With so much to do that was useful, why should Hegel resurrect a premodern notion of metaphysical evil?

Leibniz defined metaphysical evil as the imperfection of all created things, intelligent or not, solely in virtue of their being created. The fact that they are created gives them boundaries. Only God is infinite, hence perfect and complete. For Leibniz, this poses a problem of necessary evil. Post-Kantians can find it hard to understand without the problem of contingency. We have seen the contingent wreak havoc upon any of reason's demands. What better task can reason have than to overcome it? Because the contingent is infinite, and all-pervasive, our own finitude is not just a fact that good sense should accept. It's rather a source of sorrow that reason itself must reject.

Reason's task in combating contingency is daunting on two scores. One is the scope of contingency. Necessity is necessary not because failure is so great. Rather, contingency is unbearable because of the number of accidents that can destroy the best efforts of reason. The second ground on which metaphysical evil is unacceptable comes from the logic of explanation alone. To accept imperfection is to accept a world that is not as it ought to be. Why should this world exist if another were better? This question is embedded in structures of thought that reason cannot escape. For Hegel as for Leibniz, eliminating contingency means showing this world to be necessary after all. It means showing that the world as a whole, and everything within it, is purposive. Purposiveness was defined as the lawfulness of the contingent. To open any door of the world to contingency is to open the whole to chaos; if law isn't universal, it isn't really law. To accept that the world we inhabit is not the best is to accept essential unintelligibility that leaves understanding in the dark.

Hegel's rejection of finitude returns us to the problem of metaphysical evil. His refusal to accept finitude and contingency as framing the human condition was led by logic, but not confined to it. Now we cannot in fact be infinite, any more than we can be immortal, but we can be part of something that is both. So Hegel completed the appeal to history that began in Rousseau. Rousseau introduced the idea that the very history which condemns us might be the only thing which redeems us. His idea that humankind isn't fixed but subject to development was also the idea that an answer to the problem of evil is *possible* within history. Hegel wished to show that the possible is actual.

Even Kant knew that mere possibility could not keep us going forever. He had appealed to a concrete historical event—disinterested spectators' admiration for the French Revolution—as the sign we need that progress actually takes place. Hegel wanted more than signs. The idea of real history, and as much observation as was needed to give content to it, was his key to finding categories less abstract than those of Leibniz. If history is a history of progress, it would contain its own cure. The (not-quite-yet) given became the standing negation of the given. This overthrows appearances without appealing to something transcendent. The overcoming of present evils is slow, but it's immanent. For we need not appeal to another reality in order to do it. Overcoming evils is part of the process evident in history itself.

Here the reader should balk. What's evident in the claim that history makes progress that proves the goodness of the world? We do not need the events of the twentieth century, or any of their observers, to give us pause. Bayle and Voltaire, Rousseau and Kant show that doubts about progress in history presented themselves the moment anyone began to wonder about it. Put more strongly: it is history itself that presents the problem. Hegel's certainty that it presents the solution must leave us bewildered.

His initial discussion seems so sunny that it may only provoke further astonishment.

> If we admit that providence reveals itself in (nature) why should
> we not do the same in world history? Is it because history seems
> too vast a subject? . . . It is the same in plants and insects as in the
> destinies of entire nations and empires, and we must not imagine
> that God is not powerful enough to apply His wisdom to things
> of great moment. . . . Besides, nature is a theater of secondary

importance compared with that of world history. Nature is a field in which the divine Idea operates in a non-conceptual medium; the spiritual sphere is its proper province, and it is here above all that it ought to be visible. Armed with the concept of reason, we need not fear coming to grips with any subject whatsoever. (Hegel 5, 38)

Where did Hegel get his confidence in the power of the reason he recommended as weapon? In this passage he appeals to the argument from design, but it was precisely the inadequacy of the argument from design that called reason into doubt. The early eighteenth century used discoveries of modern science as evidence that the argument from design was true. Alfonso's willingness to doubt it could be cast for a time as the result of medieval ignorance. By midcentury he seemed a harbinger of modern fear. For Voltaire, the Lisbon earthquake was proof that even in nature, the world's design required improvement, and other skeptics would add conceptual battering to the attacks provided by reality. But disaster, however appalling, and speculation, however brilliant, were less threatening to the argument from design than the evidence of history. Human history always served as a standing reproach. Nature's wonders may testify to God's wisdom and goodness; the creature He designed in His image did not. Contemplating humankind's miserable record in history left God's wisdom and goodness thus doubly open to question. Rousseau was the best the Enlightenment offered by way of hope. But his ambivalent attempts to sketch ways in which the human is intrinsically good, and might become better, were at best grounds for the most cautious confidence.

Enter Hegel with the claim that if the wonders of nature reveal the workings of reason, how much more so the glories of human action! The *Lectures on the History of Philosophy* even quoted gospel to recall that Jesus disdained the fowls of the air, preferring the "divine superiority" of the human. The idea that history has meaning, one way or another, came to serve the nineteenth century much as the notion that nature has order served the eighteenth. The first will seem significantly less plausible than the second, but Hegel has several reasons for confidence in the very claim that required defense. The bright assurance that made Prometheus the nineteenth century's emblem was reflected in everything from the French Revolution to the final thought of Kant's critiques, which saw human freedom as the purpose of the universe. (Schelling's memorial address for Kant called these expressions of a single spirit.) The denial of original sin that made Rousseau's work shocking was soon taken for granted. The nineteenth century opened with an optimism the eighteenth never had.

Hegel thus had reason to be cheerful, but he wasn't, for all that, blind. It's he who described history as a slaughterbank. Using history to reveal the effects of reason in the world, and not its utter failure, required finding sense inside evil itself. This is why the struggle between slave and master in his *Phenomenology of Spirit* is a paradigm of the process he saw in history as a whole. His later speculations about the development of the World Spirit, and the role great men and their sufferings played within it, are contained in this one. The master/slave dialectic doesn't merely stand at the beginning of history; it shapes the structure of historical explanation. It asserts that Bayle's description of history as a record of crimes and misfortunes was just superficial. Bayle hadn't looked closely. Where he saw bloodshed, Hegel saw sense.

His description of the first historical event is as grand as it is eerie. There is so little description that it remains in memory like the starkness of a desert. Two men meet, and as men do, they begin to fight. For thinkers like Hobbes, such battle is expression of brute striving for power, without goal, end, or purpose. It can be suppressed but not understood, for there's nothing deep to understand. For Hegel it's the beginning of understanding itself. Each wants to realize not force but spirit. Through a willingness to give up life, each man expresses contempt for the matter of body and the contingency of death. Through a desire to force the other to yield to him, each man expresses his desire to be seen as a person, not a thing. The other's recognition is essential to one's own self-consciousness. Where Rousseau saw vanity, and resulting alienation, Hegel saw the necessary condition of identity. Our need for the other's recognition is so crucial to our sense of being that we are willing to risk our lives to attain it.

Someone blinks. The one who decided that the other's acknowledgment was not quite worth forfeiting his life will be enslaved by the one who was noble enough to disdain death for a trifle from the realm of spirit. That is, after all, what aristocrats do. But now the cunning of history begins in earnest. If battle was necessary for self-realization, defeat was even more so. The master is unhappy. Having fulfilled his only function, he has nothing left to do. All his life as agent was exhausted in one moment of prefeudal glory. Even worse, it seems to be a perfect failure, for the recognition he risked his life to attain has value only if it's recognition from an equal. By admitting defeat, the slave will avoid it, for as subordinate being, he cannot give the master what the master craved. The slave can rest easy, for this isn't disobedience but dialectic. His triumph will take place a little later, and be a little subtler: that's just what civilization means. The slave is forced to work. In so doing, he uses consciousness to give form to mere matter—the spitting image of God Himself. The master's idleness leaves him not merely bored, but obsolete as those gods whose thunder was stolen. What moves the world is something else.

Good theodicy makes everyone feel that his troubles were justified. The master has his fifteen minutes in the limelight, then consoles himself with the knowledge that his subsequent eclipse results not from a failure of his performance but from the structure of recognition itself. The slave can take pride, and revenge if he wants it, in the knowledge that he drives world history. Since increasingly refined work is a higher form of activity than battle, he is closer to the spirit and power that reflect the Creator than the master who subdued him. The World Spirit can be conscious that the design He created was the best means for pushing history forward with the right combination of freedom and necessity. And contemplating such designs, all the rest of us can feel at home in the world. What looked like two brutes on the rampage turned out to be the beginning of self-consciousness. Hegel found both sense and necessity where there seemed to be none. If there at the dawn of history, why not anywhere else?

The *Phenomenology* describes the development of human consciousness as a natural process of development. This structure was influenced by the *Emile* as well as the bildungsroman, the literary discovery of Hegel's youth. But the bildungsroman itself is a way to structure the experience of folk wisdom: through one set of trials or another, you learn the truth about yourself and the world. As an educational tool, pain has value nothing else can replace. Unlike later thinkers who viewed life as a narrative, Hegel still cared about the moral of the story—a locution we have virtually discarded. For Hegel it was clear that history must have an end. He found it in the progressive unfolding of human freedom. It may seem ironic that progress toward freedom should be absolutely necessary. But it's no more paradoxical than any other feature of the attempt to think through the combination of contingency and necessity that occupied Hegel throughout his work.

The idea that the development of humankind mirrors the development of individuals was available in Rousseau (who was very aware that in the species or the individual, education can go badly wrong). Lessing elaborated on the connections between education and progress. Kant took them so thoroughly for granted that his work is full of references to the child's growth to maturity as a paradigm of human development as a whole. His metaphors are often as clumsy as the falling toddler who forms the most famous of those references in "What Is Enlightenment?"[17] Hegel's account is much more nuanced. But he too builds on the idea implicit in the very notion of Enlightenment itself that most pain is principally growing pain, and that maturity is, finally, worth it. These are two separate claims. You may want to retain maturity as your goal while denying that pain is needed to achieve it. But unless you're especially self-deceptive or unlucky, growing up does bring progress in both awareness and freedom. Individual development is a natural metaphor for the development of humankind as a whole.

At least as surely as any theological metaphor, it's the source of the idea that the future will be better than the past. It is what we tell our children in their trouble. (You will understand how the world works, be more able to act when it doesn't.) It's an idea at least as old as the idea of the Fall—which both Hegel and Kant held necessary for the birth of humanity itself. Benjamin might have called this weakly messianic, but it's not the result of any particular form of messianism. Messianism itself is, rather, an attempt to give particular form to hope.

For Hegel, the idea of progress was heir to the idea of Providence. The relations between them have been much debated. I will return to that debate in chapter 4. One clear similarity is that both were invented not merely to explain appearances but to defy them. Both posit an order counter to the mess that experience presents. Experience offers crimes and misfortunes. Progress and Providence try to go behind (and before, and after) them. Appearances themselves are never decisive— in faith or philosophy. Both progress and Providence are read into evidence that seems to refute them. Evidence against them is not at issue, for nothing is easier to offer.

Knowing this cannot prevent some kinds of evidence from stopping us short. Even the very historical event that the late Enlightenment found redemptive (the French Revolution, for Kant, or its extension in the Battle of Jena, for Hegel) provides material for doubt. When asked whether the French Revolution signaled progress, many will second Chou En-lai: it's too soon to tell. And even should we decide that the revolution was worth it, every other decisive event looks a great deal worse. Some recent interpretations hold this objection to depend on naive readings of Hegel. His claim that modern Western history led to collective aspirations for freedom is not yet the claim that we've realized them, much less reached a state without oppression or evil.[18] One can find Hegelian indications of progress in subsequent Western history itself. The abolition of slavery, which he didn't live to see, and the demand for gender equality, which he didn't begin to imagine, can both be read as confirmation of Hegel's claims about freedom. So can many un-Hegelian attacks on Eurocentrism. And the abolition of public torture represents progress not belied by all the horrors of twentieth-century history. Foucault claimed that modern substitutes for torture are subtler forms of domination. But the fact that we can barely stand to read descriptions of things we would have brought our children to watch a few centuries earlier marks an advance in human consciousness that seems hard to reverse.

A resolute Hegelian can find signs of progress in the Hegelian system itself. The idea that modernity creates its own source of unhappiness but can also provide its own cure is new and progressive. So is the idea that self-conscious awareness is a good in itself. Both ideas can be traced to Rousseau. But Rousseau's deep ambivalence toward the very idea of modernity makes his work a prelude to the modern. Rousseau could never decide whether or not to be nostalgic. Hegel was clear. The ability to valorize the modern is itself modern, progressive, and beneficial—since turning back is not an option.

There are thus more signs to sustain claims of progress than appear at first glance. Depending on your political sympathies you will emphasize different features of modern life to support (or deny) them. But whatever you use will remain just a sign. The impulse to assert that history makes progress is not quite a form of whistling in the dark. But like claims about Providence, it arises less from belief than from doubt. Appearances suggest not God's presence in human affairs but His inexplicable absence; not progress in history but what looks like decline— or endless pointless cycles at the very best. To see this, you don't need the modern. It's been argued that the idea of Providence itself was invented in order to contend with the first great catastrophe in Jewish history. Faced with exile, the prophets sought an account that would leave intact their people's claim to be chosen.[19] This seems too specific, for the impulse is so natural that it is found throughout the Bible, beginning in much earlier books. Job's friends, for example, were faced with evidence so overwhelming that they knew no defense but to deny it, arguing that apparent injustice is a sign of God's wisdom. Turning evidence on its head is a bold move, but not a naive one.

Taking the very thing that seemed to be the problem as proof of its ultimate solution is not, therefore, a new idea. Proving it would lead to Hegel's goal for knowledge:

> The aim of knowledge is to divest the objective world that stands opposed to us of its strangeness, and as the phrase is, to find ourselves at home in it. (Hegel 3, 335)

Finding ourselves at home in the world seems so unexceptionable an aim that it's almost innocuous. The only problem is one of price: what claims on the world do you have to renounce in order to feel at home in it? The problem is not determined by Hegel's choice of means; it's implicit in his end itself. *Philosophy should help us to understand that the actual world is as it ought to be"* (Hegel 5, 66; my emphasis). If you set out to justify suffering, you may find in the end that you've justified suffering. And then you are left with consequences that Hegel was willing to draw.

We cannot fail to notice how all that is finest and noblest in the history of the world is immolated upon its altar. Reason cannot stop to consider the injuries sustained by single individuals, for particular ends are submerged in the universal end. (Hegel 5, 43)

The debate about Hegel's identification of reason and reality cannot be treated adequately here, but I hope to have offered grounds for understanding why he insisted on it. The claim that the real is rational is not, in particular, a willful confusion of the *is* and the *ought*; it is a demand. For Hegel, Kant's separation of them was timid, naive, and ultimately empty. Hegel's intention was not to idealize existing reality but to realize what Kant had left merely ideal. However complex was his discussion of real and rational, the alternatives open are few. One commentator summarizes:

Hegel's famous dictum [the real = the rational] does not . . . scandalously deify naked power: 'the actual' is not any and all existing fact (which must include the irrational, contingent and evil) but, rather, existing fact only insofar as it manifests rationality. But is Hegel's dictum not then rescued from scandalousness only at the price of being reduced to innocuous tautology? It is in the end because it can see no third alternative that Rudolf Haym's influential *Hegel und seine Zeit* chooses the first alternative and accuses Hegel of sanctifying the existing order. (Fackenheim, 208)

History seemed a vehicle not for equating real and rational but for overcoming the distinction entirely. If history is progressive, it is thereby a constant negation of given reality—not through something transcendent, but through the occurrence of more reality. To claim that history reveals its own meaning is, of course, to deny that history is just one thing after another. In practice, present reality will be negated by whatever comes next. The options for reading these facts do seem quite limited. If calling whatever is, right doesn't amount to glorifying it, then calling it right becomes empty.

There is another option, though few would wish to take it. This would be to declare that Hegel's philosophy entails the end of the human itself. Kojeve was ready to swallow this consequence with something like relish (159). The annihilation of the human is one way to stay within the demands of Hegel's logic. For many view the refusal to accept the given as given—the capacity to make demands on reality—as constitutive of being human. This gives Kant's work its distinctively tormented quality. Being human means to strive to realize a world so perfect that its realization would undo us. The best of all possible worlds is one we could never inhabit. To show the gap between *ought* and *is* slowly closing through historical process is to envision a world in which the characteristics we take to be most human become superfluous and disappear with other anachronisms.

Hegel is more commonly accused of glorifying existing power relations. If this alternative produces a more palatable interpretation of Hegel, few will find it a preferable political position. Hegel said the equation of rational and actual was the conviction on which the plain man and the philosopher simply had to take a stand (Hegel 4, 10). Arendt succinctly described the alternative they face when they take such stands:

> Since Hegel and Marx, these questions have been treated in the perspective of history and on the assumption that there is such a thing as progress of the human race. Finally we shall be left with the only alternative there is in these matters—we can either say with Hegel: *Die Weltgeschichte ist das Weltgericht*, leaving the ultimate judgement to success, or we can maintain with Kant the autonomy of the minds of men and their possible independence of things as they are or have come into being. (Arendt 4, 216)

Arendt's statement expressed her lifelong anti-Hegelian conviction that Hegel's alternative resigns us to the triumph of things as they are. She never took seriously Hegel's argument that Kant's alternative seems to resign us to simple failure. By opting for transcendence, Kant began by abandoning hope that ideas can be fulfilled. Is Hegel resigned to reality, or Kant to the mere critique of it? We can imagine the argument: *Your transcendence is empty.—Your immanence blind.* Only an intellectual intuition could directly realize the merely ideal. But such intuition cannot even be conceived, much less used by us. In the end, it hardly matters, for the question of whether World Spirit or self is the actor has disappeared in the squabble. There's very little acting going on. We are left with a debate over who was more in need of consolation: Hegel for the failures of given reality or Kant for the impotence of protest. Even without Marx, each was turning the other upside down. If this isn't antinomy, it's hard to see a way out of it.

Stating something both short and sensible about Marx is no less daunting than trying to do the same for any other major philosopher, not least because the scholarly debates are no less voluminous for him than for others. But Marx made it easier by leaving the best summary of his own approach to the problem of evil. "Philosophers have hitherto interpreted the world. The point, however, is to change it." Hegel was aware that his system was a refined form of theodicy. Marx made us aware that this could be a reason to reject it. All the heady debates of Hegel's heirs were just opiate of the salon: justifications that lulled intellectuals into accepting given reality rather than forming a plan to change it.

It's common enough to describe Marxism as a religion, or to attack it as the god that failed. Like most vulgarizations, this contains a piece of truth. But to acknowledge religious elements in Marx's view is not to oppose it to philosophy. It's often suggested that Marxism was born of disappointment with religion's failure to satisfy human longing for redemption. Philosophy, by contrast, is said to seek truth for truth's sake alone. It's further claimed that Marxism is maintained with the tenacity and disregard for evidence that marks religious faith, while philosophy is measured, rational, and responsible to evidence. Some hold that Marx's territory is close to that of religion, which explains its refusal to cover what philosophy should discuss. In particular, it's often noted that though Marx's tone conveys constant moral indignation, he has no moral philosophy in any standard sense—no definitions of right or justice, no attempts to establish moral foundations in general or to argue for the rightness of any action in particular. Thus his fervor is that of the prophet or preacher, not of the moral philosopher.[20]

All these charges take on a different cast if we place Marx where he placed himself, in the thick of attempts to explain evil. Calling it philosophical theology is acceptable as long as you remember that

Marx himself was aware that philosophical theology was supposed to be passé. To describe Marxism as the god that failed can be a way of suppressing Marx's simplest insight, for it implies that Marx's readiness to substitute human for divine agency was not self-conscious. Then his willingness to assume positions that should be hazarded, at most, within theology, would be a mixture of bravado and oversight. But—to risk the rhetorical inversion of which he was so fond—Marxism can't be described as the god that failed without first acknowledging Marx's point: God's own failure is the starting point for the history of philosophy.

Cataloging that failure is an empirical business which will occupy the next chapter. Marx belongs in the theodical tradition of this chapter, despite his merciless attacks on theodicy, because God's failure was merely his starting point. Like other rationalists, he offered both an explanation of that failure and a proposal for preventing it. More exactly, he thought that earlier philosophy was double expression of failure. After creating idols to take responsibility for human misery, it spent itself creating excuses for them. Even the most radical of young Hegelians arguing about the relations between human and God thereby forgot the point. Marx's resolve to devote himself to solving the problem rather than explaining it should not obscure his very clear view of its structure and origin, which now seems so simple it is easy to ignore. If his rejection of philosophy was simple, his reading of it was deep. Marx understood what he was abandoning.

More than anyone other than Nietzsche, Marx perceived the web binding philosophy and theology. Kantian criticisms cannot shatter it as long as those criticisms remain intellectual exercises. Mere arguments can't address the needs that found expression in theodicy. The God Kant forbade us to mention stands all the more surely behind the scenes. For transcendental idealism never transformed the reality that made us long to transcend it. Perhaps Kant's prohibitions only made problems worse: the more hopelessly elusive the object, the more longing for it grows. Hegel tried to strip the veil that Kant had provided, and demanded that philosophy face the relation between human and God. Marx argued that his boldness was only in thought. So he wrote that criticism of religion is the first premise of all criticism.

Religion, for Marx, includes a great deal:

Religion is the general theory of this world, its encyclopedia, its logic in popular form, its spiritualistic *point d'honneur*, its enthusiasm, its moral sanction, its solemn complement, and the general ground for the consummation and justification of this world. . . . Religious suffering is at once the *expression* of real suffering and the protest against real suffering. Religion is the sigh of the oppressed creature, the heart of a heartless world, just as it is the spirit of spiritless conditions. It is the *opium* of the people. (Marx, 115)

This is a lot to be said in praise of opium. Religion appears as neither trick nor narcotic but head, heart, and spirit. It is applied philosophy, the live and popular expression of a single human need. He believed it to be the consciousness of transcendence that arises from *real* necessity. Meaningless suffering is unacceptable, so both philosophy and religion go to work to give it meaning.

Some descriptions of this process sound conspiratorial. Since unexplained suffering threatens to explode established order, those interested in maintaining the order had better find explanations fast. "A theodicy justifies the happiness of the powerful and the suffering of the powerless" (Gunneman, 43). Theodicy thereby preserves each group in the place it's accustomed to occupy. But it's important to note that Marx held this process to work so naturally it didn't even require intention. One version of the process is both crude and complex: suffering people take refuge in religion, who turn to philosophy when religion begins to look illegitimate. It's a picture we'll find captured by Walter Benjamin's hunchback: behind Marxist philosophy of history lies an old religious phantom that can't be admitted to plain view. This picture assumes more discontinuity between philosophy and theology than we have been able to define. A cloudier and simpler picture does more justice to the facts. Both religion and philosophy can give meaning to suffering by distinguishing natural from moral evils and dividing responsibility accordingly. From the sigh of the oppressed to the system of Hegel there's an increase in abstraction, but each obscures our real needs. Both religion and philosophy conceal our real task: to take responsibility for the world rather than to explain it, to transform rather than to endure. The continuity in the tasks of religion and philosophy seemed so self-evident that Engels could write:

> Hitherto the question has always stood: what is God?—and German philosophy has resolved it as follows: God is man. Having grasped this truth, man must now arrange the world in a truly human way, according to the demands of his nature—and then the riddle of our time will be resolved by him. (Quoted in Tucker, 73)

Engels expressed what most left Hegelians believed. God Himself could not play the role of Redeemer He was created to fulfill. Even worse, He took up all the power and space available, so that nobody else could redeem us either. Humankind cannot be free until it takes back the power it gave to God.

Note that we have moved with extraordinary speed. If modern philosophy began by taking power from God in order to lighten His share of responsibility for evil, it soon reached the idea that all power was ours to allocate in the first place. Marx and Engels could move so quickly because they knew the discussion that consumed Hegel's heirs. Hegel had demanded mergers: philosophy should become theodicy; man should become God. Since this was the agenda, arguments could quickly turn to the question of how much was left to complete.

Debates about whether Marx was a moral philosopher should be seen against this background. Many readers are disturbed by the contrast between the tone in which Marx denounces instances of injustice and the means by which he asserts they will be overcome. While the first reflects moral indignation, often outrage, the second insists that the process of change is a matter not of moral demand but of natural law. Thus many take the late Marx, in particular, at face value. He claimed he was not a philosopher but an economist, and said his claims were not even intended to be normative, just statements of fact. The tension between the tone and the content of Marx's claims is lessened in light of the debate about natural law discussed above. For the question of which evils should be considered natural and which moral is central to that discussion.

Tension pulls in two directions. The more things are designated as moral evils, the greater our responsibility for them grows. This seems a natural process of accepting the privileges and demands of maturity—the process of Enlightenment—until we reflect that our responsibility has little relation to our power. If we don't control the natural world, we can take all the responsibility we like in thought, but it will remain without force. The price of absolute freedom becomes so high that the impulse to designate more evils as part of nature returns. Even Kant, whose insistence on separating freedom and nature was second to none, responded to this state of affairs with the categorical imperative. Directing us to act as if our moral principles were universal laws of nature is a way to imagine moral principles as efficacious. Marx was impatient with imagination.

He believed the time had come when human beings could do more than pretend to replace God as a moral hypothesis. Changes the industrial revolution had wrought in the world itself brought double fruit. Technological advances let us abolish most sources of misery. This, of course, is good in itself. But these advances themselves can create a deeper sense of liberation. The realization that progress is the product of our own creative activity should finally show that suffering and redemption are in our hands alone. Neither need be left to the grace of a Being we ourselves invented, or to the mercies of the theoretical resources of a group of philosophers. Concrete advances in material conditions allow us to control nature in ways only gods could have imagined. The industrial revolution makes further theoretical revolutions superfluous. The distinction between natural and moral evil began as a debate about how much of the world's misery was God's fault, how much of it ours. Once God was overcome as a human projection, the distinction itself must be overturned.

Engels wrote that communism was the unavoidable conclusion of German philosophy (3:448). Here three points seem to confirm him. Hegel had suggested that God was dead, along with the idea that the human should replace Him and be responsible for more of the world than we'd hitherto imagined. Similarly, the claim that ideas which remain transcendent remain mere pious wishes is found in Hegel's critique of Kant—now applied to Hegel himself. In Marx as in Hegel, the morality and nature that Kant tried to keep separate fuse. Finally, Marx was influenced by the *Phenomenology*'s suggestion that the slave and his work are the forces that transform the world.[21] In all these ideas, Marx's intention remains the same: to reproduce in the material world the movement Hegel made in thought. For Hegel represents but Prometheus manqué: he made it to the heavens, but forgot to take the fire.

In one mood, Marx's rejection of philosophy looks as simple as Dr. Johnson's. The English doctor dismissed skeptical arguments that material objects are unreal by kicking a stone, saying, "I refute Berkeley thus." This is not a part of philosophical argument but a rejection of it altogether—which itself can be part of philosophy. Marx's rejection of philosophy is accompanied by a profound narrative of its history. To claim we've forgotten that the point was not to interpret the world but to change it is to make a philosophical point. For it rests on the understanding of past philosophy as theodicy. By understanding this with an accuracy missing in others, Marx eliminated philosophy with an assurance others lacked, for he proposed to eliminate the needs from which it arises. Kant proclaimed the end of metaphysics but insisted on perpetuating the questions that produce it. Those questions, he thought, can never be answered by reason. Marx would only agree. The questions that drive philosophy are fundamental to human existence. Just because they are real questions, they demand real, not rational, solutions.

These solutions should incorporate whatever is productive in the structure of philosophical theodicies while removing the need for theodicy. Rousseau gave us the idea that historical processes made us authors of our own suffering who could become the authors of our own happiness. The idea was vastly refined in Hegel, whose view of the slave's work as the beginning of history was the basis of Marx's. Labor distinguishes us from animals, making us the creative beings we projected onto the heavens. While some animals can make particular products at random, only humans produce their own means of production. This is the source of our ability to replace the God we invented. Producing those means ensures our status as creators, for it makes us self-conscious and self-sufficient—just those qualities we projected onto God. Those who produce the means of production can foresee the future, and demand a share in it.

The alienation of labor enslaved the means of production—precisely that feature of human existence which should make us free and divine. Thus it is the basis of all the other ways human beings create their own chains and call them natural necessity. Every philosophical theodicy addresses the question of which evils are natural and which ones are moral. Marx was no exception, and his answer redrew boundaries that seemed fixed. What looked as immutable as an earthquake turned out to be merely property relations. The understanding we acquired, and technology we created, could rearrange something that seemed as objective and independent of us as the institution of private property. If we could do all that, who would set limits to the changes we could impose on the world? Like other theodicies, Marx's justified suffering in the present by showing how it was necessary to overcome suffering in the future. Marx's praises of capitalism are thus neither ironic nor paradoxical. They are part of a tradition whose goal is to make sense of suffering. Giving meaning to the past and hope to the future is the task of any ground on which religion and philosophy meet. Marx stood as firmly on such ground as anyone. In one respect, however, he broke with every preceding form of theodicy. What others left implicit, half-thought or half-dared, was for Marx as serene as an axiom. Theodicies had hitherto defended God; the point was to replace Him.

Marx's attraction to Prometheus is easy to understand, for it wasn't just anything that the Titan stole. The nineteenth century found no better dream of bringing heaven down to earth. Lightning symbolized all the majesty and terror of Providence. To transform the unpredictable force that strikes at random from above into a perfectly prosaic form of power was to put fate itself in human hands.

IN CONCLUSION

The demands of reason led to consequences that explode them. We began with Alfonso, whose fantasy looked close to common sense. Alfonso's wish to advise God quickly led to Leibniz's wish to be his advocate, a more complex form of displacement. Rousseau's wish to defend Him was a step toward making Him obsolete. Kant was the first to name the wish to be God as driving force behind much of meta-physics. His first *Critique* unmasked it, his second made it the testing ground of morality, and his third simultaneously validated it and showed it up for the hopeless piece of blasphemy that it is. No wonder his legacy was hard to decipher. We saw Hegel announce God's death and his own willingness to replace Him, and Marx demand that the replacement become real.

The same story could be told in more measured tones. In the forego-ing I have tried to show how the demands to make sense of the world threaten the limits of sense itself. The attempt to stay within reason is doomed here to failure, and forms of expression are anything but accidental. I have made little attempt to trace causal connections in the history of ideas, though I have drawn on histories of others. Rather, I have tried to show something about the logic implicit in the very ordi-nary wish to change a piece of the world.

Here there's more than one slope to slip down. Feuerbach provided cold links for a chain of argument. Providence, he argued, concerns God's relation to humans. General Providence, the claim that God's wisdom is manifest in the very existence of unchanging laws of nature, was a claim he found too weak. Rather, he took the notion of personal Providence seriously. God may intervene daily, as He sees fit. Every hair on *your* head is numbered. If God is willing to interrupt the laws of nature for your sake, you have infinite worth in His eyes. Well, then, here's nothing less than His word for it: you have infinite worth.

> Consequently, the belief in God is nothing but the belief in human dignity, the belief in the absolute reality and significance of human nature. (Feuerbach, 103)

Feuerbach concluded his discussion of Providence with a word to those Christians who might damn such views as expressions of pride. Is it more humble to imagine God becoming human for the sake of saving humankind? Feuerbach saw himself as merely leaving out the middleman. Since Leibniz gave Him little to do but pick out combina-tions already determined by necessary essences, God had become little but a middleman anyway.

If one axis on which reason falters is the increasing impotence of God, the other is the power of contingency. Rousseau's tutor was needed to eliminate it, but it was a lifelong, full-time job. The later Kant knew that accident makes short work of small changes; or, rather, that there is no way to know which changes will be small ones. So Hegel called philosophy's task the elimination of contingency—and the philosopher's goal a knowledge as absolute as that once ascribed to God. Between these two axes there is no *logical* space for humility. Wherever one moves, one is caught. The demand to change the world cannot remain a moral imperative. It will quickly move from Kant's proposal to imagine we are creating laws of nature to Marx's demand that we go ahead and change nature itself. But exchanging the demand to change the world for the insistence on being reconciled with it brings little relief. Hegel's announcement of the death of God, and of redemption through the future, would soon give way to Nietzsche's announcement of the murder of God, and the need to seek redemption through the past. Those who talk most about the owl of Minerva long most to replace the goddess of wisdom herself.

This is all the more remarkable when we recall where philosophy began. Its founding hero's claim to fame was a claim of absolute humility: only Socrates knows that he knows nothing. Socrates' uncertain shuffle between diffidence and swagger is itself a matter for study. It cannot be accidental. For even thoroughly modest characters like Kant knew that this confusion belongs to the discipline, whose goal is always to close the gap between *ought* and *is*—from one side or another. Kant's vision of metaphysics as unending rests on his view that the gap is permanent. Thus he described his relation to the subject as that of an unsatisfied yet unwavering lover (A850/B878). But tolerance for tormented love is varied; Kant's seemed to be higher than most. Hegel would at once proclaim the end of philosophy and of the gap between real and rational. Marx attacked endings that remained endings in thought; once the gap really closed, there would be no more to discuss.

The presumption involved in the wish to replace God may lead to dangers that refuse to stay in the realm of theology. This would become clearer in the following century. The wish would be condemned not as blasphemy but as pathology—the latter now considered the greater problem. So it has been argued that Nietzsche's misappropriation by fascism wasn't merely bad luck. The search for the wrong sort of power creates confusion between human and divine prerogative that must end in something damned.

All this is good reason to back down before the problems start, and to resist the fantasy of outdoing the Creator by improving on Creation before it gets out of hand. The next chapter will examine a different sort of reservation. Some thinkers rejected the wish to replace God not because it was absurd or impious, but because they thought it beneath them. On their views, the world we were given is so outrageous that no reasonable being would want credit as its Author. Giving accounts that show how the world is, or can be made, rational is a way of being accountable for it. This is responsibility they would not accept.

Chapter Two
CONDEMNING THE ARCHITECT

> Regarding nature as though it were a proof of God's
> goodness and providence; interpreting history in honor of
> divine reason; as a constant testimonial to an ethical world
> order and ethical ultimate purpose; explaining all one's own
> experiences in the way pious folk have done for long enough,
> as though everything were providence, a sign, intended, and
> sent for the salvation of the soul: now all that is *over*, it
> has conscience *against* it, every sensitive conscience sees it
> as indecent, dishonest, a pack of lies, feminism, weakness,
> cowardice—this severity makes us *good* Europeans if anything
> does, and heir to Europe's most protracted and bravest
> self-overcoming!
>
> —Nietzsche, *On the Genealogy of Morals*

Modern philosophy was full of them: good Europeans determined to be tough. They lived in cosmopolitan space. Bayle had pressing reasons for changing countries; Voltaire looked long and hard before retreating to something like his own. Schopenhauer was a German who read Indian philosophy, Hume a Scot who succeeded in Parisian society. They talked about myth with wit and detachment. All used their forms of rootless internationalism to make claims about the world. They'd been around, seen what variety one could reach in days of slow post and rough roads, and they were not impressed. Voltaire described it through the eyes of Candide, who crossed the globe in search of something better than the pettiness and cruelty of his native Westphalia. Except for a brief excursion into fantasy that leaves him bored and longing, the picture his experience presented was relentless. The universalism of this comer of Enlightenment is bleak. Human fate and human nature are pretty much the same wherever one looks. Alas.

Nietzsche's fervor was out of date. They didn't need his encouragement in order to face facts with open eyes. Rejecting the notion of Providence as something quite literally indecent began, at the latest, when Bayle's *Dictionary* was published in 1697. The analogies he used to describe the God of the orthodox could make a believer long for the bland and tasteful assertions of nonexistence that later atheists came to offer. Better to have no God at all than to have one like this.

That there is something problematic about any possible version of the project considered in the previous chapter is hardly news. The wish to displace God that is contained in every attempt to re-create the world is the very essence of the sin of pride. It's pride that can lead to rebellion caused by the contemplation of all the evil in Creation. If God failed to get it right, why don't we do without Him and take over the job ourselves? The urge to humility is a product of acquiescence, if not terror: we agree not to understand why there is evil. Dostoevsky saw this clearly. But even those who view humility as an old-fashioned, slavish virtue have a simpler problem with the wish to be God. We are so conspicuously lacking in His major virtues, benevolence and omnipotence, that even imitation is probably out of reach.

So this is one set of facts that was faced long ago. Religious attacks against humanism are older than the Renaissance, but their pious wrath was misdirected. Even the proudest of early Renaissance thinkers knew we had limits, and Enlightenment thinkers agreed. The wish to be God will not bring us anything but trouble.

Yet the urge to leave Him in His heaven, as if all were right with the world, is no solution either. Any form of theodicy—including the assertion that God's ways are beyond understanding—involves some form of bad faith. This is what Kant saw when he said that such assertions require no refutation but the feeling for morality. The other set of facts that seem to cry for recognition concern the utter irrationality of the real. This chapter discusses a group of writers who rejected all attempts to seek transcendence and insisted on staying with the appearances. You might call them empiricists, were it not for the ways this discussion casts the division of philosophers into rationalists and empiricists in doubt. You could also divide them according to directions in time. Those in the last chapter looked to the past, as a source of explanation, and then to the future, as a source of hope. Those in the present chapter focused on what Schopenhauer called the small dark cloud of the present. However we divide them, we will see that the group here considered was determined to insist that things are indeed what they seem. If the distinction is not quite contiguous with the distinction between empiricists and rationalists, it shows much of what's at stake in the latter. Appearance gives us a world of misery. Reason gives us the grounds for it, along with ideas that might show it redeemed. The arguments between them concern what to take more seriously: the stark and painful awareness that we have for a moment when confronted with any form of evil; or the ideas and explanations that allow us to transcend it.

This chapter considers one figure central to the current philosophical canon and three on its fringes. Each could be called a good European determined to reject every reference to Providence as a sign of cowardice. Each demanded that we face appearances, and argued that if we begin from the facts and forge ahead without self-deception, we will end by way of theory with gnosticism at the very best. I'll begin by examining Bayle, who scandalized early modern Europe by arguing that Manichaeism is the most reasonable explanation of the data. Therefore, he hastened to add, it makes sense to reject reason altogether. Bayle was greatly admired by David Hume, who honed Bayle's arguments into his devastating critique of the argument from design. Next to Hume's hypotheses, Manichaeism is tame. Did the world bear witness to a wise and magnificent Creator? Did it really? Wouldn't facts suggest instead the workings of an infant deity, practicing world making and producing models he could throw away? Perhaps a senile deity who's finally lost his touch? Hume's discussion of the problem of evil is, I shall argue, the centerpiece of his attack on human reason in general, and it was powerful enough to give Kant nightmares.

Those who demand that we confront appearances without illusion will care about describing details, one after another, with an eye for the example that often takes more literary than philosophical skill.[1] So I include two thinkers who are neither summits of philosophical nor

literary achievement, but who cannot be ignored by either discipline—
if neither discipline quite knows what to do with them. Voltaire has a
place both as central figure of the Enlightenment and as one who first
cried loudly against it. His poem "The Lisbon Earthquake" is baroque,
perhaps maudlin, but its passion and rage make the case against the
equation of intelligibility and hope—the cardinal assumption of the
Enlightenment. Four years later, *Candide* made the same point with
bitter humor. By any means, Voltaire wished to convince us that philosophy is vain. It may even be cruel. For all its attempts to make sense
of the vanity and cruelty in our lives only mock those lives themselves.
The Marquis de Sade took this position to its outer limit. His work
presented an argument from design in reverse: wherever you look,
you see miracles of horror. Moral and natural evil merge in his vision
because God Himself—should He be out there—is just what Descartes
feared, an utterly malevolent genius. Adorno and Horkheimer were
right to place Sade at a crucial point in the history of philosophy, wrong
about his ancestry. Sade's work, I will argue, is less a logical extension
of Kant's vision than a logical extension of Hume's. One claim should
be clear at the close of this chapter. If the problem of evil dominated
eighteenth-century thought, it was not from naïveté. No twentieth-century dismissal of its discussion compares in force or profanity with the
critics who were there at the time.

RAW MATERIAL: BAYLE'S *DICTIONARY*

It doesn't look like philosophy. It is lewd, loud, long, rambling, and
very, very funny. It never sticks to a point. It interrupts itself with endless
digression. It often seems blithely ad hominem, offering disquisitions
that cannot decide whether they are biographies of persons whose
names are now forgotten or argument about questions that still perplex
us. But Bayle's *Historical and Critical Dictionary* is breathtakingly
sharp, often unanswerable, and full of the air of excitement which is all
that gives life to intellectual debate, and that can be sensed centuries
later, in what has become another world. No wonder Voltaire called him
"the immortal Bayle," and devoted more than half the entry ostensibly
devoted to "The Philosopher" in his own *Philosophical Dictionary* to a

discussion of Bayle himself. Voltaire was not alone in his estimation. Bayle's *Dictionary* was called the most-read book of the eighteenth century and the arsenal of the Enlightenment (Gay 1, 1:293). Whether or not the philosophers who revered him were faithful to his intentions, they happily raided Bayle's book for theoretical ammunition.

If you believe that history is nothing but a record of crimes and misfortunes, you might think it sufficient to list them. Bayle's own experience contained more than enough. He was born to a Protestant pastor in southern France at a time when French Protestants were subject to severe persecution. Seventeenth-century Europe believed that reliance on the Inquisition had caused Spain's decline as a major power, so France turned to gentler forms of religious repression. Restricting access to education, holding of offices, and economic advancement to Catholics was substituted for the auto-da-fé. Dismayed Protestants who tried to leave for more hospitable countries like Prussia or the Netherlands were sent to the galleys, if male, and to the prisons, if female, for the rest of their miserable lives. Among those who succeeded in fleeing was the self-taught Pierre Bayle, who, safe in Rotterdam, produced page after page that would have been banned anywhere but the Netherlands. He nevertheless published anonymously, a very common practice, to avoid the sort of thing that happened when his cover was eventually blown. His brother in France was arrested in his stead and presumably tortured to death in the prison where he perished five months later. Scholars hold this to be the signal event in Bayle's life, undermining any possible belief in a just God who rewards the righteous and punishes the vile.

Though he was happy to write about others' life stories, he was silent about his own. How to measure the effect of such experiences on one's general view of experience itself is in any case an open question. He did not think one needed to have seen much in order to observe the joy with which nations celebrate the massacres their soldiers commit. His descriptions of the festivities surrounding military victories are particularly brutal. Such scenes are, for Bayle, hard data, and one needn't even change the details to find his description contemporary. Bayle, like Hume, turned skeptic from commitments to appearances. His article "Manicheans" held these criteria of inquiry to be self-evident:

> Every theory has need of two things in order to be considered a
> good one: first, its ideas must be distinct; and second, it must
> account for experience. (Bayle 1, 145)

Good theories must account for experience, and Bayle used all his
irony in a backhanded plea for what he called a posteriori arguments.
What must be accounted for is experience that's oddly mixed. The
problem of evil arises through contemplation of the mixture of happiness and virtue with wickedness and pain that experience makes evident. If this description of experience is indisputable, inference to the
best explanation gives you Manichaeism. The view that the universe is
ruled by two principles—call them God and Satan—locked in constant
struggle for domination is less an explanation of experience than a
reflection of it. But Bayle never thought that explanations run deep.
His "Pyrrho" argued that the view that all things are comprehensible
was the only really wise one. Manichaeism makes most sense of ordinary experience, if sense is what you want to make. As we will see, it
also provides the strongest reason for giving up the attempt. Therefore,
Bayle added, in one of his beautifully ambiguous passages, it is fortu-
nate that Augustine, "so well versed in all the arts of controversy"
(Bayle 1, 144), decided to abandon Manichaeism, since he could have
defended it so well.

If Bayle had rested there, it would have been bad enough, but he
wasn't content to point out the data. Rather, he recast the classical
statement of the problem of evil that his readers knew from Lactantius
and Epicurus.

> God is either willing to remove evil and cannot; or he can and is
> unwilling; or he is neither willing nor able to do so; or else he is
> both willing and able. If he is willing and not able, he must then
> be weak, which cannot be affirmed of God. If he is able and not
> willing, he must be envious, which is also contrary to the nature
> of God. If he is neither willing nor able, he must be both envious
> and weak, and consequently not be God. If he is both willing and
> able—the only possibility that agrees with the nature of God—
> then where does evil come from? (Bayle 1, 169)

Let's put this argument into schematic form. The problem of evil occurs when you try to maintain three propositions that don't fit together.

1. Evil exists.
2. God is benevolent.
3. God is omnipotent.

Bend and maul and move them as you will, they cannot be held in union. One of them has to go.

For Bayle, the first claim was description too apparent to call into question. So he left it alone, without bothering to defend it by amassing much evidence. Examples like human joy in contemplating massive murder were offered merely as reminders. "Manicheans" generalized such examples with the laconic indication that Bayle knew whereof he spoke:

> Travel gives continual lessons of this. Monuments to human mis-
> ery and wickedness are found everywhere—prisons, hospitals,
> gallows, and beggars. Here you see the ruins of a flourishing city;
> in other places you cannot even find the ruins. (Bayle 1, 146)

Bayle added a few quotations from the Romans, but his haphazard reference to the classics suggests he did not believe these claims to need proof. The second and third claims, however, result not from a posteriori but from a priori reflection. They proceed from hypothesis or faith, and Bayle went to work on undermining them. His book brings life to references that are today familiar to few but historians of theology, for it shows what was at stake in differences between Socinians and Arminians, or other apparently obscure forms of heresy. Living in the middle of the most violent of such debates, Bayle recast them as a matter of how to combine the three propositions above. If you drop benevolence, you're left with one heresy; drop omnipotence, you're stuck with another. The alternatives are so maddening that one almost begins to understand the temptation to burn one's opponent over a particularly tenacious assertion of one of them. Everyone was desperate to make sense of the world. Without those two premises, one could take one's sense from Manichaeism; but theology ruled out this option.

Bayle was particularly brilliant in showing how traditional attempts to solve the problem of evil abandon belief in God's benevolence. His first analogy opens a window on the terror implicit in orthodox religion.

> If you say that God has permitted sin in order to manifest his wisdom, which shines forth more in the midst of the disorders that man's wickedness produces every day than it would in a state of innocence, you will be answered that this is to compare God either to a father who allows his children to break their legs so he can show everyone his great skill in mending their broken bones, or to a king who allows seditions and disorders to develop in his kingdom so that he can gain glory by overcoming them. (Bayle 1, 176)

A father who lets his children break their legs so he can show his skill at healing. This is the God in whom we put our trust? Does the doctrine of a Being whose justice, wisdom, and mercy are shown in His redeeming only some of the creatures He allowed to fall into mortal sin really suggest something better? Bayle ran through other attempts to combine our urge to assert God's goodness with our certain knowledge of what's bad in the world. There's the argument that we need to feel pain in order to feel pleasure. Bayle thought this was nonsense, contradicting all that Scripture, reason, and experience have to teach us. Did Adam and Eve need pain to feel the joys of paradise before they fell from it? Does logic ground the claim that we cannot experience one of two contradictories without the other? Does experience really show that pleasure becomes insipid if it lasts long—or is this just the sort of thing we say for comfort because it usually doesn't?

These attempts, Bayle knew, were relatively feeble. Augustine was the real challenge. After making short work of other solutions, Bayle opened his fire on the free will defense. The first premise of that defense is that natural evil, starting with Adam's mortality, is always punishment for moral evil.

> Then it is not God who is the cause of moral evil; but he is the cause of physical evil, that is to say, the punishment of moral

evil—punishment which, far from being incompatible with the supremely good principle, necessarily flows from one of God's Attributes, I mean that of justice, which is no less essential to man than God's goodness. (Bayle 1, 149)

For very many centuries, this argument seemed unexceptionable. The premise that natural evil is punishment was accepted without blinking, and still persists in whatever premodern relics of consciousness survive in many of us. As we saw when considering Leibniz, what elicited question was something else. If God invented natural evil as fair punishment for moral evil, why did He invent moral evil? Augustine's answer seemed both moving and sane. God doesn't will moral evil, but He has to permit it, for it's a necessary condition of the greatest gift He ever gave us. God gave us respect, and the chance to become worthy of it. In giving us free will, He gave us something ennobling. We are not beasts or machines but beings made in His image. To be real freedom, it must be freedom to err. And we did.

Much of Leibniz's *Theodicy* attempted to renew Augustine's answer against Bayle's onslaught. How God's foreknowledge is meant to be compatible with freedom, and which conception of necessity eludes objections, are questions that occupied church fathers and still interest Leibniz scholars today. Their very subtlety, for Bayle, is a sign of fear and enervation, for it seeks to evade retorts of any common sense.

> Those who say that God permitted sin because he could not have prevented it without destroying the free will that he had given to man, and which was the best present he made to them, expose themselves greatly. The reason they give is lovely. It has a *je ne sais quoi*, an indefinable something, that is dazzling. It has grandeur. But in the end it can be opposed by arguments more easily opposed by all men, and based more on common sense and the ideas of order. (Bayle 1, 177)

The free will defense works with both flattery and pathos. It plays with our desire to appear in God's image, along with our need to find meaning in the world. But if it was meant to preserve the belief in God's goodness, Bayle thought the free will defense begs every question.

Once common sense steps back from its own vanity, its response is quite simple. Next to gifts like these, the Trojan horse looks benign. Here Bayle was explicit: who wouldn't load his enemies with gifts sure to bring about their ruin? Bayle didn't stop with this question but saved his lewdest analogy for this argument.

> There is no good mother who, having given her daughters permission to go to a dance, would not revoke that permission if she were assured that they would succumb to temptations and lose their virginity there. And any mother who, knowing for sure that this would come to pass, allowed them to go to the dance and was satisfied with exhorting them to be virtuous and with threatening to disown them if they were no longer virgins when they returned home, would, at the very least, bring upon herself the just charge that she loved neither her daughters nor chastity. (Bayle 1, 177–78)

Bayle was clearly delighted with the metaphor and played with it for several pages. He knew, of course, that it would seem outrageous. In the second edition he added yet another footnote, which looks intended to soothe at least the Protestants among his readers. These should consider his remark about the wanton mother as giving Catholic critics a taste of their own medicine. Hadn't Jesuits compared the God of the Calvinists to arbitrary human tyrants like Caligula and Tiberius? Why shouldn't they be answered in kind? It's a clever retort, for it adds another layer of equivocation and puzzlement. You think my God is cruel? Take a good look at yours. Can *anyone* maintain a consistent assertion of God's benevolence? To excuse His apparent lack of love for us by appealing to his alleged respect will in the end be very feeble.

> It would be in vain for [the mother] to try to justify herself by saying that she had not wished to restrain the freedom of her daughters or to indicate that she distrusted them. She would be told that this type of behavior was preposterous and was more indicative of a provoked, cruel stepmother than of a mother. (Bayle 1, 178)

Traditional belief is said to play on childhood fantasy. We want a world ordered by wise and loving parents who fulfill the needs we're not aware of, guard the interests we do not see. This is, after all, the promise of Providence:[2] God knows more than you do, and arranges events to work for that long-term interest you are not foresighted or mature enough to perceive. Bayle moved from children's dreams of safe landing to their most dreadful apparitions. Supposing God were not a sage and nurturing father, but one who let you fall to the bottom for his own narcissistic needs? Supposing God were not a protective and loving mother, but one who allowed you to ruin yourself forever— perhaps out of envy? Does any attempt to maintain God's benevolence by claiming He was only trying to offer us presents provide a better picture? Bayle elaborated various options for God's defense, adapting his analogies to traditional theological positions on God's foreknowledge. He concluded with a position he ascribed to common sense. If God even suspected we could so abuse our freedom as to cause our eternal damnation, He should have kept His gifts to Himself.

The consequences of belief in God's omnipotence are thus terrifying. Bayle's metaphors were meant to show how much we lose if we lose benevolence. But supposing we go the other route, maintaining our belief in God's benevolence and softening our demands for His omnipotence? Bayle tried to show that such a solution is equally repugnant to theology and to common sense. Suppose God cannot do or know as much as we thought. Suppose He knows less about the consequences of His actions than the average human being. Was God not quite certain that Adam and Eve would fall? Here Bayle returned to his favorite analogy.

> If this mother went to the ball, and if she should see and hear through a window that one of her girls was defending herself only weakly in the corner of a study against the demands of a young lover; if she should see that her daughter was but a step away from giving in to the desires of her tempter, and if she would not go to her aid and rescue her from that trap, would we not rightly say that she would be acting like a cruel stepmother and that she would be quite capable of selling her daughter's

honor? . . . There are no people so little experienced who, without seeing what goes on in the heart, cannot tell by signs when
a woman is ready to yield, if they should happen to see through
a window how she defends herself when her fall is imminent.
(Bayle 1, 181)

The idea that God didn't know we would abuse His gift turns the Lord
of Hosts into a pitiful slave—with less *Menschenkenntnis* than a mod-
erately experienced voyeur.

The willingness to soften traditional claims of God's omnipotence
leads to a God who is unworthy of our worship, in very short order.
Bayle also thought it led straight to Manichaeism after all. For if God is
too benevolent to have caused all the evil in the world, something else
did. That nothing comes from nothing is, for Bayle, a first rule of
thought. Some source must be responsible for evil. If it isn't God, it
must be a power whose strength is equivalent. In the end he thought
the choice to be merely one between more and less reasonable versions of Manichaeism. For a Christianity that maintains God's benevolence must give up His omnipotence. But this is Manichaeism around
the edges, pushed to incoherence. Far better to split the difference,
Bayle argued, and locate good and evil principles in two different substances rather than combining them in one. One way or another, there
is evil power. Better to call it Satan than to call it God Himself.

According to you, the sole principle, which you admit, desired
from all eternity that man should sin, and that the first sin should
be contagious, that it should ceaselessly and endlessly produce
all imaginable crimes over the entire face of the earth. In consequence of which he prepared all the misfortunes that can be conceived for the human race in this lifetime—plague, war, famine,
pain, trouble—and after this life a hell in which almost all men
will be eternally tormented in such a way that makes our hair
stand on end when we read descriptions of it. (Bayle 1, 185)

The vision of the orthodox makes God appear a monster. Bayle argued
that Calvinism would have created more converts to Manichaeism than
anything earlier theologians accomplished. Wouldn't reason prefer

two warring substances to the Calvinist God? A Being who makes the torments of hell eternal, restricts the number of those who escape them to a tiny minority, and determines who gets what without regard to merit, makes Manichaeism look positively sunny. Here we should note that Bayle belonged to Calvinist churches for most of his life. The question of the sincerity of his religious beliefs is one we'll discuss shortly, but his writing suggests that hell is part of the world he inhabits. It is one part of the argument for his final conclusion.

For what's left to reject? The first of his premises, that evil exists, is a matter of observation. Bayle thought nobody willing to face experience could call evil into doubt. Drop the second premise, God's benevolence, and you're left with a nightmare. Drop the third, God's omnipotence, and you're left with Manichaeism—covertly or not. If the rejection of any of these claims is unacceptable, the only recourse is to reject that very reason which insists on making sense of them. The urge to combine the claims of common sense and reason with the claims of faith is entirely reasonable. Still it cannot be met. Between reason and faith, one must simply choose. Bayle thought the choice was clear. He compared reason to a corrosive powder that begins by attacking the infected flesh of a wound but goes on to destroy living flesh and bone. Though reason begins by refuting error, it soon leads us astray. The confusion and contradiction left in its wake bring immediate misery and produce neither truth nor virtue. Faith, by contrast, might just possibly save.

The problem of evil is not Bayle's only argument against the value of human reason, merely his strongest. His "Pyrrho" offered other grounds for abandoning the intellect, for all but minor technical purposes. One is especially extraordinary and leads us back to the problem of evil after all. Bayle thought that the new philosophy—that is, Cartesianism—put final touches on skepticism. For it showed that objects of our senses are not what they seem. Bodies are utterly different from the way they appear. Appearance gives us qualities like heat, smells, and color; Cartesian science tells us that all these are but "modifications of the soul." It is true, Bayle continued, that Cartesianism asserts the real existence of primary properties, extension and motion. But here (you can almost see Bayle smiling) it's on shaky ground. For its only proof of the existence of bodies is that without them, God would be a deceiver. If nothing corresponded to the secondary qualities we experience, God would have given us ideas of real objects without anything to back them. But

> [e]ver since the beginning of the world, all mankind, except perhaps one out of two hundred millions, has firmly believed that bodies are colored, and this is an error. I ask, does God deceive mankind with regard to colors? If he deceives them about this, what prevents him from doing so with regard to extension? (Bayle 1, 198)

Bayle used Descartes's work to provide more grounds for doubt. If Descartes is right, he's given us reasons to believe that God is a deceiver after all. The epistemological apparatus with which He equipped us does not pick out extension without a long chain of reasons. What we experience, day after day, are bright colors, sharp tastes, strong smells. Now we know all that to be mere illusion, and continue to perceive them nonetheless. If God could deceive us about secondary qualities, why not primary qualities? Why not anything?

Earlier skeptics merely *worried* about the gap between appearance and reality; Descartes wrote it into physics. What's a bent stick in the water next to seventeenth-century optics? We saw Leibniz, among others, turn the spectacular discoveries of early modern science into grounds for faith in the increasing powers of human reason. Bayle saw them as one more ground for despair. Refusing to let up, he attacked the Cartesians from the other direction. When pushed to the limit, Descartes chose voluntarism: part of the privilege of being God is just the privilege of not having to act in accord with human reason. God's fundamental choices, like the laws of mathematics or ethics, are products of His will. They require and receive no other grounding. Bayle thought that this belief undercut the Cartesian's own foundation. For the more you insist on God's incomprehensibility, the more you allow that He could be and do anything. In particular: couldn't He be a deceiver?

What did Bayle want? He used extraordinary skill to undercut all traditional positions, while refraining from arguing a positive view of his own. Perhaps he knew how easily he would find objections to any view he might construct. His stated conclusion is to refrain from argument altogether. He told readers to look not toward reason but toward faith. Some scholars think this advice was merely prudential— in regard both to his own immediate interests and to those of his readers. Bayle claimed to defend a Christian skeptical tradition, with arguments only directed to refuting rationalist theology. But it's argued that he made such claims simply to stay out of jail. On this view all his professions of faith amounted to pure subterfuge. Rather than clearing the ground for leaps of faith, he undermined it entirely.

This view of Bayle influenced Voltaire and Hume. It's the view implied less by his claims than by the tone in which he stated them. Unlike great fideists like Pascal or Kierkegaard, Bayle betrayed no shred of religious emotion. Where he showed passion, it was passion for irony. He simply took too much pleasure in pointing out the obscene behavior of King David, or the futile and tortuous idiocies of traditional theodicy. (Nowhere else is the claim that faith requires crucifixion of the intellect more resonant than in Bayle.) This tone, as much as any particular content, was inherited by Voltaire and Hume, whose standpoints toward religion were considerably less ambiguous.

Yet significant modern scholars take Bayle at his word. There are grounds for viewing him as the believer he said he was. Elisabeth Labrousse, for instance, insists on the importance of context. Bayle wrote at a time when terrible wars of religion had been succeeded by nothing better than severe persecution. Personal experience of the latter, she argues, moved him to condemn every form of religious fanaticism, and to advocate degrees of religious toleration in advance of his time. Accordingly, his arguments against orthodox theology were designed to show that we can never know the truth of any significant religious questions. This is an argument for tolerance. For if knowledge is impossible, each should be allowed to choose faith according to conscience. On this view, Bayle was a Christian philosopher who destroyed every intelligible form of Christian theology. Humiliation of human reason was preparation not just for faith but for religious humility and political moderation.[3]

It's a question we may never settle. Most interesting is that, for present purposes, we have no need to settle it. Bayle may have been an atheist or a Christian fideist. It has even been argued that he was a secret Jew or a survivor of the Albigensian massacres. The content of his religious belief is irrelevant. Skeptical arguments like Bayle's can lead you either way: to reject God in general, and any religion in particular, in rage or disgust; or to embrace them in a leap of faith taken in desperation or ecstasy. *For the more fundamental question at issue is not skepticism about religion but skepticism about human reason.* Each of the three Western religions has both rationalist and fideist traditions; each can be taken up or rejected on either ground. The problem of evil cannot determine your religious standpoint, nor is it determined by that standpoint. This will become clearest when we turn to Hume, who took Bayle's arguments as the strongest case for rejecting God. Perhaps Bayle didn't take them that way but meant just what he said, intending to persuade us to reject argument altogether in favor of blind faith. Either response is possible. You can retain your faith in God, while acknowledging that faith to be at odds with reason and experience; you can reject that faith altogether. What you cannot retain is your wholehearted faith in human reason. After Bayle lacerated the latter on the problem of evil, it demanded a restoration of deepest proportions.

VOLTAIRE'S DESTINIES

Voltaire would not be the one to provide it. Where he does defend reason, he makes Pangloss look skeptical. Let us glance at his tale *Zadig; or, Destiny*, written twelve years before *Candide; or, Optimism*. As a character, Zadig bears less resemblance to Candide than to Job. He's described as the best and the wisest of men. Zadig is no callow disciple, but—by virtue of his own evident abilities—the treasured adviser of kings as well as gangsters from Babylon to Egypt. But as with the hero of Voltaire's more famous story, Zadig's improbable adventures take him across much of the globe, suspended amid more reversals of fortune than you can count. "So at last I am happy!" Zadig exclaims, when his virtues have brought him to some new position that leaves him powerful, useful, and beloved. He is always mistaken, for the greatest good fortune is quickly followed by exile, or slavery, or the narrowest escape from a miserable death. All these things take place through mechanisms that seem inexplicable. Zadig's righteous actions lead to his downfall, the wickedness of others leads to their happiness, and many events happen merely at random. Most of the elements of *Candide* are in place: worldwide wandering, and the hope of reunion with a distant beloved as the motor behind the hero's travels and travails. Like Candide's, Zadig's experience reveals murder, greed, and ideological warfare to be the motor that drives most of the rest of the world. Both books describe a search for the cunning of reason. Like *Candide*, *Zadig* echoed Bayle almost verbatim: "Is it necessary that there should always be crimes and misfortunes?"

Unlike Candide, Zadig gets an answer. He asks the question of the angel who appears at the end of the story. The angel answers with an account that resembles the world according to Leibniz. The universe in its immense diversity was necessarily created by supreme wisdom.

> There is no chance; all is test, or punishment, or reward, or fore-seeing. . . . Frail mortal, cease to argue against what you must worship. (Voltaire 1, 169)

The angel, however, can do things Leibniz cannot, and as representative of Providence proceeds to enact the logic of the world. Leibniz refused to give any details. In asking for a little evidence that this world is the best of all possible ones, Bayle was, he thought, too demanding. So Leibniz wrote that Bayle's request for a detailed exposition of *how* evil is compatible with the best possible world-schema is "asking too much":

> It is sufficient for me to point out that there is nothing to *prevent* the connection of a certain individual evil with what is the best on the whole. (Leibniz, 214; my emphasis)

Formally, of course, Leibniz was quite right. Here as elsewhere, his answers show the limits of the formal—as none other than Bertrand Russell complained.[4] Unlike Leibniz, Zadig's angel has power, in both practical and theoretical realms. He burns down the house of a particularly generous host and drowns the attractive youth who was a virtuous widow's only consolation. When Zadig protests in outrage, the angel reveals the truth behind appearances. An immense treasure lay buried under the house, which the owner could find only after his home was in ruins. Had the drowned boy lived, he would have murdered his aunt the next year, and Zadig himself in the following one. Zadig's virtues gave him privileged access to truths that are hidden from the rest of us. When angels descend to give explanations, you needn't your take sufficient reasons on faith. Zadig himself, moreover, is completely rewarded for his fortitude. Despite the tricks of rivals he is crowned king of Babylon, acclaimed as the bravest and wisest of its citizens, and given the hand of the beautiful and virtuous queen who loved him from a distance throughout the years.

Here *Zadig* may remind us of the epilogue to Job, an ending so crass that biblical scholars usually dismiss it as a late addition to satisfy the orthodox. As reward for his troubles, Job's possessions are restored with high interest: the Lord gives him 14,000 sheep to replace the original 7,000 burned up by lightning, 6,000 camels to make good on the 3,000 plundered by the Chaldeans. This can sound like Parisian satire, but *Zadig* itself is not. Voltaire is perfectly deadpan:

> The empire enjoyed peace, glory and abundance, it was the earth's finest century, it was governed by justice and love. Men blessed Zadig, and Zadig blessed heaven. (Voltaire 1, 172)

In 1747 the world seemed to be in order. To be sure, the ending of *Candide* is no less a fairy tale: all the battered characters reassembled from the ends of the earth to join forces in a garden. But if the ending of *Candide* served to mock aspirations of optimists like Leibniz and Rousseau, the ending of *Zadig* only confirmed them.

What happened between *Zadig* and *Candide*? The data are virtually identical, yet the reader is left with nearly opposite conclusions. The crimes and misfortunes explained and redeemed in the former tale are left hanging in the latter. If *Candide* contains a voice of wisdom, it's that of the Manichaean Martin who concludes that the world exists to drive us mad. The shift in Voltaire's views has been explained as a result of shifts in his personal affairs. Voltaire had achieved fortune and power, friendship and love. But in 1749, the remarkable woman with whom he had happily lived died giving birth to another man's child.

A few years later, his sojourn at the Prussian court in Potsdam ended in a violent quarrel with Frederick the Great. Pointing out such facts may be ad hominem, but Voltaire couldn't have minded. He would be the first to insist that immediate surroundings influence general worldviews.

> The pleasure of complaining and exaggerating is so great that at the slightest scratch you cry out that the world runs over with blood. Have you been deceived? Then all men are perjurers. A melancholy soul who has suffered some injustice sees the universe covered with the damned, as a young voluptuary, having supper with his lady after the opera, can't imagine that there are unfortunate men. (Voltaire 6, 381)

The claim that we map our moods onto the cosmos, and call them worldviews, is repeated in tales like "The World as It Is" and *Candide*.[5] But the change in Voltaire's views wasn't produced simply by a change in his fortunes. To begin with, things weren't all that bad. It was *after* Voltaire's poem on the Lisbon earthquake that Rousseau commented on the mismatch between the blessings that the world bestowed on Voltaire and Voltaire's gratitude toward the world. From Rousseau's perspective, Voltaire had every reason to sound like Pangloss.[6] And this wasn't simply envy, for Rousseau wasn't simply wrong. Voltaire had a remarkable capacity to repulse the arrows of outrageous fortune, recovering from bad luck almost as quickly as Candide recovered from the blows of the Bulgur regiment. In writing that episode, Voltaire was surely thinking of his own bad treatment at the hands of the Prussian soldier-king. But even after the forced flight from Sans Souci, and the death of his one true love, Voltaire wrote that his life was so happy he was almost ashamed.

Thus no ordinary autobiographical inferences can explain the shift in his views. And neither can any other simple view of the relations between experience and theory. If Voltaire was faithful to any tradition, it's the one that began with Bayle. Both hold that clear-eyed description of reality should precede any speculation about it. Candide's blind speculation showed that he never learned to think for himself. He sees the world through the lessons of Pangloss, whose fame as the world's greatest philosopher derived from being the tutor on call in a Westphalian castle. Candide gains a measure of wisdom when, guided by the skeptical Martin, he rejects speculation entirely in favor of hard and simple labor. And one claim of "The Lisbon Earthquake" is that cold observation—of mangled bodies and children's cries—is enough by itself to prove philosophy vain.

The reader might conclude that Voltaire got older and wiser, counted up the number of evils in the world, and grew correspondingly skeptical about making any sense of them. Such a conclusion suggests that the description of experience in later pieces like *Candide* or "The Lisbon Earthquake" will be harder, more brutal, than the description available earlier. Now *Candide*'s description of the Seven Years' War is a perfect echo of Bayle.

> Nothing could have been so fine, so brisk, so brilliant, so well-drilled as the two armies. The trumpets, the fifes, the oboes, the drums, and the cannon produced such a harmony as was never heard in hell. First the cannons battered down about six thousand men on each side; then volleys of musket fire removed from the best of worlds about nine or ten thousand rascals who were cluttering up its surface. . . . Finally, while the two kings in their respective camps celebrated the victory by having *Te Deums* sung, Candide undertook to do his reasoning of cause and effect elsewhere. (Voltaire 5, 20)

But *Candide*'s exaggerated scenes of horror are not very different from those Voltaire offered earlier. Zadig can "visualize men as they really are, insects devouring one another on a little atom of mud" (Voltaire 2, 129). And a tale written one year later, emphatically named "The World as It Is," describes a traveler entrusted with reporting the state of the world to an angel who must decide whether the world should be destroyed. The litany of war and blood and betrayal is much the same as that we encounter in later works. The denouement is laconic. The angel decides that if all is not good, it is at least passable. Destroying a city because of its sins makes no more sense than destroying an artwork because it is not exclusively composed of jewels and gold. If

Voltaire came to view matters differently, it's not for a difference in what he had *seen*.

Is the picture of experience available in these tales realistic? If *Candide* belongs to a genre, it seems to be satire. Realism, at least, looks inappropriate. The events of the tale, and the speed at which they follow one another, do more than merely defy probability. The rapid succession of apparent deaths and miraculous recoveries, unexpected revelations, fabulous wealth, unbearable torments, is all so impossible it doesn't even try to obtain the reader's confidence. We are left free to reflect on Voltaire's intentions in writing the piece, since we can't be meant to pay certain kinds of attention to the story itself. In street conversation, calling one description of the world more realistic than another is a covert way of declaring your allegiance to pessimism. The subtitle of *Candide* is *or, Optimism*. Voltaire made no commitments, juggling the triad optimism/pessimism/realism like so many balls in the air. The utter absurdity of the combinations of events that befall *Candide*'s characters is matched only by the utter veracity of the events themselves. The characters may be invented, but what they experience is not—down to the stories of the six deposed kings in Venice whose appearance is so funny that Candide himself thinks he is watching a masquerade. The book begins with the Seven Years' War, in which people really were butchered for no reason whatsoever. The Inquisition really did burn strangers in the name of God. European conquerors really did murder millions of native inhabitants in the search for gold. African slaves really were mutilated in the colonies of such enlightened countries as Holland, and progressive countries like England really executed their officers for failing to win crucial battles. Women really are raped as a matter of course in wartime. No less genuine are the minor examples of evil cataloged in *Candide*: an aristocracy so graceless and idiotic that it would rather murder and die than abandon its notions of privilege; the ordinary sorts of theft and betrayal that abound in the book; natural events like the earthquake at Lisbon, and especially the scene just before it, in which the tale's first genuinely good soul drowns in the storm survived by an unprincipled thug.

This is all just to say: *Candide* is short, compressed, and satirical, but it isn't for that reason *false*. As a description of reality, it's remarkably accurate. Any good European could have drawn up a similar list of atrocities by reading a newspaper. Voltaire refrained from creating the literary depth and texture that lead us to empathize with characters, or show indignation on their behalf, to create a report that is all the more chilling. He thereby anticipated modern media, providing a series of short takes on human misery across the globe. Like modern media reporting whatever crimes come their way, whatever their sources, Voltaire claimed to be impartial. Like modern media, he reveled in documenting the same crimes committed by rival princes and churches, civilized and savage peoples. Voltaire's age, like ours, was full of a sense of its universality: travel and commerce gave peoples unprecedented access to one another. The Enlightenment fed eagerly on accounts, both real and invented, of the mores of other continents. Was *Candide* a mockery of such accounts or simply a continuation of them? Either way, the lesson it draws seems clear. If there's common humanity to be found in diversity, it's one of common crime and misfortune.

So much for description. Indeed, Voltaire's description of reality in the earlier, more cheerful works is so similar to the description in the later and bleaker ones that it seems he took description to be relatively straightforward. At issue is what we make of it. Voltaire was aware that we incline to complain. A central claim of *Candide*, in fact, is that we all enjoy believing our own troubles are the worst. The old woman whose rough wisdom is for Cunegonde what Martin's tutorials are for Candide proposes this way of passing time during the voyage from the Old to the New World:

> Have some fun, get each passenger to tell you his story; and if there's not a single one who has not often cursed his life, who has not often said to himself that he was the unhappiest of men, you can throw me into the sea headfirst. (Voltaire 5, 41)

Cunegonde takes up the wager and persuades everyone on shipboard to tell his adventures. Afterward she agrees that the old woman was right. Such exercises in comparative suffering abound in the book.[7] Pangloss and Cunegonde's brother the Baron receive twenty lashes a day from a bullwhip for fighting over who suffered the greater injustice, and continue to do it nonetheless. Long before twentieth-century society began to regard victimization as a source of rights, Voltaire portrayed six deposed kings at a carnival, each vying for the honor of being more miserable than the rest. This scene marks how far humankind has come by the end of *Candide*. The problem of evil began with one single and majestic Job, in a text that never permits us to question the claim that he is the unhappiest of men. Were it not for Job's case, the world might be in order—or so it is implied. By mid–eighteenth century, misfortune was multiplied. Not even literal royalty gave one a claim to nobility, or majesty, or even solemnity. Lost glory only increased the wretchedness as well as the ridiculousness of one's plight.

It's an audacious reading, but I'm going to risk it: Voltaire was fighting his own tendency to be complacent. He knew, first, that he'd been blessed by fortune. He knew, second, that we all tend to complain. For Voltaire, this could sometimes be a virtue. The sharpest claim in the Lisbon poem is that our complaints stem from the nobler sorts of emotions that human beings can feel—not from vanity or pride. Pope, along with more traditional defenders of the cosmic order, had alleged the latter. He even called anyone who questioned that order "Vile worm!"—a particularly cruel epithet not merely in its immediate evaluation of humanity but in its implicit reminder of what will become of us all. Voltaire's subtitles are signposts; "The Lisbon Earthquake" is subtitled "An Inquiry into the Maxim, 'Whatever is, is right.'" In its preface Voltaire asserts his "love and admiration" for "the illustrious Pope," whom he earlier translated and tried to imitate. He says that he still agrees with him. So Voltaire writes that he

> acknowledges with all mankind that there is evil as well as good on the earth; he owns that no philosopher has ever been able to explain the nature of moral and physical evil. He asserts that Bayle, the greatest master of the art of reasoning that ever wrote, has only taught us to doubt, and that he combats himself; he owns that man's understanding is as weak as his life is miserable. (Voltaire 3, preface)

All this and more he shared with any reading of Pope. He thought that Pope failed not in understanding or observation but in compassion. It's generosity and sympathy, not arrogance or presumption, that lead us to cry out against natural evil. The doctrines of Leibniz and Pope merely add mockery to misery.

> If when Lisbon, Moquinxa, Tetuan and other cities were swal-lowed up with a great number of their inhabitants in the month of November, 1755, philosophers had cried out to the wretches who with difficulty escaped from the ruins 'all this is productive of general good; the heirs of those who have perished will in-crease their fortune; masons will earn money by rebuilding the houses, beasts will feed on the carcasses buried under the ruins; it is necessary effect of necessary causes; your particular misfor-tune is nothing, it contributes to universal good', *such a ha-rangue would have doubtless been cruel as the earthquake was fatal, and all that the author of the poem on the destruction of Lisbon has said amounts only to this.* (Ibid., my emphasis)

Those who point out the ways in which the world is not the best at least acknowledge the pain of others, even if they cannot alleviate it. To allege that they act from less savory motives is simply wrong.

Voltaire went still further. Not only did Pope's view fail to console us; it left us forlorn. If evil is necessary, we have all the more reason to despair. For this sort of optimism crushes hope for a better world.[8] The poem ended by calling hope our only happiness on earth. Voltaire left the object of such hope suitably ambiguous. Whether happiness depended on the hope of heaven, or the possibility of improvement in the world below, was not a matter he wished to address. As a com-mitted anti-Christian, he probably meant the latter, though he couldn't have put it in print.[9] But perhaps Voltaire too held the hope of another life to be all that keeps us from despairing in this one.

In sum: Voltaire's description of reality in *Candide* was congruent not just with that of Pope, and quite possibly that of Leibniz, but with his own works across time. They show little disagreement over the facts about the world, and even over the capacities of current theories to order them. What's at stake is not the truth or falsity of particular claims, or even the truth or falsity of one's most general theoretical commitments. At moments Voltaire seems to simply maintain that un-varnished experience is prior to any theories attempting to order it. But

Voltaire, like Pope, was not a metaphysician, so he can't quite be an empiricist either. Empiricism and rationalism are too crude and too general to delineate the positions available in the effort to decide the place of experience in our worldviews. The issue is not whether one looks at experience, but the distance from which one sees.

Francis Bacon claimed that scientific progress began when scientists began to look at experience. But modern historians of science point out that if you start from experience without theoretical presuppositions, you are more likely to discover Aristotle's mechanics than Galileo's.[10] Kant attributed the revolutions in modern science to Copernicus's courage to *contradict* the testimony of the senses (Kant 3, Bxxii). The ideology that encourages us to stop looking at old books and start looking at the world has long been under fire. But even when unobstructed perception of experience is the one thing that will help us, the question is one of focus. (Those who refused to look through Galileo's telescope weren't simply obtuse. Why should *that* perspective be privileged?) How close should one stand? Voltaire's critique of Pope was a nascent critique of the ideal of objectivity. Viewed from the heavens, Pope may well be right. Looked at from sufficient height and distance, our troubles may be small and compatible with a universe where everything is ordered for the best. But after quoting Pope's *Essay on Man*, Voltaire defends our right to another perspective.

> Don't you find great comfort in Lord Shaftesbury's remark that God isn't going to disturb his eternal laws for a miserable little animal like man? But you must grant this miserable little animal the right to exclaim humbly and to seek, as he exclaims, why these eternal laws are not made for the well-being of each individual. (Voltaire 6, 121–22)

We miserable little animals have the right to wonder about our misery. Voltaire didn't stop there: a God who fails to do so but simply watches it from a distance, like the majestic and disinterested God of Deism, is a God who should be faulted for His lack of humanity—in the absence of a better word.

Given how loathsome Voltaire was to Rousseau, in particular, it's odd to view him as a champion of kindness. But their one-sided exchange on the earthquake at Lisbon leaves no other choice. In his writing on Lisbon, Rousseau blamed the victims. In his writing on Lisbon, Voltaire heard them cry. When is lack of compassion a philosophical reproach? Voltaire's philosophical poem says little more to Pope, the master of philosophical poetry, than this: there are circumstances in which writing poetry can be barbarism.

One thread uniting all the writers discussed in this chapter is a sharp and brittle humor that formed a curious counterpart to their cheerless description of appearances. Perhaps they felt they could afford it, as the passionate seekers of order behind the appearances could not. Perhaps they simply needed it more. For all the glitter, and the cosmopolitan wit, Voltaire seemed to be torn. Part of him found the principle of sufficient reason to be entirely self-evident. He saw its traces within his own life, which at points along the way looked as multiply blessed as Zadig's. Along the way, to be sure. The belief that there's a reason for everything that happens can be variously parsed. For all that he played with it, Voltaire was no more careless in interpreting the principle of sufficient reason than Leibniz himself, and possibly less. Leibniz never gave a consistent reading of the claim he called his great principle. When he said that nothing ever happens without a reason, he left the reader bewildered, for he never adequately marked the distinction between final and efficient causes, and he may even have deliberately equivocated between them.[11] Voltaire was fascinated by improbable causal chains. He was clearly drawn to belief in destiny, half sister to Providence, and returned to address it throughout his work. The sequence of adventures that leads Candide into Cunegonde's arms after the disaster at Lisbon is the sort of thing that prevents readers from taking the story seriously. When it has a happy ending, it's less likely to be called literature than cartoon or farce. But recall Kant's discussion of lying to assassins. Just such improbabilities, when they go wrong, are what make something tragic. (Oedipus arriving at the crossroads a quarter of an hour later would have led to a simple epic. Juliet's waking a quarter of an hour earlier would have left her adventures a place in the annals of Harlequin romance.) Second: no matter what their outcome, improbable chains form the fabric of history. Voltaire's *Dictionary* devoted an entry to the subject. The king of Naples owed his crown, and possibly his existence, to a series of events that began with a petty quarrel between two ladies-in-waiting. After this example Voltaire concluded:

> Examine the situations of all the nations in the universe: they are thus founded on a sequence of facts which seem to have no connection and which are connected in everything. In this immense machine, all is wheels, pulleys, cords, springs. (Voltaire 6, 164)

Voltaire held these networks of chains to be no less at bottom of the natural order than of human history. All his work emphasized the sort of crazy contingency inhabiting the world which seems so utterly fortuitous that it surely cannot be.

Or can it? My suggestion that destiny is Providence's poor relation was deliberately evasive. Voltaire, in the end, was not. The clearest difference between the earlier and the later writings is Voltaire's later insistence on distinguishing between reasons and causes. Works like *Zadig* and the *Dictionary* see wisdom behind all those incredible chains of events. Works like "The Lisbon Earthquake" and *Candide* do not. Voltaire was still *tempted* to seek the hand of Providence behind all improbability. But he was merciless with his reader as with himself. *Candide*, in particular, builds up our expectations of finding meaning in history only to dash them. Again and again, it creates hopes for the discovery of Providence: the Grand Inquisitor who ordered the hanging of Pangloss is slain by Candide; the Dutch pirate who robs him is drowned with his treasures in a sea battle. But Voltaire raised hopes just to mock them, for innocents die just as easily, and plenty of evils go unpunished. There is no order to be found here at all. What's left of sufficient reason is the barest sort of efficient causality detailed at length when Pangloss explains the genealogy of his syphilis.

Pangloss's illness is a denial of Providence, not simply agnosticism about it. (Perhaps a vindictively Voltairean deity would say that the pompous doctor had it coming to him, but such a reading seems forced.) The syphilis example is no accident. Consider Voltaire's *Dictionary* entry "Love":

Most of the animals that copulate taste pleasure only through a single sense; and when that appetite is satisfied, all is extinguished. No animal, besides yourself, knows embraces; your whole body is susceptible; your lips especially enjoy a pleasure that nothing wearies, and this pleasure belongs to your species alone; finally, you can give yourself to love at all times while animals have only a definite period. If you reflect on these advantages, you will say, with the Earl of Rochester: "Love would make a nation of atheists worship the Divinity". (Voltaire 6, 74)

Voltaire went on to describe in detail the wonders of erotic love, and the advantages it gives us over other species. Love develops talents of body and mind from material provided by nature. The ways in which inclination and art combine to make erotic love the glory of human life should make us bow our heads in grateful awe. Until we consider: if animals never know the pleasures of love, they are equally unaware of its pains. Syphilis is the means through which "nature has poisoned the pleasures of love and the sources of life"—and thereby our efforts to find order in them.

If one could ever accuse nature of despising its work, thwarting its plan, acting against its design, it would be in this instance. Is this the best of all possible worlds? Very well! If Caesar, Antony, Octavius never had this disease, wasn't it possible to prevent Francis I from *dying* of it? No, people *say*, things were so ordained for the best: I want to believe it, but it is sad for those to whom Rabelais dedicated his book. (Voltaire 6, 75)

Here in prose is the movement *Candide* would provide in fable. Voltaire offered evidence for the argument from design to move his readers close to tears. Just when we're ready to sing those psalms that Kant thought would put King David to shame, Voltaire shuts our mouths. This is no attempt to make us look foolish. On the contrary: Voltaire would hardly pull this trick so often were he not struggling with himself. In the passage just quoted, he was explicit: *I want to believe it*. Here *it* refers to the whole complex of eighteenth-century optimism that looks at ordinary wonders, calls the order they reveal a miracle, and infers straight to the best explanation of an ordinary won-der-working God. Human hands and eyes served as standard Deist examples of things whose structure is so marvelous that they must have been planned. Voltaire adds the lips. What better proof of a Designer who'd arranged things for the advantage of His chosen species? But before you can linger on the ordinary wonder of a kiss, Voltaire re-minds you of its frequent outcome.

For the eighteenth century, belief in Providence was essential to any form of religion. In the *Dictionary* entry "Theism," Voltaire acknowl-edged that no difficulties in the notion of Providence will shake a the-ist's faith, for they will always remain difficulties, not disproofs.[12] With-out insight into the nature of a world to come—in this life or another—the idea of a just, rewarding God *cannot* be disproved. The core of this idea is needed for any religion to consider itself rational. In asserting a clear and certain link between moral and natural evils, the idea of Providence denies the notion of grace as well as that of atheism. Both grace and atheism leave the connection of virtue and happiness up to chance. Reason demands that the connection be systematic. Systematic connection between what you do and what befalls you is at least as important for Deism as for any form of Christianity. If the link between virtue and reward were accidental, the watch wouldn't work—to use another favorite Deist metaphor. What watchmaker would design a mechanism in which the wheels and cogs turned randomly one way, then sometimes another, without any warning whatsoever?

Both love and Lisbon belie the existence of Providence, for they belie a connection between natural and moral evil. Now Voltaire be-lieves that moral evils are by far the greater problem. On December 16, 1755, he wrote to a Protestant pastor:

> I pity the Portuguese, like you, but men do still more harm to each other on their little molehill than nature does to them. Our wars massacre more men than are swallowed up by earthquakes. If we had to fear only the Lisbon adventure in this world, we should still be tolerably well off. (Voltaire 7, vol. 4)

In *Candide* itself, the earthquake is less horrible than the subsequent auto-da-fé staged by the Inquisition to avert further disaster. And it's striking that the one Christian myth to which Voltaire wished to cling was the myth of the Fall. He held the notion of original sin to be a truer reflection of human experience than the optimistic doctrines of Pope or the Socinians.[13] It's a thought that Voltaire expressed in the earlier as well as the later work: what men do to each other is far worse than anything nature does to them. He did not need Rousseau to remind him that we'd have enough to do in eradicating those moral evils that are within our power to alter, without worrying about the natural evils that are not. Nor should we forget that, for all his irritating failures of tone, Voltaire spent an estimable amount of his time on the business of eradicating moral evils, in long and repeated campaigns against abuses of power that give him claim to be called the first modern politically engaged intellectual. Nevertheless. If the spread of moral evil is what most leads us to despair, the absence of any connection between moral evils and natural ones is what may drive us mad. What people can bear is finite. Even Job, whose patience became proverbial, curses his birth when disease strikes his body. When natural evils befall us, moral evils seem to multiply, and even the righteous among us may lose confidence about being able to struggle with them.

There's no doubt that the denial of systematic connections between moral and natural evils contains progressive elements. The syphilis example shows this especially well. For puritanical cultures in Voltaire's time as in ours, sexually transmitted diseases were indeed proof of Providence. Those who had sinned by sleeping with whoever was off-limits didn't have to wait until the next world to witness the reality of divine justice. Now in denying that syphilis has meaning, Voltaire denied that sex is a sin.

> This pestilence is not like so many other maladies that are the consequences of our excesses. It was not introduced into the world by debauchery; it was born in islands where men lived in innocence, and has spread from there throughout the old world. (Voltaire 6, 75)

But the lessons Voltaire drew show why Madame de Staël accused him of "diabolical gaiety." Suppose you applaud his refusal to connect moral and natural evils, for you share Voltaire's refusal to view fornication as an evil. Suppose you incline to share the view that it is, on the contrary, the sort of good that ought to turn us into theists. Is the world any brighter for consisting of simple causal chains that do not reward and punish, but blindly allow such good to be followed by such evil? (Voltaire doesn't even begin to meditate on the subject of broken hearts, perhaps because he held them to belong to the category of nonnatural evils that could, with some effort, be avoided.) At Candide's first reunion with Pangloss, he draws back from the pox-ridden pedant in terror. Having returned to his senses,

> he asked about the cause and effect, the sufficient reason which had reduced Pangloss to his present pitiful state.
> —Alas, said he, it was love; love, the consolation of the human race, the preservative of the universe, the soul of all sensitive beings, love, gentle love.
> —Unhappy man, said Candide, I too have had some experience of this love, the sovereign of hearts, the soul of our souls; and it never got me anything but a single kiss and twenty kicks in the rear. How could this lovely cause produce in you such a disgusting effect? Pangloss replied as follows.—My dear Candide! You knew Paquette, that pretty maidservant to our august Baroness. In her arms I tasted the delights of paradise, which directly caused these torments of hell, from which I am now suffering. (Voltaire 5, 23)

Pangloss traces the sources of his syphilis in a long genealogy of efficient causes that foils every effort to seek final ones. He is interrupted by Candide, who reasonably asks whether the devil is behind the whole thing. Pangloss thinks not. He is still undeterred from launching into another discourse explaining why syphilis is necessary in this best of all possible worlds, though it "strikes at and defeats the greatest end of nature itself." At the close of the chapter they set sail for Lisbon. Does the reader want more?

Candide is, among other things, a roman à clef, and there is no lack of speculation seeking keys. Martin the Manichaean must be based on Bayle, but some have argued about whether Leibniz or Pope should bear the burden of having modeled for Pangloss. Leibniz's defenders claimed that Voltaire could not have set his sights on the sophisticated system of the master but must have been attacking one of its simple-headed popularizers like Pope. Partisans of Pope, by contrast, were sure that Pangloss was expounding not the rich and ambiguous lessons of the *Essay on Man* but only the dry and dogmatic *Theodicy*. I suspect that Voltaire was out for both, and with them, the very possibility that words can help us with the problem of evil. Words of any kind.

Who else makes an appearance? The earnest young man without name or fortune who gives the tale its title might well be Rousseau. His travels, his worldview, and his infuriating naïveté all suggest it. Moreover, the virtues of Cunegonde are evident only to Candide. Unable to deserve his trust and incapable of writing a letter, she's a good sketch of how the *philosophes* regarded Rousseau's mistress Thérèse Levasseur. If Rousseau *was* the protagonist's model, the author is unexpectedly kind to him at the end, allowing him not only peace but a measure of wisdom. It takes time, but Candide is capable of learning.

Just what does he learn? After all Voltaire's didactic clarity when attacking his opponents, he left his own positive view quite a blur. Any reading of Voltaire's conclusion must include an answer to the question: How big is your garden? Initially we're inclined to view it as small. The injunction to cultivate our gardens thus seems part of a vision of life that is grim. Martin's conclusion—"Let us work without reasoning, it is the only way to make life endurable"—seems to be Voltaire's own. Life is a choice between "the convulsions of anxiety and the lethargy of boredom." Cultivating your garden is a way of averting three great evils—boredom, vice, and need—but it will not yield more positive fruit. The hopes for something better are the hopes of clumsy youth. Great love and passion become a dull and ugly marriage. The pursuit of understanding leads to the judgment that the world exists to drive us mad. The search for a new world reveals the vices of the old. Those enlightened nations for whose rights the French bourgeoisie yearned show no more humanity than those still under the burdens of absolutism. Wealth, and experience, and even high culture end in misery and boredom. What's left is the claim that a bit of human decency, and hard work to dull the painful memory of better hopes, are the best we can expect from the world. Most of us were raised to call this sort of vision mature.

So *Candide*, as stick-figure precursor of the bildungsroman, is read as a proof or a plea for such visions. If you do not begin with such a vision, however, you needn't read *Candide* as confirming it. It's possible to sketch a reading of the book that is well-nigh utopian. To see this we must focus on the question of description. The problem with optimism is not that it misdescribes experience. As we saw, the optimist's catalog of the furniture of the universe may be no different from anyone else's. For he claims not that this world is so much to write home about, but that any other world would be worse. He thus denies both the necessity and the possibility of making any improvements on experience. Leibniz made this point most clearly, telling us that if we understood how God made the world, we could not even wish that anything in it were different. As Voltaire emphasized, calling such a doctrine optimistic is highly misleading; it seems, rather, to destroy every chance for hope.

Candide, by contrast, contains scathing critiques of the church, the aristocracy, imperialism, and war. These were all objects of Voltaire's attacks in other parts of his work, where he sought to make real changes in the lives of real human beings. Thus the work can be read as radical demand that we stop viewing the present state of reality as determined by Providence; that we stop describing it as the best world in the service of making it a better one. For we saw that Voltaire held moral evils to be more numerous, more important, and more tractable than natural ones. *Candide*'s irony is at least as much directed against established political institutions as against established metaphysics. And Candide's education is designed to make him something close to the critical, self-made bourgeois liberal who is the Enlightenment's ideal hero. His childhood in the castle trained him to never think for himself—thus representing the self-incurred immaturity that Kant thought Enlightenment's antithesis (Voltaire 5, 61). At its beginning, the hero has no doubt about the sources of authority. In the all-encompassing anthill of a Westphalian barony, aristocratic birth and the philosophical system of Pangloss give meaning and order to life as a whole. The book takes aim at everything that combined to make such authority function, climaxing with the six kings whose only claim to attention is the assertion of their powerlessness. By the close of the book, authority comes from human hands; labor is the only real basis of order or respect. The book shifts from examining the sources of human happiness to creating them. Voltaire seized the moment when the human stopped being spectator of a vast, all-encompassing universe and began to be producer of the world. So *Candide* can be viewed as description of the path from feudal to modern order.

To expand such a view, one would need to decide that the garden we are meant to tend is quite extensive. Peter Gay believes that Voltaire's garden was all of Europe. One reason to agree with him is the presence of classical Enlightenment virtues in the group that forms *Candide*'s last tableau. Far from being traditional heroes, the members of this garden society are emphatically imperfect: a bastard, a whore, a renegade priest, a half-breed servant, a professor with the pox. It's the unsung and outcast who will take up their own destiny, constructing new social order with their hands. Their garden is unguarded. It could be sacked or ruined like so many others. Voltaire's message thus cannot be a call to retreat behind smaller borders, to lead your life without regard for the wider world, trading space for peace and certainty. Since the very same group tried to do just that in their Westphalian beginnings, they cannot be meant to embrace provincial isolation in the end. *Candide* is a meditation on the futility of guarantees. After reading it, we should be aware of the fragility of anything that looks stable.

Candide as realistically utopian? It's a possible reading, but its author leaves us wondering. For his utopianism, if it is such, is less realistic than dry. When can irony support hope, and when does it undermine it? Voltaire's rhetoric is antiheroic, again and again. Even worse, he left us this comment on the chances for radical change:

> If you could unsettle the destiny of one fly, there would be no reason on earth why you couldn't fashion the fate of all other flies, all the animals, mankind, and nature; finally you would find yourself more powerful than God. (Voltaire 6, 235)

It's a thought left to underline the suggestions that concluded the previous chapter. Today Alfonso will strike us as respectful, even modest. But any wish to improve Creation may overstep our bounds. The fact that this didn't stop Voltaire from trying made his life the more admirable. It may have left him without anything to stand on.

Reason, in particular, seems to be in shreds. Over and over, Voltaire underlined two claims. As an instrument of truth, reason leads us astray, for it is inattentive to the claims of the world. As an instrument of action, reason leads us nowhere at all, for it's too weak to move anyone to anything. Reason, in short, is both false and feeble. What human beings need, and use, is something else. In a splendid commentary on natural law Candide tries to save himself from cannibals by appealing to universal principles of humanity. His guide Cacambo knows better and rescues them by appealing both to pragmatism and to thirst for the right sort of blood. The cannibals are directed to go out and eat a *real* Jesuit. They "found this discourse perfectly reasonable," and Voltaire's readers are left to wonder. Whence his reputation as paradigmatic Enlightenment thinker? For his aim at the most central of Enlightenment beliefs was as straight as it's clear: reason can't explain the world, and reason can't help us to navigate it.

At the same time he blocked the most immediate avenue of escape, that which was historically taken in response to perceived Enlightenment weaknesses. If reason is too weak to help us, perhaps sentiment or passion is not? Now Voltaire thought that we are moved by passions, and some of them are even good ones. It's not the search for truth or wisdom but the search for Cunegonde that literally and figuratively keeps Candide going. But passions are more often base than benign, and even benign passions bring little but disappointment in their train. Candide's desire can never reach its object. He is doomed to disaffection, from the first kick that follows the kiss behind the screen to the deeper pain of realization when he finally finds her. She is desirable because she is absent and so long as she's absent. When regained, Cunegonde is an ugly shrew whom Candide no longer desires. Her former charms are replaced by the most pedestrian form of seduction: she's become an excellent pastry cook. Candide's decision to marry her anyway is motivated not by love, and barely by obligation. He's moved, rather, by his own injured pride on learning that her brother still finds the marriage beneath their rank. Candide's search for Cunegonde might easily have ended in the sort of tragedy that leaves hopes for passion itself intact. That, at least, is the promise of romanticism. Instead, it fizzles out in the despair of the everyday which corrodes even that.

Voltaire's attack on hopes for any sort of wholeness was positively savage. His characters' very bodies belie order and harmony. Pangloss loses "merely" an eye and an ear; the old woman loses a buttock. Imperfection and irregularity are part of the universe. Nothing matches the harmonious pattern that poets and metaphysicians wish to impose. Voltaire underlined this with mismatches awash with cosmic excess. The Grand Inquisitor sends those who don't like bacon to the flames as suspected Marranos, but shares his mistress with a Jew. Priests who hand out the harshest of punishments for dissipation debauch themselves regularly with boys and with girls. Willingly or not, every woman is a prostitute. The caricatures are not arbitrary. By the time we have run through them, we incline to abandon every search for ideals—be they persons or more abstract sorts of object—along with every search for sense and system.

THE IMPOTENCE OF REASON: DAVID HUME

Kant's insights into the history of philosophy were as deep as his insights into philosophy itself. Some of his remarks about what's at stake in his predecessors' work are so deep and so sharp that they obviate libraries full of later commentary. His comments about Rousseau and Newton were brief and illuminating. Here is what the *Critique of Practical Reason* says about Hume:

> [H]e desired, as is well known, nothing more than that a merely subjectively necessary concept of cause, i.e. habit, be assumed in place of all objective meaning of necessity in the causal concept; he did this in order to deny to reason any judgement concerning God, freedom, and immortality; and he knew very well how to

draw conclusions with complete cogency when once the principles were conceded. (Kant 6, A13)

The remark has received little attention, and is likely to be puzzling.
Hume's attack on the notion of cause is the heart of his work, but the
causal relation usually mentioned is that which takes place between
billiard balls. What did Kant think it had to do with God?

Though there is evidence enough in earlier works like the *Enquiry*
and the *Natural History of Religion*, it is Hume's *Dialogues Concerning
Natural Religion* that shows how these questions connect.[14] Hume's
friends judged the *Dialogues* to be the best thing he ever wrote, and
it's easy to agree. The *Dialogues* are one of the more precise and devastating examples of human reasoning in modern thought. Hume went
to great lengths to ensure that it would be published posthumously,
and his last extant letter, written to Adam Smith two days before his
death, was full of concern for it. Hume overestimated neither the value
of the *Dialogues* nor their potential for wreaking havoc. To begin to
grasp the latter, consider this letter from Smith:

> A single, and as I thought, a very harmless Sheet of paper which
> I happened to write concerning the death of our late friend, Mr.
> Hume, brought upon me ten times more abuse than the very vio-
> lent attack I had made upon the whole commercial system of
> Great Britain. (Quoted in Mossner, 605)

Smith's letter describing Hume's pagan cheerfulness in the face of his
approaching death was indeed harmless next to the work whose publication was his friend's last wish.

The *Dialogues* take aim at the natural religion that was the Enlightenment's best hope. The previous century had suffered one war of
religion after another. Slaughtering your neighbor to save his eternal
soul, or any rate your own, had been the order of business from the
farthest corner of Prussia to Europe's southern coasts. It was held in
check by sullen and tenuous agreements. Natural religion was meant
to do away with the misery caused by revealed religion, serving as a
force for unity instead of division. It would contain just those truths
that could be grounded by naked reason unaided by revelation. Hence

it could be shared universally, independent of accidents of birth. Natural religion comes as naturally to the common man as it does to the scholar, and is as evident in Paris as in Constantinople.

Natural religion offered hope not merely as an object that all could agree on, but as an ideology that sprang from the best in us. Traditional religion, it was claimed, led to fear and hatred because it stemmed from fear and hatred. Primitive man was fixed in terror before the forces of nature and needed to be controlled by terror in turn. With a new age dawning, brighter forces were assembled. Natural religion could lead to better outcomes, for it grew from better soil. Awe and gratitude at the wonders of Creation were the motives for worshiping the Deist God. And as anyone could be led to such gratitude by the clear light of reason, so anyone could, with some training, be governed by it.

Natural religion was no tepid, instrumental compromise but a breath of air and promise. All the grim apparatus of the northern Calvinism on which Hume was raised was to be dismantled by conviction in the fit between human and divine justice. All the wild articles of faith, from Real Presence to reliquaries, with which southern Catholicism had overwhelmed reason, were to be replaced by those truths any baby could see. The impulse to natural religion was more reverent than pragmatic, a far cry from the attitude that Diderot described as the English tendency to believe in God *un peu*. Real worship and wonder, as distinct from superstition, were not opposed to reason but derived from it. Rousseau's classic defense of natural religion, the "Creed of the Savoyard Vicar," argued this clearly, but it was even better displayed by Voltaire.

The one safe haven in Candide's travels is the kingdom of Eldorado, a good place to view Enlightenment daydreams about the shape of the state of nature. Travelers are welcomed with the twelve-course meals a Parisian chef would make in South America, children play with precious stones as if they were marbles, palaces of scientific learning exist in place of courts, and the king's remarks all sound witty—even in translation. Candide and his guide marvel over all the evils that are absent in Eldorado.

What is this country then, they said one to another, unknown to the rest of the world, and where nature itself is so different from our own? This probably is the country where everything is for the best. (Voltaire 5, 54)

But one thing remains unchanged even in Eldorado, as Candide and Cacambo learn when they meet the kingdom's wisest man.

> The conversation was a long one; it turned on the form of the government, the national customs, on women, public shows, the arts. At last Candide, whose taste always ran to metaphysics, told Cacambo to ask if the country had any religion.
>
> The old man grew a bit red.—How's that? He said. Can you have any doubt of it? Do you suppose we are altogether thankless scoundrels?
>
> Cacambo asked meekly what was the religion of Eldorado. The old man flushed again.
>
> —Can there be two religions? He asked. I suppose our religion is the same as everyone's, we worship God from morning to evening.
>
> —Then you worship a single deity? Said Cacambo, who acted throughout as interpreter of the questions of Candide.
>
> —It's obvious, said the old man, that there aren't two or three or four of them. I must say the people of your world ask very remarkable questions.
>
> Candide could not weary of putting questions to this good old man; he wanted to know how the people of Eldorado prayed to God.
>
> —We don't pray to him at all, said the good and respectable sage; we have nothing to ask Him for, since everything we need has already been granted; we thank God continually. (Voltaire 5, 56)

Voltaire's stance of choice is ceaseless irreverence. If *he* holds this much natural religion to be self-evident for anyone who isn't a "thankless scoundrel," its sources must run very deep.

It would be misleading to call the argument from design the foundation of natural religion, for this suggests that the argument could, in principle, be detached from it. Rather, the argument from design is so nearly the heart of natural religion that it is hard to imagine the one without the other. Nor did the eighteenth century experience the argument as *argument*. Until Hume, it seemed a self-evident statement of fact. It's a statement so common as to be almost vulgar, as Hume implied when letting Demea, spokesman for the orthodox, demand a priori proofs of God's existence. Should we leave such a crucial matter to the vagaries of mere experience? Hume offered the orthodox a critique of their favorite proofs of God, but he didn't really care about them. A priori proofs are not only easy to demolish; they never moved anyone but metaphysicians anyway. The interesting target is the claim that experience itself presents so many proofs of God's presence and goodness that we need no complex reasoning to establish them. For, says Philo, Hume's spokesman in the *Dialogues*, the problem is not that the argument from design is an inferior sort of argument, since it's based not on reason but on vulgar experience. It's not even a good argument from experience—as only a great empiricist could show.

The argument from design requires one quick inference. It's based on the testimony of what we seem to plainly see: a natural order of such fineness and complexity that it cannot have developed by accident. We needn't look to the heavens to find instances of such order. The parts of our own bodies will do just as well. Nor need we understand much natural law to admire the workmanship with which the universe was constructed. Kant's best example was the preservation of life through the changing of the seasons.

> No one can have such a good conceit of his insight as to wish to assert definitely that, for example, the most admirable conservation of the species in the plant and animal kingdoms, whereby each new generation re-presents, every spring, its original, anew and undiminished, with all the inner perfection of mechanism and (as in the plant kingdom) even with their delicate beauty of color, without the forces of inorganic nature, otherwise so destructive, in the bad weather of autumn and winter being able to harm their seed at all in this respect—no one, I say, will assert that this is a mere result of natural laws; no one, indeed, can claim to *comprehend* whether or not the direct influence of the Creator is required on each occasion. (Kant 9, A116)

Kant's theoretical insight that the argument from design depends on a brief, fallacious inference did not change his sight. When he looked at a flower blooming after a long Prussian winter, what he saw was a miracle. If all the complexity of his speculative reservations cannot prevent Kant from seeing something so simple, and simply self-evident, how much more convincing it must have appeared to those untouched by speculation. Once more, design served to unite people regardless of fortune or estate. Scholar and simpleton, Catholic and Protestant could all be moved to common devotion by the common sense of wonder at common experience.

Hume began by denying all that.

> Even in this day, and in Europe, ask any of the vulgar, why he believes in an omnipotent Creator of the world; he will never mention the beauty of final causes, of which he is wholly ignorant; He will not hold out his hand, and bid you contemplate the suppleness and variety of joints in his fingers, their bending all one way, the counterpoise which they receive from the thumb, the softness and fleshy parts of the inside of his hand, with all the other circumstances, which render that member fit for the use, to which it was destined. To these he has long been accustomed; and he beholds them with listlessness and unconcern. He will tell you of the sudden and unexpected death of such a one; the fall and bruise of such another; the excessive drought of this season; the cold and rains of another. These he ascribes to the immediate operation of providence. And such events, as, with good reasoners, are the chief difficulties in admitting a supreme intelligence, are with him the sole arguments—for it. (Hume 3, 153)

Common wonders are too common to cause reverence. It is melancholy, not the brighter emotions, that throws us on our knees (ibid., 143). Natural religion was meant to be religion stripped of superstition; Hume says it is moved by the same sorts of fear and trembling that lead to darker varieties of worship. Fear that the argument from design might be false is more likely to make us pray than conviction that it's true. We are frightened by mischance and accident, examples of disorder, and rush to ward off their blows. This movement is as natural, superstitious, and vulgar as the movements of any old-fashioned ido-lator. Or as Kant put it: we praise the order of the universe in the hope that God is listening and will reward us by making it run the way we want.

These sorts of claims concern psychology. Deep psychology, insofar as they're true, but psychology nonetheless. For most philosophers, psychological insights are ways of weakening one's prey rather than dispatching it. Hume's real arguments are elsewhere. Like the very careful, methodical, and solid builder he held the universe to be lacking, Hume deconstructed every brick and every beam with which the argument from design is composed.

The argument rests on an inference from effect to cause. Such an effect (an ordered universe) must have an appropriate cause (an ordering First Cause). If you want to block that inference, one place to begin would be the mysteries in the notion of causation. What does causation come to? We think we have a clear idea of one thing's really causing another. Once we start to ponder, all clarity evaporates. No ordinary rules of logic tell us that events need causes. Why ever not suppose that something came from nothing? The claim that every event must have a cause—one way of reading the principle of sufficient reason—is not itself a claim of reason. Nor does experience give us grounds for it. For where does experience present us with causes? When one billiard ball hits another, we see two round objects, but nothing between them that counts as a relation. If they hit often enough, with similar results, we see constant conjunction, but this is not the relation we sought.

Kant said that Hume's notion of causality lacks a notion of dignity. Today we would call it deflated. If causality is no more than constant conjunction, the very aura surrounding all ideas of First Cause will start to fade. But Hume had no need to rely on aura and rhetoric. If there is, in the end, nothing more to the concept of cause than constant conjunction, there must *at least* be constant conjunction. Otherwise causality evaporates entirely. The conjunction had better be constant, for otherwise there's no testimony to the presence of causes at all.

Here Hume's conclusions almost draw themselves. When the event under discussion is sui generis—say, the Creation of the universe—

there is no basis whatsoever for attributing causes. Our conviction that it has one should dissolve, for what can be said about causes of events that only happened once? When the *meaning* of cause has been shown to be constant conjunction, we do not, in such a case, entirely know what we're talking about. Note that this argument is different from Hume's argument on induction. The latter undermines our certainty that *like causes have like effects*. The former seeks to undermine belief that *every event has some cause or another*. Hume undermined the foundations of both these claims to make his point. Bent on demolition of the entire structure of natural religion, he took any tool at hand. However impressive the argument based on the problems with induction may be, it is less devastating than that based on the unclarity in the notion of causality itself. Inductive evidence is always problematic, and nothing here would be good inductive evidence anyway. This is bad but not decisive. For defenders of the faith might return from such arguments armed with a notion of cause they claimed was deeper or more intrinsic than that presented in mere empirical sequences. Hume's prior argument against every other notion of causality left tradition no place to retreat. All he allowed was the observation of humdrum recurring constant conjunctions. Cause *without* constant conjunction is a name without sense.

Hume sought to show that, in this instance, only unthinking anthropomorphism makes us think it has some sense. The natural religion that tried to undo magic thinking turns out to be as rife with it as any other. When we make the argument from design, we put ourselves in God's shoes. If we were making an object, especially a very large one, we'd require intention and foresight. And once we were finished, we'd like to be praised for our judgment and skill. But

> [w]isdom, thought, design, knowledge—these we justly ascribe to him—because these words are honorable among men, and we have no other language or other conceptions by which we can express our adoration of him. (Hume 3, 44)

There we are, wildly, projecting. We have no evidence whatsoever that God is like us at all.

The reminder that we do not know God's nature would be neither new nor impressive. The *Dialogues* make us experience our lack of knowledge by suggesting other options. Our belief in the austere benign wisdom of the Lord of natural religion is based on anthropomorphic wishful thinking. We imagine a Creator as we'd like to imagine ourselves, or at least our fathers or sovereigns. Once we stop viewing such a hypothesis as a self-evident product of reason, what other alternatives arise? The *Natural History* shocked readers by depicting Christianity as merely one religious alternative among others. Hume had compared the moral effects of monotheism and polytheism and concluded that the latter was healthier. It promoted tolerance rather than fanaticism, gallant virtues like courage and activity rather than monkish virtues like humility and passivity. Hume argued that the very similarity of pagan gods to humans is itself an advantage. Where the gods are viewed as only somewhat superior to frail mortals, they can function as role models. *Imitatio Dei* is easier when the object is closer to hand. Even the sins ascribed to pagan gods are worthier of imitation than those with which monotheism must cope. What are lust and adultery next to the cruelty and vengeance ascribed to the Christian god of love?

Polytheism, therefore, is more compatible with the demands of practical reason. The *Natural Religion* suggested that it also makes more theoretical sense. There, however, Hume relied on the absurder articles of faith required, in particular, by Catholicism. He described the innocent heathen's view of the doctrine of the Real Presence to suggest that mythological religions do less violence to intellect. Later he attacked most any form of conventional worship by suggesting that all ascribe to God "the lowest of human passions, a restless appetite for applause" (Hume 3, 128). But traditional dogma was an easy target in England. The *Dialogues* were bolder. They proceeded to show that the natural religion allegedly founded on common sense is in fact less reasonable than other hypotheses. As myths go, monotheism is not only less salutary but less scientific than alternatives. Natural inductive procedures will lead us to polytheism.

Suppose we accept the claim Hume called the experimental principle: like effects prove like causes. That principle is generally problematic, but in this case it's no use at all. For the effect to be explained has no class for comparison. We compare the Creation of the world to our own creation of artifacts as a result of that relentless anthropomorphism which leads us to see faces in the moon. The argument from design has no more force than that. Suppose we also grant the premise that it takes to be a matter of observation: the natural world presents evidence of order. Without a series of worlds and their causes to compare and draw conclusions from, we must rely on speculation. Which hypotheses make most sense?

> If we survey a ship, what an exalted idea must we form of the ingenuity of the carpenter, who framed so complicated, useful, and beautiful a machine? And what surprise must we entertain, when we find him a stupid mechanic, who imitated others, and copied an art, which, through a long succession of ages, after multiplied trials, mistakes, corrections, deliberations, and controversies, had been gradually improving? Many worlds might have been botched and bungled, throughout an eternity, ere this system was struck out: Much labor lost: Many fruitless trials made; And a slow, but continued improvement carried on during infinite ages in the art of world-making. (Hume 3, 69)

In fact, Hume concluded, the ship analogy leads straight to polytheism. If something as fine as a schooner cannot be produced by one man alone but requires a whole crew of them, why not suppose that several deities assembled to fabricate the world? If we're being anthropomorphic, why not do it right?

And while we're considering similarities of cause, Hume suggests we consider similarities of effect and reevaluate the suggestion that the universe resembles an artifact to begin with. Deists compared the world to a watch or a ship, but isn't it more like a vegetable? When we look at the world as a whole, it seems more organic than mechanical. Mightn't it have been generated organically? Suppose a comet were the seed of a world. After it has been fully ripened by passing from star to star, it is finally tossed into the unformed elements and sprouts into a new system. And if the world is organic, why shouldn't it be an animal? If it were, we might suppose that

a comet is the egg of this animal; and in like manner as an ostrich
lays its egg in the sand, which, without any farther care, hatches
the egg, and produces a new animal; so . . . (Hume 3, 79)

Here Demea interrupts Philo's speculations in vexation. The implicit
comparison of the Lord of Creation to an ostrich is too much to bear.
What *data*, he asks, does anyone have for such wild and arbitrary conclusions? None whatsoever, replies Philo cheerfully; that's just the
point. Data are what you have when you have scientific procedures
based on causal analyses and inductive evidence. None of this is present for events that happen only once. There everything rests on speculation. And if we're going to be speculative, no hypothesis is wilder
than another. A planet inhabited entirely by spiders (and why shouldn't
there be one?) will conclude that the universe is spun like a web from
the bowels of an infinite spider.

Why an orderly system may not be spun from the belly as well
as from the brain, it will be difficult to give a satisfactory reason.
(Hume 3, 83)

Even before reaching his discussion of human affairs, Hume hinted
that he had yet better cards in his hand. If his discussion showed that
even the appearances of order in the world permit no inferences about
its cause, it is harmless compared to his discussion of the appearances
of disorder. If we're considering the world as organic phenomenon,
doesn't it resemble a feeble embryo, or a rotten carcass, as much as
anything whole? If we view it as artifact, does it look like the work of
a master? Couldn't it, rather, be the production of a doddering old deity,
who should have retired before leaving such embarrassing last work?
Or the first attempt of some infant deity, who afterward abandoned it,
ashamed of his lame performance? As soon as we admit that God is
finite, such hypotheses are allowable. And if we call Him infinite, we'd
do better to say nothing at all. Through most of the *Dialogues* these
remain dark hints. Hume himself was tempted by a notion of the order
and beauty in the natural world. The *Dialogues* did little to question
it, though they provide convincing epistemological strictures on what
we're permitted to conclude from it. To be sure, Hume diverged from

the common view that Newton and others provided new evidence for the argument from design. The new astronomical discoveries prove the immense grandeur of the world, but Hume could use this for his own fire as well. For the larger and grander the universe appears, the less it resembles a human artifact. And it was on such resemblance that the argument from design hung.

More exactly, it hung on the claim that the universe is a good artifact. It needn't be the best one; Hume left it to his continental colleagues to knock down straw men. Cleanthes, the attractive thinker who's given the task of defending natural religion, is always quite sensible. He admits that the world isn't perfect; he simply points out that it's good, in a way that can hardly be accident. The universe, he allows, isn't *exactly* like a house.

> But is the whole adjustment of means to ends in a house and the universe so slight a resemblance? The economy of final causes? The order, proportion, and arrangement of every part? Steps of a stair are plainly contrived that human legs may use them in mounting; and this inference is certain and infallible. (Hume 3, 47)

The simile was introduced in discussion of the original inference: is there enough evidence to conclude from effect to its cause? But there Hume reserved his description of the effect. Once he began to challenge the Deist description, he was almost invincible. Description of the natural world made the argument from design a reasonable inference, if inference were possible. Even Philo is drawn to it, and says he requires all his metaphysical subtlety to elude it. But once we begin to describe the human world, we're at a loss to explain how the argument ever found a hearing. For here, says Philo, I triumph.

> Did I show you a house or palace, where there was not one apartment convenient or agreeable; where the windows, doors, fires, passages, stairs, and the whole economy of the building were the source of noise, confusion, fatigue, darkness, and the extremes of heat and cold; you would certainly blame the contrivance, without any further examination. The architect would in vain dis-

play his subtilty, and prove to you, that if this door or that window were altered, greater ills would ensue. What he says may be strictly true: The alteration of one particular, while the other parts of the building remain, may only augment the inconveniences. But still you would assert in general, that, if the architect had had skill and good intentions, he might have formed such a plan of the whole, and might have adjusted the parts in such a manner, as would have remedied all or most of these inconveniences. His ignorance, or even your own ignorance of such a plan, will never convince you of the impossibility of it. If you find many inconveniences and deformities in the building, you will always, without entering into any detail, condemn the architect. (Hume 3, 106)

We've entered the modern world. For all Bayle's obscenity, or Voltaire's patent rage, a touch of awe endured. God remained a sovereign against whom one might with reason rebel. He had not yet become a contractor whom one might decide to fire. Apart from infrequent exceptions like the Lisbon earthquake, the eighteenth century extolled His workmanship as a matter of course, convinced that all its qualities were evident on its face. Hume suggested that we look more closely. The roof leaks. The stairs slope. The windows jam. Make your own inventory.

Hume's use of the dialogue allowed him some distance, and he used it to greatest advantage. The placid rhetoric that can be annoying elsewhere is here entirely convincing. The bourgeois everydayness of his metaphor and the calm of his description leave behind a persuasive chill. For Hume himself never ranted about the miseries of life nor inveighed against atrocities. He was, notoriously, cheerful. Hume's description of the quality of the world to be judged thus functions as report. He simply recorded the general view. It's no accident that the section devoted to proving the universality of human misery begins with the testimony of the orthodox.

Were a stranger to drop, on a sudden, into this world, I would show him, as a specimen of ills, an hospital full of diseases, a prison crowded with malfactors and debtors, a field of battle strewn with carcasses, a fleet floundering in the ocean, a nation languishing under tyranny, famine, or pestilence. To turn the gay side of life to him, and give him a notion of its pleasures—whither should I conduct him? To a ball, to an opera, to court? He might justly think I was only showing him a diversity of distress and sorrow. (Hume 3, 98)

We have heard this before, in more or less elegant terms. That is Hume's point. Here he put it in the mouth of the dour Demea, while Philo need play but a supporting role. As Demea intones the "great and melancholy truth" of the misery of life, Philo adds that it's universal, and hardly confined to the orthodox. Pagans asserted it no less often than Christians; on no point was there ever more agreement between the learned and the vulgar. As Demea recites the standard catalog of woes, Philo adds new ones. When Demea describes the terror with which the strong prey on the weak in every corner of the planet, Philo reminds us that the weak torment the strong. What about mosquitoes? The great chain of being is composed of infinite gradations of enemies, each seeking the others' destruction from above and below. When Demea recalls peculiarly human capacities to overcome natural enemies, Philo recalls the peculiarly human capacities for self-made suffering. Only the human adds to his real enemies the pain of imaginary ones who blast his life with superstitious terrors. Only the human invents guilt, by inventing demons who turn his own pleasures into crimes. Only the human has nightmares.—At Philo's prodding, Demea lets loose. It's a perfect duet. Think of war and oppression. Think of sickness and death. And speaking of sickness: is the body more dismal than the soul? Count up human emotions. Think of shame, rage, despair. Does joy last as long? Take such pitch? Seize our memory?

Apart from the reminder of mosquitoes, and just possibly of guilt, Hume's litany is standard fare. He even thinks that the modern age has become *less* melancholy. This makes it all the harder to answer. If this judgment of human life is so widely accepted, whence the wide acceptance of the argument from design? The argument depends on the view of Creation as gift. Such a wonderful artifact testifies to a wonderful benefactor, whom none but thankless scoundrels would scruple to praise. Hume places this assumption next to all the timeworn portraits of the gift itself. In what respect—he concluded ever so elegantly—do the benevolence and mercy of this donor resemble benevolence and mercy of men?

After using the assumptions of traditional religion to undermine itself, Hume turned to the natural. Orthodoxy avowed that contemplation of sin and suffering must lead us to faith. Hume asked us to contemplate them a little longer, and consider whether worship is the proper response. Natural religion bid us observe the machinery of the universe and consider whether it could have arisen without intention. Hume asked us to state what, exactly, the purpose of this strange machinery might be. If it points to intention, it points at most to several: how else could storms ruin those harvests the sun nourished, or the sun destroy that growth so gently fostered by the rains? Here the reasonable inference runs straight to polytheism, a plurality of gods whose purposes are cross-purposes. Each has his own province, and none is entirely reliable. "Today he protects, tomorrow he abandons us" (Hume 3, 139). Wouldn't such a system more nearly fit that experience and reason which natural religion invokes? The sensible rationalist can argue that appearances are mixed; the world presents neither simply pleasure nor pain. Very well, then, a mixed group of deities is the best explanation of their causes. For what experience gives us is just enough to save conviction that there is *some* benevolence and wisdom in the forces of nature, if we are convinced of it already. But could experience—as we all observe it—lead to such a conviction alone?

Hume's prose exudes a ghostly sort of calm that conceals the ferocity of his attack. By taking on the attributes of reasonableness, he undermines all the interests of reason. Both traditional and natural religion relied on an implicit challenge: if you don't like this world, could you design a better one? Not a fairy tale, a *world*. A thing with constraints. Where different parts must fit together, different claims must be adjudicated, different interests reconciled. Pushed to the limit, defenders of faith argued that God too has His. Within the limits of reason, could you make a better plan?

Hume might choose to reject the question as outside his field of competence. You needn't study engineering to see that a building is a disaster, nor know how to fix it in order to condemn the one who constructed it. He was hired, after all, to bring you peace of mind. But Hume took the challenge. Perhaps he was Alfonso's heir. Hundreds of years later, he was prepared for the consequences. A better design? Nothing's simpler. It won't yield a palace, still less a castle in the air, just an ordinary dwelling-house built with goodwill and foresight. In the earlier *Dialogues* Hume gave imagination free play, inventing one cosmological fantasy after the next. In the last sections he sought the mediocrity of instrumental rationality, commonsense homespun planning. What factors do good designers need to take into account? With magisterial equanimity Hume claimed that all evils of the world depend on four circumstances. All appear to human reason to be, with good planning, entirely avoidable. A good designer would contrive better means to his ends.

The first circumstance that introduces evil is the mechanism that uses pain as a spur to action, and indeed to preservation itself. All theodicies remind us of the economy of pain. But why not design a universe in which we felt nothing but degrees of pleasure? If you were hungry, the mechanisms that drive you to nourish yourself could lead the intensity of your happiness to decrease. This would lead you toward that food which, once ingested, would send you back to ecstasy. If we can be free of pain for an hour, why not for a lifetime? Does reason require that motivation be unpleasant? Couldn't a finer mechanism be devised?

Defenders of order like Leibniz and Pope urged the necessity of general law, which Hume named as the second cause of evil. As things now stand, demands for improvement might demand breaks in natural law. Here Leibniz had been particularly indignant. Should God suspend the law of gravity to spare annoyance to the owner of a costly vase? His theoretical qualms about natural law notwithstanding, Hume knew that a predictable world has obvious advantages. A really perfect builder might, to be sure, have designed general laws that always worked to everyone's advantage. But perhaps a world in which gravity both worked to keep us from flying off into space and was suspended to protect our artworks would be a fable, not a world. Hume therefore didn't propose it but reminded us of our own. His examples are far more trenchant than those of Leibniz. Perhaps exquisitely regular general laws control the secret springs of the universe, but we have yet to find them. Apart from a few recent discoveries about things like gravity, what we notice in life is the prevalence of accident. The more we reflect, the more we are bound to be struck by the power of contingency as determining force in human affairs. It's the sway of irregularity, not the scope of regularity, that seems ever more clear. If life is so dependent on the accidental, why couldn't the accidents be happy?

> A fleet, whose purposes were always salutory, might always meet with a fair wind; Good princes enjoy sound health and long life; Persons born to power and authority be framed with good tempers and virtuous dispositions. A few events such as these, regularly and wisely conducted, would change the face of the world; and yet would no more seem to disturb the course of nature or confound human conduct than the present economy of things. (Hume 3, 108)

Hume never requested utopia, or proposed radical change. His suggestions were as modest as they were consequential. How much evil is caused by some contingency so small that its very superfluity is heartbreaking? Contractors whose neglect of modern building codes caused such loss of life in the 1999 Turkish earthquake were not excused by the fact that earthquakes are rare. Wouldn't a good designer create a universe less vulnerable to accident? Or ensure that the ones that occurred were benign?

Hume makes similar work of natural religion's claims about God's generosity. Early on, Cleanthes had extolled it. How much of Creation is superfluous! Take another look at our bodies, those Deist marvels of design. Though we could have survived without it, God gave us not just one eye but two. Not to mention two ears. Nature, to be sure, was designed with the frugality needed to fit the requirements of Ockham's razor. But instances like these show repeated proof of the munificence of God's design. He could have made us, but made us less than we are. Instead he showered us not only with proofs of His existence but His affection as well.

Hume begged to differ. The third circumstance that leads to evil is the fact that nature is so very stingy. When distributing properties, its Author seemed to have given each species the bare minimum needed to survive. Animals who are swift are proportionally frail. Animals who can reason have no bodily defense. Wouldn't an affectionate parent have given us a little something in reserve? With the knowledge of all we have to cope with, couldn't the resources for coping have been extended just a bit? Traditional religion was quick to remind us that we are not alone in the universe. Job's friends, as we saw, mentioned the long hours God spends taking care of His other creatures and warned us against demanding too great a share of His attention. Anticipating such objections, Hume was relentless. Is God's power so limited? His resources so finite? The set of properties available for distribution among His species so small? Then He'd have done better to produce fewer creatures, to ensure that each had more faculties available for securing happiness. It's a reckless builder who undertakes projects beyond his means. Conscientious ones know how to estimate and never embark upon ostentatious edifices before calculating their stocks. Here the tiles don't reach the baseboard; the pipes won't carry the sewage. Once more, you decide: goodwill or competence? In this builder, one of them is conspicuously absent.

> In order to cure most of the ills of human life, I require not that man should have the wings of the eagle, the swiftness of the stag, the force of the ox, the arms of the lion, the scales of the crocodile or rhinoceros; much less do I demand the sagacity of an angel or cherubim. I am contented to take an increase in one single power or faculty of his soul. Let him be endowed with a greater propensity to industry and labor; a more vigorous spring and activity of mind; a more constant bent to business and application. (Hume 3, 110)

Hume's choice of diligence as the attribute he would give us had he been in charge of design may not suit your taste. His claim that most moral as well as natural evils arise from idleness bears the scent of the environment in which he was raised. Still his general point is hard to dispute. Let us renounce fantasies of perfection, suppress the longing for something rare: better judgment, finer taste, greater friendship, truer love. Isn't it hard to be thrown into a world so wanting without some modest, prosaic addition to our powers?

Just in case he'd overlooked something in the first three circumstances that produced our evils, Hume added a fourth: the workmanship of the great machine of nature was never accurately adjusted. You can see that *some* purpose was intended by most of its parts, but the builder seems to have been in such a hurry to finish the job that he rushed through construction before completing the final touches. Winds may be required for nature to function, but how often do they become hurricanes? Passions are surely useful, but how often do they break their bounds? Everything in the universe may have its advantage, but everything seems to bring disadvantage by occurring in the wrong proportions. Would a good designer rush through a task without checking his measurements?

Hume had said it in the *Enquiry*: humankind worked long and hard to save the honor of the gods at the cost of denying the reality of the evil and disorder surrounding us (Hume 2, 107). His recommendation was evident enough. It is not entirely clear to which end our industry should be directed. Hume seems to have found diligence to be as close to an end in itself as he was willing to name, for at least it prevents the laziness that breeds trouble. The *Natural History* concluded with a warning against higher hopes, for they make way for crueler disappointments, as great joy is likely to produce the deeper melancholy.

> And, in general, no course of life has such safety (for happiness is not to be dreamed of) as the temperate and moderate, which maintains, as far as possible, a mediocrity, and a kind of insensibility, in every thing.
> (Hume 3, 184)

Presumably Hume's advice would be to cultivate a smallish garden, since idle hands are the devil's workshop. He would offer no grounds for cultivating *this* plot but the fact that it's the one you were born on, and it nourished your parents adequately enough. Such industry may bring some advantage; toiling on behalf of the gods will not.

Hume's rejection of religion will strike us as clear and biting, although earlier readers were reluctant to acknowledge it.[15] Hume never went so far as to call himself an atheist. Though Kemp Smith questioned the content of Hume's late, eviscerated theism, he reminded us that Hume's method was that of Bayle. Both were more interested in undermining everyone else's conclusions than in establishing any of their own. This is skepticism at its greatest, rather than anything you can identify as metaphysics. Between the demands imposed by the form of skeptical argument itself, eighteenth-century conventions imposed by censorship, and Hume's own lack of conviction in the value of sincerity,[16] it may be impossible to determine his religious beliefs.

What is here most important: it doesn't matter. The content of Hume's religious beliefs has only biographical interest. Hume himself, in an argument that he originally intended to be the last page of the *Dialogues*, made a claim as shocking as any other in the book: differences between atheism and theism themselves are only differences in degree and tone. In the history of the problem of evil, Hume's relation to God is as unimportant as Bayle's. My own conviction is that Bayle was the skeptical fideist he claimed to be while Hume was not. You may judge them differently. But even more than in Bayle's case, it is reason, not God, that was the primary target of Hume's work. All his care and zeal in attacking the latter had the former in view from the start. Human reason, said Hume, can find no ground why a universe could not be designed without those four circumstances that lead to all its evils. (All four, mind you. Hume left it to his readers to add: *at least one?*) If after reading Hume you want to praise the design of Creation, and worship its Designer, Hume would be the last to stop you. He never believed that most people were moved by reason anyway.

Nor did he seem to hold that they should be. For his very reasonable explication of the circumstances giving rise to the world's evils showed that human reason leads you wrong. If you follow human reason, you expect the world to be one way. If you open your eyes, you see that it's another. For those wishing to get about with a measure of safety (Hume's word, see above), which instrument recommends itself? The customs and habits that guided generations of mediocre but tolerable lives before you, or a compass that, fixed on an unknown object, always seems to indicate the wrong direction?

The injunction *Be reasonable!* has come to mean *Decrease your expectations.* The demand that we be realistic became a demand that we prepare for disappointment. How this came to pass is worth study on its own. Here I wish merely to note it, and to note that Hume happily acceded to both demands. With this conception of reasonableness, Hume sought the overthrow of all notions of reason. He was perfectly open in stating this; it's explicit in the elegant harangue with which Philo begins part 1 of the book.

> Let us become thoroughly sensible of the weakness, blindness, and narrow limits of human reason; Let us duly consider its uncertainty and needless contrarieties; even in subjects of common life and practice. . . . When these topics are displayed in their full light, as they are by some philosophers and almost all divines; who can retain such confidence in this frail faculty of reason? (Hume 3, 33)

Hume displayed reason's helplessness time after time. His first book, the *Treatise of Human Nature*, described reason as "perfectly inert," "wholly inactive," and "utterly impotent" (Hume 1, 457–58). It cannot penetrate common mysteries, like the existence of causes, that seem to be self-evident; it cannot establish banal truths about things like sunrises on which our lives depend. But all those are worries with which one can cope. A British gentleman can dispel them with a glass of sherry and a game of sheshbesh. It's on the problem of evil that reason truly stumbles, and skepticism truly triumphs. For here reason is not merely in trouble but in pain. However it tries to reduce them, its expectations are all wrong. Nothing in the world turns out to correspond to the assumptions of what appears, in the end, an absurd little faculty, whose purpose is as murky as, say, the human appendix. (Just another little shot at the Deist's favorite set of objects. For *what* purpose does this organ exist?) The world could have been designed so much more reasonably, in any sense of the word: more humane, more systematic, more receptive to law. The fact that it wasn't is the source of daily suffering caused by everything from bad temper to tyranny. Should reason hang its head in shame? Condemn the world that leaves no place for its ventures, and withdraw to something otherworldly?

Wherever it turns, it will be no use in approaching the problem of evil. That problem can still be abandoned. If you wish to maintain God's existence and benevolence, you may continue to do so on faith, without anything that looks like a reason. Then explanation is not your overriding interest anyway, and appearances of evil become something secondary. Or you may retain the framework of the problem, but as something unanswerable: for reason, evil becomes thoroughly opaque. Either evils are close to illusion, in which case there is no problem, or reason is utterly helpless, in which case there is no answer.

One sort of answer might seem to be left open by the structure of the *Dialogues* themselves. This would be to better divide the world's evils into natural and moral ones, and apportion responsibility accordingly. It's the solution we saw in Rousseau, and it would be tried in later eras by lesser figures. At first it seems not only to help us out of fundamental difficulties but also to avoid the embarrassing contradiction to which Hume's work points. As he made clear, the only thing that the eighteenth century found more obvious than the argument from design was the view that life was miserable. The only way to try to maintain both convictions at once would be to restrict the argument from design to admiration for the natural world. The defects in the moral world might then be dismissed with a reference to our own mortal failings, and the claim that even good designers have their limits.— It's a valiant, if guilt-tinged, effort, but the good Europeans knew better. Attempts to maintain hard distinctions between natural and moral evils did not succeed. Hume himself began by dividing them. The first nine books of the *Dialogues* focus on the natural world. All he needed were books 10 and 11 to destroy our faith in the design of the human one. Yet he knew as well as others that nothing remains in place. Fleets on good missions founder in the ocean; good princes die young. And where are mosquitoes and syphilis to be ordered? The eighteenth century was no more certain about its ability to distinguish the natural from the unnatural than we are. They were beginning to test limits.

END OF THE TUNNEL: THE MARQUIS DE SADE

Sade longed to be more criminal than he was. Indeed, he longed to be more criminal than was conceivable. For he often noted, with a mixture of rage and pleasure, that true crimes against nature are impossible. If the impulse to crime is natural, mustn't nature cooperate in any urge to its own destruction? There may be a way around this objection, and Sade sought it without rest. His Juliette, like the emperor Tiberius, wishes that all of humankind had a single neck so she could slash it; his books strain to outdo themselves in imagining one thing worse than the last. Frustrated with the finite joys of torture, murder, and betrayal, one character seeks a crime whose effects would be eternal, causing

> a chaos of such proportions that it would provoke a general cor- ruption or a disturbance so formal that even after my death its effects would still be felt. (Sade 1, 57)

Her friend Juliette proposes that she try her hand

> at moral crime, the crime one commits in writing.

Most commentators have waded through the 1,190 pages of *Juliette* to pick out this sentence as central: Sade was clearly speaking in his own voice. And though he may not have acted out many of his other fantasies, he surely succeeded in this. His writings are criminal. It's not accident or prudishness that led people to ban them. They titillate and repel in ways you shouldn't be titillated and repelled. They appeal to the meanest and worst of desires: whether you react with disgust or with boredom, you are implicated as voyeur of acts that should not see the light of day. The question of whether they actually cause anyone to imitate them is one best left to some other form of investigation. But if you actually get through all ten volumes of *Juliette*, you will be left with a set of images foul enough to make you wish you'd stopped halfway. *Justine*, comparatively restrained as well as shorter, is more readable, but all the more depressing. For even if you're used to think- ing about Job and his descendants, the spectacle of that much tortured innocence may grind you down. Tell yourself that Sade exaggerates:

this is cartoon, parody, cheap fairy tale in reverse. Forget the maddening rejoinder made by Horkheimer and Adorno: only the exaggerated is true. After finishing one of Sade's novels, you can feel imagination itself as indictment. If such stuff could be invented, something in the human soul is so vile that it's easy to share Sade's expression of the very strongest answer to the problem we will see the eighteenth century raise often:

> [D]isgust with life becomes so strong in the soul that there is not a single man who would want to live again, even if such an offer were made on the day of his death. (Quoted in Klossowski, 82)

Sade wanted his reader to suffer. We may not agree with de Beauvoir, who came close to suggesting that being subject to a Sadean villain's endless speeches is almost as unpleasant as falling into his hands. Still this is writing that is meant to cause pain. We react to it with the same ambivalence Sade had the good taste to feel toward himself. On the one hand, he dreamed of criminality so infinite it would outlast him. Few writers' dreams came so true. Sustained fascination with his works, and the use of his name as the signpost for all of humanity's worst urges provide a kind of immortality that is seldom granted. On the other hand, his last will and testament recorded self-loathing so great that it spared no attention to detail: his body should be buried without ceremony in a specified ditch:

> The ditch covered over, above it acorns shall be strewn, in order that the spot may become green again, and the copse grown back thick over it, the traces of my grave may disappear from the face of the earth as I trust the memory of me shall fade out of the minds of all men save nevertheless for those few who in their goodness have loved me until the last, and of whom I carry away a sweet remembrance with me to the grave. (Sade 1, 157)

Perhaps the pain his works cause is so great as to demand repression. It's repression, at any rate, that dominates much of the Sade literature. He's defended as an honest reporter, willing to say out loud what others did or dreamed in secret. As successor to the Encyclopedists and precursor to Freud, Sade is said to have continued the project of demasking central to Enlightenment. The lords and ladies of the old regime really did bleed the people white for their own debauched pleasures; Sade, as political critic—and didn't he put himself in the service of the Revolution?—merely recorded it, with a little polemical hyperbole. When they weren't restricted to Europeans, the criminals were even less restrained. Paulhan remarks that European literature didn't hesitate to esteem a work that makes Sade's crimes look paltry. De Las Casas's *Brief Relation of the Destruction of the Indies* recorded the slow torture of victims not in fantasy but in fact, and in numbers totaling not hundreds but millions. Blanchot reminds us that whatever the conquistadores did in the New World could be surpassed by God Himself in the world to come. Sade often regretted that enlightened theologians had done away with hell, for only hell contained the resources to prolong choice victims' agonies, but not even he dwelt on the consignment of unbaptized infants to it, which some Christian sects took as a matter of course.

Sade himself played with the posture of authenticity's apostle. His works contain passages styling him as inside critic of the French aristocracy as well as a sort of Kraft-Ebbing *avant la lettre*. For the first, take the footnote that accompanies Saint-Fond's declaration: If I thought gold flowed in their veins, I'd have every one of the people bled to death.

> There, by such tokens you may recognize them, those monsters that abounded under the *ancien regime* and personified it. We have not promised to portray them as beauties, but authentically; we shall keep our word. (Sade 2, 234)

And to portray himself as a bold researcher venturing into uncharted depths, he occasionally provided exclamations like these:

> Oh my friends, how am I to describe the horrors we witnessed? Describe them I must, however, they are aberrances of the human heart I am exposing, and I am bound to expose every nook and cranny. (Sade 2, 1046)

But there are plenty of reasons not to take Sade at his word. Among others, he was a liar. That he was a passionate and subtle liar, if seldom a very convincing one, is clear from his denial that he authored his best work, *Justine*. How could he be the author of a book in which all the philosophers are villains, when he himself was a philosopher (Sade 1, 153)? Sade's characters spend so much time justifying lies and betrayal that we'd be as naive as Justine herself if we simply believed him. This is a writer who played with all categories of concealment. And viewing him as a particularly daring exposer overlooks his writings' normative thrust. Critics who call him a fighter for freedom, enemy of guilt, privilege, and mediocrity, or a lover of everything from the concrete in itself to the abstractness of transgression in general ignore half the content of his work. For those who didn't make it to the end of *Juliette*: Sade's heroes celebrate torturing to death their own children, and anybody else's they can get their hands on, as means to a better orgasm. He tried very hard to stop at nothing. Our willingness to aestheticize Sade may itself have limits. I am not certain, for example, that the late twentieth century would have tolerated a Sade industry among German intellectuals as easily as it tolerated a French one.

Finding the object of all this rage is probably hopeless, and may involve more straying into the psychobiographical than my interests include. But one object requires more attention than it has received. We must take at least one of Sade's own claims at face value: he was a philosopher. Not a great philosopher, but an original one. For the philosopher, even descriptive writing has normative force. If your only desire is to reveal the world, you will seek models such as Isaac Newton or Jane Austen. (Whether even they succeeded in being purely descriptive is, of course, another question.) But Sade very clearly believed that his descriptions had consequences. Consider more carefully his disavowal of the authorship of *Justine*. All the philosophical personages in that book, he wrote, are villains to the core. Whereas

[e]veryone acquainted with me will certify that I consider philosophy my profession and my glory. . . . And can anyone for an instant, save he suppose me mad, can anyone, I say, suppose for one minute that I could bring myself to present what I hold to be the noblest of all callings under colors so loathsome and in a shape so execrable? What would you say of him who were delib-

erately to go befoul in the mire the costume he was fondest of
and in which he thought he struck the finest figure? (Sade 1, 153)

One could say, of course, that befouling things of which one is fond
is a particularly Sadean pastime. But the note continues with clearer
clues.

> On the contrary, all the villains I have described are devout be-
> cause the devout are all villains and all philosophers are decent
> folk, because most decent folk are philosophers.

Let us leave the truth-value of such claims to others and take a look
at their function. As a means of persuading anticlerical tribunals to
release you from prison, they are probably worth trying, though nobody seemed to believe him. Like the thunderbolt that forms the final
event in *Justine* itself, the argument invites a more natural interpretation. Sade could not be the author of a work in which all the philosophers are villains? The old regime claimed that philosophy leads to
villainy, and used this claim as ground for censorship throughout Europe and beyond. Sade didn't merely confirm the worst fear of traditional authorities; he rubbed their noses in it. For he was willing not
only to accept the consequences of philosophy—the deliberate dispas-
sionate questioning of the foundations of established ideology—but to
positively revel in them. Does philosophy lead to villainy? *Justine*'s
sequel *Juliette* is far less guarded. One of its most wicked creatures is
described like this:

> A very lofty intelligence, I have never known her peer for an
> enemy to prejudices, and I have never known a woman to carry
> philosophy so far. (Sade 2, 273)

Toward the story's beginning Juliette begs a more experienced criminal
for instruction.

> Will you be my guide in this delicious journey? Will you hold aloft
> the lamp of philosophy to light the way? (Sade 2, 180)

Whatever else the lamp of philosophy illuminated in Sade's world,
religious beliefs were first in line. In the passage quoted from the

"Note," the opposite of *philosophical* is *devout*. Here Sade was conventional. There can be no stable agreement between philosophy and religion, for the two are fundamentally at war. The Deism of which the Enlightenment was so enamored is a coward's compromise. When examined coolly, the truths of religion cannot be supported by reason or experience.

Enlightened thinkers had devoted more than a century to rationalizing religion. What remained was the natural religion whose central truth was some form of the argument from design. As if the argument hadn't suffered enough in the hands of Hume, it became primary target of Sade's twin novels *Justine* and *Juliette*. Those novels contain an argument. (Perhaps it's more accurate to say that their flaws as literary productions are due to the fact that they *consist* of an argument.) It is mercilessly simple, and often simply crude, but to be certain we don't miss it, Sade gave the novels subtitles. *Justine*'s is *The Misfortunes of Virtue*; *Juliette*'s *The Prosperities of Vice*. The plot, or the argument, is just this. Two orphaned sisters must make their way in the world. The elder chooses a path of increasing crime, which brings her every sort of happiness. The younger grips onto faith and morals all the harder for the fact that they bring her nothing but torment. After many years of separation they meet by accident and compare notes. Initially they fail to recognize each other, and this should be no surprise. Justine is on her way to be executed for a crime she not only never committed, but risked her life trying to prevent. Juliette radiates the casual confidence of those blessed by fortune, in the form of health, beauty, vast wealth, and a lover no less devoted than he is noble and powerful. She asks the poor girl to tell her life's story.

> "To recount you the story of my life, Madame", this lovely one in distress said to the Countess, "Is to offer you the most striking example of innocence oppressed, is to accuse the hand of heaven, is to bear complaint against the Supreme Being's will, is, in a sense, to rebel against his sacred designs . . . I dare not . . ." Tears gathered in this interesting girl's eyes, and after having given vent to them for a moment, she began her recitation. (Sade 1, 468)

And Sade commenced the story, that is, to do just the thing Justine does not dare. If it's crime he sought by writing, it's a crime against heaven: to tell Justine's story is to rebel against sacred design.

There is no better way to see this than to put Sade in the company of his contemporaries. Robert Darnton drew attention to a rich body of eighteenth-century literature that straddled and defied borders between philosophy and pornography. Because both were banned by the censors, both were referred to in the vast illegal book trade as "philosophical books." This is more than merely piquant. As Darnton has shown, philosophy and pornography performed subversive functions. The fact that exigencies of law grouped them together served to radicalize each one. To judge from the bedroom conversation portrayed there, the theories of d'Holbach or Diderot worked as eighteenth-century aphrodisiacs, as did any sort of attack on the Catholic Church. All these signaled challenge to order and rejection of restraint which are generally erotic. One can imagine cynical reasons to blend philosophy and porn: a dull philosopher might hope to market his long-winded materialism, a sharp pornographer to evade the censor by burying his smut in speeches few have patience to read to the end. But these are twentieth-century surmises, full of built-in dissociation. Darnton shows, rather, that "muckraking journalism, social commentary, political polemics, bawdy anti-clericalism, utopian fantasies, theoretical speculations, and raw pornography—all cohabited promiscuously under the same label, *livres philosophiques*."

This blend, he argues, could undermine the old regime in part because it mixed reason and rhetoric to produce a heady demand for more freedom in general, extending to a larger group the pleasures of this world now enjoyed by the upper classes. The fewer the number of the illiterate, the fewer the number of those willing to defer their rewards to another life. Moreover, the spectacle of heartlessly debauched aristocracy and clergy—a standard trope in this literature—was willfully seditious. In an era still inclined to believe that kings had divine rights, any work revealing just how earthy their feet had become is sure to undermine. Unmasking authority and debasing the sacred are political acts. Varying theoretical demonstration with obscene example is an obvious form of illustration. The tales of corruption described in, for example, *Anecdotes sur Mme la comtesse du Barry* look like a historical version of a Sade novel. Here aristocrats live to rob the people for a moment of pleasure. They are happy to take vast sums from the national treasury for a whore employed for a night, or a golden carriage never even used that often. Everyone seems to be pimping for others, or using refinements of sexual technique to manipulate matters of state. What, but a bit of violence, did Sade add to this standard genre?

Something very crucial: in Sade's novels, God does it too. The subversion in the earlier literature was in fact succinctly limited. Its goals are the moderate Deism and bourgeoise republicanism that most of the Enlightenment shared. Voltaire used erotic examples to further such aims, and Rousseau carried them to the brink of metaphysics. Both appealed to a vision of the natural that was obscured by centuries of superstition. Once humankind was freed of the ideologies formed by clergy and aristocracy, the natural light of reason could show Deism and republicanism to be true. To be true here means to be part of, or to follow from, nature itself. The misery caused by enslaving a free and sound human being was hardly seen as worse than that caused by forcing the intellect to accept doctrines as unnatural as transubstantiation or divine right.

For most eighteenth-century pornography, sexual repression was part of the same violence that both reason and nature opposed. It was produced by those forces that upheld superstition and absolutism, and it led to similar unhappiness. Liberation could be all of one piece, for it was a matter of expressing all the natural desires that had been frustrated by history and tradition. Once they were free to be expressed, the result would be a general web of pleasure and harmony. "Man is born free, and he is everywhere in chains" could as easily serve as a demand for open marriage as for bourgeois rights. In themselves, reason and nature are as much in tune in the bedroom as they are in the rest of the cosmos. Only ancient prejudice prevents both from coming to their rights—and to each other.

Recall that Voltaire saw human erotic life as an argument for theism—if only it didn't sometimes lead to syphilis. Syphilis is a quirk of nature, albeit one, like earthquakes, that is neither as rare nor as harmless as it should be. Erotic love itself, abstracted from such consequences, was proof of the argument from design. While Voltaire imagined sex as a pillar of natural religion, Rousseau imagined it as the basis of civil society. For erotic love provides the only link between us that is natural as well as reasonable—in principle if not in practice. The desire for another's pleasure as a part of your own is the paradigm of the bond that could tie members of society together as contracts cannot.

Rousseau recorded reading the philosophical pornography so popular in his day, and Voltaire even wrote some of it. What we know of their views is easy to combine with the epigraph of the most famous of such novels, *Thérèse philosophe*.

> Voluptuousness and philosophy produce the happiness of the sensible man. He embraces voluptuousness by taste. He loves philosophy by reason. (Quoted in Darnton, 100)

This is a story with a happy ending. In learning to become a philosopher, the heroine Thérèse gets an education in pleasure, overcoming her fear of pregnancy as well as convention to find happiness in the bed of her enlightened count. Sade described it as charming, indeed as the only work that linked luxuriousness and impiety to provide the idea of an immoral book (ibid., 89). One wonders whether Justine's choice of "Thérèse" as nom de guerre was made with this book in mind. If so, it is no accident that in Sade's work not Justine but her sister becomes a philosopher. Justine never learns anything, and the nature she confronts is one whose lessons are brutal. If the occasional touch of pain to be found in other authors confirms Sade's claims that *some* urge to this sort of thing is natural, none of the earlier philosophical pornography comes even close to resembling Sade. Darnton is right to think we can learn from reading it, but one of the things we learn is that Sade is new.

Sade's own awareness of his relation to tradition was signaled in the letter he wrote to his wife upon learning that the volume of Rousseau he'd requested from prison had been denied.

> To refuse me Jean-Jacques' *Confessions*, now there's an excellent thing, above all after having sent me Lucretius and the dialogues

of Voltaire; that demonstrates great judiciousness, profound dis-
cernment in your spiritual guides. Alas, they do me too much
honor in reckoning that the writings of a deist can be dangerous
to me; would that I were still at that stage . . . while Rousseau
may represent a threat for dull-witted bigots of your species, he
is a salutory author for me. Jean-Jacques is to me what *The Imitation of Christ* is to you. (Sade 1, 134)

Sade was perfectly correct. As we saw, all of Rousseau's work was a
paean to the glory of Creation. Kant thought it answered Alfonso and
justified God. When stripped of the chaos and corruption human beings created in the course of their history, the world in itself is as good
as God saw it to be on the day that He made it. Philosophy, and whatever political conclusions are to follow from it, strip away appearances
to reveal something better and truer behind them. Though experienced
as radical by the established order, Rousseau's work never threatened
the notion of order in general. (On the contrary.) Sade's did.

His is a world of violence and split. The insistence on disharmony
already seen in Voltaire was carried to every limit Sade could imagine.
Human bodies are more brutally and deliberately dismembered than
they were in *Candide*; when there is symmetry in the world at all, it's
the grisly sort of parody of his geometrically structured orgies. For earlier writers, sex itself could be testimony to everything the Enlightenment held dear: the harmony between individual desires and the true
interests of society, the unity of thought and emotion. Sade tore all that
apart. It was not only personal taste that fueled his endless praise of
sodomy as the perfect erotic act. He was often explicit in explaining
why: he viewed it as the antiteleological exercise par excellence. Sodomy was celebrated because it is sterile; it leads to nothing, and were
it practiced more widely, it would counter humanity's own interest in
self-preservation. All the more reason to promote it.

Choosing a pornographic vehicle for philosophical argument was
thus a natural and established move. It sold well, and it sold for reasons
besides prurient ones. If the eighteenth century was obsessed with
determining what's natural, sex must reflect all its terms. Let's take a
closer look at the argument Sade offered. Next to the points he wants

to make about materialism and morality one line stands out, particularly in *Justine* and *Juliette*. The former draws it clearly in three different beginnings the novel contains: epigraph, dedication, and preface. All build on deception that should have fooled no one. The epigraph recalls the treacherous properties of lightning:

> O thou my friend! The prosperity of Crime is like unto the lightning, whose traitorous brilliancies embellish the atmosphere but for an instant, in order to hurl into death's very depths the luckless one they have dazzled. (Sade 1, 453)

For those who know the ending, the sentence is radiant with irony. It's Justine, as virtuous as she's hapless, who will be struck by lightning, an event Sade subjected to multiple interpretation. It's a sure clue that the stated point of the book is a lie. For, as he wrote in the dedication,

> The scheme of this novel (yet, 'tis less a novel than one might suppose) is doubtless new; the victory gained by Virtue over Vice, the rewarding of good, the punishment of evil, such is the usual scheme in other work of this species: ah! The lesson cannot be too often dinned in our ears! (Sade 1, 455)

Sade wanted nothing to do with lessons so trite. His message was not the usual one, for he had loftier goals in view. Rather than presenting virtue triumphant, he sought to show it in despair. For only when love of virtue is disconnected from all questions of reward can it be seen as sublime. Such revelation is particularly needed by those of us who live in corrupted ages. If we expect virtue to be rewarded, we may easily abandon it when it's not. If we know in advance how often it is ill-requited, we'll be prepared to meet adversity with the virtue that is its own reward. Were he telling the truth here, he could almost pass for Kant.

So the first sentence of *Justine* proper is this one:

> The very masterpiece of philosophy would be to develop the means Providence employs to arrive at the ends she designs for man, and from this construction to deduce some rules of conduct acquainting this wretched two-footed individual with the manner wherein he must proceed along life's thorny path. (Sade 1, 457)

To trace the design of Providence and draw conclusions for our conduct from it: this was Sade's stated goal. The two were always connected. Sade disavowed (by simultaneously proposing) the more villainous conclusions one can draw from theodicy. The spectacle of evil rewarded by good tempts individual virtue and even seems to have the sanction of heaven. For true theodicy shows how everything happens for the best:

> [W]ill they not say, as did the angel Jesrad in Zadig, that there is no evil whereof some good is not born? And will they not declare, that this being the case, they can give themselves over to evil since, indeed, it is but one of the fashions of producing good? (Ibid.)

This is not the quietism sometimes feared as result of theodicy but something even worse. If even evil has its purpose, every crime you commit is a brick in the wall of providential design. This is cynicism far beyond the indifference expressed as *Whatever is, is right*, and Sade proclaimed his intention to reject it. Doing this required an even greater degree of cynicism. Sade's real goal was buried, not very deeply, in the words of Justine quoted above. To tell her story is to rebel against Heaven, for it's Heaven that designed a world where so much virtue is rewarded with so much misery.

The book opens by claiming to be less literature than philosophy. If it's a novel, it's a bildungsroman manqué. Its heroine should make Candide look savvy: she learns absolutely nothing. The world presents her with lessons any idiot could master, but she's incapable of getting an education. Justine begins her journeys by resolving to maintain the virtue of her childhood and her trust that Providence will reward her for it. She ends where she began, though her trust was betrayed without limit. She has a penchant for saving the lives of villains who rape, torture, and enslave her in return, while subjecting her to speeches about the absurdity of gratitude. By the third or fourth episode, the reader is almost tempted to cry out a warning to the unsuspecting ingenue. It would be useless—not because this is fiction, but because Justine is inured to experience, imprisoned in faith. It's no surprise that her faith is betrayed by one swine after another, for they are all of them agents of the great Betrayer. She puts her trust in Providence to reward her virtue with a world that deserves virtue like hers. And every time she offers thanks for Heaven's designs, they are shown to be treacherous.

Justine doesn't lack for teachers willing to enlighten her. The first of these is Dubois, a woman she meets in the prison where they're awaiting execution—Justine for a theft she refused to commit. Dubois saves them both by burning down the prison in an act of arson that costs many lives, then offers to take Justine under her wing to a career of further crime. When Justine refuses, avowing that Providence will reward her adherence to "the thorns of virtue," Dubois urges: "[B]ecome better acquainted with your Providence, my child." It will land her on a dung heap, but that isn't all. Providence is a tool invented by the rich to lull those whom they oppress into silent endurance. The rich have no need of virtue or faith, for their desires are met without them.

> But we, Thérèse, we whom the barbaric Providence you are mad enough to idolize, has condemned to slink in the dust of humiliation as doth the serpent in the grass, we who are beheld with disdain only because we are poor . . . you would have it that, while this class dominating us has to itself all the blessings of fortune, we reserve for ourselves naught but pain. (Sade 1, 482)

Justine admits she was tempted. On this argument, Providence is either a tool invented for oppression or itself an instrument of injustice. If it isn't a fraud, it serves fraudulent interests. But she falters for only a moment before rejecting such thoughts as sophistries, and affirming her commitment to virtue. She isn't allowed to keep it for an instant, for she's immediately abused by a gang of bandits, who leave her no choice but to join them. Theoretical refutation is increasingly superfluous. Life itself refutes Providence, in long chains of suffering without sense and without end.

Sade's means are rather heavy-handed for adult literature; they draw on the resources of fairy tale. For like very primitive fairy tales, this work is didactic, and its author was at pains to make his lessons clear. The connection between reward and virtue is never in fact just random.

Justine cannot do a good deed without being immediately punished for it. When she stops to give alms to a crippled old woman, that old woman, not so crippled after all, attacks the benefactress and steals her every sou. Rarely does Justine get off so lightly. Having defended her virginity against a troop of bandits, she loses it to the count whom she saved from the gang's clutches. Having nursed a wounded traveler back to life, she is led to the lonely château where he works to death those women whom he doesn't destroy by more gruesome means. Here Justine interrupts her account to her sister.

> "But how can I abuse your patience by relating these new horrors? Have I not already more than soiled your imagination with infamous recitations?"
> "Yes, Thérèse—"

puts in Juliette's lover, who sits captivated, with Juliette, by the narrative.

> "Yes, we insist upon these details, you veil them with a decency that removes all their edge of horror. You may not fully apprehend how these tableaux help toward the development of the human spirit; our backwardness in this branch of learning may very well be due to the stupid restraint of those who venture to write upon such matters." (Sade 1, 670)

So Sade obliges with details.

If her virtue is always punished, her faith is always mocked. The next form of torment always begins when she is on her knees thanking God for deliverance from the last one. Justine's hopes are always raised to be dashed again more surely. But when her trust in Providence falters, it's only for an instant, and she kneels to beg forgiveness for it later. Early on she prays to Heaven to reveal its design. If she could understand her guilt, she could accept her suffering; otherwise, she fears, she will begin to rebel (Sade 1, 575). There she is answered by the assertion of accident. She is captive in a monastery where the clergy rape and torment a large group of women according to elaborate protocol that mirrors the rites of a religious order. Periodically, a new woman is kidnapped, and a veteran retired to make room for her; those retired are never seen again. An older victim explains to Justine that caprice is all that governs their fate. No behavior can be prescribed, no future predicted. Docile women may be dispatched as quickly as rebellious ones, the most beautiful as slowly as the most indifferent. Whimsy and aberration form the monks' only law. Their arbitrary decrees, of course, are meant as example. What are these divines doing but imitating the Lord? Justine knows she is stubborn; the conclusions she refuses to draw come from the very best addresses.

> [It is] as if Providence had assumed the task of demonstrating to me the inutility of virtue. . . . Baleful lessons which however did not correct me, no, I wavered not; lessons which, should I once again escape from the blade poised above my head, will not prevent me from forever remaining the slave of my heart's Divinity. (Sade 1, 621)

How many fools are so proud of their commitment to ignorance?

The insight she seeks into God's design is never granted. In its place is no end of instruction on the nature of moral order. The arguments she hears are bad parodies of those that were in circulation. For example: the orthodox hold evil to be compatible with the claim that this world is a good one, for Providence works through it, converting everything to good purpose. In that case, why not turn criminal and become an agent of Heaven? (Sade 1, 695). Or how about this: Nature cares equally for all of its creatures; it's pride and folly to say that she takes the interests of one more to heart than another. This has been standard fare ever since Job's friends argued that complaints about cosmic injustice were narcissistic. Why not go one step further and argue that it's only human pride which makes murder into crime? For the murderer just turns the mass of flesh that today appears as a person into tomorrow's clump of earthworms. Does nature care more about one than the other? (Sade 1, 519). Along with a priori forms of persuasion her would-be tutors offer empirical ones. Virtue and vice are merely matters of opinion and geography. Justine is scorned as hopelessly provincial. Her insistence on maintaining virtue is just writing schoolgirl manners into the world as a whole. A little travel, a little history should convince her that virtue and vice are but schemes for getting along in the world. *Juliette* explicates this with encyclopedic parody. Every philosophical disquisition on some ordinary virtue is followed by a catalog of anthropological revelation. After one ogre is depicted eating his guests, the monster declaims against hospitality and offers two pages of scientifically illustrated relativism to back his view. Some of the examples Sade offers: the Egyptian government killed any foreigner found along its border. The blacks of Loango are even less welcoming, for they refuse to allow a stranger to be buried on their soil. To this day Arabs sell into slavery all survivors of ships wrecked on their coasts. Sade's lists are sometimes accompanied by footnotes. Is this a parody of the Enlightenment cosmopolitanism embodied by Diderot or just a rejoinder to it? It really doesn't matter whether any particular claim is true. The general point is quite clear: virtue and vice are but custom and habit. That being the case, why not adopt customs best adjusted to the world?

All attempts to teach her prove unavailing. As time continues, Justine begins to attribute the awful lessons life has offered to Providence itself. When the cruelest of her tormentors receives yet greater wealth, she begins to learn irony:

> This was the new piece of evidence Providence had prepared for me. This was the latest manner in which it wished to convince me that prosperity belongs to crime and indigence to virtue. (Sade 1, 686)

But belief in Providence is never based on evidence. As we saw when considering Hegel, it's usually developed in spite of it. Efforts to fathom the cunning of reason prove too great for Justine, so when her pleas for understanding remain unheeded, she decides to live without it. Didn't faith preach blind surrender to the will of the Lord? More than once she avows her attempt to imitate the life of Jesus, or finds consolation in the thought that her torments are not as severe as those of her savior. In truth she meets life with a Nazarene innocence, so the reader is unsurprised when her final torture involves multiple rape on a thorn-studded cross. Jesus exists to console the believer: not only because his death will serve as salvation, but because his torments are so great as to make the rest of us look lucky. In depicting Justine's ever-increasing suffering, Sade sought not only to attack the Father, but to compete with the Son as well.

Juliette, by contrast, is all that's unholy. She is also quick to learn. (Sade's *Philosophy in the Bedroom* had defined the word *whores* as "the only authentic philosophers" [Sade 1, 208].) The further Juliette sinks into crime, the more the world rewards her. If she loses a fortune, it's only to gain a larger one; if she pushes a loyal friend into a volcano, it's only to find one more powerful and devoted. At thirty, her body is just the lovelier for all its adventures, her soul the more tranquil for being in harmony with nature. She and her lover rescue her hapless sister from the executioner's hands and take her to their château. There Justine ends her days—struck through by a bolt of lightning.

No less. On the very slim chance that we might have missed his message, Sade concluded by letting Providence speak in its own voice. A thunderbolt finishes Justine, and both novels, but everything else about the endings is different. In *Justine*, lightning strikes the heroine inside the house where her sister has found joy in nursing her back to health and happiness. Upon awaking from her swoon, the latter decides to retire to a convent to atone for her sins. Juliette reads the lightning as eye-opening warning. If Heaven treated innocent Justine so cruelly, what awful punishment must await her libertine sister! And here she utters a variation on the statement that Sade used as epigraph:

> O thou my friend! The prosperity of Crime is but an ordeal to which Providence would expose virtue, it is like unto the lightning, whose traitorous brilliancies but for an instant embellish the atmosphere, in order to hurl into death's very deeps the luckless one they have dazzled. And there, before our very eyes, is the example of it. (Sade 1, 742)

But there is, of course, a more straightforward interpretation, and the ending of *Justine* is stretched beyond the limits of creative hermeneutics. Sade must have expected a certain cultural literacy from his readers. What does tradition infer from bolts of lightning? It's far more likely to come to the conclusions drawn at the end of *Juliette*, where lightning strikes Justine on the lane outside the château. There she was sent by Juliette and her friends, who had debated whether to immolate her in the course of diverse orgies. "My friends," said [Noirceuil] to that joyous society, "In cases like the present one I have often found it extremely instructive to allow Nature to take her own course. There is, you have noticed, a storm brewing in the sky; let us entrust this personage to the elements. I shall embrace the true faith if they spare her." (Sade 2, 1190)

Heaven sends its calling card to answer such a threat. Justine is immolated immediately, and Sade could not resist a last low blow. Inspecting the fallen victim, one of the villains sees the hand of Providence in the fact that her body is not so disfigured as to preclude an opportunity for necrophilia—which he seizes, of course, on the spot. Providence itself has ratified all their principles, and nothing remains but the last edifying assessments.

"Come, good friends, let us all rejoice together, from all this I see nothing but happiness accruing to all save only virtue—but we would perhaps not dare say so were it a novel we were writing."

"Why dread publishing it," said Juliette, "When the truth itself, and the truth alone, lays bare the secrets of Nature, however mankind may tremble before those revelations. Philosophy must never shrink from speaking out." (Ibid.)

Justine's voice is no longer around to be heard. It will be hard to find a replacement.

While his goals were those of the philosopher, Sade chose the form of the novel. One thing this allowed him was multiplicity of voice. He was free to try out positions without committing himself to any of them. His beliefs about God, in particular, seemed a matter of flux. Was He merely absent entirely, or positively malevolent? Was the evil in the world due to random bad luck or the result of deliberate intention? Sade's own uncertainty on the subject is often expressed in nearly incoherent exclamations: "Yes, vain illusion, how my soul detests you!" The reader cannot miss the fact that Sade's works are full of dialogues with a being whose existential status is murky. Juliette, it's been noted, "deifies sin. Her libertinage is as marked by Catholicism as the nun's ecstasy is by paganism" (Adorno and Horkheimer, 106). Bataille, less lucidly, described Sade's works as prayer books. Certainly if Sade was an atheist, he was a God-obsessed one. His expressions of atheism occurred in his moments of optimism. For any alternative is much worse. Dubois, who tries to tutor Justine, explains:

> "I believe," this dangerous woman answered, "that if there were a God there would be less evil on earth; I believe that since evil exists, these disorders are either expressly ordained by God, and there you have a barbarous fellow, or he is incapable of preventing them and right away you have a feeble God; in either case, an abominable being, a being whose lightning I should defy and whose laws contemn. Ah, Thérèse! Is not atheism preferable to the one and the other of these extremes?" (Sade 1, 698)

Indeed it is. For the alternative to God's absence is His presence. If He should be known by His works, what must we infer about His nature? Sade took the standard litanies that had been brewing since Bayle and drew conclusions no predecessor had dared to draw. Klossowski notes the presence of gnostic themes throughout Sade's writings. These can also be found in his view that Creation bears the seed of a curse, and in the thoroughgoing hatred of the body that none of Sade's tributes to pleasure ever hides (Klossowski, 100). But most gnostics admitted at least *two* powers. Where Sade believed that a higher force existed, it was a force of unremitting evil. Such a being must be

> very vindictive, very barbarous, very unjust, very cruel . . . more cruel than any mortal because acting without any motives a mortal might have. (Sade 2, 397)

Human criminals are usually merely base. They act to advance their own banal interests, to increase their fortunes or, at worst, their power. But God is omnipotent. What needs can be served by the steady trampling over weaker beings that fills the universe? Sheer lust for cruelty is all that explains it—which is why some take refuge in the mystery of grace. The conclusions Sade drew were foreshadowed in more than one tradition. Nietzsche described Greek gods watching human suffering as we watch tragedy at the theater. Nor can one stop at Calvinists and pagans. Can't we trace features of a Sadean hero in the Being portrayed in the prologue to Job, who allows His righteous servant to be tortured for the sake of . . . ?

Sade's most radical theological proposal is made by the minister Saint-Fond. He points out that the standard arguments of Juliette and her friend Clairwil all beg the question. For their arguments against God's existence are tied to traditional assumptions: if there is a God, His primary attribute will be benevolence. This is the foundation of their arguments against absurdities found in notions of hell. Its purpose can only be sheerly vindictive, since it's too remote to serve as warning, too eternal to serve as corrective. Saint-Fond dares them to be more radical: why not reject the assumption that God is benevolent? He commences with a marvelous mirror of the Deism that had claimed to reject superstition in favor of philosophy, a priori argument in favor of straight and simple observation. Saint-Fond is a man who prides himself on large-scale theft, so it is fitting that his intellectual weapons are stolen:

> More of a philosopher than you, Clairwil, I do not have to apply, as you seem obliged to do, either to that rogue Jesus or to that insipid novel, the Holy Scripture, in order to demonstrate my system; my study of the universe alone provides me with weapons to oppose you . . . I raise up my eyes to the universe: I see *evil, disorder, crime* reigning as despots everywhere. My gaze descends, and it bends upon that most interesting of this universe's creatures. I behold him likewise devoured by vices, by contradictions, by infamies; what ideas result from this examination . . . there exists a God; some hand or other has necessarily created all that I see, but has not created it save for *evil; evil* is his essence; and all that he causes us to commit is indispensable to his plans. (Sade 2, 399)

How can evil be essential to these interests? Saint-Fond has answers for everything. Evil is increased when it encounters more evil, hence is moved to create itself infinitely. He toys with a bit of hasty metaphysics, in the form of something called maleficent molecules, to support this claim. His own life gives example of whatever truth it may contain.

The worst sort of evil makes its victims accomplice to crime. So he forces lovers to torture their beloved, signing their souls over to the devil before being murdered themselves. Similarly, he dispatches other objections to his system. Doesn't the presence of some good in the world suggest at least a cosmos that's mixed? Rubbish, he returns, what's called good is merely feeble, and feebleness is an evil itself. By 1797 readers were used to reading catalogs of descriptions that undermine views of the world as benign; *Juliette* was published exactly one hundred years after Bayle. Here Sade needed do little more than drive it home, through a God who berates humankind for misreading the evidence. Didn't His world give clear enough indication of His designs? Couldn't they discover what sort of behavior would accord with His intentions? So Saint-Fond's God speaks:

> Did not the perpetual miseries with which I inundate the universe convince you that I love only disorder, and that to please me one must emulate me? . . . In what aspect of my conduct have you noticed benevolence? Is it in sending you plagues, blights, civil wars, earthquakes, tempests? Fool! why did you not imitate my ways? Why did you resist those passions I put into you for no reason other than to prove to you how great is the necessity for evil? (Sade 2, 399)

Saint-Fond's statement of the relations between natural and moral evils is a crude one, and for that reason instructive. His dark Creator taunts us for misinterpretation, but His assumptions about those relations are conventional. The natural world is a clue to its Creator's intentions for the moral one. Like the best religious traditions, it forms an example for imitation; like philosophical searches for foundation, it offers support for any decision we might make on our own. Recall *Justine*'s first sentence: the masterpiece of philosophy would be to show the means Providence uses to arrive at the ends she derives for us, and to deduce from those some rules for conduct.[17]

Sade's work became a synonym for radical moral evil taken past limits anyone else imagined. I have suggested that his ambitions were fulfilled. His attack on God was reckless beyond measure. His portrait of Justine gave the lie to the gospel's claim to have portrayed, in Jesus, the case of greatest sorrow. And his torment of human reason itself was thereby more brutal than anything anyone else had achieved. Like any great criminal, he managed to implicate all the rest of us in the fascination for his work that shows no sign of abating. So much for broad outlines; his details too give him claim to preeminence. Next to a Sadean orgy, the trysts portrayed in the standard pornography of his day are models of comportment.

The success of Sade's attempt to portray moral evil more extreme than anything imagined before him should not blind us to the conventional ways in which he tied it to natural evil. More exactly, he left conventional ties unbroken, and with them the hopes for harmony that the rest of his century still held. Providence is the attempt to give just form to destiny—whatever it is that befalls you in return for whatever it is you've done. It takes the form of interpretation, and vulgar readings seek to show how every natural event is reward for a moral one. Justine and Juliette meet the world with traditional assumptions and spend their lives constructing just such vulgar readings. They differ, of course, in their constructions. Tutored by experience and the wicked Saint-Fond, Juliette concludes that Providence wants evil behavior, since that's what it rewards. Tutored by convention, Justine has nothing to fall back on but the conventional assurance that Providence's ways are mysterious. Sade caricatures their fates for pedagogical purposes, for the randomness of real life can leave us confused. But one needn't view the relations between moral and natural evils to be as simple or straightforward as the simple and straightforward sisters. The eighteenth century's obsession with determining the natural, and deriving guidance for our conduct that conforms to it, reflects a desire to be in tune with the world. Perhaps the desire grew in proportion to the fear that humankind was growing increasingly distant from nature. My point is that Sade, for all that he loved to rip through things, never embraced this particular split.

Much to the contrary: he longed to hear his echo in the world, to see his reflection in the structure of nature. Despite all bravado, Sade wasn't really inclined to set himself against the powers that be. He had neither the gallantry nor the guts of Don Juan, and he didn't believe that hell was waiting. But one way or another, he felt the need to prove it, to show morality and nature in endless reflection. If there is a God, He wants creatures in His own sadistic image. If there is simply blind nature, it had better be all of a piece. Sade never failed to draw a consequence:

> Murderers are in nature as are war, famine, and cholera; they are one of the means Nature disposes of, like all the hostile forces she pits against us . . . we cannot flog or burn or brand or hang cholera or famine, whereas we can do all of these things to a man; that is why he is wrong. (Sade 2, 777)

This could be a massive way of exculpating the human—if it weren't part of a massive indictment of nature. Most important is the unspoken demand that they conform to each other's image. To call this narcissistic is in order if you admit the existence of transcendental narcissism. Most philosophers posit selves that mirror the world. Leibniz rescued final causes from Spinozan critique, and attributed purpose not only to humans but to the units that compose the universe. Hume's little bundles of selves reflect the little bundles of objects they lack the conditions to perceive. Not even Kant could entirely suppress the longing for harmony between the self and the world, but he did manage to withstand it.

This is as good a point as any to face the claim that Sade and Kant are kindred souls. The charge was made famous in Adorno and Horkheimer's *Dialectic of Enlightenment*, and it's tempting to simply dismiss it: while both Kant and Sade can show extremes of self-torment, there's all the difference in the world between those who extend it to others and those who don't. *The Dialectic of Enlightenment*'s outline of similarities proceeds less by argument than by innuendo. The "cold law" of Kant and Moses does not proclaim feeling and knows neither love nor the stake (Adorno and Horkheimer, 114). Would it be more or less Sadean if we added the stake? Is the coldness that links Sade to Königsberg and Sinai something we'd rather replace by the heat of passion? In Sade's terms or Rousseau's? Sade and Kant are linked because both traffic in formal structures. Perhaps one ought to add Bach as well, and denounce him for tormenting harmony by subjecting it to the precision of rule.

If there is an argument in addition to an atmosphere, it isn't a good one. True, Adorno and Horkheimer are right to note that Sade's villains are more attracted by the idea of crime than by the sensations it causes. Juliette is encouraged to repeat in cold blood the crime she committed in passion, so as to strike at the heart of virtue. She and her cohorts are often portrayed in acts that overcome both sentiment and disgust. This is clearly an attempt to overcome the merely human. Their pleasure comes from transgression, and transgression requires obstacles. The heroes of books like *Thérèse philosophe* want to abolish precisely the obstacles to pleasure that Sade finds erotic. In all this self-overcoming and mastery one may see parody of Kant but not kinship with him. For *The Dialectic of Enlightenment*, Kant's reason has no substantial goals; hence no argument against murder can be derived from it. Its authors conclude that Kant shares the same room as Sade.

Only the hastiest reading of Kant's work could miss his attack on instrumental conceptions of reason. These, he argued, are merely prag-matic and empirical, while the real task of reason is precisely to set ends. *The Dialectic of Enlightenment* views reason as an old pocket calculator, not even complex enough to function as a good model of instrumental reason. This is so far from Kant's view that no claim based on it can be successful in attacking him. Yet even a more accurate de-scription of Kant's notion of reason must acknowledge one of Adorno and Horkheimer's claims: Kant's moral law has no basis in the structure of reality. It rests instead on what he calls the fact of reason. This means that reason justifies itself. Kant would not justify morality on instrumen-tal grounds, so he offers no arguments to persuade us to be moral. Rather, he says, it's a fact of reason that we should be. But as Adorno and Horkheimer point out, facts do not help us when they're not there.

Neither, however, do emotions. By way of comparison, consider the following:

Let us chuse any inanimate object, such as an oak or an elm; and let us suppose, that by the dropping of its seed it produces a sapling below it, which springing up by degrees, at last overtops and destroys the parent tree: I ask, if in this instance there be wanting any relation, which is discoverable in parricide or ingratitude? Is not the one tree the cause of the other's existence; and the latter the cause of the destruction of the former, in the same manner as when a child murders a parent? (Hume 1, 467)

Sade's readers know that only a little obscenity is missing to draw one of his favorite conclusions. The biological act that sometimes leads to conception creates no obligations. Since it's undertaken only for reasons of pleasure, it cannot be a source of relations between the parties involved. Any such relation must result from mutual inclination, not the brute accident of kinship. For reason finds no path from the one to the other. If inclination may lead you to cherish your child or your parent, it may just as easily lead you to destroy them. So Sade was particularly fond of accompanying incest with murder. Of course he knew that even without reason, custom and habit erect taboos against both. (Without the pleasure of violating taboos, he would find little cause to engage in them.) But as he argued, in the course of encouraging a girl to abuse her mother,

> [i]f, by chance, you should hear some inner voice speaking to you—whether it is custom that inspires these announcements, whether it is your character's moral effect that produces these twinges—unhesitatingly, remorselessly throttle those absurd sentiments . . . local sentiments, the fruit of geographical accident, climate, which nature repudiates and reason disavows always! (Sade 1, 354)

Sade's reason, like Hume's, is the tool of the skeptic. Good at unmasking other people's views, it is perfectly inept at everything else. Hume wished to humiliate reason by demonstrating its myriad weaknesses. It is unable to establish the simplest truths. Only habit can show that events have causes, or that killing your father is a crime. Reason's expectations of the world lead to disorientation and error. Anticipating an order in the world that it cannot affect, reason prevents us from seeing the world as it is and acting accordingly. Reason is the compass that keeps steering us wrong—if it's capable of steering at all.

While Hume undertook to humiliate reason, Sade sought to torture it. The exaggeration that marks *Juliette* and *Justine* is meant not only for didactic purposes. The reader would get Sade's point were it made with a lighter hand. Hume coolly said that reason cannot comprehend why the world was constructed with so many evils. Kant argued that reason cannot stand it. In showing a world where crime always pays while virtue always suffers, Sade rakes reason over coals.

Since medieval times, rationalists used faith in reason and the argument from design to support one another. If God gave us reason, He meant us to use it. Early rationalists used this teleological strategy to dismiss their orthodox critics. But skeptics brought arguments that were harder to answer. Hume let design and reason cancel each other out. Eyes and hands may bear witness to creation. But if reason does nothing but lead us astray, we possess at least one organ that's distinctly counterpurposive—put in the world to work against us. Another ground to suspect that we live in a world without purpose is another blow against the argument from design. Sade went much further, taking up the fear Descartes only hinted at. An evil God might be a deceiver, who endowed us with a faculty He intended to be treacherous. What if reason were meant to lead us astray—to turn us into Justines, for example, naive enough to serve as prey (Sade 2, 39)?[18]

From Hume's humiliation of reason it's but a short step to punishment. But the question of whether Hume or Kant deserves more blame for having led to Sade is less important than asking which view will be better equipped to deal with Sade. *Justine* can be read as the empiricist's warning. Look what happens to those who refuse to take their cues from experience, who try to impose principles on a world that resists them. Far better to proceed in the other direction. Let experience dictate your view of the world and give you rules for acting within it. This is the message that Hume-inspired Edmund Burke drew from the Terror, and it's one you might draw from violent upheaval in general. Sade makes sure that you cannot draw it through him. For he was far more aware of the consequences implicit in modern experience. You cannot take refuge in custom and habit when custom and habit have been undermined. Having used up the tools of Enlightenment skepticism to discredit traditional positions, Hume was left with no resources he hadn't helped to destroy. The traditions we drew on have no basis but history and accident. It will do no good to say that history and accident let us muddle through this far and can therefore be trusted to keep us going. For the upheaval that makes up the modern is the very act of questioning whether history and accident are the sort of things that should count as justification. Hume's brilliant attacks on religion demand we conclude that they shouldn't. His dual solution—prescribing for the mass of humanity those crutches the wise few can forgo—is bound to appear cynical. And cynicism is ultimately unstable. To undercut our faith in traditional experience with one hand, and urge us to rely on it with the other, is a solution you need not be Sade to reject.

Far better to be wholehearted in accepting disjuncture, if you've got to accept it at all. As we will see in chapter 4, this is one way to follow Kant. Maintaining the gap between reason and nature is not without cost, but Sade's work provides a glimpse of another alternative. The price of closing gaps between the moral and the natural is even higher than that of retaining them. The only challenge Sade found to nature's ends is the end of nature as a whole. Some of his works imagine a final state where nature itself is overcome in a massive act of self-destruction. If nature leads to its own obliteration, you may, of course, decide to view annihilation itself as a natural goal. This may be a consistent defense of the unity of nature and purpose. But it's hardly a source of solace.

SCHOPENHAUER: THE WORLD AS TRIBUNAL

Consider Schopenhauer as exclamation point. He was out of touch with his times, a century he saw scrambling to get rid of Kant and drink to Leibniz (Schopenhauer 1:510). Kant gave metaphysical expression to crisis and fracture. Those following him sought to heal it. Old models of Providence could not survive attacks like those of Hume and Sade. Struggling to articulate those attacks, the late eighteenth century showed its awareness that those models had broken down. The nineteenth century, by contrast, struggled to find a replacement for them. In the process, thinkers tried everything from history to economics to biology. No wonder Schopenhauer felt out of place. In an age bent on inventing whole sciences to detect signs of progress, his vision of a cosmic trend toward self-destruction was bound to be ignored.

Schopenhauer's dry elegance masks a despair so thoroughgoing that it may even remain untimely for darker epochs. In all of his writings,

> [l]ife presents itself as a continual deception, in small matters as in great. If it has promised, it does not keep its word, unless to show how little desireable the object was; hence we are deluded now by hope, now by what was hoped for. If it has given, it did so in order to take. The enchantment of distance shows us paradises that vanish like optical illusions, when we have allowed ourselves to be fooled by them. Accordingly happiness lies always in the future, or else in the past, and the present may be compared to a small dark cloud driven by the wind over the sunny plain; in front of and behind the cloud everything is bright, only it itself always casts a shadow. (Schopenhauer, 2:573)

His work was devoted to showing that suffering is the essence of existence. Only the form of the pain is a matter of accident. Our lives move between pain and boredom; we are pushed toward the one in an effort to avoid the other. These elements of reality are so fundamental that we even project them into that afterworld in which Schopenhauer had no faith.

> [A]fter man had placed all pains and torments in hell, there was nothing left for heaven but boredom. (Schopenhauer, 1:312)

Schopenhauer was casual about the means he used to establish his claims. He was happy to blend empirical observation and a priori argument, happiest of all when he could present some perverse contradiction built into the nature of things. He was convinced that all these support him.

He was well aware of those who preceded him. Though his plans to translate Hume's *Dialogues* came to naught, he was full of praise for Voltaire. His gratitude toward his predecessors was matched by his lack of mercy toward the views he opposed. He called Rousseau's work the superficial philosophy of a Protestant pastor (Schopenhauer, 2:585). Everything was fuel for his fire. To anyone who viewed the sexual impulse as a sign of harmony between human and natural purposes, he offered alternatives. He maintained that the sexual impulse is "the real lord of the world." But he thought that even satisfied passion brings more unhappiness than its opposite, for the will of the individual and that of the species show not unity but conflict (Schopenhauer, 2:555 ff.). Those who seek salvation by denying nature only confirm Schopenhauer more directly. Hatred of body and matter and all that's bound to this world proves his views: the universe is so ruled by suffering that Christianity cannot even represent itself except through a symbol of torture. After refusing "to give out Jewish mythology as philosophy," he turned to optimists who attack the Christian view that the world is a vale of tears. Schopenhauer found them simply laughable. Leibniz's view had no merit besides having given rise to "the immortal *Candide*"; the *Theodicy* is so palpably sophistical that it ought to be negated. So Schopenhauer, his tongue only half in cheek, presented an argument that this world is *the worst* of all possible. For a world slightly worse would cease to exist. The earthquake at Lisbon was but a "small, playful hint" at the destructive forces of nature; scientists know how easily some small change of heat or motion could bring the world to an end (Schopenhauer 2, 582 ff.). Existence is so precarious that any number of changes could render it entirely impossible.

> Consequently the world is as bad as it can possibly be, if it is to exist at all. Q.E.D. (Schopenhauer 2, 584)

Uncharacteristically, he forgot to add that this fact itself is fresh proof of life's perversity. For if this is how things are, why should there be something rather than nothing at all? Why shouldn't the universe go directly to the annihilation toward which it tends, and spare us all the torture on the way? Life is a battle we are certain to lose, for it consists in a struggle for existence that is destined to fail. Presumably, the long slow torment that precedes our deaths was Schopenhauer's substitute for hell.

Schopenhauer prided himself on being the first true atheist in German philosophy, and scorned his contemporaries' attempts to substitute a world spirit for a bankrupt deity. Yet he never abandoned a notion of cosmic justice. As in Sade, this remained when every other convention was violated. The first of Nietzsche's good Europeans,

Schopenhauer had no trouble rejecting a notion of Providence. What remains is Providence reversed.

> If we want to know what human beings, morally considered, are worth as a whole and in general, let us consider their fate as a whole and in general. This fate is want, wretchedness, misery, lamentation and death. Eternal justice prevails; if they were not as a whole contemptible, their fate as a whole would not be so melancholy. In this sense we can say that the world itself is the tribunal of the world. If we could lay all the misery of the world in one pan of the scales, and all its guilt in the other, the pointer would surely show them to be in equilibrium. (Schopenhauer, 1:352)

Moral and natural evils are perfectly balanced. The scales of justice remain when the judge is entirely absent: *the world itself is tribunal of the world*.

Belief in Providence presumes that we are innocent long after we've begun to look very suspicious. It does so by offering hope for an order behind appearances that will right the wrongs the appearances present. Rather than simply denying appearances, belief in Providence is belief that there's reason behind them. What looks like chance will be shown to make sense. Schopenhauer proposed something similar. We know that human lives consist of chains of misery. Could that much punishment be accidental? He was persuaded of eternal justice. What looks like its absence is but superficial appearance. He admitted that wicked people lead lives of pleasure, while good ones often suffer without vengeance or end. Schopenhauer set out to provide them with comfort. Unlike others, he offered no hope for redemption. Rather, he argued that their innocence, like individuality itself, was merely illusion. In reality, he thought tormentor and tormented are one. This is consolation so black it begins to be funny. Are you dismayed by a world full of innocent suffering? Don't despair: it's not so innocent. Of what is everyone guilty? There he turned to the poets: our greatest offense is having been born. How can life not be criminal, when it's always followed by capital punishment?

If we are infinitely deserving of the infinite misery that is our lot, then suicide is too good for us. Consequently Schopenhauer argued against it. Suicide contains an element of affirmation. One who takes his life rebels against the conditions he's been given, by refusing to live amid permanent pain. Thus suicide is still expression of will, for it remains an act of protest against the world as it is. Confronted by suffering, the suicide refuses to seize an opportunity:

> Suffering approaches, and as such, offers the possibility of a denial of the will; but he rejects it by destroying the will's phenomenon, the body, so that the will may remain unbroken. (Schopenhauer, 1:399)

Instead of suicide Schopenhauer recommended practices that destroy the will itself. He praised the Indian mystic who, after extirpating all other desire, is finally directed not to lie down too often under the same tree, lest he acquire a preference for it rather than another. Willing brings pain. In a conclusion more masochistic than coherent, Schopenhauer urged slow destruction of desire rather than the immediate self-destruction that kills the body but not the soul.

> Every fulfillment of our wishes won from the world is only like the alms that keep the beggar alive today so that he may starve again tomorrow. Resignation, on the other hand, is like the inherited estate; it frees its owner from all care and anxiety forever. (Schopenhauer, 1:390)

Such a standpoint expresses the kind of decadence only rich men's sons enjoy. But this criticism cannot be devastating when literal decadence, as in *decay*, is at issue. Schopenhauer's position refutes itself as little as Sade's does. The categorical imperative has nothing to say against resolute nihilism. Would a world built on such principles incline to self-destruct? No doubt about it. What lets us assume we can let matters rest there? For Schopenhauer as for Sade, destruction was the only desirable goal.

We are left to conclude that what's in need of justification is life itself.[19] This makes the problem of evil most urgent for those who insist that it has no solution. Chapter 1 considered the wish to change some piece of the world, in order to justify the world as a whole. I argued that such wishes cannot be contained. The thinkers considered in this chapter opposed theoretical attempts to change the world: philosophy, in this sense, leaves everything as it is. They were also dedicated to destroying ordinary belief in God. The shift of focus from God to reason showed that traditional theodicy was not the real object of attention, nor did shifting focus dissolve the problem. The conclusion that life, not God, is in need of defense, will seem very tempting—even if we can imagine no other defense of life than the living of it.

The wish to be God seems to require no refutation, and nothing will seem further from contemporary concerns. You are unlikely to share the tame and confident Deism of the eighteenth century. You may even view it as akin to cowardice, the response of those who cannot bear to imagine a world without a kind, all-seeing father. I have argued that eighteenth-century thinkers could bear a great deal. They subjected both Creator and Creation to ever-increasing fire and found their weapons in facts provided by life itself. Bayle used examples to show that human history consists of crime and misfortune. Though he used them for added emphasis, Schopenhauer thought examples superfluous: birth itself was crime and misfortune at once. If the arguments condemning Creation were increasingly brutal, descriptions of the Creator were worse. Bayle pictured God as a father who lets his child break his bones so as to show his skill at healing, then decided not to picture Him at all. Hume gave us pictures to arouse scorn and derision: God as ostrich, dumb shipwright, vain doddering fool. Sade's visions can cause terror. God is a vampire, an evil genius whose goal is to deceive us *and* to set a bad example. Against such images, the twentieth century looks dull and pale.

If modern philosophers continued to be engaged with theodicy, it was not out of innocence. They could imagine even darker scenarios than we managed to put into practice. Earlier thinkers were no more gullible than you are. Those occupied with theodicy knew every objection to it. Theodicy is never blind to critiques of God's goodness; it arises in response to them. Leibniz began writing about it in order to answer Bayle. Job's friends kept their mouths shut until Job began to curse. Theodicy is rarely naive. Is it for all that superstitious? Philoso-

phers often return to things they should have transcended. Even knowing they know nothing is not always guarantee of wisdom on that
score. Socrates was a symbol of skepticism toward traditional religion,
and the Athenians put him to death for it. But Hegel reminds us that
the last thing he did before dying was to offer the god Aesclepius a
sacrificial cock (Hegel 7, 1:116).

Chapter Three
ENDS OF AN ILLUSION

> Philosophy, like the overture to *Don Giovanni*, starts with a
> minor chord. . . . The more specific character of the astonish-
> ment that urges us to philosophize obviously springs from
> the sight of the evil and wickedness in the world. If our life
> were without end and free from pain, it would possibly not occur
> to anyone to ask why the world exists.
> —Schopenhauer, *The World as Will and Representation*

Chapter 1 examined philosophers who sought some reason or other behind the world's appearances that would explain or redeem or justify our experience. Whether they sought to show that the world could be accepted or that it could be changed can make all the difference in the world. My interest in dividing them was not worldly but metaphysical: to underline the differences between those philosophers, in chapter 1, who insist that reality is not what it seems, and those, in chapter 2, who insist that it is. The problem with appearances is not that they are flimsy, but that they are unyielding—indeed, often inexorable. The drive to metaphysics is a drive to find a real order behind the apparent one, in which all the things we long for—the good and the true and the beautiful—will be connected and revealed.

So described, this may be a project only Plato would admit to undertaking. But one needn't get stuck on the cave metaphor; above all, it's meant to teach us that our vision is blurred. What we see is not quite right, in both senses of the word. Philosophy begins with the demand that truth and goodness coincide. Leibniz held the right to consist in an order existing behind the appearances that only God—at the moment—knows how to decode. Marx held the right to consist in an order that humankind could establish only after it stops looking for signs of an order created by someone else. In practice, the difference between them could not be greater. In metaphysics, they were closer than they seem, for each denied that appearances are final. Whether they placed it in heaven or in history, each believed there was another court of appeal.

The alternative is the demand to stay with appearances; as Schopenhauer put it, to let the world itself be tribunal of the world. Its judgment could scarcely be bleaker. Those who insisted on remaining with that judgment could be as different as those who didn't. Voltaire's rejection of attempts to reconcile us to the world by appealing to Providence was clearly motivated by solidarity with the victims. For him, to defend God is to betray justice. Sade reveled in betrayal. Where his descriptions of the awfulness of appearance had normative thrust, he wished to provide us with role models. The search for reasons to explain appearances to us, or to reconcile us with appearances, can be refused on many grounds. The thinkers considered in chapter 2 rejected every form of mediation. Facing the world honestly meant facing it raw: experience is just what it seems.

Dividing thinkers into those who search for reasons independent of experience and those who refuse to do so ignores many important distinctions between them—as does the more traditional division of philosophers into rationalists and empiricists. Neither division makes any sense of Nietzsche, which is surely one reason why so many historians of philosophy left him alone for so long. As he predicted, his stature increased with time. Reading his work as centered on epistemology would require interpretive contortions too daunting to be tried very often. The question of whether he's rationalist or empiricist thus spares itself. But fitting him into the schema I've sketched is still more problematic. Nobody was more vehement in denying the existence of an order behind appearances, or in denouncing the attempt to find one as a denial of life. Yet nobody struggled harder against passively accepting appearances, nor warned more actively against nihilism. I do not find Nietzsche's alternative successful, but it's significant enough to undermine every effort to classify him as belonging to either group. In placing him outside them, I wish to underscore his allegiances to both. Nietzsche drew the consequences of both traditions. It was he who first diagnosed the narrative I recounted. He subjected the longing for order behind appearances to scrutiny so devastating that it can never be done innocently again.

But he knew that simply accepting the appearances is no solution either. Those who don't *do* something with them remain Stoics or slaves. Schopenhauer could serve as an educator, but like the appearances he was mired in, he must be overcome. Once you've diagnosed the sick longing that seeks reason behind appearances as well as the feeble resignation that preaches acceptance of them, what's the alternative? You may try to will appearances themselves. Nietzsche fulfilled the hopes and fears of all those who ever dreamed of taking a piece of Creation into their own hands.

Nietzsche's work revealed the centrality of the problem of evil precisely for those who recognized the futility of attempts to solve it. His obsession with the problem resulted not from nostalgia but from very clear sight. Nietzsche called the problem of evil

> my *a priori*. Indeed, as a thirteen year old boy, I was preoccupied with the problem of the origin of evil: at an age when one's heart was 'half-filled with childish games, half-filled with God' I dedicated my first literary childish game, my first philosophical essay, to this problem, and as regards my 'solution' to the problem at the time, I quite properly gave God credit for it and made him the *father* of evil. (Nietzsche 5, 16)

After outlining the solutions he developed over time, Nietzsche sketched the genealogical approach we know as Nietzschean.

> Out of my answers there grew new questions, inquiries, conjectures, probabilities—until at length I had a country of my own, a soil of my own, an entire discrete, thriving, flourishing world. (Nietzsche 5, 17)

To examine that world would be to examine Nietzsche's work as a whole. This might be necessary to thoroughly understand the transformation of the problem of evil that underpins all his work. Instead of trying to do so here, I wish to enter that world by sketching how his transformation of the problem of evil leads to the most radical of wishes to re-create the world. It's a transformation that puts him close enough to Freud to warrant our discussing them together. Both turned to genealogy in a moment of unmasking and thereby turned the problem of evil into a problem about us. Why and how we explore it reveals worlds about who we are.

ETERNAL CHOICES: NIETZSCHE ON REDEMPTION

The question could be raised during a conversational lull in a good salon: would you live your life over, if given the chance? Eighteenth-century thinkers took a rest from more serious business by discussing it. Few of them were entirely clear about the form of the question. Were they seeking an empirical survey, or a normative claim? Were they asking whether people in general, and any one of us in particular, would in fact repeat their lives over—or whether it would, on balance, be reasonable to do so? Either question might raise itself naturally, and either might be traced to classical sources. *Oedipus at Colonus*, one of the earliest, is suitably ambiguous: not to be born is the best thing. To die very quickly is a close runner-up. And

> This the truth, not for me only
> But for this blind and ruined man.
> (Sophocles, line 1224)[1]

Admittedly, it is Oedipus to whom the chorus is speaking. What about the rest of us?

Leibniz was interesting, and interestingly clear.

> Had we not knowledge of the life to come, I believe there would be few persons who, being on the point of death, were not content to take up life again, on condition of passing through the same amount of good and evil, provided always that it were not the same kind: one would be content with variety, without requiring a better condition than that wherein one had been. (Leibniz, 130)

The caveat is significant. Leibniz thought that the knowledge we have of the life to come must discontent us with the life we have. That aside, he was as clear about what such a survey would mean as he was certain of its results. Most people would repeat lives that contained the same quantity of good and evil, if they were assured of variety in form. Leibniz took this as evidence that the amount of evil in the world is smaller than the amount of good. One wonders what would follow if it weren't. Hadn't Leibniz said that whatever evil is, is necessary? Even if evil were something quantifiable, the quantities may not matter. His claim that this world is the best of all possible ones rests on arguments about possibility. Numbers are irrelevant. If x evils are a necessary part of the best possible world, the fact that x turns out to be plus or minus one (or a hundred, or . . .) should make no difference. But even Leibniz sometimes left the realm of logic to take up persuasion. The fact that most of us would choose to repeat our lives cannot be for him a proof, but it ought to be a suggestion. It functions like the fact that the world contains more houses than prisons—a fact he thought should give Bayle some pause. If most of us are settled in cosy domestic arrangements, can the world really be made up of so much crime? If most lives would be voluntarily lived over, Leibniz concluded those lives aren't so bad.

Voltaire disagreed. He admitted that most of us would, at death's door, choose to take our lives back. But this is a wish born from terror, fear of the unknown. Even then he thought variation was needed. People would rather die at once than die of boredom. Voltaire's remarks could be a comment on Hobbes: if life is solitary, poor, nasty, and brutish, who can complain if it's short? But complain we do, without stint or measure. Our reluctance to leave life is not the fruit of love. It's part of the network of fear and perversity that accompanies us from cradle to grave.

Hume denied he was expressing an opinion; ever the good empiricist, he just wished to report. Thus he both sharpened the question and recorded others' claims. After quoting classical sources on the subject, he let Demea, the *Dialogues*' voice of orthodox opinion, say the following:

Ask yourself, ask any of your acquaintance, whether they would live over again the last ten or twenty years of their life. No! but the next twenty, they say, will be better:

'And from the dregs of life, hope to receive
What the first sprightly running could not give.' (Dryden, *Aurengzebe*)

Thus at last they find (such is the greatness of human misery; it reconciles even contradictions) that they complain, at once, of the shortness of life, and of its vanity and sorrow. (Hume 3, 99–100)

Hume's own Philo reports that it was *formerly* very common to maintain that life was nothing but vanity and misery. Earlier ages exaggerated life's ills. He claims that worldviews have become more sanguine.

Divines, we find, begin to retract this position, and maintain, though still with some hesitation, that there are more goods than evils, more pleasures than pains, even in this life. (Hume 3, 115)

Reading the dismal views of Hume and his contemporaries should make us wonder: if this judgment is correct, how very bleak was the *seventeenth* century? Hume was more resolute than most in recommending an alternative. When life becomes unbearable, he saw no objection to suicide. Despite his evident satisfaction with life, Hume faced his own death with a self-conscious cheer unrivaled by anyone but Socrates.

Kant was predictable. He believed that nobody would repeat his life as a matter of pleasure. For a hedonist, little intelligence is needed to see that reliving would be against simple self-interest. Thank heaven for the existence of duty, since nothing else would ensure the continued existence of the species. Schopenhauer's position is equally foreseeable. He thought that we hide our misery just to save face. If we conceal the fact that our own lives confirm that "every life-history is a history of suffering," it's only to be spared other people's schadenfreude. But no one who is "sincere and in possession of his faculties" at the time of his death would choose to repeat that chain of misery he has experienced. In support of this conclusion Schopenhauer continued the conversation across several epochs:

> What has been said by the father of history (Herodotus) has not since been refuted, namely that no person has existed who has not wished more than once that he had not to live through the following day. Accordingly the shortness of life, so often lamented, may be perhaps the very best thing about it. If, finally, we were to bring to the sight of everyone the terrible sufferings and afflictions to which his life is constantly exposed, he would be seized with horror. If we were to conduct the most hardened and calloused optimist through hospitals, infirmaries, operating theaters, through prisons, torture-chambers, and slave-hovels, over battlefields and to places of execution; if we were to open to him all the dark abodes of misery, where it shuns the gaze of cold curiosity, and finally were to allow him to glance into the dungeons of Ugolino where prisoners starved to death, he too would certainly see in the end what kind of world is this *meilleur des mondes possibles*. For whence did Dante get the material for his hell, if not from this actual world of ours? (Schopenhauer, 1:324–25)

This is what one expects to find in Schopenhauer, at considerable length. But the view was hardly confined to him. Rather, it seemed so common that it was viewed as hard data. Its most surprising supporter may be Goethe, who is quoted in conversation with a historian.

> In all times and all countries things have been miserable. Men have always been in fear and trouble, they have pained and tortured each other; what little life they had, they made sour one to the other. The beauty of the world and the sweetness of existence which the beauty of the world offered them, they were not able to esteem or enjoy. Only to a few life became comfortable and enjoyable. Most people, after having played the game of life for a time, preferred to depart rather than to begin anew. That which perhaps gave or gives them some degree of attachment to life was and is the fear of death. Thus life is; thus it always

was; thus it will always remain. That is the lot of man. (Quoted
in Loewith, 229)

The text leaves us uncertain. It's hard to know whether Goethe condemned the standpoint he thought most people held, or whether he
shared it. But that ambiguity hardly saves him. His remarks are amaz-
ing. For they come from a man who received, in one lifetime, all the
world has to offer: love and friendship, chances to see the world and
to act upon it, creative achievement and the honors that ought to ac-
crue to it. Were you given a choice about *which* life to live over (and
over and over), you could hardly do better. Yet the dismal judgment
just quoted was not an aberration. He also wrote the prologue to *Faust*,
a good candidate for being the greatest general statement of world-
weariness in modern literature. At least in moments, his disgust with
life's evils and indifference to its goods was so great that he could
imagine selling his soul for the chance to affirm not life as a whole but
one single moment of it.[2]

Voltaire acknowledged that our stance toward life is affected by circumstance. Rousseau was the first to suggest that it may be a matter of
temperament. The question of whether we'd live our lives over doesn't
seem to be affected by any particular facts about them. Rousseau's
were extremely tough, as he never quite let anyone forget. Nor was he
willing to take refuge in any form of Stoicism urging that what's truly
important are not the goods of the world but our ability to be detached
from them. (Rousseau's distinctive suffering may have resulted from
his having been the first thinker who wished to unite, in one person,
all the things that life can give you. Goethe actually seems to have got
them.) Yet the clear-sighted view of the distance between what he
longed for and what he got never made Rousseau really bitter. His
description of the contrast between his own attitude and Voltaire's borders on the self-righteous, but it's nevertheless quite right.

That discussion takes place in his letter attacking Voltaire's poem
"The Lisbon Earthquake." The poem was received as a masterpiece of
despair. While some of its elements were new, its view of the value of
life was not: Voltaire simply stated, with unusual length and pathos,
the melancholy litany we have already heard. Rousseau's was the one

robust dissenting voice. He insisted that life is a gift, and asked why Voltaire hadn't noticed.

> I cannot help noticing, in conclusion, a very strange opposition between you and me in the subject of this letter. Rewarded with glory, and disabused of vain airs, you live freely in the breast of abandon. . . . Nevertheless you find nothing but evil in the world. And me, in obscurity, poor, alone, tormented by a suffering without remedy, I meditate with pleasure in my retreat and find that all is well. From where do these apparent contradictions come? You yourself have explained it—you rejoice, while I hope, and hope embellishes everything. (Rousseau 5, letter to Voltaire, August 18, 1756)

Rousseau was correct: the opposition is strange. Voltaire had his share of troubles, but they were, as Hebrew idiom puts it, troubles of rich men. His jeremiads didn't correspond to the blessings life gave him. Are those beside the point—perhaps even counter to it? Rousseau argued that those who live as nature intended estimate life itself differently.

> I daresay that there may not be in the upper Valais a single mountaineer who is unhappy with his life, and who would not voluntarily accept, even in place of paradise, an unending cycle of rebirth. (Ibid.)

Voltaire's conclusions were skewed by his samples. Instead of the sick, reflective aristocracy whose lives Rousseau had begun to diagnose, Voltaire should have looked to honest working people. Unlike the *philosophes*, they would gladly repeat their lives. Rousseau's letter contained an edge of resentment, and an appeal to simple folk that can become tedious, but he raised the right question. What allows some of us to affirm life in the face of disaster while the rest of us shuffle between cynicism and despair? You may call the question psychological as long as you remember that the answer may be mysterious; it can be called grace. What will be decisive is also a matter of description: how the world is seen long before it becomes an object of judgment. The bon mot about optimists and pessimists is tired but not false: even a stupid glass of water can be seen in radically different ways. Is optimism a matter of attitude?

Relations between philosophy and psychology are more than ever in need of investigation. No philosopher ever refuted Socrates' claim that the task of philosophy is self-knowledge. Indeed, much of philosophy's history can be seen as attempts to find a model for it. Hume's *Treatise*, Kant's first *Critique*, Hegel's *Phenomenology*, and Wittgenstein's *Investigations* offer very different pictures of what knowing the self might come to. Perhaps the only thing uniting them is a passionate determination to avoid the "merely" psychological. Rather, all maintained that the explorations of the soul they offered must be something else. The hostility toward psychologism in a field concerned with self-knowledge is deep and striking. For all the great differences between them, one thing uniting Rousseau and Nietzsche is disdain for other philosophers' distinctions between philosophy and psychology. Neither cared in the least about distinguishing between the self-knowledge that's the province of philosophy and that which comes from other kinds of reflection. In calling himself a psychologist, Nietzsche was almost as provocative as Rousseau was in writing the *Confessions*. For if what's at issue in the problem of evil is related to temperament, psychology would be the heir of metaphysics.

His *Twilight of the Idols* begins with the claim:

> In every age the wisest have passed the identical judgment on life: *it is worthless.* . . . Everywhere and always their mouths have uttered the same sound—a sound full of doubt, full of melancholy, full of weariness with life, full of opposition to life. (Nietzsche 6, 29)

Nietzsche thought the judgment that life is worthless revealed more about the judges than about life itself. Perhaps all the sages were decadents, old men too weak for life and literally sick of it? If so, they sought revenge. By positing a world beyond this one, they spoiled this one for the rest of us. "Why not a Beyond if not as a means of befouling the Here-and-Now?" (ibid.). Those who condemn this world just reflect their own impotence. The sage's response is nothing if not clever: it's a cosmic version of the fox's decision that the grapes were sour.

Instead of saying simply '*I* am no longer worth anything' the moral lie in the mouth of the decadent says: 'Nothing is worth anything—*life* is not worth anything.' (Nietzsche 6, 87)

Nietzsche thought that the problem of evil wasn't given but created—by those who were unequal to life. They thus created an ideal world to oppose to the real one. Values became inverted; in the light of the ideal world, the real world was despised. The clearest example of this process is Christianity, which saw the natural world as the locus of everything wrong: the misery we constantly suffer as punishment for the harm we constantly inflict. The supernatural world is the opposite, a negation of this one that redeems all its ills. But Christianity was just the lucid expression of a much wider view. Nietzsche called it Platonism for the people, but he didn't even think the standpoint was confined to Platonists. The longing for a life other than this one characterized most past sages. Nietzsche's deepest longing was to overcome them.

One thing at issue was a move from theory to practice, reflection to consequence, conviction to courage. What allows us to make it? Nietzsche's *The Birth of Tragedy* captured early Greek thought:

Thus do the gods justify the life of man: they themselves live it—the only satisfactory theodicy! (Nietzsche 1, 43)

Nietzsche's own work brought theodicy to life, moving among metaphysics, ethics, and psychology in ways that bound them irrevocably. After Nietzsche, *proving* that life is good should be beside the point. Anybody tempted to do so should be able to show it, for no other theodicy counts. (Anybody arguing the opposite should, presumably, be asked to consider how far he is prepared to go in meaning it.) Greek gods, argued Nietzsche, were willing to share human lives. That kind of theodicy makes theoretical justification redundant.

Nietzsche's eternal return turned a salon game into a method. Whether the world is a world that should be willed is no longer the question. Can you will it? Earlier sages could not. Their loathing and self-loathing were too close to disentangle. The world was despised by despicable people, who beguiled all the rest of us with life-destroying concepts. Who has the strength to will the world? Nietzsche used the question to reveal the essence of cultures as well as individuals. Consider the lives of the Olympians. Greek gods suffered the kinds of experiences you can imagine taking up and calling life interesting: betrayals of love and honor and power, treasures lost and stolen, plans failed, promises broken. The smaller sorts of heartbreak that really only matter when you're mortal. Given world enough, and time on your hands, you might choose to repeat them—again and again. By contrast, what Jesus took up was so fearful and awesome that not even eternity may suffice to redeem it. Imagine the choice now: you will give all of yourself out of love for the Other and in return have your flesh slowly tortured, your person despised. Could you will such a life—or would it be truly God-forsaken?

Nietzsche thought that such a life-world could be willed only by a deeply sick soul. Here conceptions of God and of Creation mirror each other too reciprocally to be separated. The picture of life and that of the God who gives it determine each other without end. Early Greeks lived in a world so rich with glory that in it, "lamentation itself became a song of praise" (Nietzsche 1, 43). What better gift could they give their gods than a never-ending share in it? When Christians imagine their god descending to dwell among them, the only life they can offer might make the most selfless among us long for another world.

It may have been one of Hegel's lectures that provoked Nietzsche's beloved Heine to scorn: "Berliner dialectics couldn't even kill a cat; how could they effect the death of God?" (Heine, 509). Nietzsche, like Heine, believed that earlier discussions were harmless. By mid–nineteenth century, calling God a human projection was almost trite. Nietzsche thought we needed stronger stuff. He was fond of Stendhal, who wrote that God's only excuse is that He doesn't exist. But to say that we killed Him is very far from saying we invented Him and finally owned up to our little fiction—the view of many a thinker before Nietzsche. He brought theodicy to a different kind of conclusion. God isn't merely absent, nor did He—pass away. He'd been on trial for some time, and judgment day was overdue.

> The 'father' in God has been thoroughly refuted; ditto the 'judge',
> the 'rewarder'. He does not hear—and if he heard he would still

not know how to help. Worst of all: he seems incapable of clear communication: is he unclear? (Nietzsche 4, 66)

After centuries of waiting for an answer less murky than what Job got from the Voice from the Whirlwind, humankind had had enough. Unafraid of images—all the horror of the Crucifixion, the dismembering of Dionysus—Nietzsche was obsessed with a god that dies.

Nietzsche was graphic, but not entirely explicit. After centuries of theodicy one might decide to let the defense rest, call in the verdict, and condemn the accused to execution. But Nietzsche was of two minds about whether we had just cause. The priests in his story were at least as culpable as the Being they served. He thus left questions of guilt open. For guilt is a concept Nietzsche sought to revise. He insisted that the consequences of God's death had not been measured. Earlier formulations of the problem of evil could agree on a question: How can there be justice and meaning in Creation when good people suffer? Nietzsche subjected all of these terms to radical questioning. Neither justice nor meaning nor good nor suffering would ever look the same. The death of God means that their senses must shift. Nietzsche made us conscious both of the religious origin of the problem of evil and of the fact that abolishing religion cannot solve it—except at the price of world-destroying nihilism.

It's easy to see that the loss of God entails the loss of grounding. Without a Creator to put it there, meaning can no longer be part of the world. But the cheerful humanist response is one Nietzsche could not share. To acknowledge that old values had no foundation, and continue to maintain them all the same, seemed to him bad faith. Not even Kant could abandon the idea that morality should be reflected in nature, though he denied that it was grounded in it. Nietzsche thought that to look toward nature for signs to guide us is a relic of slave morality: we want to be commanded. Earlier thinkers walked up to the opposition between reason and nature, but they couldn't really face it. Nietzsche makes the opposition clear. Real and rational are not merely unrelated; they stand with daggers drawn. One of them must give in.

There is no mediation between *is* and *ought*. Life and morality cannot be reconciled; one always condemns the other. Nietzsche thought that two millennia provided variation on one kind of surrender. The real was condemned by the rational, again and again.

> For confronted with morality (especially Christian or uncondi-tional morality) life *must* continually and inevitably be in the wrong, because life *is* something essentially amoral—and eventu-ally, crushed by the weight of contempt and the eternal No, life *must* then be felt to be unworthy of desire and altogether worth-less. Morality itself—how now? Might not morality be a will to negate life; a secret instinct of annihilation, a principle of decay, diminution and slander—the beginning of the end? Hence the danger of dangers? (Nietzsche 1, 23)

For morality, the existence of suffering is a condemnation of life itself. Nietzsche suggested we try the other alternative. Humankind became sick by letting suffering serve as an argument against life. Why not let life serve as refutation of suffering?

Nietzsche shared the goal of the thinkers we saw in chapter 1. Like them he sought to redeem reality, not simply to acquiesce in it or cry against it. But the difference between them is enormous. For Nietzsche, reality must be redeemed not from any intrinsic failings but from the curse placed on it by the ideal. Humanism, the attempt to retain tradi-tional ideals within an atheist framework, maintained the curse against reality. It just abandoned the forces that give curses power. By continu-ing to oppose an ideal of life to the reality of it, humanism continues to condemn life with every breath.

The problem of evil is thus the problem of evil itself.[3] It's a problem humankind brought on itself by creating ideals that put life in the wrong. If we created the problem, we should be able to resolve it, when we recognize the depth of transformation we must undergo. The problem of evil was *meaningless* suffering. Pain that makes sense is not hard to bear. Making sense of it involved finding both good cause for it and good consequences of it. So we invented sin and redemption. Sin gave pain an origin, and redemption gave it a telos. Humankind prefers masochism to meaninglessness. We took the blame for suffer-ing on ourselves in order to give life meaning. Christianity held such sacrifice to be so profound that it projected the act onto God Himself.

Volunteering for torture to save humankind was the early Christian paradigm, and later souls did to spirit what the saints did to flesh.

Nietzsche sometimes described guilt as an act of revenge: moral denunciation was the product of slaves determined to spoil for others the life they could not enjoy. More interesting passages describe martyrdom in the service of meaning as something that almost made sense. Indeed, it did make sense, which is why the demand for sense itself must be altered.

> Except for the ascetic ideal: man, the animal man, had no meaning up to now. His existence on earth had no purpose; 'What is man for, actually?' was a question without an answer; there was no will for man and earth; behind every great human destiny sounded the even louder refrain 'in vain!' This is what the ascetic ideal meant: something was missing, there was an immense lacuna around man. . . . suffering itself was not his problem, but the fact that there was no answer to the question he screamed 'Suffering for what?' . . . The meaninglessness of suffering, not the suffering, was the curse which has so far blanketed mankind—and *the ascetic ideal offered man a meaning!* . . . Within it, suffering was given an interpretation; the enormous emptiness seemed filled; the door was shut on suicidal nihilism. (Nietzsche 5, 162)

The ascetic ideal divided suffering in two and thereby gave it meaning. If the natural evil you suffer results from the moral evil you do, all your suffering is intelligible. Modern thought tried to restructure the relation but retained the demand for sense. The view of natural evils as punishment for moral evils could not survive the Lisbon earthquake. The impulse to disconnect them entirely, and to mark the disconnection by abolishing the very term 'natural evil', was thus easy to follow. Still the urge to relate moral and natural evils remained powerful even for those who naturalized both. Rousseau took the idea that you suffer for your sins, and built it into natural law. Though he praised Rousseau's account, and often presupposed it, Kant's separation of natural and moral evil was more decisive. He was consequently tormented by how to relate them. In the end he left us with little but the claim that reason has a need for them to be related—a claim that skeptics could argue was the place where the problem began.

After Kant the focus shifted. The demand that we reject theodicy by considering human, not divine, responsibility increased in force. Until we have eradicated the evil that's in our hands, why worry about the evil that isn't? Even Hegel's attempt to make philosophy become theodicy turned to human history. Nietzsche's work radicalized the modern attempt to take increasing responsibility for the world. For Nietzsche, we are responsible not only for particular moral evils but for the very concept of evil itself.

In moments he sounds like Feuerbach gone to the opera, a sort of humanist for aesthetes. If he were, his message would be simpler: redemption lies in our hands. We need only take on the role of Creator we once gave to God, making objects redolent with meaning as we thought He made worlds. Life has no meaning? Very well, then, let's give it some. That's what it means to be modern. God is dead? He'd been getting feebler every decade. Did you expect Him to last forever?

But this is not Nietzsche's standpoint. It belongs to those Last Men for whom Nietzsche's message will seem mad. And the Last Men are unspeakably vulgar. For a philosopher who thought life justified as aesthetic phenomenon, vulgarity is a philosophical reproach. But it's not the only possible reproach to this do-it-yourself meaning. Nietzsche insisted that the move to the modern was neither natural nor inevitable. The demand to displace God and call it maturity will thus not be enough. Both his denial of progress and his claim that God did not simply wither away require something stronger. If God died at our hand, we cannot take His place without further ado. We must undergo a process of divinization ourselves.

Nietzsche spent a lifetime wondering which god to become. Many of his texts suggest Dionysus as the clear favorite. But why call his intellectual autobiography *Ecce Homo*, or write *Zarathustra* in the style of the Gospels, choked with allusions to the Sermon on the Mount? Let us say he couldn't decide it with precision. He was clear, however, that religion cannot be merely abandoned. We cannot get rid of its power until we get rid of the needs that created it.

So far, this is almost Marx. To see why Nietzsche would dismiss a Marxist solution as coarse and pointless, we must think about time. The metaphysical wound created in the struggle between reason and reality cannot be healed by the future so long as the pain of the past remains. This pain creates resentment and all its bitter consequences. To think that suffering can be redeemed by the demonstration that it's necessary for future good is not only to be instrumentalist; it shows you know nothing about pain. Time itself does not heal; it only buries. Nineteenth-century discussions of the problem of evil turned to history, in part, because history is unbearable. The future is still undetermined. If it's not easy to face it with hope, it's not hard to face it with confidence. But *past* horror and sorrow threaten to overwhelm us with rage and despair. Both Hegel and Marx tried to redeem the past by showing it to be a necessary bridge to the future. If this worked, ordinary human beings would be enough for salvation. Superhuman ones are needed because salvation is not a matter of reparations. You cannot do anything to make good that which is not. Nor can the past be repaired. The stumbling block is that which was. In the chapter of *Zarathustra* called "On Redemption" Nietzsche explained:

> To redeem the past and to turn every "It was" into a "Thus I willed it"—that would be what I call redemption! I teach you will, my friends—this is the name of the liberator and bearer of joy! But learn this as well: the will itself is still a prisoner. Will liberates—but what is the name of that which still puts the liberator in chains? "It was": this is the name of the will's gnashing teeth and misery. Powerless against that which happened, it is a bitter observer of all the past. (Nietzsche 3, 142)

We cannot will backward. This fact drives the will to rage and revenge. *Move on and think about the future.* Advice that is trite as psychology gets no deeper if you make it into metaphysics. This is not redemption of pain but repression of it. And Nietzsche is too good a psychologist to ignore what becomes of pain repressed.

The question that began as elevated diversion became the key to redemption. Nietzsche's doctrine of eternal return is meant to save your soul. The eternal return is "only a thought experiment," as is sometimes suggested, if you call heaven and hell thought experiments too. For the Christian, life is justified in light of the afterworld. All events in his life's narrative gain their meaning through the ending: did they lead to heaven or hell? The ease with which Providence became progress served Nietzsche as warning. Theological conceptions condition our experience. Only a deliberate countertheology is powerful enough to combat them. Proof is beside the point, for the claim that history has no end is as easy to prove as the claim that it has one. Neither will ever be known. Both are standpoints that frame our lives. In one case, life has meaning through a telos that is other than itself. The significance of each moment derives from moments that came before and after it.

Nietzsche could have attacked this conception without offering another. Why not forget time altogether? Meaning might be found in every moment. Why did Nietzsche ask us to suppose that every moment recurs? First, he believed that when joy is genuine, we cannot let it go. Joy demands eternity. If you will an instant you will the world as a whole, for the urge to call *Verweile doch* to a passing moment is not one that can be contained. (Stay awhile. For an hour? A weekend?) Second, the eternal return is needed to replace cosmological conceptions whose staying power proved remarkable. Kant abolished God from the realm of discourse, but Hegel thought Him more present in modern philosophy than ever before. Years after Hegel wrote that God was dead, Marx was still certain that religion was the place for criticism to begin. And in the midst of all the furor, Heine could not write a history of philosophy without writing a history of religion at the same time. If God was murdered, and analyzed to death, why did His shadows remain?

Nietzsche thought we could not forsake God because we cannot forsake the past. If there were gods, cries Zarathustra, how could I bear not to be one? True redemption isn't humble. It won't rest content with willing the future. As genealogist, Nietzsche knew how thoroughly the future is conditioned by the past. If we cannot create the past, we are not real creators at all. Earlier attempts at *imitatio Dei* were halfhearted. If you cannot will the world as it was in the beginning, you will be poisoned by your own impotence.

The will must be entirely active. Any Stoic can accept his fate. Nietzsche challenged us to love it. The presence of contingency demands that fate be loved as a whole. If you never know which events will turn out to determine your life, all of them are significant. Terrible moments and trivial ones must equally become objects of will. Giving up the problem of evil means giving up the opposition that created it. This means abandoning the contrast between the ideal that evil should not exist and the real which reminds us that it does. To do this would be to will evil itself, both that which we do and that which we suffer.

Nietzsche's defense of willing the evil we do cannot be discussed fully here. For the present I will only note that radical elitism lightens the burden of theodicy. If you don't feel bound to redeem everybody's suffering equally, half the work is done before you start. But though the menace implied by his praise of blond beasts caused no end of trouble, his discussion of the evils we suffer is in fact more extensive. The two are closely connected, but his praise of the evils we suffer may be in the end more puzzling. What does it mean to will your pain?

Though he called himself a Stoic at least once, Nietzsche was usually at pains to distinguish his conception from a Stoic one. *Accepting* suffering is not enough. His works are full of great one-liners about the value of pain: how profoundly you can suffer determines your nobility; whatever doesn't kill you makes you stronger.

> The discipline of suffering, of great suffering—do you not know that only this discipline has created all enhancements of man so far? That tension of the soul in unhappiness which cultivates its strength, its shudders face to face with great ruin, its inventiveness and courage in enduring, persevering, interpreting, and exploiting suffering, and whatever has been granted to it of profundity, secret, mask, spirit, cunning, greatness—was it not granted to it through suffering, through the discipline of great suffering? In man *creature* and *creator* are united: in man there is material, fragment, excess, clay, dirt, nonsense, chaos; but in man there is also creator, form-giver, hammer hardness, spectator divinity, and seventh day; do you understand this contrast? And that *your* pity is for the "creature in man", for what must be formed, broken,

forged, torn, burnt, made incandescent, and purified—that which *necessarily* must and *should* suffer? And *our* pity—do you not comprehend for whom our converse pity is when it resists your pity as the worst of all pamperings and weaknesses? (Nietzsche 4, 154)

But which god was it who took on the deepest suffering—not merely accepting but choosing it? His praise of suffering can easily raise the question: If you like suffering all that much, why don't you just go out and be a Christian?[4] Why not Christ himself? Nietzsche's later work is full of fantasies about the option.

Thinking about Nietzsche provokes impieties in every direction. If he could never quite decide which god he wished to become, he was equally uncertain about the value of divine humility. While his praise of great suffering could veer toward the Christlike, he urged an acceptance of the given that is second to none. To will the world in all its detail requires a dizzying mixture of exaltation and submission.

What exactly is the difference between willing the world forever and calling it the best of all possible ones? Nietzsche's work tried to overcome theodicy by offering a bolder version of it. Kant allowed us to imagine creating laws of nature. Nietzsche urged us to become creators of the whole world, not just the good parts; the past as well as the future. Loving the fate you cannot change may be a sign of good taste. But the very elegance of the attitude Nietzsche calls life-affirming leaves his view suspicious. Did Nietzsche cherish a view close to Leibniz's after all—a sort of hyper-Stoicism, slave morality for aristocrats?

Of course Leibniz believed in truth, and if foundations are your worry, you may find this difference decisive. To call this world the best possible is to say there could have been others. For Nietzsche, necessity and accident turn out to converge. Praise of one and praise of the other are less in conflict than they seemed. All the more reason to fear that his views end in titanic submission. At least hypothetically, Leibniz's view left room to imagine other worlds. Nietzsche's may deny us even that.

To insist that this world is the only one available is not to start on the road to theodicy but to refuse to take it. A theodicy does more by way of justification. It must show why things that seemed to be re-proaches against the world are not. Leibniz was roundly attacked for doing so little on this score, but even he made concessions. To be reconciled to evils, he knew, we needed to hear more than the general claim that they're necessary. So he sometimes argued they were neces-sary for particular goods. Leibniz reminded us that in order to perceive light, there has to be shadow, that a life containing nothing but sweet-ness would be cloying. One must wonder about his choice of example. This sort of thing may help reconcile you to bad weather, or publishers' rejections. Not even Job's friends would try it on hard cases.

Nietzsche did make general claims that seem eerily Leibnizian: hap-piness and unhappiness are sisters, even twins. On occasion it could be rousing: if you don't embrace unhappiness, you will never know happiness, but at best merely comfort. When picking examples, he tried to talk tough. He knew that what must be faced is not just unpleas-ant but actually evil, the sort of thing that led other eras to celebrate triumphs with autos-da-fé. Now Leibniz sometimes bit bullets too. He insisted that this world was the best one even if it turned out to include the burning of unbaptized babies in hell. Usually, however, he avoided hard cases as Nietzsche did not.

But despite his attempt to pick outrageous examples, Nietzsche's paradigms of suffering sound more like weltschmerz than anything else. And weltschmerz may be acceptable where suffering is not. You may be willing to embrace pain in the course of a life that is richer than one where you feel very little at all. But your willingness may stop at the sort of pain that annihilates great souls instead of ennobling them. (To say that they wouldn't have been annihilated if they'd been greater is to beg too many questions, which Nietzsche sometimes does.) To put the problem differently: one can't help suspecting that Nietzsche sometimes imagined himself on the wrong side of the auto-da-fé. Em-bracing the evil involved in watching (not to mention causing) suffer-ing is another matter than embracing what's involved when you're con-sumed by it.

Leave—for the moment—such objections aside. Suppose Nietzsche's view is talking about suffering, not weltschmerz, and suf-fering from the standpoint of one who actually suffers. This suffering will be applauded as a condition of greatness of soul. But isn't this the sort of instrumentalist redemption he elsewhere attacks? Is suffering significant only as a means to greater ends?

Nietzsche often returned to the metaphor of childbirth. For the Greeks, he argued,

> [e]very individual detail in the act of procreation, pregnancy, birth, awoke the most exalted and solemn feelings. In the teachings of the mysteries *pain* is sanctified: the "pains of childbirth" sanctify pain in general—all becoming and growing, all that guarantees the future, *postulates* pain. . . . For the eternal joy in creating to exist, for the will to life eternally to affirm itself, the "torment of childbirth" must also exist eternally. . . . All this is contained in the word "Dionysus." (Nietzsche 6, 109–10)

Christianity, Nietzsche concluded, needed to find a meaning for the pain of childbirth. Common senseless suffering was too hard to bear. Christianity discovered its meaning by looking backward to causes. It concluded that procreation must be evil, since it leads to suffering like that. A freer, noble, Hellenic worldview reverses the process. It found the meaning of suffering by looking toward the future. Thus suffering became necessary and exalted, for it belongs to the process of creation itself.

With such metaphors Nietzsche came so close to Christian views that sanctify suffering that it is hard to tell them apart. But that objection is mild next to problems posed by the metaphor itself. For were all suffering like suffering in childbirth, it would always make perfect sense. The pain is so brief, the end is so good, that a lifetime of misery in return for eternal paradise is scarcely a better exchange. Childbirth is the paradigm of *meaningful* suffering—in simple and straightforward terms. It's a paradigm that informed Nietzsche's discussion even as he recognized that the problem of evil concerns *meaningless* suffering. And so it leaves untouched the question: What if evil creates nothing?

At times, Nietzsche's claims can appear *crudely* instrumental: evils provide poets with topics as the Trojan War provided the gods with entertainment. Nietzsche wasn't alone in viewing tragedy as the highest form of human narrative. Unlike others, he simply refused to shrink from conclusions: if there's going to be tragedy, there's got to be raw material for it. Your pain is a model. If you don't find a way to use it, a better artist will. Even when put less crudely, Nietzsche's claims can look instrumental. To say that suffering is needed to ennoble your soul seems still to give it meaning by making it something other than it is.

If Nietzsche had an answer to this worry, it was aesthetic. He knew we have yet to understand the phenomenon of tragedy. Aristotle's discussion of catharsis came too close to suggesting that we watch it out of schadenfreude. But Nietzsche thought tragedy produced real joy.

There is no such thing as pessimistic art. Art affirms. Job affirms. (Nietzsche 9, 435)

If tragedy affirms life, it serves as a model as nothing else can. Nietzsche said it gives metaphysical comfort. For only art can turn horror into something sublime. It does so by refusing to make sense of it. Tragedy offers form in place of meaning. The tragic worldview declined after Socrates introduced the idea that beauty and intelligibility go together. Plato followed him by banning tragedy because it was an unreasonable genre. Why should his republic permit stories full of causes without effects and effects without causes (Nietzsche 1, 84–89)?

Nietzsche wrote that life could be justified only as an aesthetic phenomenon. This amounts to giving up the demand that it be intelligible. For the aesthetic is exactly that which has no meaning. Here music served him as constant example. Any attempt to state the *meaning* of a piece of music is less false than off-key. Music makes apparent what all great art reveals: to speak of its meaning is more than mistaken. Meaning can be expressed independently, but the meaning of tragedy is not even unstatable. Ditto, the meaning of life. As in a work of art, it will be present in every note and line, every moment and every measure—or it will not be present at all. To insist that life is justified as art is not to find a new way of giving life meaning but to demand that we stop seeking it.

So Nietzsche claimed that to will one moment is to will every moment. For to will a moment is to will it for itself, not for anything to which it points or from which it follows. Initially, you might think Faust's bargain too cheap. Shouldn't he have demanded at least a year?

Nietzsche always returned to Faust's longing to affirm just *one* moment in time. This is not a Leibnizian point: you cannot pick and choose your sequences, will pleasure without pain. Rather, whenever you will sequences, you will things that have meaning through causes and consequences. To will one moment would be to affirm it without seeking its meaning. If you could do that, you could affirm the world as a whole.

So willing your suffering is aesthetic through and through. If the quality of the story is all that matters, explaining all your misery by reference to Prometheus is simply more attractive than explaining it through the Fall.

> That man should freely dispose of fire without receiving it as a present from heaven, either as a lightning bolt or as the warming rays of the sun, struck these primitive men as sacrilege, as a robbery of divine nature. Thus the very first philosophical problem immediately produces a painful and irresolvable contradiction between man and god and moves it before the gate of every culture, like a huge boulder. The best and highest possession mankind can acquire is obtained by sacrilege and must be paid for with consequences that involve the whole flood of sufferings and sorrows with which the offended divinities have to afflict the nobly aspiring race of men. This is a harsh idea which, by the dignity it confers on sacrilege, contrasts strangely with the Semitic myth of the fall in which curiosity, mendacious deception, susceptibility to seduction, lust—in short, a series of preeminently feminine affects was considered the origin of evil. What distinguishes the Aryan notion is the sublime view of active sin as the characteristically Promethean virtue. With that, the ethical basis for pessimistic tragedy has been found: the justification of human evil, meaning both human guilt and the suffering it entails. (Nietzsche 1, 71)

How would you prefer to imagine the forebears who got you in trouble? Kicked out of God's kingdom in shame and confusion, bent over clutched fig leaves and seeking others to blame? Or proud and defiant, conscious and bold? Put like that, the answer looks easy. Remember, you are to imagine absolutely nothing, without form and void. Which beginning can you will from it, which origin of woe? It's hardly even a question, until you remember the end of the story: Prometheus chained to a boulder, his liver devoured. (Earning one's bread by the sweat of one's brow is, after all, something to which most of us have become accustomed. Marx went so far as to call it fundamentally human.) If Nietzsche wished to abolish meaning the way art abolishes meaning, he must insist that stories are whole: who wills the beginning, wills the end. This is a test.

ON CONSOLATION: FREUD VS. PROVIDENCE

Nietzsche's work revealed the resonance of the problem of evil. Long after it was found to be unsolvable, we could not let it go. Its sources were too deep, its orbit too wide. Too many needs fueled it; too many concepts were conditioned by it. It was simply too big to be defeated by argument—or even by the death of its leading protagonist. Nietzsche confirmed that the problem of evil may engage you most in the moments when you reject its most central premises. Indeed, he thought that the demand to abolish religion itself arose from religious impulses. *Beyond Good and Evil* described the death of God as a religious sacrifice. Freud called Nietzsche the most self-knowing man who ever lived. But the fact that he was conscious of his religious impulses made them no less religious. Nietzsche's very obsession with the death of God was a way to ensure His survival. The richness of his work, and all the ambiguity indicated it, left many paths open. In *Zarathustra* he created a prophet. Freud refused to be one.

Even more than Nietzsche, Freud created the most widespread assumptions that determine contemporary thought on the subject. Two centuries of thinkers' hacking away at the truth-value of statements about Providence were less effective in undermining belief in them than two decades of psychoanalytically oriented culture. For belief in Providence arose not because it seemed to fit the evidence but just because it didn't. A simple believer like Justine knows as well as a sophisticated theorist like Hegel: you're most inclined to argue that there's reason in the world in the moments you're afraid there isn't. Hence even after Nietzsche, you could take the world's resistance to the reasonable not as refutation but as challenge. Of course the ways of Providence are hard to fathom; that's the point where labor started. The very fact that work continues, despite the poverty of its results, seems to show we're on the right track. We may never understand how everything that happens, happens for the best, but that's no cause to stop trying. For mustn't there be a reason why such efforts have persisted against all the evidence that defies our hopes?

Freud offered a reason, and it wasn't very attractive. Our massive attempts to seek sense in misery are fueled by childhood fantasies and feelings of loss. Since these experiences are at least as universal and persistent as the belief in Providence itself, they're the right sorts of thing to explain it. Not until the belief in Providence was uncovered as a function of universal needs could we begin to let it go. For nothing works so well in getting someone to give up a position as making him feel ashamed of it. Kant and Hegel said we seek to be at home in the world. Freud took the homeless metaphor seriously and said that we were infantile. We really do long to go home—possibly all the way home—but we can't. The metaphor lost the depth and wit it had in Kant's work, and the dreamy effulgence it acquired with the Romantics. We are not, as Hegel put it, adventurous mariners on stormy seas—just lost children seeking protection we never really had. Earlier empiricists condemned the architect. Freud sought the source of the assumption that somebody owes us a home. The very longing to be at home in the world must be based on a model of Creation. Only a notion of a Creator, who does things according to intentions, gives rise to a theodicy problem at all. For homes are the products of conscious, indeed beneficent thought. Of course we long for a world to feel at home in. Freud makes the desire seem not deep but embarrassing.

The Future of an Illusion put the view baldly: religion is a universal obsessional neurosis of humanity, stemming from the Oedipus complex. It will inevitably be abandoned at the moment we acknowledge that we can't retain our youth. To be sure, abandoning illusions will cause pain. It hurts people to admit they are

no longer the object of tender care on the part of a beneficent Providence. They will be in the same position as a child who has left the parental house where he was so warm and comfortable. But surely infantilism was destined to be surmounted. Men cannot remain children forever; they must in the end go out into 'hostile life'. We may call this *'education to reality'*. Need I confess to you that the sole purpose of my book is to point out the necessity for this forward step? (Freud 1, 233)

For any other question at all—even one that affects us so little as the question whether whales lay eggs—we demand more proof than we have for Providence. What leads us to clasp so strongly claims so unsupported by evidence? Having posed the question that way, Freud found the answer simple. The intensity of belief in Providence derives from the intensity of the terror and helplessness felt by the child. These emotions are so powerful that he invents an even more powerful father to whom he can cling throughout a lifetime. The "oceanic feeling" of oneness with the universe, sometimes a spur to religious emotion, may be experienced by a few. But infantile helplessness and need for a father's protection are felt by us all, and

the feeling is not simply prolonged from childhood days, but is permanently sustained by fear of the superior power of fate. (Freud 2, 20)

Fate, for Freud, is our word for untamed nature, and it is always superior to us. Civilization is an attempt to defend us against nature and remove all its terrors. It begins by anthropomorphizing: projecting will and intention into the blind and impersonal forces that threaten us makes them less distant and frightening. We can thereby feel "at home in the *unheimlich*." The powers remain superior to us, but at least we can react to them. And who knows? Perhaps the same tricks and negotiations that sometimes succeed in controlling hostile forces in the social world will function in the cosmos at large. So we try to bribe and appease the forces we've projected onto nature just as we try to influence the human powers that be.

We are so desperate to find a way of controlling the terrors that beset us that we invented guilt as a keystone of explanation. We prefer a system of self-punishment to remaining in the dark. Here Freud followed Nietzsche and added his own brilliant set of reflections. Primitive man beats his fetish when he meets with misfortune; civilized man beats himself. Israel's commitment to its role as the favorite child of a divine father didn't waver in the least when it met one misery after the next. Rather, it invented the prophets. They claimed that its suffering resulted from its guilt, and gave it a list of commands to avert future misfortune. Since the list was so long, the likelihood of the commandments' ever being followed by the entire people was very slim. Thus Israel could continue to feel in control of its suffering *in principle* while continuing to suffer nevertheless.

In so doing, it followed a universal process Freud thought emerged with the Greeks. Their gods were invented to serve three functions: to exorcize the terrors of nature, to reconcile us to the cruelty of fate, and to compensate us for the suffering that civilization itself imposes. But the functions gradually shifted. Nascent science revealed internal laws within nature, allowing us to substitute natural for supernatural explanation. And all the burnt entrails and entreaties notwithstanding, the gods seemed to be utterly inept at fulfilling their second function, controlling our fate.

> As regards the apportioning of destinies, an unpleasant suspicion persisted that the perplexity and helplessness of the human race could not be remedied. It was here that the gods were most apt to fail. If they themselves created Fate, then their counsels must be deemed inscrutable. The notion dawned on the most gifted people of antiquity that Moira (Fate) stood above the gods and that the gods themselves had their own destinies. And the more autonomous nature became and the more the gods withdrew from it, the more earnestly were all expectations directed to the third function of the gods—the more did morality become their true domain. (Freud 1, 198)

Freud suggested that morality was invented to give the gods something to do. Unnecessary in their first task and incompetent in the second, they were increasingly employed in the third one. Making the gods responsible for the defects of civilization by legitimizing the repression we suffer was a wonderful use of otherwise idle powers. The gods' new occupation was to sanction morality, which now appeared as the result of divine prohibition. This explained our suffering as a consequence of our sin in a way that allowed us to go on suffering *and* sinning—while keeping sinning within bounds required for civil society to function.

Freud knew that none of these considerations constitutes an argument against belief in an order of cosmic justice. One can continue to believe in some version of Providence despite Freud's description of the source of belief, just as one can continue to maintain it despite Hume's description of its irrationality. The difference is only, as it were, psychological. After we uncover the process through which we develop those beliefs

> our attitude to the problem of religion will undergo marked displacement. We shall tell ourselves that it would be very nice if there were a God who created the world and was a benevolent Providence, and if there were a moral order in the universe and an after-life; but it is a very striking fact that all this is exactly as we are bound to wish it would be. And it would be more remarkable still if our wretched, ignorant and down-trodden ancestors had succeeded in solving all these difficult riddles of the universe. (Freud 1, 215)

Our beliefs may not be false, but they are certainly humiliating. In *Civilization and Its Discontents*, written three years later, Freud was even more devastating. It *hurts* to realize that the majority of humankind lives with a worldview structured and determined by infantile terror.

> The whole thing is so patently infantile, so foreign to reality, that to anyone with a friendly attitude to humanity it is painful to think that the great majority of mortals will never be able to rise above this view of life. It is still more humiliating to discover how large a number of people living today, who cannot but see that this religion is not tenable, nevertheless try to defend it piece by piece in a series of pitiful rearguard actions. One would like to mix among the ranks of the believers in order to meet these philosophers, who think they can rescue the God of religion by replacing

him by an impersonal, shadowy and abstract principle, and to address them with the warning words: "Thou shalt not take the name of the Lord thy God in vain!" (Freud 2, 23)

Notice the rough way Freud rides over distinctions among natural, moral, and metaphysical evils. From the point of view of the affected individual, all these are just instances of a simple fact:

Life, as we find it, is too hard for us; it brings us too many pains, disappointments, and impossible tasks. (Freud 2, 23)

This is the perspective of the child, who has not yet learned to make the distinctions we use to try to bring our suffering under control. We are threatened with misery from three directions: our own bodies bring pain, eventually decay and dissolution; the external world rages against us with merciless forces of destruction; other people make us suffer. Freud called the last the most painful because we experience it as gratuitous. Surely cruelty at the hands of beings like ourselves could be avoided, if earthquakes and tempests cannot? He believed the one to be as inevitable as the other. Most interesting is his view that they are two species of a common threat to our purposes—the happiness that comes from the satisfaction of needs embodied in the pleasure principle. Freud thought that we share the same, straightforward view of the purpose of life. We wish to become happy and remain so. But

[t]here is no possibility at all of its being carried through; all the regulations of the universe run counter to it. One feels inclined to say that the intention that man should be 'happy' is not in-cluded in the plan of 'Creation'. (Freud 2, 25)

From the point of view of the pleasure principle we remain undiscrimi-nating babies. An earthquake and a war equally thwart our intentions and may cause us equal pain. All suffering is, finally, a matter of sensa-tion that exists just as long as we feel it. It should follow that any activity which decreases painful sensations is ipso facto good. Some means of palliating our miserable reality is clearly indispensable. Freud refrained from making recommendations. The reduced sense of happiness he thought may be possible will depend on the economics of the individual libido. In contrast to religion, which holds one form of coping with suffering to be valid for everyone, Freud preached tolerance. He thought each must discover the best way to be saved.

Intoxicating substances and simple mania are, Freud wrote, the most effective means of coping with suffering. For both produce the greatest degree of independence from the external world. They allow us to withdraw at any time from painful reality and find refuge in our own. Their effectiveness is also their danger. This limits their use in the social economics of libido. Though Freud thought they will always have a place in civilization, the injury and waste caused by intoxication and madness led us to seek more useful forms of flight. In particular, we invented culture.

As an effective form of compensating the frustration created by miserable reality, culture has much to recommend it. This is what Voltaire meant, said Freud, by ending *Candide* with the advice to cultivate one's garden.

> One gains the most if one can sufficiently heighten the yield of pleasure from the sources of psychical and intellectual work. When that is so, fate can do little against one. A satisfaction of this kind, such as an artist's joy in creating, in giving his fantasies body, or a scientist's in solving problems or discovering truths, has a special quality which we shall certainly one day be able to characterize in metapsychological terms. (Freud 2, 29)

Such satisfactions are limited. Withdrawing from the world through the production of culture is a method accessible to only a few gifted people. Even for those with luck and talent, the method gives no "complete protection from suffering" (ibid.). For the joys of creating are mild in comparison with cruder, instinctual joys, and they habitually fail to help us when the body is the source of suffering. Freud thought love to be a better means of gaining independence from fate, but it offers little promise. Though more effective as a way to happiness, a life centered on loving is even harder to maintain than a life centered on science and art.

> The weak side of this technique of living is easy to see; otherwise no human being would have thought of abandoning this path to

happiness for any other. It is that we are never so defenseless against suffering as when we love, never so helplessly unhappy as when we have lost our loved object or its love. (Freud 2, 33)

Did Freud offer a form of theodicy after all? His picture of the natural cycle is remarkably efficient. We are attacked from within and without by forces that cause us nearly constant pain, and we seek to flee from reality by the best available means. Drugs are too risky, love is too rare. Though culture is less effective than either, at least it is steady. So far, this could be a modern version of Stoicism. Freud added that the very steadiness of culture leads to benefits that remedy at least one source of evil. For by creating what we call conscience, it controls the more violent impulses with which people torment each other when they're not being tormented by something else. By splitting the self into pieces and having the superego do to the ego what the ego longs to do to someone else, civilization can turn destructive forces into something useful.

Civilization, therefore, obtains mastery over the individual's dangerous desire for aggression by weakening and disarming it and by setting up an agency within him to watch over it, like a garrison in a conquered city. (Freud 2, 84)

But Freud's economy was bleak. He knew it would not satisfy. For his system would work as theodicy only if he held civilization to be a value. In that case, producing civilization would be a worthy goal. It might even be fair exchange for the amount of suffering that goes into making it. This is just the move Freud refused to make, and he was brutally explicit about the reason: the price we pay for the advance of civilization is the loss of happiness. And since civilization itself arose as a flight from reality, it can't even be justified as related to truth. The more civilized we become, the more we seem to suffer—without clearly gaining in knowledge. Calling what happens to you fate, and blaming it on Athena's quarrel with Poseidon, is a way of giving meaning to your suffering from outside. Calling it Providence is a way of internalizing. Better to blame your misery on yourself than remain utterly without meaning—but the price of such meaning is immense. So Freud concluded unremitting:

Thus I have not the courage to rise up before my fellow-men as a prophet, and I bow to their reproach that I can offer them no consolation: for at bottom that is what they are all demanding— the wildest revolutionaries no less passionately than the most virtuous believers. (Freud 2, 111)

For many, Freud's view came to seem self-evident. Mention the problem of evil, and any group is likely to split. Some will confess to seeking reason in the world, while others are certain that such searches reveal childish weakness of which the others should be ashamed. The division doesn't reflect education or class background, and it seems impervious to national and religious differences. Still it's always as sharp as it is clear and passionate. For one group, the world is so thoroughly disenchanted that the absence of reason in it isn't worth mentioning. For the other that absence is the source of permanent frustration and pain. Members of the first group describe their loss as natural. Does that make them Freud's adults—or Nietzsche's Last Men?

For those influenced by Freud, reason and nature are so thoroughly different that the demand to connect them is a category mistake. If we expect justice from the world, it's only because we project childhood structures onto the universe at large. They insist that the world is not the sort of thing that has to do with justice, and those who think otherwise are just counting their losses and nursing their wounds. This standpoint requires the idea that the world is comprehensible without normative categories.

Yet the urge to naturalize the world arose from the same process that issued in theology. Taking the spirits out of nature is a different way of making yourself comfortable than putting them into nature in the first place. Both arise from the need to make the world less *unheimlich*. Recall Rousseau's project. The idea of radically separating natural from moral evil, and calling whatever is left over the human condition, was part of a search to show that events like earthquakes were events without meaning. What began as a plan to absolve God of responsibility for evil actually reduced the quantity of evil itself. Earthquakes became flat. Categorizing an event as natural gives us hope of predicting and controlling it through natural law. But whether or not we actually succeed in doing so, calling something natural is a way of making it tame. Supernatural events have depth and dimension. Even if they occur regularly, they are experienced as extraordinary. Natural events are common events. They are very literally insignificant—not representations of something beside themselves, nor signals we need to decode. We are freed from the burden of thinking about them because there is nothing in them to interpret. We can only manage our lives around them as best we can.

Ordinary events are what the order of the world consists in, not whatever is a threat to it. The more pieces of the world become ordinary, the less threatening the world as a whole. The more things can be viewed as *natural* evils, the less evil the world contains—until the term 'natural evil' drops out. An insignificant event may cause a great deal of damage, but the damage is merely unfortunate. It leaves the realm of evil to join the merely bad. The paradox is just this: the urge to naturalize evil arose from the desire to tame and control it. But the more it is tamed, the more the quality of evil disappears. This leaves us with the fear that evil wasn't captured but trivialized. The banal doesn't shatter the world; it composes it.

In demystifying natural and metaphysical evils, Rousseau also decriminalized them. But the more psychology strove to become a science of nature, the more the distinction between moral and natural evils broke down. The problem was dissolved but raised in different form: can we trust a world where human nature is subject to such despicable tendencies? The very naturalism that was the pride of those who sought to disenchant the world undermines hard distinctions they sought to establish. The more human beings become part of the natural world, the more we, like earthquakes, become one more unfortunate fact about it. The more evil itself seems explicable in terms of natural processes, the more nature itself is implicated. Naturalism is a way of dividing responsibility for the world as well as making us comfortable in it, in one crude blow. Few were as crude about this as Sade was: if nature can do it, so can I. But the consequences of naturalism can be overlooked only at the cost of a radical dualism few are willing to maintain. Science may have abolished the sense that the world is inhabited by forces with wills of their own, and in this way reduced the *unheimlich*. But the price is enormous, for all nature stands condemned. Human beings themselves become walking indictments of creation.

The older Freud was at once the most articulate proponent of naturalization and the author of one of the darker views of human nature. It is thus little surprise that principled distinctions between different kinds of evil melt away in his work. They are all merely instances of countless ways in which life is too hard for us: the whole world presents obstacles to thwart our desires. Even while diagnosing it, he returns to the prereflective stance of the child. Children meet the world as Job did. Little matter if devastation comes at the hands of marauding Chaldeans or a great wind from the desert. Each belongs to a world that is, as usual, opposed to us.

Chapter Four
HOMELESS

> ZEUS: You are not in your own home, intruder; you are
> a foreign body in the world, like a splinter in the flesh, or a
> poacher in his lordship's forest.
>
> —Sartre, *The Flies*

Voltaire wrote poetry after Lisbon, but the catastrophes of the twentieth century seemed to resist expression. Most descriptions of contemporary evil emphasize its radical difference from everything that preceded it. Something about the crimes and misfortunes of the present shook our bearings so thoroughly that doing anything but describing them seems wrong. Adorno, most famously, wrote that poetry after Auschwitz would be barbarism; Arendt said the impossible became true. To seek understanding, explanation, catharsis, consolation—all goals of philosophical and literary reflection about earlier forms of evil—seems out of place. An almost obsessive, sometimes questionable interest in cataloging twentieth-century horrors continues to fill the world with testimony in all the forms modern media has at its disposal. But most agree that we lack the conceptual resources to do more than bear witness. Contemporary evil left us helpless.

For Levinas,

[p]erhaps the most revolutionary fact of the twentieth-century consciousness . . . is that of the destruction of all balance between explicit and implicit theodicy of Western thought. (Levinas 2, 161)

The claim that whatever was left of religious faith before Auschwitz could not survive it became famous in works of witnesses like Elie Wiesel's *Night*, or of theologians like Richard Rubinstein's *After Ausch- witz*. The arguments that both Jewish and Christian paradigms of faith were destroyed there are not uncontroversial, but they have been well treated elsewhere, and I will not review them here.[1] But unlike most contemporary thinkers, Levinas did not restrict the word *theodicy* to justifications of God's goodness that were modeled by Leibniz. Rather, he drew as much on secular forms of theodicy, which persisted without religion as attempts to reconcile us to suffering. Theodicy, in the nar- row sense, allows the believer to maintain faith in God in face of the world's evils. Theodicy, in the broad sense, is any way of giving mean- ing to evil that helps us face despair. Theodicies place evils within structures that allow us to go on in the world. Ideally, they should reconcile us to past evils while providing direction in preventing future ones. Levinas claimed that the first task could not be maintained in good conscience after Auschwitz. He thus gave philosophical expres- sion to an idea shared by many: the forms of evil that appeared in the twentieth century made demands modern consciousness could not meet.

In order to understand what is true in such claims and what is not, we should look more closely at Lisbon. For Lisbon too made something impossible. Understanding what ended there can help us to under- stand more clearly what is new about contemporary evil, and what resources remain for thinking about it. In the preceding chapters, I described an intellectual drama that spanned two centuries. Against this background, I now turn to discuss two cases, each of which was seen by its era as paradigmatic of evil. Each case shattered what had allowed those who lived through it to negotiate their ways through the world. Events are always located in distinct conceptual space. Both Lisbon and Auschwitz occurred in contexts of massive intellectual fer- ment. In both cases, catastrophe tipped the bucket of assumptions that were already precarious. But in both cases, the events themselves cre- ated boundaries between what could and what could not be thought.

Lisbon shocked the eighteenth century as larger and more destruc- tive earthquakes did not move the twentieth. And though the Thirty

Years' War was barbaric and ravaging, it did not leave those who lived through it feeling *conceptually* devastated. Auschwitz did. The difference in response, I will argue, lies in the difference between the structures that each era had used to make sense of suffering. The very differences in the nature of the events caused differences in the kinds of shock they produced. Lisbon revealed how remote the world is from the human; Auschwitz revealed the remoteness of humans from themselves. If disentangling the natural from the human is part of the modern project, the distance between Lisbon and Auschwitz showed how difficult it was to keep them apart. After Lisbon, the scope of moral categories contracted. Before Lisbon, they could be applied to the world as a whole; it made sense to call earthquakes evils. Afterward moral categories were confined to one small piece of the world, those human beings who may be able to realize them. Auschwitz raised doubts about the sense in which we apply moral categories at all.

This chapter is structured as follows. The first section examines responses to the Lisbon earthquake, while section 2 discusses why the event named by the word *Auschwitz* stands for contemporary evil. The third supports Levinas's claim by showing how Auschwitz destroyed two central responses to evil that can be viewed as secular theodicies. The fourth section goes further in showing that Auschwitz undermined the modern rejection of theodicy that locates evil in intention. The fifth argues that despite the dangers technology lends to terrorism, terrorism itself is not a new form of evil. The sixth considers some thinkers who took up traditional questions about evil after Auschwitz. In trying to elucidate why they did so after every form of theodicy had been rejected, the final section argues that the problem of evil is driven by ties not to religion but to the principle of sufficient reason.

EARTHQUAKES: WHY LISBON?

The Lisbon earthquake was said to shock Western civilization more than any event since the fall of Rome.[2] Earthquakes clearly have metaphorical resonance. We are always trying to determine just what in the world we can trust. When the ground disappears from under our feet, anyone may incline to say: very little. But fifty years before Lisbon, an earthquake had destroyed Port Royal, Jamaica, and nothing else at all. No conceptual damage occurred.

Viewed from the capitals of Europe, the West Indies had it coming. An anonymous pamphlet entitled *Verses on the late Earthquakes: addressed to Great Britain* announced that Jamaica, like Sodom, deserved whatever destruction it got. A place full of pirates and half-breeds was ripe for the hand of Providence and could be easily fit into any explanation invoking it. But Lisbon was neither so profligate as to merit the special attention of Providence nor so distant as to elude the attention of the arbiters of intellectual judgment. As example, it was both ordinary and representative enough to provoke general alarm.

Lisbon in 1755 was no backwater. Commerce had made it one of the world's wealthier cities. Posed on the edge of Europe, it was the natural starting point for the exploration and colonization of the preceding centuries, which had made it powerful and cosmopolitan as well. A busy port with a large foreign population was an ideal place from which to broadcast any message to the rest of the world—which confirmed many observers' view that the messenger must have been God. *Qui n'a pas vu Lisbonne, n'a rien vu de bon.* The fact that this claim was reported in French in a book published in England confirmed the feeling of globalization the earthquake inspired. Lisbon's reputation as queen of the seas was underscored by the inventory of goods that were destroyed. The wealth lost was vast. In addition to gold and silver totaling millions, chroniclers recorded the destruction of hundreds of pictures, including works by Titian, Correggio and Rubens; thousands of books and manuscripts, including a history written by Emperor Charles V in his own hand; and furniture, tapestries, and ornaments from churches and palaces as well as simpler homes. Loss of life was less well documented than loss of property, but even conservative estimates counted fifteen thousand dead.

The sequence of disaster was unremitting. The earthquake itself struck the city on the morning of November 1 and lasted about ten minutes. This was long enough to destroy a vast number of buildings, bury thousands of people in the ruins, and turn the sky dark with dust. But a great deal could have been saved had the quake not been followed by terrible fires. These raged over the city, killing many inhabitants of poorer districts as well as destroying the treasures busy merchants had dragged from the ruins to salvage in the public squares. Descriptions of the day's events suggest that the final disaster was the most terrifying. For even as the fires ravaged parts of the city, a series of tidal waves smashed the port, tearing ships from their anchors and drowning hundreds of people who sought shelter on the coast. Earth, fire, and water were together perfectly relentless. With all the elements combined to orchestrate destruction, even coolheaded observers might suspect a design.

Lisbon was a more natural candidate than Port Royal for intellectual disaster, for by the time it occurred, the Enlightenment was well underway. The earthquake shook up fertile ground. It didn't create debate out of nothing but happened in the middle of it. Orthodox theologians welcomed the earthquake in terms they barely troubled to disguise. For years they had battled Deism, natural religion, and anything else that tried to explain the world in natural terms alone—or in terms of the vague general Providence that Enlightenment thinkers loved. God's goodness was manifest in the system of order and harmony He occasionally revealed to prophets like Newton. Viewing Him as speaking directly to ordinary sinners was regarded less as false than as tacky. Who was so self-satisfied as to suppose his own crimes and misfortunes deserved cosmic attention? Leibniz thought the progress of science would allow the rest of us access to the general message; those inclined more to Pope believed that mysteries would endure. All were nevertheless far from holding the position we now take for granted: however it may be awful, it's only an earthquake. For the eighteenth century, the whole of nature was invested with meaning. The meaning and glory of nature were so great as to make belief in particular Providence seem petty. Rousseau was the clearest but far from the only thinker to invest nature itself with moral authority. Traditional theologians' faith in miracles and wonders was not what was threatened at Lisbon. What was shattered, rather, were liberal views about the miracle and wonder of nature itself.

In this context orthodox theologians saw the earthquake as a double gift from Heaven. Not only could it punish particular transgressions; it would show those who thought God's works exhausted by the abstract and distant Creation that He still played a role in the world. Those within Portugal inclined to believe that the Portuguese had sinned quite enough to merit this punishment, and more. Those outside it inclined more to ask why Lisbon should have suffered a worse fate than Paris or London. But in Portugal and abroad, theologians took the opportunity to return to the sort of explanation that had just begun to go out of fashion.

If earthquakes are paradigms of natural evil, what kind of moral evil must have occurred to produce this one? Some poets thought it enough to point to the original relationship between human beings and the dust from which we came. "O Earth, why do you tremble?" was a question put rhetorically; if humans were made of clay, how could the earth fail to convulse with the weight of human crime? At least one observer pointed a finger at something we can regard as sin: "Think, O Spain, O Portugal, of the millions of poor Indians that your forefathers butchered for the sake of gold" (quoted in Kendrick). But this English pastor's reminder was the exception. Most pointed to traditional sins that Lisbon shared with other locations. Ordinary greed and licentiousness seemed enough to explain the devastation. After years of watching the Portuguese prefer the goods of this world to God's word, He determined to speak a little louder. Most divines viewed the event as proof of God's mercy. The earthquake's survivors were given a chance to repent before the general apocalypse visited everyone. So one Johann Gottlob Krüger, professor of philosophy at Helmstedt and member of the Prussian Academy, wrote a book called *Virtue Awakened by the Earthquake*. It argued that Lisbon was an unmistakable warning. Anyone seeking to explain it as a merely natural event should note that not only Christian but Stoic sources agree that the end of the world will be heralded by massive conflagarations.

> It is true that Lisbon was not destroyed by underground fire. Fire was either already burning in hearths, which ignited fallen beams and boards; or it was in part set by godless and wicked villains. But the underground fire was indeed the cause of the earthquake itself. . . . Doesn't our Savior himself mention the earthquake not

just as prelude but as cause of the destruction of the world? (Quoted in Breidert, 41)

After quoting apocalyptic scenes from the Gospels, Krüger concluded:

What was missing on the night of November 1 to make visible the whole force of these words to Lisbon and the world? Nothing but roaring thunder in the clouds. This stood already mobilized like a wild horse before battle. But the Lord of Nature restrained it out of fatherly pity. (Ibid., 42)

Many devout souls turned to number mysticism to predict the timing of the next disaster. Dates were invested with meaning in violent doctrinal debates. Jansenists used the fact that Portugal was a Jesuit hotbed to show that God wished to crush the Inquisition. In choosing All Saints' Day to strike His blow, God signaled that the saints themselves had begged Him to punish Lisbon for its religious perversions. One divine explained why so many churches were shattered while a street full of brothels remained standing: God more easily forgives the wretched creatures who frequent such places than those who profane His own house. Such explanations are invaluable, for they can be applied by opposing confessions ad nauseam. Jesuits had no trouble responding with the counterargument that the earthquake was God's reaction to an Inquisition that had grown too lax—nor in following the quake with an auto-da-fé.

Even serious thinkers could think about Lisbon and continue to think about their world much as they'd done before. Consider Immanuel Kant. At the time of the earthquake he was a private scholar of little means in a provincial capital at the other end of Europe. His intellectual commitments were determined by the system of Christian Wolff, who had expanded on Leibniz's views in fifty-nine volumes. Wolff's influence was evident in the three essays Kant produced on earthquakes for the Königsberg weekly paper in 1756, which sought to assure readers that earthquakes don't happen in Prussia. Kant's reasons were taken from natural science, for his essays were written to show that earthquakes are not supernatural events. If they could be explained without reference to God's judgment, Enlightenment views about general Providence could be maintained without raising troubling questions about particular Providence. So Kant elected to stay in the realm of science by expanding on the embryonic fault theory developing in the wake of Lisbon. For readers not convinced that earthquakes are perfectly natural, Kant offered instructions for experiment. All they need do to produce a little earthquake themselves was take twenty-five pounds of sulfur and twenty-five pounds of iron filings, mix them with ordinary water, and bury the whole mess a foot or so in the ground. This shows that earthquakes work according to general laws, the virtues of which are too well known to require repetition.

Leibnizian arguments about the goodness of systematic law in general were enough to support claims about the necessity of earthquakes in particular. But occasionally, Kant even tried to show that in this case as in others, apparent evils can have good effects. His example of goods that result from earthquakes—the creation of a mineral spring with healing properties—was, thankfully, brief. Kant spared his readers much of that sort of speculation by concluding that the main benefit of Lisbon was the knowledge that the world is not made for our advantage. Lisbon proved we cannot understand God's purposes. The last of the earthquake essays ended with a reminder of our finitude that began at last to sound almost Kantian. After tirelessly insisting that earthquakes are the product of natural causes, Kant expressed skepticism about the possibility of preventing them through natural means. For

> [f]rom the Prometheus of modern times, Mr. Franklin, who wanted to disarm thunder, to those who want to extinguish the fire in the vulcan's workshop, all such attempts are proofs of the audacity of the human being, who is fitted with abilities that stand in small relation to it. These proofs bring him in the end to the humiliating recollection with which he ought to begin: that he will never be more than human. (Quoted in Breidert, 143)

These are hints of work he would write decades later. They reveal the young Kant as nothing worse than a complacently enlightened liberal. In the context of works like those of the professor in Helmstedt, or even more zealous colleagues to the south, Kant's views were by no means embarrassing. Still he wrote, years later, that his writings in defense of optimism were the only works of which he was ashamed.

Kant's shame marks the beginning of the modern. It signals awareness that understanding has limits. Lisbon didn't create such awareness, but it crystallized it. Lisbon made sense—or failed to make sense—against the background of debate I've described. Later centuries would have encountered it differently, and earlier ones would have given it little notice. The premodern world experienced earthquakes with fear and trembling that not only didn't threaten religion but often enhanced it. The random force of lightning is part of what made it a fitting symbol of divine power. Given the appropriate worldview, the sense that earthquakes are thoroughly inexplicable could increase the sense of mystery that furthers awe and wonder. Our lack of understanding of why the gods strike can be one more sign of the distance between human and divine that moves some souls to reverence. For contemporary observers, earthquakes are only a matter of plate tectonics. They threaten, at most, your faith in government building codes or geologists' predictions. They may invoke anger at lazy inspectors, or pity for those stuck in the wrong place at the wrong time. But these are ordinary emotions.

At one particular moment in Europe, by contrast, an earthquake could shake the foundations of faith and call the goodness of Creation into question. What challenges one's sense of intelligibility underscores particular worldviews. This challenge owed less to the weight of disaster than to the burden of increased expectations. Two related developments in the history of rationality turned the earthquake into a threat it would not have posed at another time. The first was the ways natural sciences had combined to confirm Enlightenment conviction that the universe is, as a whole, intelligible. The idea of general Providence was a response to triumphs of modern science. If the universal scientific order is such a marvel, why suffer a God who kept jumping in and out of it? A Creation that was good in the beginning should require no intervention thereafter. Particular Providence demanded too much meddling in the scientific order whose contemplation provided the Enlightenment with so much satisfaction. The wonder and gratitude earlier ages felt toward miracles was transferred to the generally miraculous system of nature. Not even Leibniz was so satisfied as to believe the system transparent. But he was confident that all the murkiness was our fault. Like Alfonso, we ascribe the confusion in our thought to Creation itself. With the passage of time, the clutter of the universe would be seen to have an order of its own.

Related to rising expectations for a transparent intellectual order was the rising demand for a social order that matched it. The bourgeoisie was busy replacing economic structures fixed by tradition with an order that sought to distribute rewards according to rational principles accessible to all. If you believe that your efforts in the marketplace will be naturally rewarded as if by an invisible hand, you'll tend to expect the same of the cosmos at large. Here it's hard to determine which expectation came first. But it's easy to see that the more Providence showed signs of functioning smoothly in the economic sphere, the more expectations would grow. For the eighteenth century, the replacement of feudal economies determined by inheritance with the principle of careers open to talent was a sign that effort and reward were generally in tune. A bourgeois world was as little inclined to bow to God's will and accept natural events by fiat as it was prepared to accept a political order on the strength of authority alone.[3]

It seems foolish to privilege one of these developments over the other. Rather, they worked together. The revelation of an increasingly transparent natural order through the discoveries of science fed expectations that a social order could be discovered which made equal sense. Conversely, demands for the replacement of structures based on tradition with those based on reason furthered demands for the discovery of rational structures in the universe as a whole. No crude expectation of reward and benefit, but the general demand that the world make sense stands behind both. As such demands were fulfilled in one realm, they were extended to another, for the inclination to the inexorable is natural to reason itself.

Rising expectations that the social and the natural worlds would be equally transparent thus made Lisbon the shock it wouldn't have been without them. Both Leibniz and Pope discussed earthquake and sin: each was an instance of the unfortunate events in the world that do not lead us to general doubt.[4] Babies had died in disasters before; this disaster led the hardened Voltaire to ask why. Lisbon could be used, of course, as a reason to protest against traditional religion. But reasons for protest existed before Lisbon. Traditional religion had answered them traditionally, by taking refuge in the claim that God's ways are mysterious. The idea that they were *not* mysterious was a demand of reason embodied in natural religion as in other eighteenth-century discoveries. It was this idea that Lisbon sent stumbling.

For the government of Lisbon, none of these matters remained abstract. The question whether the earthquake was God's signal or a natural event had direct political consequences. Those who believed it was God's signal devoted their efforts to interpreting it. If God had sent the earthquake to warn of the short time remaining for repentance, the only interesting questions concerned duration and means. How much time did the Lisboners have left before the Apocalypse, and what sorts of measures would save their eternal souls?[5]

These questions undermined the work of those entrusted with restoring order. First among these was Pombal, the controversial prime minister of Portugal. When the unhappy young king asked him what could be done after the earthquake, Pombal is said to have replied: Bury the dead and feed the living. He quickly organized the disposal of corpses to prevent an outbreak of plague, commandeered stocks of grain to prevent famine, and ordered militia to prevent looting within the city and attacks by pirates from without. Pombal's efforts were so successful that he could ensure the weekly paper was published without missing an edition. He knew that information was crucial. If the public was fed by false rumors and speculation, it would resist the measures needed to return the city to normal life. Pombal was explicit in supporting naturalist explanations of the earthquake. The more earthquakes were viewed as normal events, the easier it would be to incorporate them into a normal world—or to view the return to normalcy as a merely practical problem.

Initial shock and paralysis assisted Pombal's first efforts. It was only some time after the earthquake that the tension between natural and supernatural explanation came to a very violent head. Aftershocks continued to feed fears that the earthquake had been only God's gentle warning. Priests vied with each other in suggesting causes of the original catastrophe as well as the date of the worse one yet to come. The city was sent into panic by the rumor that a new and greater quake would occur a year after the disaster on November 1, 1756. The Jesuits were widely held responsible for the rumor. One of them, an eloquent, miracle-working Italian named Malagrida, challenged the minister directly in a series of sermons. His goal was to destroy the peace of mind Pombal worked to establish. Instead of going about the prosaic business of recovery, the Portuguese should repent of their sins. Scourging and fasting, not building and distribution, were the tasks this fateful hour demanded. Pombal wished to save citizens from sickness and famine; Malagrida wished to save souls from hell. Each worked under the shadow of a ticking clock. Malagrida was bent on persuading every sinner in Lisbon to drop every other occupation and spend six days in prayer and meditation at a Jesuit retreat. If their final hours were at hand, what occupation could be more important? So his sermons repeatedly returned to the earthquake's true cause.

> It is scandalous to pretend the earthquake was just a natural event, for if that be true, there is no need to repent and to try to avert the wrath of God, and not even the Devil himself could invent a false idea more likely to lead us all to irreparable ruin. (Quoted in Kendrick, 89)

This kind of rhetoric could not remain unanswered forever. By 1758 charges were trumped up to arrest Malagrida. The daylong auto-da-fé in which he died was also the end of a form of explanation. After Lisbon, even relatively conservative Western cultures were no longer willing to tolerate God's hand in their daily affairs. Even relatively progressive cultures, of course, were unwilling to deny it entirely. Slogans like "In God We Trust" functioned as talismans long after the conceptual machinery behind them had ground to a halt. But the battle between priest and prime minister was decisive. Pombal's victory was a victory for the view that God's purposes have no public function. Even today, major earthquakes can evoke cries and speculations that will seem archaic, but they are generally confined to fundamentalist sects and hapless victims.[6] Political action will focus on corrupt officials who take bribes in exchange for relaxing building codes rather than on increasing the performance of religious rituals.

This signals a shift in consciousness so profound that it often remains unnoticed. Since Lisbon, natural evils no longer have any seemly relation to moral evils; hence they no longer have meaning at all. Natural disaster is the object of attempts at prediction and control, not of interpretation. None of the questions that tormented Europeans reflecting on Lisbon was ever directly answered or even directly rejected. People affirmed the wisdom of God's order in general without demanding to understand too many of its details. Theory proceeded much as Pombal did. It focused on eradicating those evils that could be reached by human hands. Progress, when we achieve it, involves doing just this. Enlightenment thinkers turned to praxis, for the apparent absence of justice in divine institutions was no excuse for tolerating it in human ones. If anything, it made the business of establishing justice even more pressing. But in proceeding as if questions were settled that were simply left hanging, theory left residues that cloud our attempts to eradicate evils today.

MASS MURDERS: WHY AUSCHWITZ?

Our very distance from Lisbon makes the disturbances it set in motion easier to evoke. Comparing the conceptual changes wrought by Auschwitz to those created by Lisbon, should help us recover a sense of shock. Can we summarize the changes by saying that humankind lost faith in the world at Lisbon, and faith in itself at Auschwitz? Only by making two important qualifications. The significance of the Polish death camps came to seem clear by the late twentieth century, but it was not self-evident before.

First, for many thinkers, the breakdown of the modern took place much earlier. Humankind's faith in its ability to overcome its self-incurred immaturity was dispelled long before 1945. World War I in particular seemed devastating beyond measure. As Henry James wrote in 1916, to have to take the present "for what the treacherous years were all making for and *meaning* is too tragic for any words." The sadness he expressed can seem as dated as some of his characters' dilemmas.

A world that could be shattered by Verdun and the trenches of the Somme looks almost as curiously fragile as the world of 1755. World War I now seems both intelligible and contingent, the lethal fruit of old-fashioned imperialism and early modern technology. From where we are standing, it remains within the outer limits of the normal.

Auschwitz does not. Lyotard compared it to an earthquake that destroys not only lives and buildings but also the instruments used to measure the earthquake itself, so that the devastation cannot even be adequately gauged. We can mourn the youth who died at Flanders while wondering how their officers could have thought a horse and a good education equipment enough with which to face artillery. By contrast, there is nothing a trainload of deportees arriving at a Polish ramp might have known. Auschwitz beggared expectation. The impossible became true.

The year 1945 thus marks a fundamental divide that can almost create nostalgia for the despair which followed World War I. But the divide was not immediately captured by the name *Auschwitz*, which gained its sense of uniqueness much later. The judgment at Nürnberg viewed the systematic murder of the Jews as one of many war crimes; Germany was held responsible for starting a war that caused untold devastation with unforeseeable consequences. The meaning of *Lisbon* was clear and immediate in 1755. For a good two decades after World War II, the conviction that limits had been crossed in ways from which we would never recover was captured more by the word *Hiroshima* than by *Auschwitz*. Atomic warfare disturbed the order of the universe, for it not only exceeded every prior limit to destruction but made complete and total destruction of life itself an ever-present possibility. So William Faulkner's 1950 Nobel Prize acceptance speech declared: "There are no problems of the spirit. There is only the question: when will I be blown up?" Fourteen years later Leslie Fiedler would still write, "[F]or most of the younger writers today, the only war that *counts* is World War III, the war that does not happen."[7]

In many contexts it is important to examine differences between the kinds of mass extermination that mark our world. The German Jewish philosopher Günther Anders, for example, argued that crimes like those committed at Auschwitz are greater threats to the human soul, whereas what happened at Hiroshima poses the greater threat to humanity itself. For, he wrote, it takes more hardness of heart to lead a child to a gas chamber than to drop a bomb on her. We are far from understanding what it takes to drive children into flames in which one knows one will oneself be consumed. Those who did the daily work of the death camps created an abyss between themselves and the rest of humanity. Some descriptions of them suggest an absence of soul that those who kill at greater distances from their victims need not share. But the problem is not that Nazi murderers were either particularly brutal or particularly heartless—but precisely that, by and large, they were not. Differences between them and others may be important differences for moral psychology, but they have little bearing on what Anders and others believed was the greater threat to life itself, namely, the possibility of total extinction through weapons of mass destruction *without* any of the features that once seemed essential to evil.

Comparing what happened at Auschwitz with Hiroshima or the Soviet gulags can be important for many reasons. To understand history or psychology and to draw conclusions for our futures, we will often need to examine ways in which forms of mass murder are different. Most attempts to assert that one form of mass murder is *worse* than another are motivated by political rather than philosophical concerns. In some contexts political concerns should be primary, and furthering them becomes a moral demand. During the German Historians' Debate of the 1980s, for example, emphasizing the universal element within Auschwitz functioned as a way of denying German guilt. To assert that what happened at Auschwitz was worse than what happened in the gulags was thus to take a stand against rightist attempts to avoid German responsibility for its own war crimes by pointing to those of others. Different political contexts may demand different moral responses. It can be an act of courage and compassion to underline the universal elements that were present at Auschwitz—if one is, for example, confronting those American assertions of the uniqueness of Auschwitz which are used to argue that anything short of putting children in gas chambers is relatively benign. Political discussions that compare evils can be manipulative or moral, but they are all fundamentally practical. My purpose at present is not. Rather, I seek to understand how our consciousness has and has not been changed by contemporary evil.

While the moral shock that began in 1945 had several sources, I will continue to use *Auschwitz* as shorthand. To say that political systems as different as fascism, communism, and liberal democracy were all, by 1945, implicated in cases of mass murder is not for a moment to equate them. It is to say that contemporary evil takes distinctive common forms. Like sound echoing off the walls of a closed room, the reflection of evil from vastly different sources made it seem almost inescapable. The very multiplicity suggested something new and fundamental that was common to all those forms. To use the word *Auschwitz* as an emblem of a new form of evil need not be an entrance into political debate.

Before trying to elucidate the claim that Auschwitz represents new forms of evil, it is important to mention two common ways of rejecting it. One entails viewing the Nazis as no worse than other war criminals, while the other views them as uniquely diabolical. Each is a way of dismissing the significance of Auschwitz by attempting to fit that event into traditional conceptual resources for coping with evil.

The first evokes classical religious forms of explanation. Some orthodox Jews view Auschwitz as God's judgment on European Jews, many of whom had turned away from traditional law. Here the covenant is evoked as simply as in the days of the prophets: God abandons those who abandons His ways. Why were those Galician Jews who kept the law murdered along with those Parisian Jews who did not? Since Judaism is a religion of collective responsibility, this kind of explanation can use notions of collective punishment to explain why God's judgment fell on the pious and the secular alike. On such views, the Nazis were no different a scourge from any other group of antisemites. None of them are interesting in themselves. SS officers, Russian Cossacks, and the biblical tribe of Amalek are all interchangeable instruments in God's hands. His message is always the same, and it's the message, rather than the form in which He chooses to send it, that deserves our attention. This kind of reaction is no different from traditional priests' reaction to Lisbon. Since beliefs in Providence are never built on evidence, they will always prove impervious to it. But we saw these beliefs waning in 1755. Though they resurface in moments of crisis, such beliefs do so in opposition to the modern world. For a modern atheist like Jean Améry, these reactions are forms of blasphemy.[8]

A more common way to deny the significance of Auschwitz combines a completely secular vocabulary with a curiously theological structure. While the first view regards Nazis as one more variation in the long history of antisemitism, the second views them as singularly demonic. On this view, Auschwitz reveals much about one nation in particular but nothing about humanity in general. The agitation that accompanies attempts to prove that only Germans could have produced Auschwitz betrays its own bad faith. Would that it were true. We are horrified, after all, not when beasts and devils behave like beasts and devils but when human beings do. Could it be proved that something about Auschwitz were essentially German, life would be easier for all of us.[9] A dog born with three legs casts no doubt on our normal concepts of dogs. If Auschwitz were only a national problem, the crimes of one nation would reflect nothing about the human race as a whole.

Auschwitz was conceptually devastating because it revealed a possibility in human nature that we hoped not to see. For the conditions in Germany should have led not to highly developed forms of barbarity but to genuine civilization. All philosophical discussions of it insist on this point. Since many authors of those discussions were German Jews, some critics have tried to dismiss their work by suggesting that their efforts were moved by perverse and tragic need to vindicate the culture they could not abandon. Such dismissals are not only ad hominem but odd. Whatever culture those thinkers belonged to, they all belonged to the human race—and all accepted some version of universalist principles. Vindicating Germany by implicating humankind would not have offered any solace. The assumption that insisting on the utter uniqueness of Nazism was somehow equivalent to taking Nazism seriously is an assumption that was never adequately argued but nonetheless dominated much twentieth-century discourse outside philosophy. But those philosophers who addressed the subject argued that what was terrifying were the ways in which Auschwitz threatened and implicated a larger portion of humanity than had been threatened and implicated before. They would have agreed with French philosopher David Rousset, who wrote the following four months after his liberation from Buchenwald:

> The existence of the camps is a warning . . . it would be duplicity, and criminal duplicity, to pretend that it is impossible for other nations to try a similar experiment because it would be contrary to their nature. Germany interpreted, with an originality in keeping with her history, the crisis which led to her creation of the concentration camp world. (Rousset, 112)

To say that Auschwitz stands not for particular national failures but for modern breakdown altogether is not yet to say why. It's clear that technology shapes the bounds of contemporary evil. Before the invention of automatic weapons, you normally had to see anyone you hoped to kill. Since the development of the process that began with the American Civil War, you no longer need to do so. Technologically and, even more important, psychologically, this creates opportunities for destruction once available only to nature. Before contemporary warfare, nothing but an earthquake could kill fifteen thousand people in ten minutes. One eighteenth-century Portuguese commentator tried to console his readers for Lisbon by urging them to consider earthquakes as being like wars, where human beings cause destruction they are used to taking in stride. Like wars, he suggested, earthquakes are just one more unfortunate fact about the world; numbers of innocent deaths involved in either case cannot be the thing that matters.

Technology reversed those numbers, creating opportunities for killing at rates surpassing anything other centuries imagined.[10] Today, only the more spectacular earthquakes cause as much damage as a modest bombing. But in neither case do we see evil as a matter of number. Most ethical and religious views deny that human life is quantifiable. Gratuitously killing one soul more or less cannot be what is morally decisive. The Talmud compared saving one life to saving a world. Dostoevsky argued that murdering one child might suffice to damn it. Thoughts like these belong to poetry as much as to argument. But arguments that try to rank evils according to relative numbers of deaths ignore what is crucial about the significance of each particular life.

If whatever is new about contemporary evil cannot be simply a matter of relative quantity, neither is it a matter of relative cruelty. The gas chambers were invented to spare victims more agonizing forms of dying—and the murderers sights that might trouble their consciences. For many, it is this perverted mixture of industrialization undergirded with a claim to humanity that made the death camps horrifying. Arguments about which kinds of death are worse lead to gruesome forms of competition. A moment's reflection on the history of torture makes it clear that, before and after Auschwitz, human beings showed capacities for cruelty that words fail to capture. Only the fact that we are accustomed to Jesus' death as an icon obscures the atrocity of the Crucifixion. Were it not so familiar, it could still easily serve as the paradigm for innocent suffering that early Christianity saw. To force a condemned prisoner to drag through a jeering crowd the instrument that will shortly be used to torture him to death is a refinement of cruelty that ought to take your breath away. It should be enough to stop the impulse to comparative suffering as it begins. What makes Auschwitz a problem for thinking about evil cannot be a matter of *degree*, for at this level, there are no scales.

The claim that Auschwitz represents a form of evil which is radically new persists despite all difficulties in giving reasons for it. I've suggested that uncritical faith in humankind's ability to determine its own fate was shattered by World War I, not World War II, while its certainty in its continued survival was lost in Japan, not in Poland. If it is difficult to locate what is distinctive about Auschwitz in space or in time, it seems equally fruitless to view its significance by comparing numbers of corpses or degrees of agony. Singling out any one factor in the network of atrocity that made up the death camps is likely to be misleading. Rather than asking why this particular event produced the sense of unique devastation that heralds the violent end of an era, we should look more closely at what conceptual resources were destroyed. Like Lisbon, Auschwitz acquired significance in relation to the web of beliefs in which it occurred. What seemed devastated—nay, entirely thwarted—by Auschwitz was the possibility of intellectual response itself. Thought stood still, for the tools of civilization seemed as helpless in coping with the event as they were in preventing it.

The most powerful testimony describes those tools as a hindrance to survival at Auschwitz. The humanistic intellectual skills required to build structures of sense were just the skills that proved treacherous. Seeking meaning and sense in reality could literally be fatal, for both were at odds with those skills required in a place that defied meaning and sense.[11] These accounts suggest that what did not work in helping prisoners to survive Auschwitz will not work any better in helping us to understand it.

Although old models were occasionally refurbished, no first-rate thinker proposed new forms of theodicy, in the narrow sense, after Lisbon. Even the faithful stopped seeking systematic attempts to reveal God's purposes in permitting individual suffering. But three distinct paths for theodicy, in the broad sense, remained open. None of them has the form of traditional theodicy, for all of them deny that God's purposes—should there be any—are relevant to our attempts to understand the world. All these paths, however, are ways of confronting the same questions that earlier philosophers captured in theodicy. It is these attempts to replace theodicy that contemporary evils undermine.

The first kind of attempt, taken by Hegel, sought to redeem particular evils by placing them in history. The second was taken by Nietzsche, who argued that the problem of evil is our own creation; the moral categories that resentment established demand an opposition between life and morality which poisons our days. Both these ways of approaching the problem of evil are ways of attempting to abolish the distinction between *ought* and *is*. One holds out the promise that reality will become what it should be with the passage of time. The other offers hope that we will overcome the desire to condemn reality for not being something different.

The third avenue is quite different, for it rejects every attempt to reconcile nature and morality. Rather, it insists on their utter and essential difference. Natural and moral categories do not support or reflect each other. If this is true, neither nature nor natural events are ever good or evil. This path abolishes all that was understood as natural and metaphysical evil and insists that evil is a moral category alone. In exchange for abandoning the idea that natural suffering can be understood as evil, this path is all the more certain that we know what we mean in speaking of moral evil. Of all the losses humankind sustained at Auschwitz, I will argue that this is the most devastating. Our inability to rely on a clear notion of evil intention will be the subject of section 4. Before we examine the ways in which Auschwitz threatens to undermine the modern determination to live without theodicy, let us turn to the ways in which it devastated modern attempts to replace it.

LOSSES: ENDING MODERN THEODICIES

It is often claimed that Auschwitz overturned earlier beliefs that progress was inevitable, but such claims presuppose naïveté that few texts can support. We saw skepticism about humankind's capacity to improve itself run through the work of Enlightenment thinkers as deeply opposed to each other as Voltaire and Rousseau. By 1794, at the very latest, any remaining faith in the inevitability of progress was under fire in practice, through the Terror, and in theory, through Kant's powerful argument that progress was at best an ideal. Humankind's capacity to hope was all that was left to bear witness to the existence of moral progress at the end of the eighteenth century. It is hard to view this as inevitable, or even particularly robust. And if a certain nineteenth-century cheerfulness came to replace the Enlightenment's darker expressions, it didn't last very long. Here is one description of what happened:

> [Comte] failed as completely as Saint-Simon and Fourier, whose dream that the nineteenth century would see the beginning of an epoch of harmony and happiness was to be fulfilled by a deadly struggle between capitalism and labor, the civil war in America, the war of 1870, the Commune, Russian pogroms, Armenian massacres, and finally the universal catastrophe of 1914. (Bury)

Bury's history of the idea of progress was meant as its elegy. It was written in the conviction that the idea of progress was decisively refuted by all the events he listed. Bury viewed that conviction as uncontroversial—though there were always dissenting voices. But even for more hopeful historians, these events, long before Auschwitz, were enough to dispel any unlimited faith humankind may have had in itself.

If few serious thinkers before Auschwitz believed that progress was inevitable, it isn't a belief that Auschwitz could destroy. Yet though never as naive as is sometimes suggested, any form of Hegelianism held that humankind's slow if unsteady movement toward freedom could be maintained as a whole. Backsliding into barbarism is always a possibility. But neither left- nor right-wing Hegelians questioned the identity of interest between advances in freedom and advances in knowledge that forms the core of secular faith in Enlightenment. This identity is precisely what Auschwitz threatened. For neither product of that faith—bourgeois culture or socialist revolution—had prevented the emergence of evil. On the contrary. Where civilization itself produces new forms of evil, who will dare urge another step forward? The central murders of the twentieth century were the fruit neither of passion nor of ignorance. Overcoming passion or ignorance, therefore, no longer held out the same sort of promise. When white southern Americans lynched their black neighbors, there was still hope for the *idea* of civilization. When Germans deported their Jewish neighbors, there was not even that.

But Auschwitz seems to negate Hegelianism less because of Hegelian beliefs in progress than because of two of its other elements. The first was its hostility to contingency. Recall Hegel's claim that the sole aim of philosophical inquiry is to eliminate the contingent. Observers of twentieth-century history, however, agreed on nothing so much as the degree to which the contingent resisted elimination. Soviet terror functioned by functioning at random, making it impossible to predict what actions could lead to arrest or execution. This was one crucial difference between life in the Soviet Union and life in Nazi Germany, where ordinary Aryan citizens could control much of what happened to them by following the ruling laws and procedures.[12] For non-Aryan victims of Nazi terror, nothing stood out more clearly than the contingency of survival. Life and death were so often dependent on matters of accident that every attempt to seek reason in them stopped short. The death camps revealed nightmares of contingency, thwarting the most basic assumptions instrumental rationality uses to promote survival in ordinary worlds. Your friend could be shot for doing her work properly; you could escape selection by doing the same.

Occasionally, those who were especially conscious of the role accident had played in their own survival found hope for humankind in
the very power of contingency revealed during the Third Reich.
Arendt, for instance, never ceased to be impressed that one could not
have predicted who would capitulate to Nazi authority and who would
resist it.

> And when you have made it through such times as those of totali-
> tarianism, the first thing you know is the following: you never
> know how someone will act. You always experience the surprise
> of your life! This is true at all levels of society and concerning the
> greatest differences between people. (Arendt 8, 85)

Neither age, nor class background, nor education, nor any other clear-
cut factors in one's history could determine who sold their souls.[13] This
fact could be reason to hope for the prospects of human freedom itself.
As Kant's example of king and gallows showed, only the hardest
choices reveal absolute freedom. If nothing in your past determined
whether you collapsed in the face of fascism or whether you defied it,
you are free in a way no tyrant can control. The utter randomness of
responses within German society revealed realms of the human spirit
that the most repressive dictatorship cannot reach.

But those who saw here a reason to hope for the future of humanity
saw no reason to hope for the future of Hegelianism. Much to the
contrary. If the persistence of contingent factors in saving and destroying life thwarts a Hegelian dream of a world without accident, it also
undercuts a Hegelian nightmare of a world without choice. Arendt, in
particular, scorned every remnant of Hegelianism. The kindest thing
she wrote about him was that he was the last of the old philosophers
to evade the important questions. By contrast, she claimed,

> Schelling marks the beginning of modern philosophy because he
> explicitly states that he is concerned with the individual who
> 'wants a providential God'. (Arendt 7, 169)

In *Eichmann in Jerusalem* she accused both defense and prosecution
of giving in to Hegelianism, since both were inclined to put history

more than Eichmann on trial. If pushed far enough, she held both standpoints to exonerate Eichmann. For if history was merely one anti-semitic event after another, wasn't he even a smaller cog in a larger machine than he himself claimed? Arendt maintained the Kantian view that moral responsibility demands acknowledgment of the radical contingency of moral choice. Only by sharply insisting that such choices are fully undetermined could particular people be held accountable for Nazi crimes. For worse and for better, contingency played so central a role in the Holocaust that a philosophy aimed at eliminating contingency seemed doubly condemned by experience.

Thus neither the concept of progress nor that of contingency could carry the same weight after Auschwitz. Still more problematic, however, was the concept of reconciliation underlying Hegelian replacements of theodicy. For this was the point of the first two concepts. Removing the sting of contingency by showing individual misery to be necessary for human history as a whole was a way of reconciling us to a world where such misery occurs. Twentieth-century history made the very desire for reconciliation suspect. Part of the suspicion was that justifications invented to console us for past misfortunes could too easily be used to prepare the ground for future ones. The difference between invoking collective good as a way of *consoling* us for individual suffering and invoking it as a way of *justifying* individual suffering is so fine that it is routinely ignored in political practice. Hegel knew that any consolation his theodicy provided would be collective, not individual. Now the demand to ignore individual suffering for the sake of future collective goods is always problematic. Herder called such views unfair to people of earlier epochs, who suffered for the civilization they would never live to see. This kind of charge was never adequately answered. Nor were Hegel's own remarks about individual suffering likely to assuage such concerns. He faced the consequences of his views and went so far as to state that "the finest and noblest individuals were likely to be immolated on the altar of history" (Hegel 5, 43). In nineteenth-century Berlin, such lectures could still be heard without a shudder; Hegel could not know what images those words would produce one century later. But even those who never dreamed of burning individuals themselves might have hoped to use Hegel to reconcile themselves to a world where other people did. After Auschwitz, that hope seemed decisively blocked. Thinkers like Adorno who had escaped through accidents of fortune thought the least one owed to those who hadn't was the refusal to be reconciled with the world of their murderers. His claim that poetry after Auschwitz would be barbaric refers, among other things, to this. To reject poetry is to reject whatever consolation art delivered when God did not—the shadows of the argument from design that Kant saw in the presence of beauty. To seek such consolation seemed to drown the cries of the victims in the attempt to overcome one's own dejection. Moral integrity demanded helpless silence. Reconciliation, were it possible, could occur only between the murderers and the murdered. The rest of us have no right to it.

Is this argument, or simply an expression of what is called survivor guilt? I believe it is neither but a form of disgust that is equally aesthetic and moral. Dialectics, on this view, are in execrably bad taste; every Hegelian avenue is blocked by the technological production of corpses.

> Who would dare to reconcile himself with the reality of extermination camps, or play the game of synthesis-antithesis-synthesis until his dialectics have discovered 'meaning' in slave labor? (Arendt 7, 444)

Or as Hans Jonas put it:

> The disgrace of Auschwitz is not to be charged to some all-powerful providence or to some dialectically wise necessity, as if it were an antithesis demanding a synthesis or a step on the road to salvation. . . . It remains on our account, and it is we who must again wash away the disgrace from our own disfigured faces, indeed from the very countenance of God. Don't talk to me here about the cunning of reason. (Quoted in Bernstein 2, 4)

After Auschwitz, Hegel's system came to seem like the efforts of Job's friends: useful insurance against the possibility that God may be eavesdropping. If He were, there might be a point to claiming that this bloody process is the best device for moving history forward. For any more straightforward purposes, such attempts at consolation came to seem intolerable forms of denial.

In chapter 1, I described Hegel's historical turn as an attempt to close the gap Kant's work placed in the heart of being: between the given world as we find it and the ideals that demand it be different. The appeal to history was meant to preserve both. It seemed to negate the reality that should be negated without appealing to ideas that threaten to dissolve into pale and pious wishes. The real was the rational because the real would become rational in the passage of time. What was immanent as present hope would naturally become future reality. As Hegel himself knew, redeeming present evils through the unfolding of future historical development was the closest we could come to traditional theodicy.

As every such project seemed increasingly problematic, the urge to undermine the very impulse that leads to theodicy grew stronger. Nietzsche's work proceeds from that urge. For Nietzsche, every Hegelian attempt to overcome the opposition between idea and reality was simply untenable. Not only faith in progress but even hope itself was an underground version of the love for the ideal that Nietzsche wished to subvert. Earlier generations had damned themselves and all the world by allowing reality to be judged by one ideal or another. Nietzsche proposed to end the conflict by dismissing all such ideals and willing reality as we find it.

Reality as we find it includes Dionysian carnage and autos-da-fé—two examples Nietzsche used to show he was aware of what reality includes. Willing the world without wanting it to be different must include the will to live with all of its evils. Like Hegel's occasional dismissals of the importance of individual suffering, Nietzsche's dismissals could make one uneasy in earlier eras. The exhortation to will the world eternally may just help in overcoming evils like Zarathustra's loneliness. Could it really stand up to an auto-da-fé? While the proposal may be questionable in the face of the Inquisition, it cannot even be made after Auschwitz. So Giorgio Agamben wrote:

Let us imagine repeating the experiment that Nietzsche, under the heading 'The Heaviest Weight,' proposes in *The Gay Science*. "One day or one night, a demon glides beside a survivor and asks: 'Do you want Auschwitz to return again and again, innumerable times, do you want every instant, every single detail of the camp to repeat itself for eternity, returning eternally in all the same precise sequence in which they took place? Do you want this to happen again, again and again for eternity?' This simple reformulation of the experiment suffices to refute it beyond all doubt, excluding the possibility of its even being proposed. (Agamben, 99)

Agamben's thought experiment is decisive. Once you have formulated it, you cannot imagine anyone grotesque enough to carry it out. A Nietzschean proposal that a survivor should be able to will the reality of the death camps seems even worse than the Hegelian proposal that he should be reconciled to them by contemplating some future good. Would the suggestion be equally repulsive if made to the survivor of an old-fashioned massacre? Perhaps it would be, but this isn't a question Nietzsche raised. Once the question is raised directly, the flaws in his account cannot be overlooked. Willing the world eternally, and rejecting the ideals that propose to make it different, is not a demand you can make of anyone else.

Nietzsche might accept this conclusion. For willing the world is a task he thought so hard that it may only be self-imposed. You cannot demand that anyone will the reality, let alone the recurrence, of the evil that has been done to him. But could you, after Auschwitz, make such demands on yourself?

According to Jean Améry, it depends on what was done to you. If you were a victim of Gestapo torture, for example, he thinks Nietzsche's challenge cannot be met. His essay "Resentments" was written to confront Nietzsche's claims. Améry, who survived Auschwitz, held that no one who did so could will its recurrence. Even further, he is plagued by a wish to undo past time. The survivor's engagement with the evil he witnessed is obsessive and fruitless. Nietzsche was right to view the wish as unnatural, producing the rancor and resentment he described so well. Those who cannot face the present without the wish to undo past evils are imprisoned without hope. But some evils produce states that cannot be overcome. Améry saw himself as a prisoner of events he could not undo and would not accept. Any diagnosis that tried to liberate him merely points out that his wish to undo the past conflicts with reality. But for Améry, this conflict is hardly news. Indeed, he argues that the whole worth of morality lies in that conflict.

> What happened, happened. The sentence is just as true as it is hostile to morality and the spirit. Moral resistance contains the protest, the revolt against reality, that is only reasonable as long as it is moral. The moral being demands to set aside time. (Améry 1, 116)

Améry's opposition to Nietzsche was deliberate and self-conscious. He knew all the reasons Nietzsche had to attack the very notion of transcendence. Auschwitz presented a reality, however, which demanded that transcendence be resurrected. Améry's engagement with Nietzsche is particularly troubling in its acceptance of Nietzsche's description of ressentiment. The wish to undo an evil that was done to you in the past is the very model of senseless obsession. If you cannot abandon it, you will be trapped in the sterile self-defeat of rage without revenge, pain without relief. Just this picture captures the survivor—said Améry after examining himself. He never disputed Nietzsche's claim that it's an ugly sight, though he denied Nietzsche's view that the inability to will everything is a sign of weakness. The demand to will the world as a whole cannot include every world. Nietzsche's demand relied on models of suffering that the twentieth century made obsolete.

Descriptions of Auschwitz leave little room for Nietzschean claims about the value of suffering. For nearly all observers share the view that this suffering created nothing of value, either for any individual who witnessed it or for humanity as a whole.[14] This is not a moral but an empirical claim: Auschwitz produced nothing but possibilities that should never have been opened, wounds that can never heal. Again it was Améry whose statement of this thought was most devastating:

> We did not become wiser in Auschwitz ... nor did we become 'deeper' in the camps, insofar as that fatal depth is a definable spiritual dimension at all. That we didn't become better, more human, more humane, and morally mature need not, I believe, be argued. . . . The word dies everywhere that reality makes its claim total. It died for us long ago. And we were not even left with the feeling that we had to regret its loss. (Améry 1, 45)

Améry claimed that the demand to will reality without ideals depends entirely on the character of your reality. For some forms of evil, the demand cannot be met. In chapter 3, I argued that Nietzschean remarks about the ability to suffer as criterion of nobility came dangerously close to the Christian and Stoic views he wished to oppose. But even should we be able to maintain distinctions between the view that suffering sanctifies souls and the view that suffering strengthens them, Auschwitz poses terrible problems. Postwar consensus was so adamant in denying that this sort of suffering ennobled its victims that those victims were often stigmatized.[15] Brutal as it was, both survivors and observers often repeated the claim: the best were those who did not survive. The claim that whatever doesn't kill you makes you stronger was problematically applicable to survivors: if the experience led some of them to develop strengths useful in brutal environments, every other aspect of character was often atrophied. Even those who describe how decency was maintained inside the extermination camps agree that it was also exceptional.

For the camps were very successful in performing the task to which they were dedicated: not only the fabrication of corpses but the prior destruction of souls. Many have described the *Musselmänner*—prisoners whose wills were so thoroughly extinguished that even before they died, they were no longer among the living—as the essential product of Auschwitz. Even those who escaped this fate record nothing but losses. They conclude that whatever depth or wisdom or humanity was intact after Auschwitz remained not through but in spite of it.[16] For everything was directed toward eradicating them. From the long ride in conditions barely appropriate for transporting animals, to the replacement of prisoners' names with numbers, to the disposal of corpses without any of the dignity normally accorded them, victims were subject to a process designed to destroy the very concept of humanity within them. This is not an attack that can be faced directly, with heroic moments that may triumph over death itself. It is, rather, deep and grinding, dulling response by degrees and implicating the victim in his own slow destruction. Souls may be strengthened in the confrontation with evil that acknowledges them. Evil that seeks to deny its victims all the conditions of having a soul cannot possibly further them. We can be grateful to those few who found strength to resist this massive attack on humanity. We cannot suppose them to reveal anything but the mystery of human freedom.

INTENTIONS: MEANING AND MALICE

They would have loathed one another's company, but I brought Hegel and Nietzsche together because both sought a unity between nature and morality that is at odds with modern consciousness. (Nietzsche's description of his work as untimely correctly anticipated that its importance would grow, but it also revealed longing for some ancient impulses. He was out of place in the century that surrounded him.) Both Hegel and Nietzsche represent forms of monism that seek to overcome the gap between nature and morality by abolishing one of the terms. While the opposition between nature and morality is the source of complex metaphysics, it occurs in contexts that are perfectly ordinary. Whenever one voice protests, *That should not have happened*, and another insists, *But it did*, an opposition arises that can become intolerable. Any number of paths to overcome it may present themselves as different forms of monism.

But modern thought is more typically dualistic. We have little use for different sorts of substance, but Cartesian dualism is less urgent than Kantian. What's at issue is not what reason and nature are made of, but whether it makes sense to expect them to have similar properties. If the Lisbon earthquake is a birthplace of modernity, it's because it demanded recognition that nature and morality are split. Lisbon ought not to have happened, but it did. Accepting this came to seem a minimal sign of maturity, and Voltaire's long lament about the earthquake appeared but an elegant version of the child's curse at the chair over which he stumbled. Neither earthquakes nor chairs are properly viewed as objects of outrage because neither contains any moral properties at all. Nature has no meaning; its events are not signs. We no longer expect natural objects to be objects of moral judgment, or even to reflect or harmonize with them. For those who refuse to give up moral judgments, the demand that they stop seeking the unity of nature and morality means accepting a conflict in the heart of being that nothing will ever resolve.

This was the path most often taken in the need to abandon theodicy that arose after Lisbon. For all its difficulty, it's a path which came to seem so self-evident that it forced a change of vocabulary. Before Lisbon, evils were divided into matters of nature, metaphysics, or morality. After Lisbon, the word *evil* was restricted to what was once called moral evil. Modern evil is the product of will. Restricting evil actions to those accompanied by evil intention rids the world of a number of evils in ways that made sense. Less clear were the concepts of willing and intention themselves. Falling rocks and tidal waves do not have them. What having them comes to remained murky.

Kant's ethics began from the claim that only the good will is good in itself. His shopkeeper example was illustration: a shopkeeper who refrains from cheating because good reputations are good for business is different from a shopkeeper who knows he can get away with cheating, and doesn't. Though we may never *see* the difference between them, we know that one is merely prudent, and the other is good. Suppose we accept this account of the difference between a good will and an indifferent one. The good will wants good for the sake of good alone; Kant called it acting from respect for the moral law. The indifferent will wants good when it suits its other interests. But how are we to understand an evil will?

If willing evil becomes too deliberate, we risk the return to original sin that Rousseau sought to avoid. In Rousseau's version of the Fall, humankind became wicked *without* willing evil. Our descent from innocence into civilized barbarism wasn't caused by the deliberate defiance that led Adam and Eve to ruin. The noble savages in Rousseau's story made a series of natural, understandable, and contingent mistakes. Thus Rousseau could assert the fundamental goodness of God and His creatures without denying the reality of the evils of Creation.

The account had flaws, but it had the great merit of both acknowledging the appearances and asserting that there is order behind them. It was particularly brilliant in accounting for evils like inequality, and even slavery, and providing hope that they might be overcome. For Rousseau showed how such evils were not part of the order of nature but consequences of human actions that did not emerge from incorrigibly evil wills. Now even the eighteenth century raised the question: Is there radical evil that Rousseau's account failed to capture? The origin of evil in a series of good-natured mistakes left what was *evil* elusive. It also threatened to undermine the very responsibility it set out to ground. If our mistakes arise from brutish self-interest, it is nature that made us self-interested brutes. How can there be crimes against nature, if evil is part of nature itself? You don't have to be a moralist to find this outcome unacceptable. Sade was outraged by it, and spent most of his time in prison trying to imagine a crime so unnatural that nature itself would protest.

The dilemma is grave. To view acts of evil as deliberate acts of will was to risk a return to original sin. To view acts of evil as simply mistaken was to obscure the difference between what is merely expedient and what is much worse. Kant's book *Religion within the Limits of Reason Alone* tried to solve the problem by asserting the existence of radical evil that is a matter neither of oversight nor of brute natural inclination. Rather, he held that radical evil involves the calculated desire to break the moral law. His account has been so thoroughly and critically examined elsewhere that I will not discuss it here, except to express agreement with the view that Kant's discussion of the matter is extremely disappointing. He argued that the grounds upon which anyone chooses to violate or respect the moral law will always remain inscrutable. This must be the case to preserve the absolute freedom that, for Kant, is the ground of moral responsibility. To say that heroism is as ultimately inscrutable as villainy, because both depend on the mystery of freedom, is to be honest about your limits. We'd expect no less of Immanuel Kant, but we would also expect more.

Traditional attempts to fix a distinction between nature and morality thus left many crucial questions open. But the distinction did fit and promote needs arising in a disenchanted world. As Freud showed, one goal of disenchanting the world was to solve the problem of natural evil. If there is no will behind things like earthquakes and lightning, those that turn out to strike you dead are merely bad luck. Even thinkers who, unlike Freud, still acknowledge God's presence in nature no longer hold Him accountable for His absences. With natural evil reduced to regrettable accident, and metaphysical evil transformed to recognition of the limits we expect every adult to acknowledge, the problem of evil was as far on its way to dissolution as philosophical problems ever go. Though the solution left issues unresolved, it worked well enough for the same reasons Pombal's answers worked for the people of Portugal. There's always enough to do in the business of eliminating those evils we can approach without worrying about the ones we can't. Resolving to take responsibility for some piece of the world in the absence of convincing metaphysical grounding is part of what it means to grow up in it.

In this context Auschwitz posed philosophical problems because it left the nature of assuming responsibility so very unclear. It's easy to see that evil will is absent in things like earthquakes, but what did it mean for evil to be present in humankind? Auschwitz stood for moral evil as other war crimes did not because it seemed deliberate as others did not. Sending children to fight for Britain in the mud of Flanders without grasping the power of the weapons you have put in their hands can be called gross criminal negligence. Rounding up children from all ends of Europe and shipping them to gas chambers in Poland cannot. The number of Jews herded into cattle cars was even exactly calculated; the SS wished to pay the Reichsbahn no more than economy group rates for the cost of transporting people to be murdered. It is hard to imagine an act that is more intentional, at a structural level.

For the individual, things were infinitely murkier. Jurisprudence views heinous crimes as those done with malice and forethought. Both these components of intention were often missing in many agents who carried out the daily work of extermination. Sadists, and particularly venomous antisemites, were present among the murderers, but the SS sought to avoid using those who took obvious pleasure in murder, and most of it was carried out as routine. Vicious hatred was far less in evidence than might be expected among the lower echelons of those who took over the killing. The opportunity to avoid being sent to fight at the front enlisted far more concentration camp guards than did the opportunity to torment Jews. At the highest levels, not only malice, but clear view of the consequences of one's actions was often missing as well. Eichmann is only the most famous Nazi official whose initial goals had nothing to do with mass murder and everything to do with petty desires for personal advancement. At every level, the Nazis produced more evil, with less malice, than civilization had previously known.

The apparent absence of malice or forethought has proved so disturbing that many observers prefer to argue they were present in subterranean form. Writers like Goldhagen argued that behind a mask of relative tolerance, German culture contained particularly virulent forms of antisemitism. The appeal of such claims derives less from historical accuracy than from philosophical naïveté. An old-fashioned picture of evil as inevitably connected to evil intention is more soothing than alternatives. Similarly, ordinary Germans who insist that they never knew what crimes were committed in the east in their names are dismissed as merely dishonest. Bureaucrats who claim to have joined the Nazi party without awareness of its final aims are dismissed as merely despicable. It is easier to appeal to unconscious hatred and unconscious knowledge than to admit the more disturbing view. They really *didn't* mean it—and it really doesn't matter. Auschwitz embodied evil that confuted two centuries of modern assumptions about intention.

Those assumptions identify evil and evil intention so thoroughly that denying the latter is normally viewed as a way of denying the former. Where evil intention is absent, we may hold agents liable for the wrongs they inflict, but we view them as matters of criminal negligence. Alternatively, anyone who denies that criminal intention is present in a particular action is thought to exonerate the criminal. This is the source of the furor that still surrounds Arendt's *Eichmann in Jerusalem*, the twentieth century's most important philosophical contribution to the problem of evil. The conviction that guilt requires malice and forethought led most readers to conclude that Arendt denied guilt because she denied malice and forethought—though she often repeated that Eichmann was guilty, and was convinced that he ought to hang. Her main point is that Eichmann's harmless intentions did *not* mitigate his responsibility. Both the prosecution and the defense proceeded on the assumption that they would. So the prosecution tried to show that Eichmann was both more brutal and more knowledgeable than he claimed to be. Just as surely, the defense tried to show that Eichmann's relatively high position in the hierarchy of the Final Solution resulted from good intentions: Eichmann was moved by nothing worse than the desire to please his superiors by doing his job well. So, it was argued, he never hated Jews, he never set out to murder them, and the one time he watched others do so seemed to have made him sick. Eichmann's trial focused on the question of whether these claims were true. In doing so, Arendt argued, it ignored the most important questions.

> Foremost among the larger issues at stake in the Eichmann trial was the assumption current in all modern legal systems that intent to do wrong is necessary for the commission of a crime. On nothing, perhaps, has civilized jurisprudence prided itself more than on this taking into account of the subjective factor. Where this intent is absent, where, for whatever reasons, even reasons of moral insanity, the ability to distinguish between right and wrong is impaired, we feel no crime has been committed. We refuse, and consider as barbaric, the propositions 'that a great crime offends nature, so that the very earth cries out for vengeance; that evil violates a natural harmony which only retribution can restore; that a wrong collectivity owes a duty to the moral order to punish the criminal' (Yosal Rogat). And yet I think it is undeniable that it was precisely on the ground of these long-forgotten propositions that Eichmann was brought to justice to begin with, and that they were, in fact, the supreme justification for the death penalty. (Arendt 2, 277)

Earlier legal conceptions tied crime to intention in different ways. Oedipus's best efforts to elude his fate may have mitigated his guilt, but they did not erase it, for his crime damaged the order on which

Greek life depended. Now Greek audiences too would have judged Oedipus, who did everything possible to avoid his crimes, differently from Eichmann, who did not. Eichmann caused tragedy; he wasn't fit to be a subject of it. Thus Oedipus is anything but Eichmann's equal, but his example reminds us that the moral consequences of intending an action are no more self-evident than the concept of intention itself. Both can change significantly, and with them the ways we cut up the world.

Arendt's account was crucial in revealing what makes Auschwitz emblematic for contemporary evil. It showed that today, even crimes so immense that the earth itself cries out for retribution are committed by people with motives that are no worse than banal. Flamboyant villainy is easy to recognize, and not too hard to avoid. The lines between wickedness and decency, in yourself or in others, can be drawn with relative clarity. Criminals like Eichmann have none of the subjective traits we use to identify evildoers, yet his crimes were so objectively massive that they made subjective factors irrelevant. His attempts to prove he was perfectly normal were as arduous as the prosecution's attempt to prove he was not. Both attempts were wasted, if what's at issue is what's appalling: the most unprecedented crimes can be committed by the most ordinary people.[17] It is this factor that Auschwitz shares with other contemporary cases of mass murder—for all the other differences between them. In contemporary evil, individuals' intentions rarely correspond to the magnitude of evil individuals are able to cause.

Again it's important to distinguish between metaphysical and political kinds of discussion. Neither should be privileged over the other; each, rather, gains different significance in different contexts. Much of the anger that often attends comparative discussion of twentieth-century evils arises from the failure to distinguish between political and metaphysical comparisons. Arendt's discussion of the role of the Jewish Councils in carrying out the Final Solution is an important case in point. These councils organized by the Nazis often used respected members of already extant Jewish governing bodies to administer the details of deportation. *Eichmann in Jerusalem* aroused particular outrage by claiming that the Jewish Councils were instrumental in ensuring the smooth organization of mass murder. Because she denied that Eichmann's intentions were evil, then turned to discuss the behavior of the Jewish Councils, Arendt was widely accused of excusing the murderers and blaming the victims. At the very least, she was thought to propose the vague and unacceptable claim that in war, everybody is guilty of something or other.[18]

Arendt herself failed to distinguish between political and metaphysical discussion. When pressed, she retreated to the claim that she was only engaged in journalism. This underestimated the depth and force of her own work and allowed criticism to continue that missed her own point. Later historical work, largely sparked by *Eichmann in Jerusalem* itself, showed that the dichotomy it posed between armed resistance and cooperation through the Jewish Councils was too simplistic. But growing sympathy for the moral dilemmas faced by members of the Jewish Councils cannot obscure the fact that their strategies rarely worked. Though their goals were to save lives and reduce suffering through the very limited means at their disposal, their well-intended actions helped the Nazis to murder Jews with an efficiency and thoroughness that the Final Solution would otherwise have lacked. The Nazi capacity to implicate victims, or those who would elsewhere remain innocent bystanders, is the feature of the regime that most resembles traditional forms of evil. This suggests that not the *Musselmann* but the *Sonderkommando* is its most terrible product. Condemning the victim to participate in the mechanics of murder was one way of obliterating morality itself. But here too, the Nazis' intentions were rarely actively diabolical, but merely a dull desire to let others do the dirtiest work.

Nazis forced everyone from passive bystanders to victims to participate in the vast network of destruction. Their success in doing so revealed the impotence of intention on its own. To shut your eyes to Nazism, and even to profit from it, is *not* the same thing as to will the sequence of events that ended at Auschwitz. Auschwitz was nevertheless the product of discrete actions decided upon by particular agents. Debate about moral responsibility during the Third Reich is often sidetracked by discussions of authenticity. If all the Germans who claimed to have privately loathed the regime were telling the truth, it could hardly have retained power for twelve days. But suppose that many bystanders' claims to have been "inwardly opposed" to the Nazi regime were perfectly genuine. Most people desired nothing better or worse than to be left alone to pursue their own private and harmless ends. Much evidence suggests that Eichmann himself was perfectly sincere. He may have been more willing than many of us to ignore other people's interests in the drive to advance his own, but he took no special pleasure in causing suffering, and seems to have actively disliked contemplating it. What better proof can there be that subjective states are not here decisive? What counts is not what your road is paved with, but whether it leads to hell.

Precisely the belief that evil actions require evil intentions allowed totalitarian regimes to convince people to override moral objections that might otherwise have functioned. Massive propaganda efforts undertook to convince people that the criminal actions in which they participated were guided by acceptable, even noble motives. Himmler's exhortation to SS troops at Posen is only the most famous and extreme instance of propaganda that worked by inverting moral values. He proclaimed that it was the very difficulty of overcoming their normal reluctance to shoot women and children that revealed the sublime and significant nature of the historical enterprise in which the troops were involved. Less incredible instances worked in similar ways. Of course it's always possible to betray someone for the prospect of petty personal gain. But if you believe your betrayal is required by loyalty to higher values, it's that much easier to live with. The *feeling* of guilt is so unreliable that it can often serve as an index of innocence. The best of bystanders are those whose consciences are most tormented. Indifferent souls are rarely troubled by the thought of having done too little to prevent crimes.

Like most Nazi officials, Eichmann felt little guilt. This feeling (or its absence) was subjective. Inspecting his conscience, he discovered nothing worse than the ordinary wish to get ahead and even the admirable desire to fulfill obligations that sometimes countered his own private feelings. Suppose he was sincere: the contents of his soul were just as meager as he reported. This is no reason to deny his responsibility, but to look for responsibility elsewhere than in the contents of the soul.

Inspecting your soul is not like unpacking your suitcase. Philosophy long ago abandoned the picture of intentions as mental objects that are ghostly versions of physical ones. But once intentions are no longer viewed as inner objects, how are they to be understood? Frustrated with the vagueness of the concept of intention, some philosophers suggested that intentions be analyzed as dispositions or potentials. Your intention to do something comes to nothing else than your potential, under appropriate circumstances, to do something. But in the crimes we are considering, the distinction between potential and actual evil is exactly the difference that morality demands we preserve. Eichmann argued that in other circumstances he would have behaved no worse than others. Bad luck placed him at a desk where signing a form could become an act of murder. Potentially, he could have lived a life as harmless as his inner world, just as others more fortunately situated might have realized the evil for which he was responsible. This is what it means to engage in ordinary complicity—just as refusing to give in to this kind of bad luck is what it means to engage in ordinary heroism. But determining what complicity and heroism now mean is vital, for Nazi attempts to obliterate moral distinctions between actual and potential criminals make it all the more crucial to preserve them. Of all those who might have become criminals, only some actually participated in the Final Solution. Of all those who might potentially have been heroes, even fewer actually defied the powers that were. Guilt and innocence depend on these very simple truths. When the notion of intention is tied to a notion of potential, the distinction between actual and potential evil becomes even more obscure. So, Arendt argued, the court should have addressed Eichmann:

> We are concerned only with what you did, and not with the possible noncriminal nature of your inner life and of your motives or with the criminal potentialities of those around you. (Arendt 2, 278)

It's not accidental that analysis of the concept of intention occupied much of late-twentieth-century philosophy and jurisprudence. Various authors have offered accounts of intention designed to avoid both Cartesian pictures of intentions as ghostly objects and the problems generated when we view intentions as potential. Some accounts are better than others, but none has yet led to consensus on how we are to understand historical responsibility. A moment's reflection reveals how much is at stake here. Debates between the functionalist and intentionalist schools of Holocaust historiography betray a lack of clarity about the concept of intention itself. For they ask whether what is at issue is guilt (*Schuld*) or negligence (*Fahrlässigkeit*)—when what was present in most people was both. Recurring arguments about whether Nazi slave camps were worse than Soviet ones, whether the bombing of Hiroshima was comparable to the Axis slaughter of civilians, are questions about how to weight the role of intention itself. Much of the fury surrounding such debates results from the desire to retain a connection between evil and intention that is not theoretically defensible. Those reluctant to describe the bombing of Hiroshima as evil emphasize the fact that nearly everyone with any responsibility for it acted from acceptable, even good intentions. It is just this identification of evil with evil intention that led to the widespread misreading of Arendt. Because she argued that Eichmann's intentions were only trivially bad ones, she was held to have argued that his actions were nothing worse. Her point was not to deny responsibility but to demand that we understand responsibility anew. The sheer number of questions that can be raised here reveals how very shaky our understanding has become. Post-Lisbon thinkers used intention as the concept that determined good and evil, turning what had once been natural evil into mere disaster, and evil into that which was somebody's fault. But the concept cannot help without consensus about what it comes to, apart from agreement that it isn't found in earth or water.

Eichmann's case is interesting because it represents the worst case. Others who helped to carry out the Final Solution may have had better intentions—the genuine desire, for example, to hinder more, or more gruesome death. Once we turn away from Nazi crimes to look at others, we will find murders carried out for motives that many of us share. Perhaps the most frightening consequence of pondering these considerations is that the self itself retreats from view. The mass murderer turns individuals into numbered corpses, but he himself, as individual, is scarcely more present.

Sade's works have grown steadily more popular since the war. One reason is surely a deep desire for models of villains who are both clear-cut and full-bodied. The claim that evil is easier to portray than goodness has become a cliché, but literature gives us surprisingly few examples of pure and radical evil. Iago is notoriously mysterious, too small and opaque for the degree of destruction he is able to cause. Sade's criminals, by contrast, compete to outdo each other in transparent displays of evil will. Sade's opponent was always God, even when he was skeptical about His existence. He thus sought to create criminals large enough to hit his target. Sade's villains are neither subtle nor slimy. They are conscious about their motives, which they discuss at interminable length. Evil, for them, is a means to physical pleasure, the only drive that ever moves them. They are men and women with large and unusual appetites. You like lemon pie; Juliette likes torturing children. Saint-Fond, Sade's most successful portrait of pure evil, adds intellectual refinements to torment as other people add spices. He particularly enjoys implicating victims in his crimes. Forcing a man to whip his beloved while being tortured to death extends Saint-Fond's pleasure, through contemplation, a little longer. We have two minds about whether heat or coolness marks a more evil will. In creatures like Saint-Fond, Sade united perverse unbridled appetite with cold-blooded forethought. Whatever is more essential to evil, he had the bases covered.

Sade's portraits of pure evil fascinate because they are rare. Literature gives us fewer models than we'd imagine, for even the devil himself is usually disappointing. Consider modern literature's greatest attempts to depict him. Both Goethe's and Dostoevsky's devils exude airs of shabbiness. Each is significantly smaller than the hero he means to seduce. Both offer themselves not as masters but as particularly obsequious servants. They represent not malicious impulses but mean ones. Faust is a thinker; Mephistopheles is a pedant. He is so constrained by rule that he cannot enter Faust's study without finding a loophole. He limps, complains, makes vulgar jokes. Every word and every gesture signal impotence, not power. The spirit who always denies, Mephistopheles destroys what others create. He says himself that he's not one of the great ones, and he claims—perhaps truly—that he cannot move anything at all. Faust sets ends; Mephistopheles provides means. When he describes himself as *playing* the devil, one wonders whether he's ever capable of *being* it. Faust calls him a poor devil. It's an ironic twist on a common expression, but it underlines all the difference between them. The figure of size and stature is Faust himself.

Goethe suggested that Faust's search for meaning made him prey to temptations that leave others cold, and Dostoevsky said so clearly. The devil who visits Ivan Karamazov "loves the dreams of [his] passionate young friends, quivering with a quavering for life!" This devil is failure itself. Ivan describes him as a sponger, a flunky, a clown. The devil responds by taunting Ivan for his disappointment. Didn't he know we live in a disenchanted world? Not even the devil appears in flames. Instead he comes in threadbare coat and dirty linen. He's subject to colds and severe self-pity; the devil is the very sum of human weakness. He is so far from being a fallen angel that even his attempts to look like a gentleman dissolve on examination. He isn't clearly driven by any motive worse than an indiscriminate desire to make himself agreeable. In the famous chapter "Rebellion" Ivan is prepared to reject God for the sake of Creation. When he finally meets the devil, he has no heroic choices. The devil is the expression of base urges, not defiant ones.

Both devils are remarkably concerned with their own existence. Dostoevsky's devil recounts meeting with journalists who denied his existence outright. "Why, I said to them, 'It's reactionary to believe in God in our age. But I'm the devil. You can believe in me." The devil's need to demonstrate his reality is a comment on our unwillingness to see the presence of evil. Both devils defend their *right* to exist with traditional theodicy. Mephistopheles is the force that always wants evil and always does good nonetheless. What begins as evil is always re-vealed to end as its opposite. How can we complain about evil, in a world that functions so well? Dostoevsky cited Goethe's text and tried to improve on it. His devil would prefer to do good, but he has another job: keeping the world in motion. Without evil there would be no events at all. The world would grind to a halt in a dull burst of loud praise. For, he intones, suffering is life. Here theodicy itself is the work of the devil. Mean and self-seeking apologetics replace active sedition. Romantic rhetoric is out of place.

The devil's banality is designed to make us uncomfortable. Both Goethe and Dostoevsky said this clearly. Sade captured twentieth-century imagination because he described the devils we'd prefer. It's often said that we long for lost heroes, but our need for the right kind of villain is no less urgent. We long for a picture of what went wrong in the world. Fortunately or not, villains like Sade's are comparatively infrequent. The greatest destruction is caused by men who look more like Dostoevsky's devil than they look like Saint-Fond. We are threatened more often by those with indifferent or misguided intentions than by those with malevolent ones; even deliberate forms of malice are often so petty as to bewilder. Brute sadists administered daily life in concentration camps everywhere, but they did not build them. *Bad* intentions and thoughtlessness were present enough in the architects. They do not add up to the magnitude of the evil they caused.

The banality of evil is a new phrase, but it isn't a new discovery. At Auschwitz the devil showed the face that earlier literature merely suspected. What he did there resists the conceptual categories we have available. The Holocaust did not take place by accident, or by oversight. But the vast and careful design at some levels crumbles on examination at others. Who was the designer? Few Nazis showed the signs that traditionally made evil tempting. Out of uniform, they were rather pathetic, which mitigates their otherwise sickening tendency to feel sorry for themselves. Auschwitz revealed the gaps between the pieces of our concepts of intention. Neither malice nor foresight was sufficient to account for all of the evil they were meant to explain. Struck by the absence of sufficient signs of individual evil intention, some have tried to explain evil by a collective will, or structural intention. Appeals to structural processes that lead to evil remind us of our roles as parts of systems where divisions of labor, and simple distance, obscure individual responsibility. Auschwitz was hardly the only example of evil produced by human cogs—just the clearest one. But calls for awareness are not yet accounts, and substituting collective for individual intention is an attempt to preserve an old framework simply for the sake of having one. Recognizing this means recognizing that we have very clear paradigms of moral evil but nothing close to an adequate account of them. Sade and Auschwitz have little in common. It is unlikely that a general formula will be found to unite them, and any attempt to do so may obscure what is morally important in each.

The absence of a general account of intention and evil is profoundly disturbing because the hope for it was a minimalist demand. The problem of evil began by trying to penetrate God's intentions. Now it appears we cannot make sense of our own. If Auschwitz leaves us more helpless than Lisbon, it is because our conceptual resources seem exhausted. After Lisbon, one could pick up shattered pieces of worldview and decide to live bravely, taking responsibility for a disenchanted world. After Auschwitz, even our attempts to do this much seem doomed to failure. The long philosophical silence on the subject will surprise no one who recognizes the consequences of the attack on intention. The notion cannot carry the weight that contemporary forms of evil bring to bear on it. Nor can we simply do without it—nor collapse the distinction between natural and moral evil.

We should admit the extent of our losses. If Lisbon marked the moment of recognition that traditional theodicy was hopeless, Auschwitz signaled the recognition that every replacement fared no better. In each case there was complex interplay between the shock of confrontation with evil and the intellectual resources present to cope with it. Lisbon exhausted classic attempts to connect natural and moral evil, and with them hopes of finding systematic justification of individual suffering. There remained three very different ways of closing the gap between the evil that happens and reason's demand that it be otherwise. In the last section I argued that Auschwitz blocked both the path taken by Hegel and that proposed by Nietzsche. Finally and most troubling, as the present section argued, it undermined the most common modern response to the end of theodicy. For where the notion that evil requires evil intention is thrown into confusion, attempts to take responsibility for suffering will seem precarious.

TERROR: AFTER SEPTEMBER 11

One late autumn evening a student from Paris sat in my kitchen in Berlin and asked, apropos of nothing, where I had been when I heard the news. He might have come from Boston or Santiago or Zagreb.

Wherever we were, whoever we are, it is a moment we will not forget, and need to recall over and over—as we needed to watch the World Trade Center fall, over and over on television, until we felt sick enough to be sure it was real. This is globalization. Is it Lisbon?

The parallels are undeniable. The suddenness and speed of the attack resembled natural catastrophe. There was no warning. There was also no message. The absence of both created the kind of fear that made most of us know we had not, until then, understood the meaning of the word terror. Like earthquakes, terrorists strike at random: who lives and who does not depends on contingencies that cannot be deserved or prevented. Thinkers like Voltaire raged at God for His failure to uphold the elementary moral rules human beings try to follow. Children should not be suddenly and brutally tormented; something as big as the difference between life and death should not depend on something as small as chance. Natural disaster is blind to moral distinctions that even crude justice draws. Terrorism deliberately defies them. In underscoring contingency, September 11 underscored our infinite fragility. Even in New York, many people knew no one who was in the World Trade Center at the time of the attack, but everyone seemed to know someone who was sleeping off a hangover or taking a child to kindergarten. Where failure to get to work becomes a way of saving one's life, our sense of powerlessness becomes overwhelming. The terrorists chose targets sure to increase it. Wall Street and the Pentagon are at once symbol and reality of Western force, and it is unclear which was more frightening: the collapse of the glaringly conspicuous twin towers or the assault on the impenetrable recesses of military might. Neither visibility nor invisibility provided protection. Watching both shatter so quickly, no one could possibly feel safe. Ordinary people everywhere echoed Arendt: the impossible became true.

So it was said and written, on streets and papers in more languages than are worth counting, that the world will not be the same. It is too soon to know what this means. This is partly because the consequences are not all clear. It is also because the only way to hold a world together is to deny it has been shattered. We cannot know whether an epoch has been ended by an event when *not* viewing the event as epochal is essential to going on. This is part of maintaining order in defiance of attempts to destroy it. Pombal had to underplay the earth-quake's significance in order to return Lisbon to normalcy. His exhorta-tions to go back to business had the same source as Giuliani's: where all the odds are against it, making life ordinary can be an act of heroism. For a day or so after the catastrophe, language itself seemed useless. At midday on September 12, CNN showed silent pictures above a running band of caption: NO COMMENT   NO COMMENT   NO COMMENT   NO COMMENT NO COMMENT   NO COMMENT. By nightfall there was ordinary newscasting discussing everything from economic losses to the appropriateness of discussing anything at all. Pombal simply kept the Portuguese newspa-per in print. In our self-reflective era, the media rushed to defend their own return to business as usual. It wasn't necessary. Terror is meant to strike us dumb. Finding words with which to face it is an act of reconstruction.

Still we cannot say how much the world will change. We face new forms of danger. But they are not, I submit, new forms of evil. The difficulties of coping with terrorism are not conceptual difficulties. Those who carried out the mass murder on September 11 embodied a form of evil so old-fashioned that its reappearance is part of our shock. It is old-fashioned not because it was carried out by those who held fundamentalist ideologies untouched by modern scruples. Seeing the power of belief in a god who rewards those who destroy his enemies with a rancid caricature of paradise can only make us grateful for skep-ticism, but the content of the terrorists' beliefs is not central. Some Nazis' decisions to die rather than surrender in the final days of the war drew on primitive chiliastic fantasies, yet I have argued that the Third Reich embodied contemporary evil. September 11 provided an instance of evil that was old-fashioned in structure. Banal evil emerges from the fabric of ordinary life that September 11 ripped through.

Most important: it was awesomely intentional. The foresight in-volved was massive. The murderers focused their end precisely in view, and they went to every imaginable length to achieve it—from the exact planning required for years of coordination to the preparation of their own certain deaths. The clearest use of instrumental rationality was matched by the clearest flaunting of moral reasoning. Nature disre-gards distinctions between every kind of guilt and every kind of innocence; the terrorists actively scorned them. Without even a demand that was put forth for negotiation, there wasn't the flimsiest of excuses for the destruction of ordinary lives. The terrorists' goals were, rather, to produce what morality tries to prevent: death and fear. (Rousseau thought the fear of death worse than death itself, since fear threatens our freedom and poisons our lives.) Malice and forethought, the classic components of evil intention, have rarely been so well combined. The terrorists bypassed complex models like Mephistopheles and took us back to Sade. Some will doubtless counter that they believed their cause was just. But the absence of so much as an ultimatum renders every attempt to make a case for just terrorism hopeless—even for those who like defending contradictions. Destroying random members of a culture you find unacceptable does not count as a permissible cause.

Later, it seemed foreboding. The slow and inexorable destruction of the giant double Buddhas in Afghanistan sent shivers down the spine of a world long inured to watching children starve before cameras. The Taliban explosion of what was, after all, only stone and statue, captured days of unexplained global attention. Did it foreshadow the imploding towers a few months later? Heine wrote that anyone willing to burn books will not hesitate to burn people. The sentence was written long before joyful Nazi students piled banned books onto public bonfires, and its prescience came to seem eerie. To take that pure an aim at human culture—what makes us free, according to Hegel, and able to assume the role of creators, according to Marx—is to aim at humanity itself.

But the parallels stop there. The Taliban and the terrorists they supported are not *complex* thugs. Their appearance on a sunny morning in the center of civilization was shocking because we were used to more sophistication as well as to more safety. Those whose intellectual nourishment isn't confined to old Westerns were no longer accustomed to such straightforward moral judgments. When forced to choose between simplification and cynicism, educated people incline to the latter. There was plenty of evidence to make it look reasonable. Wall Street seemed determined to show that everything could be bought and sold, the Pentagon bent on renewing the pre-Socratic belief that justice means helping your friends and hurting your enemies. After 1989, only interests, not ideas, seemed objects of real conflict. Easy enough to conclude that any conflict between good and evil themselves was nothing but hype.

This paralyzed moral reaction. Those whose conceptions of evil were always simple and demonic were happy to see them confirmed. It gave them new missions, and new excuses to carry out old ones. Those whose conceptions of evil had been shaped less by Hollywood than by Chile and Vietnam and Auschwitz and Cambodia are at more of a loss. We have learned how easily crimes are committed through bureaucratic structures of ordinary people who do not let themselves acknowledge, exactly, what it is that they do. Arendt's analysis of Eichmann was never completely elaborated. But the description of evil as thoughtless captured so many cases of contemporary evil that we were unprepared for a case of single-mindedly thoughtful evil. The sense of conceptual helplessness the terrorists thus produced was almost as great as every other sense of helplessness. We seemed left with no good choices. To call what happened on September 11 evil appeared to join forces with those whose simple, demonic conceptions of evil often deliberately obscure more insidious forms of it. Not to call the murders evil appeared to relativize them, to engage in forms of calculation that make them understandable—and risked a first step toward making them justifiable.

Some were willing to take those steps, and to offer crude forms of theodicy from several directions. Christian fundamentalists blamed the secular world for weakening God's willingness to protect America. There were more numerous suggestions that New Yorkers were reaping what the Pentagon and Wall Street had sowed in all the forms of suffering they cause throughout the Third World. Only those closest to the terrorists went on to maintain that September 11 was therefore simple justice. But the lack of a coherent conclusion did not prevent many from pointing to the data, again and again, as if they should form one by themselves.

Simple theodicies are types of magic thinking. Hoping the powers that control your life are listening to what you think they want to hear is a desperate search for protection—as Kant chided the friends of Job.

Jerry Falwell never had an abortion; French critics never hurt an Iraqi child. Surely they must be safe from terrorist assault?

They are not, of course, but we understand their impulse. This way of seeking explanations of evil is part of an attempt to ward off more of it, as well as to make sense of the world as a whole. If the first urge is comprehensible, the second urge can be positively commendable. Yet both are, in this context, obscene. For both are ways of denying that what happened on September 11 was evil—when the blatant unbearable anguish stared into our faces from every haunting homemade poster on the streets of New York.

Refusing to deny this kind of evil hardly entails a refusal to deny other kinds. All to the contrary. Dividing evils into greater and lesser, and trying to weigh them, is not just pointless but impermissible. To call something evil is to say that it defies justification, and balance. Evils should not be compared, but they should be distinguished. The appearance of old forms of evil need not blind us to the appearance of other forms, and it may even sharpen our eye for them. Systematic worldwide oppression does nothing to justify terrorism; it doesn't even explain it. It surely prepares ground in which terrorism can grow. *But even if it didn't, it should be resisted as an evil on its own terms.*

For those who wanted to hear it, Auschwitz offered a moral lesson about vigilance. Very few people are prepared to destroy their own lives for the sake of destroying others. Very many are prepared to play small parts in systems that lead to evils they do not want to foresee. Many whose lives were spent opposing contemporary forms of evil were reluctant to use the word to refer to the terrorists—or to use it at all except in scare quotes. They knew that it had been used crudely by those whose lives were spent making themselves deaf to the forms of evil they and their institutions cause. But abandoning moral discourse to those with fewer scruples is a peculiar way of maintaining one's own. Those who care about resisting evils must be able to recognize them however they appear. Surrendering the word *evil* to those who perceive only its simplest forms leaves us fewer resources with which to approach the complex ones.

Evils can be acknowledged as evils without insisting that evil has an essence. Our inability to find something deep that is common to the mass murders committed by terrorists and the starvation furthered by corporate interests does not prevent us from condemning both. Thinking clearly is crucial; finding formulas is not. For contemporary possibilities threaten even early modern attempts to divide moral from natural evils. Terrorist strikes imitate nature's arbitrary blows. If combined with the deliberate reproduction of nature's worst elements, like plague, terrorism's blend of moral and natural evil is so appalling that we seem doomed to despair. Using human intention to outdo nature at its most perfidious makes earlier ways of rearranging nature seem laughable. Knowing this cannot make us forget other possibilities that threaten to blur distinctions between natural and moral evils. Slow ecological disaster is not intended by the developed nations that fail to regulate the consumption that will surely lead to it—which lessens no one's responsibility to prevent it. Debates about which blend of moral and natural evil is worse will lead us nowhere. I write in the fear and knowledge that either could destroy us all.

September 11 revealed one ground for hope they will not. The terrorists' resolve to make us feel we have no power showed that in fact we do. For they revealed how far evil as well as resistance to it remain in individual human hands. A few men with determination and pocketknives killed thousands in an instant and set events in motion that threaten the earth as a whole. This would be reason for dismay, or at best for reflection, were it not for Flight 93.

Evil is not merely the opposite of good but inimical to it. True evil aims at destroying moral distinctions themselves. One way to do so is to make victims into accomplices. The *Sonderkommandos* who did the work that allowed the gas chambers to function were implicated in them, though every opportunity for resistance was gone by the time they knew what they were doing. The worst horror of September 11 was the fact that those riding in the planes that slammed into the World Trade Center were not only torn out of ordinary lives into their own deaths, but became part of explosions that killed thousands of others. This, at least, was the judgment of a handful of passengers on board the fourth plane heading toward an uncertain Washington target. Unlike the passengers on other flights, they had knowledge on which they could act. Without it they would have been as helpless as those confronted by the unimaginable when the doors of the cattle cars opened. Before it ever happened, who could suppose that human beings would be extinguished like vermin, or transformed into living bombs?

Smashed planes leave little hope that we will ever know the whole story, but what we know already is enough. Informed via cell phone that other hijacked planes had been flown into the towers, some people determined to fight. They failed to overcome the terrorists but succeeded in assuring that the plane crashed into an empty field. They died as heroes die. Unlike the hypothetical fellow in Kant's example who prefers to die than to bear false witness, their refusal to become instruments of evil became more than a gesture. We will never know how much destruction they prevented, but we know they prevented some. They proved not only that human beings have freedom; we can use it to affect a world we fear we don't control.

This is not theodicy. It is not even consolation—though it is all the hope we have.

REMAINS: CAMUS, ARENDT, CRITICAL THEORY, RAWLS

In a tribute to King Alfonso, Hans Blumenberg wrote that the modern age began with an act of theodicy (Blumenberg 2, 307). Does it end with the realization that all such acts are forlorn? Political and historical reflection about particular causes of evil, and the hope of particular resistance that comes with them, would still be an option, but anything general seems proscribed. To be certain, theodicy's continued existence was never assured. Leibniz's stance was defensive even before Voltaire caricatured it in *Candide*. We saw theodicy come to an end, over and over, throughout the eighteenth and nineteenth centuries, only to reappear in other forms. Its persistence in the face of attack testifies to the fact that theodicy meets some deep human needs, but not to its truth, or even its stability. This demise might just turn out to be the final one; some messages take longer than others to grasp.

Changes within philosophy seem to confirm this suggestion. If any one feature distinguishes twentieth-century philosophy from its predecessors, it is the absence of explicit discussion of the problem of evil.

Despite the differences between his work and everything preceding it, Nietzsche's case makes this most clear: through the late nineteenth century you could take whatever position you wanted on the problem of evil as long as you were engaged with it. If you were not, you were not a philosopher. Engagement transcended differences between national and confessional traditions, between rationalist and empiricist, systematician and skeptic. Consider, as one surprising example, John Stuart Mill. While his lifelong concern with moral evil remains well-known, his concern with questions of natural and metaphysical evil has been largely forgotten. Here is one passage:

> In sober truth, nearly all the things which men are hanged or imprisoned for doing to one another are nature's everyday performances. Killing, the most criminal act recognized by human laws, nature does once to every being that lives, and in a large proportion of cases after protracted tortures such as only the greatest monsters whom we read of purposely inflict on their fellow living creatures. (Mill, 385)

Engagement with the problem of evil continued in British philosophy through McTaggart and Bradley, to disappear almost entirely with Bertrand Russell. Russell's example is particularly instructive because it underlines that what is at issue cannot be explained in ethical terms. His commitments to ethical and political engagement, and even to writing works discussing philosophical questions of general interest, were demonstrated throughout a long lifetime. And since he began his philosophical career as a Hegelian, his disregard for the scope of the questions of theodicy cannot be a matter of simple ignorance. Yet Russell's disinterest is so great that, like other analytic philosophers, he read it back into history: even the index to his 895-page *History of Western Philosophy* devotes more entries to *Egypt* than it does to *evil*.

Twentieth-century philosophy saw no future for theodicy and barely noticed its past. What had functioned as starting point for most philosophical speculations about appearance and reality, reason and right, became an embarrassing minor anachronism. We write the history we want to continue. Philosophers working on problems of foundationalism wished to be part of the same subject that engaged

Kant and Hegel. Standing on giants' shoulders is an old recipe for improving your vision—or at least for raising your stature. So contemporary historians described earlier philosophers' projects in terms they wished to share. Being represented with certainty was not in fact the greatest problem the external world had traditionally posed for philosophy—but it was the one most twentieth-century philosophers wanted to solve.

Of course differences in philosophical traditions made themselves felt in the historiography of philosophy. Philosophers on both sides of the Atlantic now commonly deny differences between what was called analytic and what was called continental philosophy. Certainly simple attempts to distinguish them proved wrong. Polemical charges that continental philosophy was hostile to science, or analytic philosophy indifferent to ethics, were belied by good and overlapping work in both traditions. Even more problematic for those seeking clear philosophical lines was the growing awareness of differences within these traditions themselves. If no European philosopher ever answered to the name "continental," the number of Anglo-Americans willing to regard themselves as analytic philosophers is currently in decline. Still one difference remains between philosophers trained in Europe and those trained in Britain or America. The former were likely to have learned something about the problem of evil and retained some connection to it in their own work. Contemporary analytic discussion of the problem of evil, by contrast, remains squarely confined to the marginalized field of philosophy of religion. Thus historical discussion, where it does occur, is focused largely on Leibniz and Hume, whose treatment of the problem of evil remained within traditional religious discourse. Postwar German history of philosophy, by contrast, offered rich and significant work related to many aspects of the problem.[19] Yet the conception of the problem of evil those works faced was smaller in scope than the one I have sketched here. One consequence is a different estimate of its significance for the questions of metaphysics, so that the broad narrative of the history of modern philosophy as the transformation of ontology to epistemology is still the story most often told in Europe. Our views of our pasts and our futures are mutually supporting: underestimating the scope of the problem of evil in the history of philosophy makes it easy to overlook its remnants in the present. So it was possible for a German philosopher to complain in 1997 that German philosophy had ignored Auschwitz—though German culture as a whole was obsessed with it.[20]

These shifts in focus lend weight to Levinas's claim. Shall we conclude with him that the most revolutionary change in twentieth-century consciousness was its ability to abandon theodicy? Not before considering, once again, exactly what is meant by it. Theodicy, as systematic justification of suffering, and of God's goodness in the face of it, originated not with Leibniz but with the oldest book of the Bible—in the persons of Job's friends. God's reaction shows that something about this response to the world is deeply inadequate, and possibly immoral. God Himself condemns the impulse to theodicy, for He says that not the friends but Job spoke truth.

Which truth did He mean? The literature on the Book of Job is deeply divided. What's clear is that Job's speeches are no systematic justification but a response to the same impulse that gives rise to theodicy: the need to face evil in the world without giving in to despair. If we call this impulse the drive to theodicy in the widest sense, it is far from certain that it's exhausted. Levinas's own work is part of this project.[21] Many other works are conscious attempts to take up the problems that no previous theodicy could resolve. Postwar philosophical discussion of these questions has been hesitant, in painful awareness that even the attempt to voice them may be problematic. Since reason itself has been thrown into question, the discussion takes a fragmentary, sometimes literary character. Not even theologians today attempt the sort of systematic accounts that were once central. Nevertheless, elements of traditional discussion of the problem of evil have reemerged in response to Auschwitz. This reemergence is so surprising that we must ask what moves thinkers well aware of the problems to undertake any discussion of them at all.

This section presents four examples of such reemergence. Discussing texts of Camus, Arendt, Adorno and Horkheimer, and Rawls is not a systematic overview of their work as a whole. It isn't even an attempt to survey the practical engagement with particular evils that was important to all of them. Though Camus, as I argue, offered no interesting political theory, both Arendt and the Frankfurt School devoted years of hard work to empirical investigations of politics and history. The author of *Eichmann in Jerusalem* presupposed the work she'd completed in *The Origins of Totalitarianism*. The later reflections of Adorno and Horkheimer were preceded by lifelong attempts to rethink Marxism as well as the sort of studies undertaken in *The Authoritarian Personality*. Rawls's work, of course, is as political as philosophy can be, and no serious thinker ignored the fact that contemporary evils must be treated in political terms. The thinkers I will sketch reveal something further: that political questions can emerge from, and remain entwined with, metaphysical ones. If the first moral obligation is to offer reflections that may help shape political solutions, the first philosophical obligation is to reflect on what precedes them.

The thinkers introduced here hardly exhaust twentieth-century thought on the subject, but they do represent it. A full account of these questions would include Bloch and Benjamin, Levinas and Sartre, Habermas, Lyotard, and doubtless others. Here I hope simply to present enough material to be exemplary. My interest is not to give a thorough review of the problem of evil but, rather, to shed light on the question: What makes it so central to modern philosophy?

A night watchman makes a brief appearance in Camus's novel *The Plague*.

> The man never failed to remind everyone he met that he'd foreseen what was happening. Tarrou agreed he'd predicted a disaster, but reminded him that the event predicted by him was an earthquake. To which the old fellow replied: "Ah, if only it had been an earthquake! A good bad shock, and there you are! You count the dead and the living, and that's the end of it. (Camus 3, 114)

Instead of clean-cut disaster Camus gave us something else: men filling mass graves with increasing speed and indifference, internment camps whose guards shoot to kill, the slow unendurable death of a child. Worse than these: the increasing isolation of victims from each other as tragedy saps emotional along with physical strength, the bleak unending struggle when all human desire congeals into the wish for more food. It's the insidiousness of evil—its grim persistent refusal to achieve heroic dimensions, its unremitting ugliness—that marks contemporary consciousness. Fighting it is a matter of quiet heroism, without hope of final victory. It may involve nothing more than "bearing witness . . . so that some memorial of the injustice and outrage done to them might endure" (Camus 3, 308).

We have heard this before, as Camus knew. The outrage he chose to witness was neither earthquake nor death camp but plague. Much controversy around his masterpiece was provoked by his choice. Prominent critics accused him of moral evasion. In focusing on a name-less natural enemy, *The Plague*, it was argued, taught readers to ignore history and human struggles. In response to Roland Barthes Camus wrote:

> *The Plague*, which I wanted to be read on a number of levels, nevertheless has as its obvious content the struggle of the Euro-pean resistance movements against Nazism. The proof is that al-though this enemy is nowhere named, everyone in every Euro-pean country recognized him. I will add that a long extract from *The Plague* appeared under the Occupation, in a collection of resistance texts, and that this fact alone would justify the transpo-sition I have made. *The Plague* is, in a sense, more than a chroni-cle of the resistance. But it is certainly not anything less. (Camus 5, 220)

For critics like Sartre this just begged the question. Why choose the brute blind plague to symbolize Nazism—unless you want to say that the Nazis' crime was to act as accomplices to the blind forces of the universe? The plague can be used to symbolize Nazism only if Nazis themselves become symbols: for some vague and brutal destructive force that is part of the world and constantly threatens to overwhelm it. In that case what's at issue are metaphysical conditions, not particular historical ones—which comes perilously close to absolving particular historical beings of responsibility. Sartre did not quite accuse Camus of this, or of making God responsible for human crimes. But he did say that Camus hated God more than he hated the Nazis, and complained that the latter never really counted in Camus's world. Camus's struggle in the resistance was a task he took on with reluctance, for it distracted him from the primary struggle against larger, more abstract evil (Sartre).

Sartre's description was exact. As political analysis Camus's metaphor borders on the willfully irresponsible. To fight particular evils effectively, you need to understand them. To view Nazism as comparable to microbes is to obscure understanding. Camus's essays reveal even more of the truth in Sartre's charges. Camus's discussion of moral and natural evils was the result, however, not of conceptual confusion but of self-conscious assertion. Both moral and natural evils are special cases of something worse: the metaphysical evil built into the human condition. Camus rejected the description of metaphysical evil as abstract and harmless finitude. He thought that this was a coward's attempt to reconcile us to our unacceptable fate. We are confronted with nothing so bland as a limit but with a death sentence imposed without mercy for a crime as universal as it is unspecified. So *The Plague*'s hero Tarrou, like Ivan Karamazov, hates the death penalty because it mirrors the human condition as a whole. All true rebellion is rebellion against the existence of death itself, for however it takes us, it is evil.

What drives us to rebel is not simple self-interest or the cowardly refusal to die; the rebel is less interested in life than in reasons for living. Like Platonism and Christianity, Camus would never be content with the temporal. His paeans to sensuality were always swan songs. At bottom he believed that what does not last cannot be significant. Thus he concluded that to fight against death is to insist that life has a meaning.

So *The Myth of Sisyphus* begins starkly:

> There is but one truly serious philosophical problem, and that is suicide. Judging whether life is or is not worth living amounts to answering the fundamental question of philosophy. All the rest—whether or not the world has three dimensions, whether the mind has nine or twelve categories—comes afterwards. (Camus 1, 3)

Camus held the metaphysical problem of evil to be as unyielding as it was when first raised. He thought it arose in the attempt to combine Greek and Christian worldviews.

Christ came to solve two major problems, evil and death, which are precisely the problems that preoccupy the rebel. His solution consisted, first, in experiencing them. The man-god suffers, too—with patience. Evil and death can no longer be entirely imputed to Him since He suffers and dies. (Camus 4, 32)

The Rebel argued that the Greeks found neither gods nor humans entirely innocent or guilty. Disasters were closer to error than crime. The experience of cosmic injustice provokes a sense of outrage thus lacking in Greek experience of suffering: there it was easier to submit to one's fate. Belief in a personal God and a sense of mutual responsibility go hand in hand; it's sometimes been called a covenant. The attempt to combine Greek ideas with Christian ones produced gnosticism. Camus thought that the large number of gnostic sects reflected desperation: gnostics sought to remove motives for rebellion by removing the unjust element of suffering. But real metaphysical rebellion, he argued, first appeared in the late eighteenth century. This is not the result of declining religion. For the metaphysical rebel is less atheist than blasphemer: he denounces God in the name of an order that is better than the one we know.

Camus's times demanded particular attention to distinctions among evils, and his views took shape accordingly. *The Rebel* begins by describing murder, not suicide, as the problem of the age. This was a deliberate contrast to *The Myth of Sisyphus*. The fifteen years separating the books were not random ones. The events that occurred between 1940 and 1955 focused Camus on solidarity, community struggle, and their conditions. In turning from the question of suicide to the question of political murder, he distanced himself from the earlier work. If both acts raise questions about the meaning of life, one does so in a way that the mature man could defend as a responsible citizen. Yet for all Camus's intentions, much in the later book confirms the earlier book's view that political problems are but special cases of metaphysical ones.

Nothing makes this clearer than his discussion of Ivan Karamazov. Dostoevsky's chapter "Rebellion" is the prelude to his "Grand Inquisitor." In it Ivan tells a story as unforgettable as any atrocity of more recent literature. An eight-year-old boy who threw a stone that wounded the paw of his landlord's favorite dog was hunted and torn to pieces by a pack of hounds before his mother's eyes. Ivan concludes the tale by resolving to reject truth, understanding, and salvation itself, if they come at the price of such murder. He explicitly refuses the comfort that might be won by seeing this story in political terms, as an instance of what feudalism had allowed. The abolition of serfdom should not provide comfort or reconcile us to reality. Even if political changes make a repetition of this crime impossible, the fact that it occurred once is intolerable to Ivan: he would refuse the salvation of humankind if it demands one sacrifice like this.

Ivan Karamazov became Camus's emblem of a metaphysical rebel, and this chapter of *The Brothers Karamazov* was central to his thought. Camus's echo of it in his own greatest novel thus reveals a great deal. *The Plague*'s starkest chapter is an agonizing description of one boy's death. Here the source of torment is anything but malevolent. On the contrary, the boy's death is particularly painful and prolonged because he was given experimental serum in a final effort to save his life. Knowledge of their own good intentions does no more to lessen the despair of the doctors observing the death than to lessen the suffering of the screaming child. Such despair and such suffering are indictments that no form of social reordering can answer.

We are left with what looks like paradox. Few people who ever made their living teaching philosophy were louder in their denunciations of metaphysics than Camus. But few modern writers were so deeply concerned with an evil that turns out to be metaphysical in its roots, merely moral in its manifestations. Metaphysical evil provides occasions for displaying moral evils, or for resisting them. But the former, not the latter, is the ultimate and unreachable target. Camus insisted on acknowledging the depth of metaphysical evil while leaving himself without options for redemption. Camus never viewed the transcendent as liberating. His greatest power as a writer lay in his ability to evoke the force and presence of the resolutely everyday. His early "Summer in Algiers" begins with descriptions of sky and sea so stunning they might leave you blinking; it ends by condemning hope as the worst of evils in Pandora's box. Like Nietzsche, he thinks that to hope for something better is to live in opposition to life itself. Salvation, if we find it, will reside nowhere but in the hard matter of the human senses, whose unforgivably brief appearance demands all of our strength to protest.

Camus didn't deny the transcendent; he blasted it—and gave us prose that can make one believe in an alternative. This was more the attack of an adversary struggling with a worthy enemy than that of one bent on disclaiming its existence. Camus was at war with the very idea of transcendence. Sartre's criticism was thus fitting: political battles were, for Camus, unfortunate distraction from the real ones. To a political man like Sartre, this is the ultimate failing.

It's important to note that whatever tendency Camus may have had to minimize the gravity of Nazis' crimes appeared even before he used the plague as a metaphor for them. His "Letters to a German Friend," written in 1943, reveal an astonishingly mild view of Nazism. Far from being a paradigm of absolute evil, Nazism appeared as an honorable enemy. It's an enemy capable of war crimes—though in the one he mentioned, the real villain is a French priest. But the Nazis Camus addressed were men he treated as open to persuasion through moral principles he shared in common with them. The letters are ordinary war propaganda intended to convince the enemy of the righteousness of the French cause. Camus even felt compelled to *argue* that the Germans, not the French, started the war. All this may betray a political naïveté that cannot result simply from the poverty of information available in 1943. Camus's readiness to use a natural evil like plague to symbolize a moral evil was probably supported by his underestimation of the moral evil represented by Nazism. It was a sign not of confusion between metaphysics and politics but of weaknesses in his political judgment.

In political terms, such work is useless. It will bring no understanding of the structure of the enemies who need to be fought. Its power lies in moral terms. Camus provided an unusually exact and evocative picture of the ethical weapons needed for the fight. His readers are left with an oddly hopeful picture of the human that is all the more stark against the bleakness of the cosmos. The depth and variety of quiet corporeal heroism contrasts too with the heroes of the novels written by some who criticized Camus for not engaging with history. If Sartre's metaphysical claims seem to give more room for action, his characters give no reason for optimism about its results. Sartre tells us that other people are the source of hell. Camus lets us hope they might prevent it.

If there's a key to Camus's ethic, it's found in the thought that hatred of the Creator dare not become hatred of Creation. His attempt to separate Creator and Creation determined his focus on the everyday substance of the world we are given. Camus called this attention to the banal (Camus 4, 87–88). If there were a Creator, He would be as awesome and terrible and endless as death itself. The Creation, therefore, is made out of moments. They are repetitive and finite. Without poets, they would also be nameless. *The Plague*'s finest character is the unassuming clerk whose life is exhausted in three tasks. He never forgets the woman he loved; he volunteers unhesitatingly for the dangerous work of the sanitary squads; and he devotes every evening to writing a work of literature that Camus finally reveals as endless attempts to write one perfect sentence. All, in the end, emerge as utterly ordinary, even dull. It is not accidental that he is the only one of the book's heroes to get the plague and survive it—as it cannot be accidental that his name is Grand.

The Plague's main hero is a doctor who is "on the right road—in fighting against Creation as he found it" (Camus 3, 127). Though Camus insisted on the importance of distinguishing between Creator and Creation, he seemed uncertain how to do it. Sometimes it looks as though you must hate God if you want to love His Creation. Sometimes rage against one spilled into the other. This is just the sort of muddle against which Camus himself had warned. Is that confusion we should expect from a man whose gifts were more literary than philosophical?

Arendt suggested otherwise. The slide between Creator and Creation can be made by thinkers as sharp as Leibniz.

> Thus Leibniz, with admirable consistency, finds that the sin of Judas lies not in his betrayal of Jesus but in his suicide; in condemning himself, he implicitly condemned the whole of God's creation; by hating himself, he hated the Creator. (Arendt 5, 38)

Condemn the Creation, and you've condemned the Creator. In this realm, constructive criticism is never possible. Alternatively, *all* criticism is constructive, for it implies a wish to replace the architect yourself. For this reason, tradition sought to stifle Alfonso's fantasy before it could unfold. Once you begin finding faults in the world that is given, you are on the road to rebellion that cannot be blocked.

After Nietzsche, the distinction between Creator and Creation becomes even harder to maintain. How can one battle the Creator on behalf of Creation, if there's no full-bodied Being to serve as a target? To love Creation while attacking the Creator for the faults it contains becomes worse than quixotic. Where the Creator is absent, it's not even a task that can be defined.

In writing about the problem of evil, therefore, Arendt gave little weight to the distinction between Creator and Creation. Evil raises questions about the legitimacy of both. She defined theodicies as

> those strange justifications *of God or of Being* which, ever since the seventeenth century, philosophers felt were needed to reconcile man's mind to the world in which he was to spend his life. (Arendt 5, 20; my emphasis)

Or, as she wrote on another occasion, what drives the justifications of God in theodicy is the suspicion that *life* as we know it is in great need of being justified (Arendt 9, 24).

With this in mind we can return to *Eichmann in Jerusalem* and ask the question never adequately answered in all the debate the book provoked. What exactly was on trial here, and which side did the author take? Arendt's claim that her best-known book was just a long piece of reporting was disingenuous, for her critics were right to sense that she was not merely describing but also defending *something*. The ferocity of debate obscured the object whose defense was in question. To reject her claim that she was merely a journalist is not to accept her critics' claims that she was merely a traitor. I have argued that this accusation depends on a false picture of intention, but have not yet addressed the suspicion that the book is more apologetics than report. For Arendt, neither German war crimes alone nor possible Jewish complicity in them was on trial. What was under indictment was Creation itself. In a world that produced the death camps, the impossible became true. This was not a metaphor. The world itself, therefore, could no longer be accepted as it had been in the past. *Eichmann*

in Jerusalem is a defense not of Adolf Eichmann, but of a world that
contained him. It is the best attempt at theodicy postwar philosophy
has produced.

Arendt was both determined to defend Creation and deeply troubled about the form any justification could take. For to justify life *tout
court* would be to claim that things are, on the whole, as they ought
to be. But her work expressed a constant, often simple hatred of Hegelianism in every form. She thought that human freedom depends on
the contingency Hegel saw as a curse. Arendt's willingness to embrace
contingency fueled her lifelong distance from left Hegelian movements
like Marxism, though she never belonged to the right. As we saw, she
drew consequences from metaphysical commitments. But Hegelianism is the most natural way to justify Creation when you've given up
on the Creator. What alternatives remain?

Throughout her work Arendt sought to formulate the task that might
replace theodicy. How can life itself be justified without justifying the
evils that call it into question? Knowing what we know about the magnitude of modern evil and the paucity of theoretical resources for approaching it, how can we even describe the relation toward the world
we hope to maintain? Arendt considered calling a major work *Amor
Mundi*, and the idea of loving the world was central to her thought.
But since love itself requires grace, or good fortune, it is not a relation
that can be demanded of us. So she suggested that the question is,
rather, whether human beings fit into the world—a question she saw
as central to both Camus and Kant (Arendt 7, 191; Arendt 9, 30). But
she knew it was no accident that Kant never wrote a theodicy. To show
that we are at home in the world would make us too comfortable for
anyone so profoundly cosmopolitan, as she recognized when she refused to attribute such a project to Lessing. To provide a framework
that would reconcile us to reality might support a passive stance which
threatens to acquiesce in it. Her best formulation of the goal to which
our efforts should be directed is probably this one:

> to find my way around in reality without selling my soul to it the
> way people in earlier times sold their souls to the devil. (Arendt
> 7, 213)

Eichmann sold his soul. Arendt's claim was not that such action was trivial but that souls generally go at bargain rates. Thirty shekels, another notch in a bureaucratic hierarchy—the things for which people are willing to betray everything that matters are appallingly insignificant. Her work seeks a framework to help us find our way in the world without making us too comfortable in it. To seek a frame in which to set evil is to seek something less than a full theoretical explanation of it. For an exhaustive theoretical explanation would restrict our room for freedom. To claim that evil is comprehensible is not to demand a full account but to make a commitment to naturalism. It is also to claim that our capacity for moral judgment is fundamentally sound.

Camus used plague to stand for evil in general. In a letter to Gershom Scholem, Arendt wrote that evil resembles a fungus.

> Evil possesses neither depth nor any demonic dimension. It can overgrow and lay waste the whole world precisely because it spreads like a fungus on the surface. (Arendt 3)

Arendt was far too sophisticated—and too determined to avoid causal explanation in the moral realm—to suggest that, like bacteria, evil could be given a genuinely scientific explanation. The metaphor is an attempt to defuse the *conceptually* threatening element in contemporary evil. Biological warfare could destroy humankind, but it is not the bacteria that call the value of life into question.

The fungus metaphor thus signals evil that can be comprehended. It also indicates an object that has no intention whatsoever. This, we saw, was Arendt's greatest break with modern philosophical tradition—particularly Kant's work, to which she was otherwise much indebted. Here the use of naturalist, nonintentional vocabulary is an attempt not to avoid responsibility but to develop new idioms for assuming it. Arendt was convinced that evil could be overcome only if we acknowledge that it overwhelms us in ways that are minute. Great temptations are easier to recognize and thus to resist, for resistance comes in heroic terms. Contemporary dangers begin with trivial and insidious steps. Once these are taken, they lead to consequences so vast they could hardly have been foreseen. The claim that evil is banal is a claim not about magnitude but about proportion: if crimes that great can result from causes that small, there may be hope for overcoming them.

Calling evil banal is a piece of moral rhetoric, a way of defusing the power that makes forbidden fruit attractive. Since Sade became presentable, the inclination to aestheticize evil has grown. Even Camus saw Sade's embrace of evil as an understandable revolt against God. If the Creator commands us to do good while Himself producing evil, isn't it better to reject the good itself? Camus never actually recommended such a solution, but he saw the aestheticization of evil as one way to respond to the absurd. Once evil becomes aesthetic, it's not far from becoming glamorous. For this reason, Arendt thought that gnosticism would be the most dangerous, attractive, and widespread heresy of the future. She therefore sought descriptions of evil that resist the urge to give it "Satanic greatness," for such urges are both puerile and dangerous. The ironic tone she took toward Eichmann was entirely calculated. It's a tone that creates distance in place of desire. Like Brecht, Arendt argued that comedy undermines evil more effectively than does tragedy. The diabolic can be ambiguous; the ridiculous is not. To call evil banal is to call it boring. And if it is boring, its appeal will be limited. A fungus, after all, is rarely erotic.

Not evil but goodness should be portrayed with depth and dimension. When Arendt described heroes, her use of rhetoric displayed moral passion verging on the sublime. Consider her description of Anton Schmidt, a German soldier who sacrificed his life to help Jewish partisans. As his story was told during the Eichmann trial, a hush fell over the courtroom "like a sudden burst of light in the midst of impenetrable, unfathomable darkness." For

> [t]he lesson of such stories is simple and within everybody's grasp. Politically speaking, it is that under conditions of terror most people will comply but *some people will not*, just as the lesson of the countries in which the Final Solution was proposed is that "it could happen" in most places but *it did not happen everywhere*. Humanly speaking, no more is required, and no more can reasonably be asked, for this planet to remain a place fit for human habitation. (Arendt 2, 233)

Precisely this passage shows that what's at issue is not only moral education, finding the right tools to move people to do better rather than worse. At issue are the questions that came from metaphysics as well. If the forces that produce evil have neither depth nor dimension, then gnosticism is false. But then, as she wrote to Kurt Blumenfeld,

[t]he world as God created it seems to me a good one.

To call evil banal is to offer not a definition of it but a theodicy. For it implies that the sources of evil are not mysterious or profound but fully within our grasp. If so, they do not infect the world at a depth that could make us despair of the world itself. Like a fungus, they may devastate reality by laying waste to its surface. Their roots, however, are shallow enough to pull up.

To claim that evil is comprehensible in general is not to claim that any instance of it is transparent. It is, rather, to deny that supernatural forces, divine or demonic, are required to account for it. It is also to say that while natural processes are responsible for it, natural processes can be used to prevent it. Here Arendt's project is heir to Rousseau's. By providing a framework that shows how the greatest crimes may be carried out by men with none of the marks of the criminal, *Eichmann in Jerusalem* argued that evil is not a threat to reason itself. Rather, crimes like Eichmann's depend on thoughtlessness, the refusal to use reason as we should. Like Rousseau, Arendt sought to show that our souls are built to work: our natural faculties are corruptible, but not inherently corrupt. Nor are they in principle impotent, as Hume had argued so forcefully. We have means both to understand the world and to act in it. Arendt compared the feeling of understanding to the feeling of being at home (Arendt 8, 47). Our capacity to comprehend what seemed incomprehensible is evidence for the idea that human beings and the world were made for each other. As Kant suggested when discussing natural beauty, this is as close to the argument from design as we should ever come. If it offers something less than justification, it produces something more than hope. No wonder that *Eichmann in Jerusalem* could evoke exhilaration. Mary McCarthy compared it to hearing *Figaro* or the *Messiah*, "both of which are concerned with redemption" (Arendt 10, 166). Arendt's reply is no less extraordinary:

> [Y]ou were the only reader to understand what I otherwise never admitted—namely, that I wrote this book in a curious state of euphoria. And that ever since I did it, I feel—after 20 years—light-hearted about the whole matter. Don't tell anybody; is it not proof positive that I have no 'soul'? (Arendt 10, 168)

Many voices are in play here, and it would be foolish to rule out any one of them. But euphoria can be explained only by the sense of wonder and gratitude for all that is. Arendt saw this as the beginning of thought itself. We may be at home in the world after all.

The metaphor of being at home in the world is an old one. In his essay "Das Ende aller Dinge" Kant listed four models of homes that different traditions held the world to provide us: a cheap inn, a prison, a madhouse, and a latrine. Kant's options are hardly appealing, but the metaphor persists even without acceptable images for it. Home is the normal—whatever place you happen to start from, and can return to without having to answer questions. It's a metaphor that may seem to fit reduced expectations. We no longer seek towers that would reach to the heavens; we've abandoned attempts to prove that we live in a chain of being whose every link bears witness to the glory of God. We merely seek assurance that we find ourselves in a place where we know our way about.

The absence of such assurance is a touchstone of the modern. Since Lisbon, the world has been an object of study, but it's no longer an object of trust. Despite its apparent modesty, home is too intentional a concept to be part of a disenchanted world. It's a metaphor that shows how much we lost when we lost the argument from design. God was the architect whose plans ensured that you could do all the things you take for granted in your own domain, stretch your feet on the table without waiting for permission, or checking to see whether the floor will collapse. In losing the architect, we lost not only grander structures but all of that as well.

Still it's a metaphor the twentieth century took up with particular seriousness. One famous section of Adorno's *Minima Moralia* is called "Homeless Shelter." There he wrote that whether it's a slum or a bungalow,

> [t]he house is gone. The destruction of European cities and the concentration camps merely continued the processes that the immanent development of technology decided for the houses long ago. 'It is part of my happiness not to be a homeowner,' wrote Nietzsche in *The Gay Science*. One must add today: it is part of morality not to be at home with oneself. (Adorno 1, 41)

Most important notes of the Critical Theory developed by the Frankfurt School were sounded here. Auschwitz was the completion of a process inherent in the modern, not a departure from it. Through that process we lost something too deep to be entirely fathomed. It's a process in which we are always complicitous, if not entirely responsible. Nothing in Western culture is untouched by it; according to *The Dialectic of Enlightenment* it began with the *Odyssey*. That nothing can redeem or console or distract from it is expressed in Adorno's famous aphorism condemning poetry after Auschwitz. Or, as this section concluded: there's no right way to live when everything is wrong ("es gibt kein richtiges Leben im falschen"). What remains is only the moral imperative not to deceive ourselves about the magnitude of the modern catastrophe. Decency demands that we refuse to feel at home in any particular structure the world provides to domesticate us. It also requires that we refuse to feel at home in our own skins.

This is the difference between the loss of trust in the world that occurred with Lisbon and the losses apparent today. Modern consciousness required us to stop viewing the world as a home that a stern but indulgent parent might have built us, and to grow up and build our own. If this project seemed increasingly precarious, it was maintained until the war. But the weak messianic hope that Benjamin still discerned in 1938 seemed prostrate soon afterward. For we, and all of our joys and sorrows, are implicated in the general decay. "Nothing is harmless anymore" (Adorno 1, 21).

The devastation was so extensive that Frankfurt School thinkers felt compelled to return to a notion of transcendence all had earlier rejected. For neither the sources of horror nor any object of hope that might replace them could be expressed directly. The losses are so great that any statement of them will be prey to twin dangers: the temptation to kitsch or to reconciliation. For Adorno and Horkheimer, the only solution was to be found in ideas that transcend given reality for something better beyond it. Both were well aware that such solutions resemble religious ones. Indeed, they praised traditional religion for "keeping longing alive." Horkheimer was explicit:

> What is religion in the good sense? The not-yet-strangled impulse that insists that reality should be otherwise, that the spell will be broken and turn toward the right direction. Where life points this way in every gesture, there is religion. (Horkheimer 2, 6:288)

Naturally Horkheimer argued for the need to distinguish between ideas that had their origins in religion and those that should come after them. So a fragment entitled "The Question of Philosophy" put the question thus:

> "If there is no God, nothing about me needs to be serious," argues the theologian. The horrible deed that I do, the suffering that I permit to exist, live on after the moment in which they occur only in conscious human memory and expire with it. . . . Can one admit this and live a serious but godless life? This is the question of philosophy. (Ibid., 198)

But protests that all this praise of transcendence is meant to be godless are less convincing when we look at the details. Adorno even went so far as to defend Kant's discussion of immortality, for it condemns the unbearableness of the given and strengthens the spirit that recognizes it (Adorno 2, 376). Both Jewish and Kantian traditions believe that transcendent ideas are necessary. Both hold those ideas to be necessarily inexpressible. Horkheimer recorded his debt to each in a note entitled "On Critical Theory":

> The Jewish prohibition on representing God and the Kantian prohibition on going off into intelligible worlds both contain the rec-

ognition of the absolute whose determination is impossible. The same is true for critical theory, insofar as it declares that the bad— first in the social sphere, but also in the moral sphere, that of the individual human being—can be described, but not however the good. (Ibid., 419)

Representing ideals always betrays them. For the nature of the ideal is to be more, and better, than everything that merely is. That is why all that is dearest to reason must remain unknowable. Now most twentieth-century philosophy agreed about how little we know of the objects of traditional metaphysics. It differed in its standpoint toward all those things we cannot know—everything Kant consigned to the realm of the inexpressible. For analytic philosophy, what's important is to restrict our discourse lest we stray into nonsense. For continental philosophy, what's important is the hope of other modes of articulation. The difference between them is shown by their different answers to the question: Is the urge to move beyond experience part of experience itself? Is the desire for transcendence a matter of psychology—in which case it's advisable to seek a good cure? Or is the existence of that desire fundamental to any experience we could recognize as human?[22]

By insisting on the latter, the Frankfurt School criticized not only analytic philosophy, which it never took seriously in the first place, but also Nietzsche, who was far more important to it. Recall that for Nietzsche any link to transcendence was a betrayal of life itself. Nietzsche viewed every appeal to the beyond as an expression of the theological instinct, with which he was at war. The war he waged was total. Traditional anti-Christians confined their attacks to heaven. Nietzsche's target was bigger. *Hope itself* must be combated, since hope for something better condemns whatever there is. So Nietzsche reread Pandora's box: hope is not redemption. Rather, it's the evil that should remain enclosed in the box because the Greeks considered it the only evil that was truly malignant.

Nietzsche's effort left few European thinkers unmoved. But it faltered on an event that even the very prescient Nietzsche never imagined. Auschwitz functioned as proof that some worlds are unacceptable. It demanded a return to all the machinery of transcendence that had seemed obsolete. So Adorno wrote that Auschwitz had, by itself, established a new categorical imperative: to act in such a way that Auschwitz will never be repeated. For as he noted, complaints about the bleak idleness of immanent reality are nothing new. Theologians and poets since King Solomon have expressed them. To move from complaints about the bleakness of reality to something that might take us beyond it, we need transcendent ideas. For

> [o]nly when that which is can be changed is that which is not everything. [Nur wenn, was ist, sich ändern lässt, ist das, was ist, nicht alles.] (Adorno 2, 388)

But did Critical Theory think the world could be changed? This is probably the most debated question about Adorno and Horkheimer's work. They insisted that ideas transcending reality are needed in order to protest it. Critics saw those protests as feeble celebrations of causes long lost. Earlier Critical Theory claimed that philosophy could function as a corrective of history by keeping ideals alive (Horkheimer 1, 186). But the pessimism implicit in later works, as well as their ambivalent responses to actual political protest, led many to conclude that critical theorists sought less to correct history than to elegize it. *The Dialectic of Enlightenment* can seem to describe the worst of all worlds: we have no one to blame for our misery, but the process is so swift and self-maintaining that we cannot stop what we started. After such a diagnosis, the appeal to transcendence can quickly become an excuse for inaction. The Frankfurt School's response to such criticism was always unclear.

While the urge to reinstate transcendence arose in reaction to Auschwitz, it did not end there. The contrast between immanent and transcendent reality that increasingly found voice in the Frankfurt School embraced a form of protest that cannot be contained in political terms. If the problems inherent in modern humanity's relation to the world begin with Odysseus, their solutions will not be exhausted by changes of particular social organization. Both Adorno and Horkheimer emphasized those features of disaster which were new to the twentieth century. Both stressed the need for forms of response that were not yet articulated. They very nearly reveled in the homeless metaphor and made exile an emblem of modern life in general. Yet each was emphatic in arguing that the twentieth century was only an extreme. The problems it posed were not confined to it. Thus one reason to return to elements of sacred language lies ready to hand. While Auschwitz presented a new set of problems, they are best understood through the vocabulary of the old. Though insisting that the death camps turned death into something it had never been, Adorno insisted that death itself is a problem for which there is neither meaning nor comfort—precisely because, contra Heidegger, it is foreign to human being. No human life is ever enough to realize the potential contained in it. Hence death and life are irreconcilably at war. From a different vantage point, Améry came to similar conclusions, whose expression took even starker form. After writing one of the most devastating descriptions of life at Auschwitz, he wrote a book arguing that nothing he witnessed there matched the horror of the universal process of aging and death. For the latter is not only inescapable; it involves betrayal from within. Death, for Améry, is reason's ultimate foe.[23]

In works like these we glimpse a turn in the direction of metaphysical evil, and with it all the baggage of metaphysics that most forms of modern philosophy were proud to discard. It's true that many came to agree with Wittgenstein that all the things which couldn't be said directly were the ones that mattered most. As Adorno wrote, in a wonderful piece of polemic:

> That metaphysical philosophy, which historically is essentially the same as the great systems, contains more *Glanz* than empiricism and positivism, is not merely aesthetic, nor merely psychological wish-fulfillment. The immanent quality of thought, which is manifested in power, resistance, fantasy, in unity of the critical with its opposite, is at least a clue, if not an index. That Carnap and Mies are more true than Kant and Hegel could not even be the truth if it were the case. (Adorno 2, 375)

Here the inexpressibility of metaphysics is the source of its force and radiance.

Just this passage could suggest why analytic philosophy inclined to abandon the problem of evil despite reclaiming most other topics in the history of philosophy. For the foregoing discussion seems to confirm its worst fears. Adorno's *Glanz* can be translated as *glitz* or *glamour* as well as *radiance*. Analytic philosophy set out to replace the glamour of self-indulgent metaphysics with humbler virtues, and these quotations seem to offer more grounds for doing so. For, it could be argued, all the *Glanz* of the metaphysical questions surrounding the problem of evil derives from the afterglow of religion. Isn't this just the sort of covert appeal to theology that analytic philosophy was invented to avoid? Adorno said that the problem vulgarly known as that of the meaning of life reflects the persistence of "secularized metaphysical categories" (Adorno 2, 367). Odo Marquard has offered a skeptical defense of metaphysics: metaphysics may not solve problems, but it's needed to keep questions of meaning alive (Marquard 2, 48). But if meaning now appears in the role less cautious eras reserved for God, shouldn't it be allowed, a hundred years after Nietzsche, to rest in peace?

John Rawls's work developed within the best traditions of analytic philosophy. The disinclination to classical metaphysics usually produced there was reinforced, in Rawls's case, by two factors. One was the kind of personal humility that makes grander sorts of speculation distasteful. The other was a resolute sense of moral priority. Figuring out which intentions are the right ones is more important than figuring out what intention is, and putting off the former until you've done the latter is likely to lead to wrong. Rawls's insistence on doing moral and political theory independently of metaphysics thus had deep roots and was repeated often throughout his career. It is all the more surprising to find late suggestions that the problem of evil plays a major role in his work.

This is not because he wrote the first major book of substantive ethics in English since John Stuart Mill. Analytic ethics had been paralyzed by questions about whether and how moral judgments could be justified. Rawls's *Theory of Justice* actually made some, and for anybody with lingering inclinations to believe that all moral judgments are merely expressions of feeling, it provided 587 pages of densely argued justification for them. Offering specific guidelines for solving moral and political problems can surely contribute to preventing specific evils. By itself, however, this would make Rawls's work a contribution to ethics alone. His work stands in the tradition to which this book is devoted because his ethics is written in response to two metaphysical questions that orbit the problem of evil: the problem of contingency and the problem of reconciliation.

Although easy to miss in the idioms of analytic philosophy and rational choice theory in which the book was written, the problem of contingency is central to *A Theory of Justice*. There Rawls presented a method for making fair decisions about the structure of political institutions. In deciding whether a society is just, we are to pick the society we would choose to inhabit if we knew nothing about ourselves in particular. Rawls proposes a thought experiment in which we cover our characters with a veil of ignorance. You are to choose the world you want for yourself and your children without knowing whether you or they will be rich or poor, male or female, citizens of New York or Burundi. So far, this is a version of liberal social contract theory, one tradition on which Rawls drew. But he went considerably further: in deciding on social institutions, you are to imagine knowing nothing about your talents or inclinations. You may prefer to write poetry, or to establish an ascetic community devoted to otherworldly salvation. You may be more disappointed by missing a ball game than by the UN's failure to make peace in the Balkans. You may be timid or daring, ardent or cool. You do not know any of this, so the choices you make must be right ones for whoever you turn out to be.

All this is a thought experiment for which many critics saw no point. Bad enough that it was a thought experiment that presupposed the sense of justice they hoped it would demonstrate. For like Kant, Rawls denied that there can be an answer to the question: Why should we be moral? No arguments can force you into other people's shoes. Either you decide that it's right to consider the world from somewhere other than the accidental point at which you stand in it—or you don't. Particular interests cannot compel you to take up a universal perspective; instrumental reasons cannot serve as grounds for moral ones. Now these problems were present in the categorical imperative, the other thought experiment that influenced Rawls. But in expanding on that model, many critics thought Rawls only expanded on its flaws. His ideal subjects lacked all the particular qualities that make us distinctly human. Supposing we succeeded in imagining ourselves as the disembodied creatures in his original position. Why ever would we *want* to see the world from that point of view?

The answer is available in Rawls's earliest work. The original position makes it possible to revolt against the arbitrariness of nature. Natural facts are contingent. When we allow those facts to retain social significance, we acquiesce in injustice.

> But there is no necessity for men to resign themselves to these categories. The social system is not an unchangeable order beyond human control but a pattern of human action. In justice as fairness men agree to share one another's fate. In designing institutions they undertake to avail themselves of the accidents of nature and social circumstance only when doing so is for the common benefit. The two principles are a fair way of meeting the arbitrariness of fortune. (Rawls 1, 102)

Many contingencies are unalterable accidents of nature, and we cannot even mitigate their effects. You may take the wrong train and run into an explosion—or miss it and run into an earthquake. Believing that fortune is arbitrary helps some people accept it. For others, like Rawls, this belief serves as goad to do all one can to lessen the force of natural accident. If many facts of nature cannot be changed, some of their consequences are in our hands. Your native intelligence or your willingness to take more risks than your neighbor is as much a matter of fortune as his trust fund. Neither of you deserves what you were born with. For desert and justice are not natural categories but ours to put in the world if we choose. Working to design a social world in which fortune plays no decisive role is a way of asserting your freedom. Nature may be contingent; you need not follow its lead.

Alfonso's suggestions were confined to the cosmos. A monarch, however enlightened, is unlikely to propose a world where accidents of birth do not determine the social order. But Rawls's late work revealed that Alfonso's impulse could reappear in analytic philosophy. Redesigning a piece of the world is a project undertaken in the hope of affirming the world as a whole. Kant's influence on Rawls was clear in *A Theory of Justice*. But *Justice as Fairness*, conceived as a re-statement of the earlier work, opens by invoking Hegel.

> A third role [of political philosophy], stressed by Hegel in his *Phi-losophy of Right* (1821), is that of reconciliation: political philoso-phy may try to calm our frustration and rage against our society and its history by showing us the way in which its institutions, when properly understood from a philosophical point of view, are rational, and developed over time as they did to attain their present, rational form. This fits one of Hegel's well-known say-ings: 'When we look at the world rationally, the world looks ratio-nally back'. He seeks for us reconciliation—*Versöhnung*—that is, we are to accept and affirm our social world positively, not merely to be resigned to it. (Rawls 3, 3)

Rawls avows his commitment to this role of political philosophy. If Rawls's work more openly indicates hesitations imposed by the scru-ples of analytic philosophy, Auschwitz and Hiroshima are unspoken sources of his reluctance to write sotto voce.[24]

The more we know about the history of philosophy, and about his-tory itself, the more the reasons to refuse to truck with reconciliation multiply. After the passage just quoted, Rawls warns against letting his own political philosophy serve as reconciliation in the sense Marx called ideological. We cannot allow the possibility of a decent social order to console us for the absence of an actual one. Awareness of theoretical and practical hazards has altered our expectations; even our hopes will be piecemeal. Hegel wanted to reveal the actuality of reason in the world as a whole. Rawls would be satisfied to show the possibility of reason in the social world. Yet this, he argues in *The Law of Peoples*, would be a good deal.

> To be reconciled to the social world, one must be able to see it as both reasonable and rational. (Rawls 2, 127)

Rawls describes the goal of his work as showing that a realistic utopia is possible. A realistic utopia is a society in which the greatest evils of human history—unjust war and oppression, starvation and poverty, genocide and mass murder—would be eliminated through politically just institutions. Without the hope that this can happen, "one might reasonably ask, with Kant, whether it is worthwhile to live on this earth" (Rawls 2, 128). Rawls stressed, of course, that the most his work shows is something about possibility. Unlike Hegel, there is no sense in which he holds such a world to be actual in the present or necessary in the future. Developing a model for a social system that would create justice by reducing the role of luck in our lives is not, of course, the same thing as realizing it. But if the model is not merely utopian,

> I believe that the very possibility of such a social order can itself reconcile us to the social world. The possibility is not a mere logical possibility, but one that connects with the deep tendencies and inclinations of the social world. For so long as we believe for good reasons that a self-sustaining and reasonably just political and social order both at home and abroad is possible, we can reasonably hope that we or others will someday, somewhere, achieve it; and we can then do something toward this achievement. This alone, quite apart from our success or failure, suffices to banish the dangers of resignation and cynicism. (Rawls 2, 128)

The reemergence of the problem of evil in Rawls's work, despite his own best efforts (and those of his friends) to avoid metaphysical pitfalls, may account for some of the resonance of the work as a whole.[25] The recent publication of his lectures on the history of philosophy is one testimony to Rawls's engagement with the history of philosophy. His engagement with the problem of evil shows how thoroughly he is a part of it. The fact that this engagement was increasingly unavoidable almost in spite of personal inclinations suggests something about the problem of evil itself.

ORIGINS: SUFFICIENT REASON

In the previous section I sketched works of some postwar thinkers whose discourse was reflected in theology. Of them only Arendt acknowledged "a childish trust in God" (Arendt 6, 202), while the others were avowed atheists. All of them groped toward formulating a set of problems they knew could not be discussed in theological terms. And yet, it could be argued, this very groping betrays its origins in religious assumptions the authors could not overcome.

The question of whether the problem of evil derives from religious concerns has shadowed our discussion. It's time to address it directly. Hegel was the first to emphasize the ways in which the idea of progress was continuous with the idea of Providence, but he never thought one was derived from the other. How are progress and Providence related? German discussion of this question centered in the secularization debate, which began with works like those of Karl Loewith and Jacob Taubes. Each independently noted similarities of structure and function between nineteenth-century ideas of progress and classical ideas of Providence.[26] Thus it was natural to conclude that claims about progress which drive philosophies of history were derived from theology. The cunning of reason, the invisible hand, and the proletariat are different ways to replace the hand of Providence and cannot be understood without it. Hans Blumenberg responded to such claims by defending what he called the legitimacy of the modern—the idea that many modern concepts, including progress, were independent and irreducible. While those concepts occupied the same space formerly taken by theological ones, they were not simply derived from them. Rather, they represent something new, original, and constitutive of modern consciousness.

Much of this debate, though rich and interesting, depends on the unspoken assumptions captured in the opening metaphor of Walter Benjamin's *Theses on the Philosophy of History*.

> The story is told of an automaton constructed in such a way that it could play a winning game of chess, answering each move of an opponent with a countermove. A puppet in Turkish attire and with a hookah in its mouth sat before a chessboard placed on a large table. A system of mirrors created the illusion that this table was transparent from all sides. Actually, a little hunchback who was an expert chess player sat inside and guided the puppet's hand by means of strings. One can imagine a philosophical counterpart to this device. The puppet called "historical materialism" is to win all the time. It can easily be a match for anyone if it

enlists the services of theology, which today, as we know, is wizened and has to keep out of sight. (Benjamin 3, 253)

Blumenberg was right to see that what's at stake in the argument about whether the idea of progress is derived from Providence is the question of legitimacy. For Benjamin's automaton is a fake. What looked like a genuinely modern invention (the robot we dream of, with pleasure and fear) turned out to be nothing but an ordinary human, and an old Byzantine one at that. If philosophy of history is moved by history as the chess player is moved by the little hunchback, its results are just as deceptive.

For all its literary interest, the assumptions behind Benjamin's metaphor are oddly positivist. Like Comte's discussion, the metaphor suggests that thought could be in principle divided into theological and metaphysical phases. It implies that advancing from one to another would be a form of progress—without Comte's assumption that progress actually takes place. When we return to our roots, we face decline; when we don't, we face self-deception. Benjamin left us few choices. Of course, the argument that a secular idea is born from a sacred one need not end in a demand that it be rejected. For secular readers, pointing out that the idea of progress has stale and withered origins in theology may be enough to undermine it. But other readers may urge us to accept the religious foundations of modernity and return to faith with open eyes. Enlightenment rather than progress is at issue here. Are there ghosts (or soon to be ghosts) in the machinery? The Enlightenment will have no tools to remove them if its agents are driven by the same spirit as everyone else. What's at issue is not just a scholarly question in the history of ideas. If concepts like progress, and evil itself, are reduced to religious origins, the use of them will be monopolized by religious spheres—and not likely the most scrupulous ones. The clear human need to recognize evil as evil, to seek progress as progress, cannot be met by those who doubt that the concepts can stand on their own.

Thinkers who support the secularization thesis imply that the transformation of concepts that took place was naive. In fact, it was completely self-conscious. Earlier philosophers were well aware of continuities between sacred and secular concepts even as they undertook to transform them. Kant, Hegel, and Marx all held certain questions to be essential to human reason. Those questions will be expressed and answered differently at different times. We may or may not make progress in resolving them, but whatever looks like progress in leaving them behind will simply be repression. Ideas of progress and of Providence are alternative ways of working out versions of the same problem. Neither can be reduced to or derived from the other. For they are the result not of historical accident (even a very big historical accident, like the Judeo-Christian notion of a personal God) but of something about human nature itself.

Hegel expressed this idea in his *Introduction to the Lectures on the Philosophy of World History.*

> Another of the main reasons why I have cited this earliest instance of the idea that reason rules the world [in Anaxagoras] and discussed its inadequacy is because it has also been applied more fully to another subject with which we are all familiar and of whose truth we are personally convinced—I refer, of course, to the religious truth that the world is not a prey to chance and external contingent causes but is governed by Providence. . . . The truth, then, that the world's events are controlled by a Providence, indeed a divine Providence, is consistent with the principle in question. For divine Providence is wisdom, coupled with infinite power, which realizes its ends, i.e. the absolute and rational design of the world; and reason is freely self-determining thought, or what the Greeks called *nous*. (Hegel 5, 35)

For Hegel, Providence was *one* expression of an idea that goes back to the pre-Socratics, and may receive other interpretations in other times. None of these expressions is born from another; all derive from a fundamental truth of reason itself. Kant called it a need rather than a truth, but he held it to be just as universal. On such views the problem of evil is not derived from religion; religion is one kind of attempt to solve the problem of evil. The invention of Providence was the result of the need for an engine of progress in a world that presents little space for hope.

The suggestion that Hegel's or Marx's incorporation of sacred categories was less than conscious or critical should therefore be rejected. They were well aware that they were attempting to resolve problems traditionally resolved by theology, and to do so with concepts that were developed through interaction with religion. Nineteenth-century philosophers knew they were reworking ideas that had been rejected in the form of traditional religion, and twentieth-century philosophers were not more naive. If Adorno thought that the consolation offered by poetry might be unacceptable after Auschwitz, he would hardly have accepted the consolation of theodicy. Arendt so thoroughly opposed anything resembling Hegelianism that she struggled to find a form of reconciliation that would avoid Hegelian pitfalls. Despite all other differences, such thinkers shared awareness of the failures of past philosophy. If—after Auschwitz—they nevertheless reappropriated elements of the traditional problem of evil into central parts of their work, we must conclude that something besides God is at issue.

The impulse to theodicy is not a relic of monotheism but goes deeper than either. Indeed, it is part of the same impulse that leads to monotheism itself. When we recall that similar debates continue within theology, from earliest times, we must cease to view these questions as theological. Each of the three Western religious traditions maintains debates around the question: Was reason God's greatest gift? If so, argues one side, He is bound to adhere to it; if not, argues the other, we are bound by nothing but obedience to His will.[27] Here God's presence is taken for granted by all parties; it's His relation to reason that is open to doubt. For us this becomes the question of intelligibility: Are our capacities to find and create meaning in the world adequate to a world that seems determined to thwart them?

But once you seek a source of the impulse to theodicy more basic than religion, you are likely to be sent to read Freud. Freud thought religion itself begins in the longings of the frightened child. Recall that he traced all questions of Providence to the child's need for protection against the pains that besiege her. For Freud as for the child, whether those sources can be divided into moral and natural evils is not an interesting question. Human beings and forces of nature can equally be objects of terror. The child seeks as comprehensive a source of shelter as possible. She invents the notion of Providence in the hope of protection, and where this fails, revenge. This explanation accounts for the emergence of some version of providential thinking across most cultures. Freud thought it universal, but a universal case of wishful thinking. He had particular contempt for modern thinkers who knew too much to give full voice to the child's wishes yet tried to retain them anyway. So he found the attempt to replace the hand of Providence with an impersonal abstract principle to be an act of bad faith that was little short of blasphemy. Freud's account makes sense of the fact that the problem of evil survives attacks on religion even as it condemns that survival as cowardly. For on that account, the hope of finding sense in the world is older than Athens and Jerusalem put together. Though it's thereby more elementary, it's all the less venerable. If the problem of evil begins in the child besieged by terror, our continued engagement with it is an expression of fear.

Where the child isn't frightened, she seems to be whiny. So some view the problem of evil as a demand for rewards. Because we were raised to expect payment, we are distraught when happiness and virtue fail to link up. Here Providence takes more the shape of the indulgent mother than that of the avenging father, but we remain infantile all the same. The view that Joe Hill called pie-in-the-sky-when-you-die is cruder than anything we have yet considered. You needn't be Kant to see that this much calculation is inimical to any idea of morality. Teaching children to be decent is a matter of teaching them that the world *doesn't* function by rewarding them with treats for jobs well done, and insisting that they do them anyway. Yet some suspect that this is always where we start. The child seeking the cookie becomes the adult seeking the hand of Providence. She has learned to delay gratification, but her needs are at bottom the same.

Freud himself knew that pointing out the origins of a belief is never an argument against it. The belief in Providence might arise from the child's hopes of reward for herself and punishment for others—and nevertheless be true. Yet even after we've learned to avoid the genetic fallacy, Freud's account may succeed in undermining our beliefs as arguments do not. To present the problem of evil as expression of childhood needs is to present a paradigm that makes us ashamed of it.

If the problem is a form of metaphysical whining, we can only hope to grow out of it. Then contemporary philosophy's usual distance from the problem of evil will seem one of the rare proofs of progress in the field, and its willingness to ignore the problem's centrality for earlier thinkers merely an application of the principle of charity. It's hard enough to view Kant, for instance, as bound by the philosophical theology his own metaphysics undermined. To regard him as trapped in the realm of childhood fantasy seems positively disrespectful.

When what's at issue is less a matter of argument than of origins, we need different paradigms of explanation. Suppose the problem of evil does express assumptions that emerge in childhood. Need we accept Freud's picture of childhood itself? Freud's child is a humiliated creature, driven by discomfort, dread, and shame. But the child may also be a figure of promise. She approaches the world in wonder as well as in fear. Here innocence can be a source of strength. The child's questions about why things are as they are do not cease, pace Freud, when she learns where babies come from. The urge to greet every answer with another question is one we find in children not because it's childish but because it's natural. Once you begin the search for knowledge, there is no obvious place to stop. The fact that the desire for omniscience cannot be met does not make it either foolish or pathological. Indeed, it is embodied in the principle of sufficient reason itself.

The principle of sufficient reason expresses the belief that we can find a reason for everything the world presents. It is not an idea that we derive from the world, but one that we bring to it. Kant called it a regulative principle—not a childish wish, but a drive essential to reason itself. Children display it more openly than adults because they have been less often disappointed. They will continue to ask questions even after hearing the impatient answer—*Because that's the way the world is*. Most children remain adamant. *But why is the world like that, exactly?* The only answer that will truly satisfy is this one: *Because it's the best one*. We stop asking why when everything is as it should be. No wonder Hegel called Leibniz's work a metaphysical fairy tale; children are natural Leibnizians. In the child's refusal to accept a world that makes no sense lies all the hope that ever makes us start anew.

The child emerged as a figure in philosophy at the moment when the demand for theodicy was loudest. I argued that the optimism reflected in the eighteenth-century explosion of interest in theodicy was not about the goodness of the world but only about our ability to understand it. Progress in scientific discovery created expectations that grew harder to delay. As long as most things seemed mysterious, the question of useless suffering was less acute. The more the rest of the world appeared transparent, the more pressing was the need for an account of the mystery that mattered most. From this perspective, the search for reason in the world is not derived from religious notions of Providence. Rather, the invention of Providence arises with the search for reason in the world. Making bargains with the gods is a way of trying to control your fate. It is not yet demanding that your fate make sense. By contrast, belief in justice that is written into the universe is belief in a world that makes sense as a whole.

Rousseau has been credited with inventing the idea of childhood. Whether or not he was the source of it, the figure of the child's growth to adulthood came to seem a natural metaphor for enlightenment, and indeed for civilization itself.[28] The model was not entirely new; on some readings history itself was God's form of pedagogy. The idea of human development as a process of growing up goes together with the replacement of antique conceptions of cyclical time by linear ones. Still, the metaphor was particularly appropriate for an age that experienced its understanding of the world as continually expanding. In some cases it served as a means for advancing understanding itself.[29]

I believe we should use Enlightenment resources to develop a different picture of childhood needs from the one Freud offered. The child seeks sense as well as protection. One demand is no less fundamental than the other. To trace the problem of evil back to childhood needs is thus not, by itself, to show very much about its structure. The Enlightenment itself knew that children's endless urge to find reason in the world can verge on the ridiculous. Everybody read *Candide*. But abandoning the urge altogether means abandoning the assumptions that drive humankind to grow up.

Kant distinguished between the reason that sets ends in the world and the instrumental reason that calculates means. While the latter can be mastered by any criminal, the former is a matter of seeking, and creating, what is good in itself. I follow this distinction, as well as Kant's belief that the drive to seek reason in the world—even, or especially, at the points where it seems most absent—is as deep a drive as any we have. It's this urge that keeps the problem of evil alive even after hopes of solving it are abandoned. It is not psychological, for it isn't derived from particular facts about human development, like our parents' desire to get our attention through a series of bribes and threats. Nor does it result from particular facts of historical development, like the move from polytheism to monotheism. For as Kant implied, but never actually stated, behind the principle of sufficient reason itself is the assumption that the *is* and the *ought* should coincide. The principle of sufficient reason starts its work where they fail to meet. When the world is not as it should be, we begin to ask why. Metaphysics is the drive to make very general sense of the world in face of the fact that things go intolerably wrong. If they did not, the world would make sense as it is. It would be transparent or, as the German has it, *selbstverständlich*—an untranslatable suggestion of something that is understood in and by itself. We proceed on the assumption that the true and the good, and just possibly the beautiful, coincide. Where they do not, we demand an account. The urge to unite *is* and *ought* stands behind every creative endeavor. Those who seek to unite them by force usually do more harm than they set out to prevent. Those who never seek to unite them do nothing at all.

The idea that the gap between *is* and *ought* generates metaphysics was often expressed by Schopenhauer.

> If the world were not something that, practically expressed, ought not to be, it would also not be theoretically a problem. On the contrary, its existence would require no explanation at all, since it would be so entirely self evident. (Schopenhauer, 2:579)

Levinas maintained a similar view:

> The first metaphysical question is no longer Leibniz's question *why is there something rather than nothing?* but *why is there evil rather than good?* The ontological difference is preceded by the

difference between good and evil. Difference itself is this latter;
it is the origin of the meaningful. (Levinas 1, 160)

Arendt viewed such claims as extreme. With the possible exception of
Schopenhauer, she thought that the sense of metaphysical outrage
never produced great philosophy. She did believe that metaphysical
outrage is related to its opposite, the sense of pure wonder from which
philosophy was traditionally said to spring. Let us suppose that thinking demands both. One way to understand their relation is via the principle of sufficient reason itself. We experience wonder in the moments
when we see the world is as it ought to be—an experience so deep
that the *ought* melts away. The disappearance of the *ought* in such
moments leads some thinkers to describe them as the experience of
Being freed from human demands and categories. But it is equally the
experience that all our demands have been fulfilled.

If we wish to retain traditional metaphysical language, we could call
the claim *the real should become the rational* a transcendental one. It is
transcendental because located neither in normative nor in descriptive
space. Were it a claim about reality, it could be confirmed or discon-
firmed by reality. Were it a claim within reason, it might be susceptible
to other forms of proof. It is neither but, rather, the demand that reason
be applied, and the basis of any application of reason at all. You may
call it reason's narcissism—the wish to see itself reflected wherever it
goes. Yet reason's attempt to be at home in the world is also a refusal
to abandon the world to its own devices. The demand that reason and
reality stand together is tenacious because it is no more than a demand.
Its basis is not real but rational. We are so structured as to expect a
world that comes to meet us halfway, for we cannot make meaning
alone. Being dependent on the world is so fundamentally human that
Stoicism will always threaten to slide into solipsism. Perhaps gods experience the world without caring whether *is* and *ought* coincide. If
we began to do so, we would lose the basis of every attitude and emotion that is central to the human attempt to live in the world. The demand to unite *is* and *ought* is nothing but reason's demand. Though
it doesn't come from experience, the attempt to imagine experience
without it is no easier than imagining experience that wasn't cut up

into causes and effects. Belief that there may be reason in the world is a condition of the possibility of our being able to go on in it.

The urge to unite *is* and *ought* is so deeply anchored that it's often maintained at too high a cost. Many victims of disaster would rather blame themselves for their suffering than view it as a matter of accident. And criminals found it easier to adjust to life in concentration camps than did those deported on racial grounds partly because criminals perceived their imprisonment as just.[30] Belief in versions of original sin persists because experiencing one's life as punishment is easier than experiencing it as senseless.

Even worse than blaming oneself for inexplicable suffering is the temptation to blame others. Kleist's story "The Earthquake in Chile" describes human inability to tolerate contingency. With brilliant and poignant irony, Kleist rebuked all attempts to make the earthquake a source of meaning. In his tale, the mob that smashes a baby it holds to be born of an unholy union seeks both sense and sacrifice. Unable to accept the yawning unintelligibility of natural evil, it prefers doing evil itself. Kleist was not alone. The auto-da-fé that followed the Lisbon earthquake moved Voltaire as surely as the earthquake itself. Far better, he concluded, to live without reasons at all than to risk making that kind of mistake about them. These are pathologies that may arise from the drive to unite *is* and *ought*, and they function as warnings about its limits.

Fear of this sort of abuse has been one reason to avoid the problem of evil altogether, but an even deeper argument is sometimes made. This rests on the idea that to understand something is to justify it. Two versions of the claim occur in the literature—both in French, and both in the negative. But *tout comprendre ce n'est pas tout justifier* and *s'expliquer n'est pas se justifier* are always asserted defensively. Hegel recognized the insight behind Leibniz's theodicy: full understanding of an event would show it to be part of a whole that could not possibly be better ordered than it is. If we stop scientific investigation at the point when we've achieved partial understanding, it is not only because we've learned to be content with less than our predecessors but because we suspect that understanding has moral limits.

In chapter 2, I argued that one motive driving those who insisted on remaining with the appearances was a moral one. Keeping faith with the world, and particularly with those who suffer miserably in it, seemed to require rejecting every attempt to find meaning that would make appearances seem milder. Voltaire preferred to reject philosophy rather than to accept a rosier account of appearances. Dostoevsky's Ivan Karamazov made the point even stronger: after describing cases of tortured children, he chooses to reject comprehension itself.

> "I understand nothing," Ivan went on as though in delirium, "and I don't want to understand anything now. I want to stick to facts. I made up my mind long ago not to understand. For if I should want to understand something, I'd instantly alter the facts, and I've made up my mind to stick to the facts. (Dostoevsky, 285)

Dostoevsky underlined the idea that the problem of evil is not just one more mystery. It is so central to our lives that if reason stumbles there, it must give way to faith. If you cannot understand why children are tortured, nothing else you understand really matters. But the very attempt to understand it requires at least accepting it as part of the world that must be investigated. Some hold even this much acceptance to be unacceptable. Thus the rejection of theodicy becomes the rejection of comprehension itself.

Just this realization drove contemporary thinkers to take up the question again, in full awareness of all the reasons the twentieth century provided to abandon it forever. The moral impulse expressed in Dostoevsky's refusal to understand is overridden by the impulse that sees no alternative. To abandon the attempt to comprehend evil is to abandon every basis for confronting it, in thought as in practice. The thinkers who returned to the problem of evil while knowing the limits of any discussion of it were driven by moral demands. For creatures endowed with reason, love of the world cannot be blind. The intellectual struggle is more important than any particular results that emerge from it. Practical results are unlikely without some such struggle and the demand that begins it. Belief that the world should be rational is the basis of every attempt to make it so. Political progress has metaphysical conditions. We cannot even try to understand the causes of evil, and go to work on eliminating them, without the idea that happiness and virtue should be connected. Moral reactions like guilt and indignation that lead to political actions have their basis in the principle of sufficient reason. The connection between the rise of rationalism and the demand for autonomy is not a historical accident. The demand that reason and reality come to meet is the source of whatever progress occurs in actually bringing them together. Without such a demand, we would never feel outrage—nor assume the responsibility for change to which outrage sometimes leads.

The tentative and fragmentary discussions of the problems of evil that have arisen in the wake of Auschwitz reflect the fact that abandoning discussion comes too close to abandoning the principle of sufficient reason itself. Moral and epistemological scruples destroyed our hopes for complete explanations of reality. Twentieth-century events made systematic explanations of the whole seem not only impossible but finally and decidedly wrong. Were we offered an account that shows Auschwitz to be part of the order of things, most of us would reject it. Yet any account of the world that ignores it will be worth very little.

How much reason would be sufficient? It's clear that we must make do with less than once was wanted. Some will consider themselves lucky to get any at all. It is crucial to resist the equation of rationalism and system. Kant's greatest error was to mistake the demand for reason with the demand for system. Few took his vast architectonic entirely seriously, and pointing out its flaws became the Kant scholar's minor sport. But the idea that rejecting the will to system meant rejecting the heart of rationalism was the miserable, unspoken legacy of German philosophy. Interest in the detail, analysis of the fragment, were thus left to all those who rejected reason. This proved especially fatal, for where so many structures of modern thought have been shattered, whatever sense we find must be incomplete. Attention to the pieces is now all the more important.[31]

In rejecting Kant's account of reason as systematic, I do not reject his picture of reason as uncompromising. The adamant child who wants every question answered expresses something about the nature of reason. Kant held that reason is structured so as to seek premises for every condition. Logically, it will find no place to rest until it reaches the Unconditioned—the point at which everything appears so self-evident that there are no questions left to be asked. Reason's tendency to keep going until all its demands are met is relentless. Some will dismiss it as childish; others will shrink from it as potentially totalitarian. Caution is always in order, for all the alternatives are worse. The smaller the expectations of the rational, the less it demands of the real. Where reason's demands are too humble, it concedes all the terms to reality before the struggle begins.

The picture of reason as inherently systematic is fatal to any form of philosophy we will want to preserve. If the events that determined the twentieth century left contemporary experience fractured, any conception of reason that can be salvaged must reflect fracture itself. This is an old insight, reflected in the abandonment of the great metaphysical systems of the nineteenth century. Those who followed erred in dividing philosophy into areas. The analytic division of philosophy into areas of specialization and the German division of philosophy into *Lehrstühle* reflect a will to system grown embarrassed, not a rejection of it. Where experience was truly shattered, the pieces will never be neatly ordered again. They are pieces of a whole which reflects the fact that reason, if not a system, is still a unity. Ethics and metaphysics are not *accidentally* connected. Whatever attempts we make to live rightly are attempts to live in the world.

Classical rationalism viewed our lack of understanding as itself providential. Even Lessing and Mendelssohn's attack on Pope named human ignorance as an argument for God's benevolence: instead of knowledge of the future, God gave us hope. Kant turned this thought into one of his greater arguments: if we knew that God existed, freedom and virtue would disappear. It's an act of Providence that the nature of Providence will forever remain uncertain. Einstein said the Creator was subtle; Kant's thought showed Him brilliant. Our very skepticism is a providential gift. What binds the real and the rational together must be so fragile that it will seem miraculous—and on occasion the miracle occurs. As with any other miracle, it takes something like faith to perceive it.

Learning from the history of philosophy is not a matter of appropriating it wholesale. We use its insights to shed light on our own. We cannot make the same claims that even the most modern Enlightenment thinkers asserted before us. At times the most hopeful gesture we may be able to manage is not to answer whether life is justified but merely to reject the question. Meaning is a human category, and must be won against a background. A life that was inevitably meaningful would defeat itself from the start. Between the adult who knows she won't find reason in the world, and the child who refuses to stop seeking it, lies the difference between resignation and humility.

NOTES

CHAPTER ONE
FIRE FROM HEAVEN

1. All quotations, and my account of Alfonso's life, are taken from Bayle's version in the *Historical and Critical Dictionary*, "Castile (Alphonsus X of that Name, King of)" (Bayle 2). I am indebted to Claudio Lange for another picture of the king, whom much Spanish tradition still reveres as Alfonso the Wise for his collections of law and music as well as his mediation between Christian, Jewish, and Muslim traditions.

2. See the headnote to the bibliography, below, for an explanation of the citation style used in this book.

3. Leibniz, 248. Discussion and quotations of Leibniz are based on this text.

4. For this reason, one of Bayle's opponents retracted the doctrine that the tortures of hell are eternal. Bayle added an argument to show that if his original argument about infinite amounts of torture was valid, the same could be shown for torture of any duration.

5. Oddly enough, it's Immanuel Kant, the philosopher whom Heine described as thoroughly unpoetic, who raised unresolved tension to something like the fundamental principle of human being. His occasional unforgettable passages not only approach Pope's style but convey just Pope's message. Think of "Human reason has this peculiar fate . . ." or "Two things fill the mind. . . ."

6. There are excellent exceptions. The classic discussion is found in Cassirer. I follow his account on several points. See Velkley, Schulte.

7. Voltaire and Kant, to take two examples, were tireless in arguing that Europe, America, and the Orient, savage and civilized citizen, present the same barbarous picture. For Rousseau's critique of what he takes to have become unscientific cliché, see Rousseau 1, 187, 220. Even Voltaire could be tempted by thoughts that are proto-Rousseauian; his *Dictionary* suggested that "Man is not born evil, he becomes evil, as he becomes sick" (Voltaire 6, 2:378). But such suggestions remained isolated.

8. Rousseau's account of love is marred, of course, by the claim that Sophie, unlike Emile, should attend to appearances instead of the real things that matter. It is easy to imagine a version of the book in which Sophie, true to her name, received an education like Emile's. Such an account would be less sappy as well as less sexist, but showing all this is a task for another occasion.

9. For discussion of the *Pantheismusstreit*, see Beiser, Neiman.

10. Of course this sketch is not intended to be a detailed survey of Kant's theory of knowledge or doctrine of transcendental idealism. For those interested in a good one, see Allison.

11. The relevant text is sufficiently unnoticed to be worth repeating. It occurs in the casuistic discussion of cases of action Kant had elsewhere seemed to regard

as clear. He asks his readers to consider: "An author asks one of his readers, 'How do you like my work?' One could merely seem to give an answer, by joking about the impropriety of such a question. But who has his wit always ready? The author will take the slightest hesitation in answering as an insult. May one, then, say what is expected of one?" (Kant 10, 431). Kant leaves the question open.

12. For a defense of this view, see Neiman.

13. Tucker rightly rejects what he calls the argument from propriety, which refuses to acknowledge that Hegel identifies anyone in particular with the Absolute simply because such a conclusion would be shocking. Forster gives a thorough discussion of Hegel's rejection of the notion that philosophy and common sense must share the same world.

14. See Hegel 1. Fackenheim explains it thus: "The divine redemptive act, then, must unite the Jewish transcendent Lord with the immanence and humanity of the gods of Greece. To bring about this union He cannot, like the Greek gods, be merely *represented* as human. . . . In the Christian view the Greek gods were not too anthropomorphic, but rather not anthropomorphic enough" (140).

15. Roger Garaudy argues that the Incarnation serves Hegel as the paradigm for the overcoming of all dualism—between human and God, the historical and contingent, and the absolute and necessary—which is the goal of his work as a whole. See Garaudy, 109 ff.

16. This claim has been superbly shown by Odo Marquard in his "Idealismus und Theodizee," in Marquard, 1.

17. "[The self-appointed guardians of humankind] . . . regard the step to maturity as not only difficult but also very dangerous. After they have first made their domestic creatures stupid and carefully prevented them from daring to take even one step out of the leading strings of the cart to which they are tethered, they show them the danger that threatens them if they attempt to proceed on their own. Now this danger is not so great, for by falling a few times they would indeed finally learn to walk; but an example of this sort makes them timid and usually frightens them away from all further attempts" (Kant 4, A482).

18. See especially Pippin 1 and Pippin 2.

19. See Loewith.

20. Two excellent exceptions, which read Marx in light of traditional philosophical debates about the problem of evil, are Tucker and Gunneman.

21. Tucker, 125 ff., presents textual evidence to show that this, not *The Philosophy of Right*, was the fundamental text for Marx's appropriation of Hegel.

Chapter Two
Condemning the Architect

1. But those still inclined to insist on hard-and-fast distinctions between them should consider the degree to which Hume was required to slake his chief passion, the love of literary fame, through the response to his *History* and lighter essays. Not until after his death, and the dawn of a dryer age, did his metaphysics receive the central place in his work that they are now accorded.

2. Heine portrays Providence as a Jewish mother, the worried servant running after his charge with an umbrella (Heine, vol. 3). Nietzsche makes the hint explicit and thinks piety itself should abolish the notion of "a God who cures a headcold at the right moment or tells us to get into a coach just as a downpour is about to start . . . God as a domestic servant, as a postman, as an almanac maker—at bottom a word for the saddest kind of accidental occurrence" (Nietzsche 7, #52).

3. See Labrousse, vol. 2, as well as Richard Popkin's introduction to his translation and abridgment of Bayle (Bayle 1).

4. In his *The Philosophy of Leibniz*, where he writes that Leibniz "seems to imply that existence *means* belonging to the best possible world; thus Leibniz's optimism would reduce itself to saying that *actual* is an abbreviation which it is sometimes convenient to substitute for *best possible*. If these are the consolations of philosophy, it is no wonder that philosophers cannot endure the toothache patiently!" (Russell 1, 377).

5. "When he thought of the wealth that remained in his hands, and when he talked of Cunegonde, especially just after a good dinner, [Candide] still inclined to the system of Pangloss" (Voltaire 5, 64). See also the *Dictionary's* "Well, All is Well" (Voltaire 6).

6. "Struck by seeing that poor man weighed down, so to speak, by fame and prosperity, bitterly complaining, nevertheless, against the wretchedness of this life and finding everything invariably bad, I formed the insane plan of trying to prove to him that all was well. . . . The absurdity of Voltaire's doctrine is particularly revolting in a man loaded with every kind of blessing who, living in the lap of luxury, seeks to disillusion his fellow-men by a frightening and cruel picture of all the calamities from which he himself is exempt. I, who had a better right to count up and weigh the evils of human life, examined them impartially and proved that there is not one of those evils which could be blamed *on Providence*"(Rousseau 4, bk. 8, p. 99). Rousseau is referring to the letter he wrote Voltaire in response to the poem "On the Lisbon Earthquake." He concludes by complaining that Voltaire never bothered to answer the letter directly. If he is right in suggesting that the answer, four years later, came in the form of *Candide*, it should have been some consolation.

7. I owe this term, and much discussion of the subject, to James Ponet.

8. See "Well, All is Well" (Voltaire 6). Or, as Candide asks after the Lisbon earthquake and its consequences, "If this is the best of all possible worlds, what are the others like?" (Voltaire 5, 28).

9. In private correspondence, he described the earthquake as a kick in the ass to Providence ("de cette affaire la Providence en a dans le cul") (quoted in Gourevitch).

10. See Westfall, 21 ff., for this claim, in particular.

11. For further discussion, see Neiman, chap. 1.

12. See also the entries for "Atheism" and "Religion."

13. See the open letter to the *Journal Encylopédique*, April 1, 1759, quoted in Gay, "Voltaire's Faith," in Voltaire 4; also the letter to Bertrand quoted in Mason, " 'Candide' Assembling Itself," ibid.

14. Schopenhauer was, at least in these matters, as good a reader of Kant and Hume as Kant was of Hume and Rousseau. See Schopenhauer, 2:338. Kant read Hamann's translation of the *Dialogues* shortly after they appeared in 1780, when he was finishing the writing of the *Critique of Pure Reason*.

15. For the ease with which it has come to appear self-evident, see Norton, 19–27.

16. For a revealing instance of the latter, note the following 1764 letter from Paris: "It is putting too great a respect on the vulgar, and on their superstitions, to pique oneself on sincerity with regard to them. Did one ever make it a point of honour to speak truth with regard to children or madmen? . . . Am I a liar, because I order my servant to say, I am not at home, when I do not desire to see company?" (Hume 4, 1:439). Though Kant's regard for truth telling is not as absolute as legend would have it, it is hard to avoid comparison with the tortuous vistas of his last essay.

17. One of Voltaire's darkest passages suggests that those who invented torture did just this, modeling thumbscrews and racks on the illnesses that are "executors of the vengeances of Providence" (Voltaire 6, 490). Sade was not quite as unique as he tried to be.

18. If Descartes suggested this nightmare, Goethe put it in the mouth of Mephistopheles, who attacks God for having given humankind "that appearance of heavenly light he calls reason" (Goethe 3, line 283).

19. So Nietzsche's *Schopenhauer as Educator* insists that "Genius itself is now called upon to hear whether it, as the highest fruit of life, can perhaps justify life; the magnificently creative man must answer the question: Do you affirm this existence deep in your heart? Is it sufficient for you? Will you be its advocate, its redeemer? But for a single true yes! From your mouth—and life, which is accused of such great crimes, shall be acquitted" (Nietzsche 2, 33).

Chapter Three
Ends of an Illusion

1. Nietzsche's rendering of the passage is very different. See Nietzsche 1, sec. 3. Pippin rightly sees Nietzsche's discussion of the question as central to his later work as well; see his "Truth and Lies in the Early Nietzsche," in Pippin 2.

2. Nietzsche was right to warn us against confusing authors and their creations, and against the particular temptation to do so with Goethe and Faust. But no matter what it looked like from the outside, Goethe's own description of his life was staggeringly bleak. In the *Conversations with Eckermann* he denied that he'd felt four weeks of contentment in seventy-five years. His description of his life as endless martyrdom without real pleasure in his *Sketch of an Autobiography* seems to confirm the insight of the old woman aboard ship in *Candide*.

3. I owe this formulation to Irad Kimhi.

4. Zarathustra finds it necessary to deny that his view is Leibnizian. On similarities between Nietzsche's view of reconciliation and that of Hegel, see especially Pippin 3.

CHAPTER FOUR
HOMELESS

1. See in particular Rubinstein, Katz, and Münz.

2. This statement, like most of my information about the Lisbon earthquake, is taken from T. D. Kendrick's excellent book. See also Breidert, Gunther, and Shklar for further discussion.

3. This is a subject in great need of discussion. Weber's classic study attributed the rise of capitalism itself in large part to certain beliefs about Providence, but much remains to be done. It should be mentioned that while Hume's work was often concerned with destroying beliefs in Providence, and his friend Adam Smith's may be said to give Providence a naturalist shape, their correspondence records no mention of the Lisbon earthquake. On April 12, 1759, Hume did send Smith an appreciative remark about the attack on Providence in *Candide*.

4. Leibniz wrote: "One Caligula alone, one Nero, has caused more evil than an earthquake" (Leibniz, 26).

5. It was possible for traditional theology to blame humankind for its misery in this world as well as the world to come. So *Virtue Awakened by the Earthquake* argued that most of the damage the earthquake caused could have been avoided if houses had been differently built. This proto-Rousseauian claim puts the blame for the damage on us without quite sanctifying our responsibility for it. Its focus is vindicating the Creator rather than changing anything in His world.

6. The Turkish earthquake of 1999 produced some eighty thousand victims and a rash of fundamentalist Islamic claims about God's punishment for a secular government. Similar reactions occurred in the wake of the even larger Indian earthquake two years later. Christian fundamentalist claims that the September 11 terrorist attacks were punishment for American secularism suggest that this kind of response is a universal possibility—and displays the fundamentalist rejection of the distinction between natural and moral evil.

7. For these quotations and other fine discussion of these questions, see Lifton and Mitchell, 345, 304. On the development of the idea that Auschwitz was unique, see Maier; see also Margalit and Motzkin. For Anders's view, see especially his *Besuch im Hades*.

8. See Améry 3, 101 ff.

9. Including many Germans, for—as Arendt remarked—collective guilt is a form of individual exoneration. Where everybody is guilty in general, nobody is guilty in particular. This reaction has been suggested as a reason for Goldhagen's popularity in Germany.

10. On one estimate, if spread out over the course of the century, war killed one hundred people every hour (Glover).

11. For particularly stark expressions of these claims, see Primo Levi's report of a guard's statement, "Hier ist kein warum" (Here there is no "why"), or Ruth Klüger's description of *verlorener Verstand* (lost understanding) as a condition of functioning well at Auschwitz. The classic statement of the idea that the intellect itself was defeated by Auschwitz is found in Améry 1.

12. For some of the discussion on which I have relied here, see Arendt 1, Diner 1, Diner 2, and Glover.

13. See also Klemperer. *The Authoritarian Personality* was the Frankfurt School's attempt to come to terms with just this problem through empirical study of the structures that led people to be vulnerable to Nazism, but the study's results were sufficiently general to confirm the sense of indeterminacy.

14. A surprising exception may be seen in the final pages of David Rousset's *L'Univers Concentrationnaire* (Edition du Pavois, 1946) (translated as *A World Apart*). It is dated August 1945, four months after the author, a French professor of philosophy, was released from Buchenwald. "The balance is by no means negative. It is still far too soon to draw up the positive sheet of concentration camp experience, but even now, it promises to be a rich one. A dynamic awareness of the strength and beauty of being alive, self-contained, brutal, entirely stripped of all superstructures, of being able to live even in the midst of the most appalling catastrophes or the most serious setbacks. A fresh sensual feeling of joy, arising out of the most scientific knowledge of destruction and, as a result of this, an increased firmness in action and unshakable judgments; in short, a fuller and more intensely creative state of being" (103). Rousset's voice is so unusual in the literature that its Nietzschean tones carry less force than would be the case if they were echoed elsewhere.

15. See, for example, Segev.

16. My discussion has relied primarily on the discussion of the camps found in Agamben, Améry, Hilsenrath, Klüger, and Levi.

17. "Half a dozen psychiatrists had certified him as 'normal'—'More normal, at any rate, than I am after having examined him' one of them was said to have exclaimed, while another found that his whole psychological outlook, his attitude towards his wife and children, mother and father, brothers, sisters, and friends, was 'not only normal but most desirable'—and finally the minister who had paid regular visits to him in prison after the Supreme Court had finished hearing his appeal reassured everybody by declaring Eichmann to be 'a man with very positive ideas' " (Arendt 2, 25–26).

18. No commentator has yet suggested a satisfactory explanation of Arendt's introduction of the discussion of the Jewish Councils into her analysis of the Eichmann trial at all. Benhabib says she has no answer to the question (Benhabib, 180). Bernstein suggests that Arendt wanted to show the general moral collapse of European society (Bernstein 1, 163). This is surely correct, but her further point is that this collapse was not a function of the wrong kind of intention.

19. I have learned, in particular, from the works of Blumenberg, Loewith, Marquard, and Taubes.

20. See Kuhlmann.

21. See Bernstein's perceptive essay "Evil and the Temptation of Theodicy" (Bernstein 2), which argues that Levinas's work as a whole is a response to the problem of evil. Bernstein views the nonreasonableness of Levinas's demand that we take infinite responsibility for the other as a response to the nonreasonableness of evil itself.

22. Kant himself insisted that the urge to move beyond given experience is as central a mark of the human as the fact that we are limited to it. Critical Theory recognized this, and Benjamin is particularly explicit on this point; see Benjamin 2, 164. Wittgenstein is the twentieth-century philosopher most resistant to classification for just this reason. While nobody said more clearly that the unstatable questions were the only ones of importance, nobody fought more savagely his own urges to state them.

23. See Améry 2.

24. Although his article in *Dissent* on the fiftieth anniversary of Hiroshima is the only written work in which Rawls hints at those sources, they are evident from private conversation.

25. It must be emphasized that Rawls's reluctance to engage in metaphysics was so great that the extent of his engagement with such questions was long unclear to most of his students, the present author included. In conversation and correspondence, Rawls occasionally said he was concerned with the problem of evil, and elaborated this with very fragmentary remarks in the directions sketched above. Thomas Pogge writes that "[a]ll his life, Rawls was interested in the question whether and to what extent human life is redeemable," in his excellent "Brief Sketch of Rawls' Life," in Richardson and Weithman. Pogge reports Rawls's frequent use of the word *redeem* in the interviews conducted for this sketch. But this was not the sort of language that left even an echo in earlier days, nor did the word *evils* figure significantly until *The Law of Peoples*.

26. See Loewith, Taubes. For some of the further discussion, see Blumenberg 1 and Marquard 1. Robert Pippin provided the best discussion in English; see his "Blumenberg and the Modernity Problem," in Pippin 2.

27. The idea that showing the universe to be comprehensible is a moral project is one way to read the repeated attempts to combat voluntarism described in J. B. Schneewind's magisterial book *The Invention of Autonomy*. Modern moral philosophy, it suggests, viewed autonomy and benevolence as arising in each other's service.

28. Kant's "Was heißt Aufklärung?" and Lessing's *Die Erziehung des Menschengeschlechts* are but the two most famous instances of this metaphor.

29. So Bury argued that the Romantic reevaluation of the Middle Ages arose from the need to defend claims about progress in civilization. On this view, seeking light in the Dark Ages was a matter not of validating the Counter-Enlightenment but of confirming Enlightenment hopes for more or less steady progress in history.

30. On the first question, see Shklar; on the second, see Arendt 7, 242 ff.

31. I take this to be what Adorno meant in writing that after Auschwitz it is impossible to say that truth is unchanging and illusion is *vergänglich* (transitory) (Adorno 2, 352). I believe, however, that neither Adorno nor Horkheimer took their implicit critique of Nietzsche to its proper conclusion. To argue for transcendence, conceived radically, as a feature of liberation is to deny that transcendence is a theological concept, in any but the vaguest sense; talk of secularized metaphysical categories recalls Benjamin's dwarf pulling strings behind apparently modern forces.

BIBLIOGRAPHY

Below are listed books to which direct reference is made in the text. Where standard English translations were available, I have used them, with occasional changes. Other translations are my own. Where several works of an author have been cited, I have numbered them chronologically and listed the edition used. So, for example, the reference (Nietzsche 1, 27) would refer to page 27 in the Kaufmann translation of Nietzsche's *Birth of Tragedy*. An exception was made in the citation of Kant's works. Those cited were also numbered chronologically, but I have followed standard practice in referring to pages of the *Critique of Pure Reason* as A/B, and all other works with the pagination used in the Academy edition, which readers may follow in any edition they use.

Adorno, Theodor. *Minima Moralia*. Suhrkamp, 1951. (Adorno 1)

———. *Negative Dialektik*. Suhrkamp, 1975. (Adorno 2)

Adorno, Theodor, and Max Horkheimer. *The Dialectic of Enlightenment*. Translated by John Cumming. The Seabury Press, 1972.

Agamben, Giorgio. *Remnants of Auschwitz*. Zone Books, 1999.

Allison, Henry. *Kant's Transcendental Idealism*. Yale University Press, 1983.

Améry, Jean. *Jenseits von Schuld und Sühne*, Klett-Cotta, 1977. (Améry 1)

———. *Über das Altern: Revolte und Resignation*. Klett-Cotta, 1969. (Améry 2)

———. *Hand an sich Legen*. Klett-Cotta, 1976. (Améry 3)

Anders, Günther. *Besuch im Hades*. Beck, 1967.

Arendt, Hannah. *The Origins of Totalitarianism*. Harcourt Brace Jovanovich, 1951. (Arendt 1)

———. *Eichmann in Jerusalem*. Viking, 1963. (Arendt 2)

———. "Eichmann in Jerusalem: An Exchange of Letters between Gershom Scholem and Hannah Arendt." *Encounter* 22 (January 1964): 51–56. (Arendt 3)

———. *Thinking*. Harcourt Brace Jovanovich, 1971. (Arendt 4)

———. *Willing*. Harcourt Brace Jovanovich, 1978. (Arendt 5)

———Hannah Arendt / Karl Jaspers. *Briefwechsel*. Edited by Lotte Köhler and Hans Saner. Piper, 1993. (Arendt 6)

———. *Essays in Understanding 1930–1954*. Edited by Jerome Kohn. Harcourt Brace and Company, 1994. (Arendt 7)

———. *Ich will verstehen: Selbstkritik zu Leben und Werk*. Piper, 1996. (Arendt 8)

———. *Lectures on Kant's Political Philosophy*. Edited by Ronald Beiner. University of Chicago Press, 1982. (Arendt 9)

———. *Between Friends: The Correspondence of Hannah Arendt and Mary McCarthy 1949–75*. Edited by Carol Brightman. Harcourt Brace and World, 1995. (Arendt 10)

Bayle, Pierre. *Historical and Critical Dictionary*. Selections translated with an introduction and notes by Richard Popkin. Bobbs-Merrill, 1965. (Bayle 1)

———. *Historical and Critical Dictionary*. Translated by J. J. and P. Knapton, 1738. Reprinted by Garland Press, 1984. (Bayle 2)

Beiser, Frederick C. *The Fate of Reason*. Harvard University Press, 1988.

Benhabib, Seyla. *The Reluctant Modernism of Hannah Arendt*. Sage Publications, 1996.

Benjamin, Walter. "Dialogue über die Religiosität der Gegenwart." In *Gesammelte Schriften*, Band II. Suhrkamp, 1980. (Benjamin 1)

———. "Über das Programm der kommenden Philosophie." In *Gesammelte Schriften*, Band IV. Suhrkamp, 1980. (Benjamin 2)

———. *Illuminations*. Edited by Hannah Arendt. Translated by Harry Zohn. Schocken, 1969. (Benjamin 3)

Bernasconi, Robert, and David Wood, eds. *The Provocation of Levinas*. Routledge, 1988.

Bernstein, Richard. *Hannah Arendt and the Jewish Question*. MIT Press, 1996. (Bernstein 1)

———. "Evil and the Temptation of Theodicy." In *Radical Evil: A Philosophical Investigation*. Polity Press, 2002. (Bernstein 2)

———. "Kant at War with Himself." In *Radical Evil: A Philosophical Investigation*. Polity Press, 2002. (Bernstein 3)

Blumenberg, Hans. *Die Legitimität der Neuzeit*. Suhrkamp, 1966. (Blumenberg 1)

———. *Die Genesis der kopernikanischen Welt*. Suhrkamp, 1975. (Blumenberg 2)

———. *Arbeit am Mythos*. Suhrkamp, 1979. (Blumenberg 3)

Breidert, Wolfgang. *Die Erschütterung der vollkommenen Welt*. Wissenschaftliche Buchgesellschaft Darmstadt, 1994.

Bury, J. D. *The Idea of Progress*. Dover, 1932.

Camus, Albert. *The Myth of Sisyphus*. Translated by Justin O'Brien. Knopf, 1955. (Camus 1)

———. *Lettres à un ami allemand*. Gallimard, 1948. (Camus 2)

———. *The Plague*. Translated by Stuart Gilbert. Vintage, 1991. (Camus 3)

———. *The Rebel: An Essay on Man in Revolt*. Translated by Anthony Bower. Knopf, 1956. (Camus 4)

———. *Selected Essays and Notebooks*. Penguin, 1979. (Camus 5)

Cassirer, Ernst. *The Question of Jean-Jacques Rousseau*. Indiana University Press, 1975.

Clarke, Samuel. *A Demonstration of the Being and Attributes of God*. In Cambridge Texts in the History of Philosophy and Other Writings, ed. Ezio Vailati. Cambridge University Press, 1998.

Darnton, Robert. *The Forbidden Best-Sellers of Revolutionary France*. W. W. Norton, 1996.

Diner, Dan. *Das Jahrhundert Verstehen*. Luchterhand, 1999. (Diner 1)

———. *Beyond the Conceivable*. University of California Press, 2000. (Diner 2)

Djuric and Simon, eds. *Nietzsche und Hegel*. Königshausen/Neumann, 1992.

Dostoevsky, Fyodor. *The Brothers Karamazov*. Translated by David Magarshack. Penguin, 1958.

Engels, Friedrich. *Marx-Engels Gesamtausgabe*. Edited by the Internationalen-Marx-Engels-Stiftung. Amsterdam, 1990.

Fackenheim, Emil. *The Religious Dimension of Hegel's Thought*. Indiana University Press, 1967.

Feuerbach, Ludwig. *The Essence of Christianity*. Translated by George Eliot. Harper, 1957.

Forster, Michael. *Hegel's Idea of a Phenomenology of Spirit*. University of Chicago Press, 1998.

Freud, Sigmund. *The Future of an Illusion*. In *Civilization, Society, and Religion*. Penguin, 1985. (Freud 1)

————. *Civilization and Its Discontents*. W. W. Norton, 1961. (Freud 2)

Garaudy, Roger. *Dieu est Mort*. Presses Universitaires de France, 1962.

Gay, Peter. *The Enlightenment*. Vol. 1. W. W. Norton, 1966. (Gay 1)

————. "Voltaire's Faith." In *Candide, or Optimism: A Fresh Translation*, edited by Robert M. Adams. W. W. Norton, 1991. (Gay 2)

Glover, Jonathan. *Humanity: A Moral History*. Jonathan Cape, 1999.

Goethe, Johann Wolfgang. *Conversations of Goethe with Johann Peter Eckermann*. Da Capo Press, 1998. (Goethe 1)

————. *Tag- und Jahreshefte: autobiographische Schriften aus Goethes letzten Lebensjahren*. Edited by Irmtraut Schmid. Deutscher Klassiker Verlag, 1994. (Goethe 2)

————. *Faust*, Part One. Translated by Peter Salm. Bantam, 1985. (Goethe 3)

Gourevitch, Victor. "Rousseau on Providence." In *Review of Metaphysics*, 2000.

Gunneman, Jon P. *The Moral Meaning of Revolution*. Yale University Press, 1973.

Gunther, Horst. *Das Erdbeben von Lissabon*. Wagenbach, 1994.

Hegel, G.W.F. *Early Theological Writings*. Translated by T. M. Knox. University of Pennsylvania Press, 1988. (Hegel 1)

————. *Phenomenology of Spirit*. Translated by A. V. Miller. Oxford University Press, 1977. (Hegel 2)

————. *The Science of Logic*. Translated by A. V. Miller. Humanity Books, 1998. (Hegel 3)

————. *Philosophy of Right*. Translated by T. M. Knox. Oxford University Press, 1952. (Hegel 4)

————. *Introduction to the Lectures on the Philosophy of World History*. Translated by H. B. Nisbet. Cambridge University Press, 1975. (Hegel 5)

————. *Vorlesungen über die Philosophie der Religion I*. Vol. 16 of *Hegels Werke*. Suhrkamp, 1990. (Hegel 6)

————. *Lectures on the History of Philosophy*. Translated by E. S. Haldane and F. H. Simon. University of Nebraska Press, 1975. (Hegel 7)

Heine, Heinrich. *Geschichte der Religion und Philosophie in Deutschland*. Vol. 5. In Heine, *Sämtliche Schriften*. Ullstein, 1976.

Hilsenrath, Edgar. *Nacht*. Fischer Taschenbuch Verlag, 1991.

Horkheimer, Max. *Eclipse of Reason*. Oxford University Press, 1947. (Horkheimer 1)

————. *Gesammelte Schriften*. Fischer Taschenbuch Verlag, 1991. (Horkheimer 2)

Hume, David, *A Treatise of Human Nature*. Edited by L. A. Selby-Bigge. Oxford University Press, 1978. (Hume 1)

Hume, David. *Enquiries Concerning Human Understanding and Concerning the Principles of Morals*. Edited by L. A. Selby-Bigge. Oxford University Press, 1975. (Hume 2)

———. *Dialogues Concerning Natural Religion* and *Natural History of Religion*. Edited by J.C.A. Gaskin. Oxford University Press, 1993. (Hume 3)

———. *Letters of David Hume*. Edited by J.Y.T. Greig. Clarendon Press, 1932. (Hume (4)

Kant, Immanuel. *Fortgesetzte Betrachtung*. (Kant 1)

———. *Reflektionen*. (Kant 2)

———. *Critique of Pure Reason*. (Kant 3)

———. "What Is Enlightenment?" (Kant 4)

———. *Groundwork of the Metaphysics of Morals*. (Kant 5)

———. *Critique of Practical Reason*. (Kant 6)

———. *Critique of Judgment*. (Kant 7)

———. "On the Failure of Every Possible Future Attempt at Theodicy." (Kant 8)

———. *Religion within the Limits of Reason Alone*. (Kant 9)

———. *The Metaphysics of Morals*. (Kant 10)

———. *Lectures on Philosophical Theology*. Translated by A. W. Ward and G. M. Clark. Cornell University Press, 1978. (Kant 11)

Katz, Stephan T. *Post-Holocaust Dialogues: Critical Studies in Modern Jewish Thought*. New York University Press, 1983.

Kaufmann, Walter. *Twenty German Poets*. Random House, 1962.

Kendrick, T. D. *The Lisbon Earthquake*. Methuen, 1956.

Kierkegaard, Søren. *The Sickness unto Death*. Edited by Howard V. Hong. Princeton University Press, 1983.

Klemperer, Victor. *Ich will Zeugnis ablegen bis zum letzten*. Aufbau Verlag, 1995.

Klossowski, Pierre. *Sade My Neighbor*. Northwestern University Press, 1991.

Klüger, Ruth. *Weiter leben. Ein Jugend*. Deutscher Taschenbuch Verlag, 1995.

Kojeve, Alexander. *Introduction to the Reading of Hegel*. Edited by Allan Bloom. Translated by James H. Nichols, Jr. Basic Books, 1969.

Kuhlmann, Hartmut. "Ohne Auschwitz." *International Zeitschrift für Philosophie*, 1997.

Labrousse, Elisabeth. *Pierre Bayle*. Martinus Nijhoff, 1964.

Leibniz, Gottfried Wilhelm. *Theodicy*. Edited by Austin Farrar. Translated by E. M. Huggard. Open Court, 1985.

Levi, Primo. *Survival in Auschwitz*. Translated by Stuart Woolf. Scribner, 1995.

Levinas, Emmanuel. "Transcendence and Evil." In *The Phenomenology of Man and of the Human Condition*, ed. Anna Tymienicka. D. Reidel, 1983. (Levinas 1)

———. "Useless Suffering." In *The Provocation of Levinas*, ed. Robert Bernasconi and David Wood. Routledge, 1988. (Levinas 2)

Lifton, Robert Jay, and Greg Mitchell. *Hiroshima in America: Fifty Years of Denial*. Putnam, 1995.

Loewith, Karl. *Meaning in History*. University of Chicago, 1948.

Maier, Charles S. *The Unmasterable Past*. Harvard University Press, 1988.

Margalit, Avishai, and Gabriel Motzkin. "Die Einzigartigkeit des Holocaust." *Deutsche Zeitschrift für Philosophie*, 1997.

Marquard, Odo. *Schwierigkeiten mit der Geschichtsphilosophie.* Suhrkamp, 1982. (Marquard 1)

——. *Apologie des Zufälligen.* Reclam, 1986. (Marquard 2)

Marx, Karl. *The Portable Marx.* Edited by Eugene Kamenka. Viking Penguin, 1983.

Mill, John Stuart. *Nature.* In *Three Essays on Religion, Collected Works of John Stuart Mill,* edited by J. M. Robson. University of Toronto Press, 1969.

Mossner, Ernst. *The Life of David Hume.* Thomas Nelson and Sons, 1954.

Münz, Christoph. *Der Welt ein Gedächtnis geben: Geschichtstheologisches Denken im Judentum nach Auschwitz.* Chr.Kaiser/Gütersloher Verlagshaus, 1995.

Neiman, Susan. *The Unity of Reason: Rereading Kant.* Oxford University Press, 1994.

Nietzsche, Friedrich. *The Birth of Tragedy.* Translated by Walter Kaufmann. Vintage, 1967. (Nietzsche 1)

——. *Schopenhauer as Educator.* Translated by James W. Hillesheim and Malcolm R. Simpson. Gateway Editions, 1965. (Nietzsche 2)

——. *Also sprach Zarathustra.* Insel, 1967. (Nietzsche 3)

——. *Beyond Good and Evil.* Translated by Walter Kaufmann. Vintage, 1968. (Nietzsche 4)

——. *On the Genealogy of Morals.* Translated by Walter Kaufmann. Vintage, 1969. (Nietzsche 5)

——. *Twilight of the Idols.* Translated by R. J. Hollingdale. Penguin, 1968. (Nietzsche 6)

——. *The Anti-Christ.* Translated by R. J. Hollingdale. Penguin, 1968. (Nietzsche 7)

——. *Ecce Homo.* Translated by Walter Kaufmann. Vintage, 1968. (Nietzsche 8)

——. *The Will to Power.* Translated by Walter Kaufmann and R. J. Hollingdale. Vintage, 1968. (Nietzsche 9)

Norton, David F., ed. *The Cambridge Companion to Hume.* Cambridge University Press, 1993.

Pippin, Robert. *Hegel's Idealism.* Cambridge University Press, 1983. (Pippin 1)

——. *Idealism as Modernism: Hegelian Variations.* Cambridge University Press, 1992. (Pippin 2)

——. "Selbstüberwindung, Versöhnung und Modernität bei Nietzsche und Hegel." In *Nietzsche und Hegel,* edited by Djuric and Simon. Königshausen/Neumann, 1992. (Pippin 3)

Pope, Alexander. *Essay on Man.* In *Selected Poetry and Prose,* edited by William K. Wimsatt, Jr. Holt, Rinehart and Winston, 1951.

Rawls, John. *A Theory of Justice.* Harvard University Press, 1971. (Rawls 1)

——. *The Law of Peoples.* Harvard University Press, 1999. (Rawls 2)

——. *Justice as Fairness.* Harvard University Press, 2000. (Rawls 3)

Richardson, Henry, and Paul Weithman, eds. *The Philosophy of Rawls.* New York: Garland Press, 1999.

Rousseau, Jean-Jacques. *The First and Second Discourses Together with the Replies to Critics and Essay on the Origin of Language.* Edited and translated by Victor Gourevitch. Harper and Row, 1986. (Rousseau 1)

Rousseau, Jean-Jacques. *La Nouvelle Héloïse*. Translated and abridged by Judith H. McDowell. Pennsylvania State University Press, 1968. (Rousseau 2)

———. *Emile*. Translated by Allan Bloom. Basic Books, 1979. (Rousseau 3)

———. *Confessions*. Edited by Patrick Coleman. Translated by Angela Scholar. Oxford University Press, 2000. (Rousseau 4)

———. *Oeuvres Complètes*. Edited by B. Gagnebin and M. Raymond. Pléiade, 1959. (Rousseau 5)

Rousset, David. *A World Apart*. Translated by Yvonne Moyse and Roger Senhouse. Secker and Warburg, 1951.

Rubinstein, Richard L. *After Auschwitz: History, Theology, and Contemporary Judaism*. The Johns Hopkins Press, 1992.

Russell, Bertrand. *The Philosophy of Leibniz*. George Allen and Unwin, 1937. (Russell 1)

———. *History of Western Philosophy*. Simon and Schuster, 1945. (Russell 2)

Sade, Marquis de. *Justine, Philosophy in the Bedroom and Other Writings*. Edited by Austryn Wainhouse and Richard Seaver. Grove Press, 1965. (Sade 1)

———. *Juliette*. Translated by Austryn Wainhouse. Grove Press, 1968. (Sade 2)

Sartre, Jean-Paul. "A Reply to Albert Camus." In *Situations*. Braziller, 1965.

Schneewind, J. B. *The Invention of Autonomy: A History of Modern Moral Philosophy*. Cambridge University Press, 1998.

Schopenhauer, Arthur. *The World as Will and Representation*. Translated by E.F.J. Payne, Dover, 1966.

Schulte, Christoph. "Zweckwidriges in der Erfahrung." *Kant-Studien* 82, 1991.

Segev, Tom. *The Seventh Million: The Israelis and the Holocaust*. Translated by Haim Watzman. Hill and Wong, 1993.

Shklar, Judith. *The Faces of Injustice*. Yale University Press, 1992.

Sophocles. *Oedipus at Colonnus*. Translated by Robert Fitzgerald. Harcourt Brace Jovanovich, 1941.

Taubes, Jacob. *Abendländische Eschatologie*. Mattes und Seitz Verlag, 1991.

Tucker, Robert. *Philosophy and Myth in Karl Marx*. Cambridge University Press, 1972.

Tymienicka, Anna, ed. *The Phenomenology of Man and of the Human Condition*. D. Reidel, 1983.

Velkley, Richard. *Freedom and the End of Reason*. University of Chicago Press, 1989.

Voltaire, François-Marie Arouet. *Zadig, or Destiny*. In *Candide, Zadig and Selected Stories*, translated by Donald M. Frame. Penguin, 1981. (Voltaire 1)

———. *The World as It Is*. In *Candide, Zadig and Selected Stories*, translated by Donald M. Frame. Penguin, 1981. (Voltaire 2)

———. "Poème sur la Destruction de Lisbonne, ou Examen de cet Axiome, Tout est bien." in *Journal encyclopédique*, 71–81. Liège, 1756. Reprint, Genève-Nedeln, 1967. 253–56. (Voltaire 3)

———. *Candide, or Optimism: A Fresh Translation, Backgrounds, Criticism*. Edited by Robert M. Adams. W. W. Norton, 1991. (Voltaire 4)

————. *Candide*. In *Candide, Zadig and Selected Stories*, translated by Donald M. Frame. Penguin, 1981. (Voltaire 5)

————. *Philosophical Dictionary*. Translated with an introduction by Peter Gay. Basic Books, 1962. (Voltaire 6)

————. *Correspondance*. Edited by Theodore Besterman. 13 vols. Gallimard, 1975–. (Voltaire 7)

Westfall, Richard. *The Construction of Modern Science*. Cambridge University Press, 1977.

INDEX

Compiled by Sylvia Coates

problem of evil: atheists' formulation of, 314–15; Auschwitz's presentation of, 2, 3, 273–81; Bayle on free will defense of, 120–25; Bayle's analysis of, 118–21; Christianity presented as solution to, 18–19; claims of this text regarding, 7–8; danger of denying, 41–42; danger of fragmenting, 7; death of God as Nietzsche's solution to, 215–27; development over time and solution to, 44–47; differences in philosophical traditions approaches to, 290–91; as expression of child's needs, 319–20; fears of understanding, 324–26; Hegel's use of metaphysical frame for, 86, 93–94; Hume's approach to, 168–69; Job's story and, 17; Job's story as beginning, 135; Kant's examination of assumptions for, 60–62; Marx's approach to, 103; as meaningless suffering, 216–17; modern philosophy's neglect of, 288–90; Nietzsche on creation of, 213, 257; Nietzsche's focus on centrality of, 205–6, 289; postwar intellectuals and, 2; presented in Sade's novels, 188–96; redeeming past, 219; reemergence of philosophical discussion on, 291–314; religious origins of, 315–24; replacing God as solution to, 200–201; Rousseau's shaping of, 55–57; stated in nontheist terms, 5; Voltaire on, 141–48; Voltaire's position on, 141–48. See also evil

progress: Auschwitz impact on beliefs about, 258–59; Bury's history of the idea of, 258; connection between ideas of Providence and, 98–99; Hegelian view of, 94–100, 259, 260–61; historical evidence of, 94–98, 263; legitimacy of the modern and idea of, 316

Prometheus, 58–59, 108, 109, 226, 227

Providence: classical religious judgment and belief in, 253–54; earthquakes as challenging, 246–47; Freud's examination of belief in, 227–37; General and personal, 110; Heine's portrayal as Jewish mother, 331n.3; Justine presentation of, 180–81, 182, 183, 184, 185, 187, 190; Leibniz and Pope's views of, 38–39; link between idea of progress and, 98–99; origins of ideas of, 100, 317, 319, 321; rejecting notion of, 114; rise of capitalism

and beliefs about, 333n.3; Rousseau's version of, 40–41, 50–51, 54, 57–58; Sade's stated goal to trace design of, 181; Schopenhauer's rejection of, 199; Voltaire questioning of, 33, 139, 141–48, 204. See also God; humankind

Prussian Academy, 32

punishment: of Alfonso for blasphemy, 15–16; Auschwitz viewed as classical religious, 253–54; Bayle on free will defense and, 120–21; examining Job's story for justified, 17; injustice of infinite amount of, 19–20; Kant's principle of sufficient reason and, 61–62, 138–39, 320, 326; Leibniz on sin and suffering, 22–24; Lisbon earthquake as divine, 242–45; of natural evils for moral evils, 38; Rousseau on value of childhood, 47–48; taken on by Jesus, 19

purposiveness: as lawfulness of contingent, 93; of nature, 82–83

"The Question of Philosophy" (Horkheimer), 306

quietism: denial of evil as leading to, 41; theodicy charged with leading to, 68–69, 181

rationalists, 11, 114–15, 195

Rawls, John, 292, 310–14, 335n.25

real = the rational dictum, 101

reality: accepting vs. changing, 103; Agamben's experiment on re-creation of Auschwitz, 264; Candide portrayal of, 133–34; Descartes on gap between appearance and, 126; Freud on need for education to, 229; Freud on terror-constructed, 231–32; history as negation of given, 101; Nietzsche's solution to opposition of idea and, 263–64; Nietzsche's view of, 222; ought and is gap in, 89, 101, 102, 111, 215–16, 257, 322, 323–24; theodicy function regarding, 222–23; understood through philosophy, 100–101

reason: contemporary fractured conception of, 327; demand for systematic connections by, 141; as the divine in humankind, 88–89; Eichmann in Jerusalem on evil as refusal to use, 303–4; eliminating contingency task of, 93–94; God

PAUL
RICOEUR

INTERPRETATION
THEORY:
DISCOURSE AND THE SURPLUS
OF MEANING

THE TEXAS CHRISTIAN UNIVERSITY PRESS
FORT WORTH, TEXAS 76129

The Library of Congress Cataloged the First Issue of this work
as follows:

Ricoeur, Paul.
    Interpretation theory: discourse and the surplus of
    meaning
    Paul Ricoeur. — Fort Worth: Texas Christian University
    Press, c1976.

    xii, 107 p.: port.: 24 cm

    1. Discourse analysis — Addresses, essays, lectures.
    2. Meaning (Philosophy) Addresses, essays, lectures.
    3. Languages — Philosophy — Addresses, essays,
    lectures.
    I. Title

P302.R5   410   76-29604
ISBN 0-912646-25-X   MARC
ISBN 0-912646-59-4

PAUL RICOEUR

PREFACE

IN THE FALL OF 1973 Paul Ricoeur journeyed from Paris to Fort Worth to deliver a series of lectures as part of the centennial celebration of Texas Christian University. That series bore the title "Discourse and the Surplus of Meaning." The expanded text published here under the title *Interpretation Theory* retains the earlier title as a subtitle. This change marks the development of the text into a systematic and comprehensive theory that attempts to account for the unity of human language in view of the diverse uses to which it is put.

A reasonable question is that of the location of this text within the horizon of Ricoeur's investigations of language and discourse published after *The Symbolism of Evil* (1960). That broad horizon is the search for a comprehensive philosophy of language that can account for the multiple functions of the human act of signifying and for all their interrelations. No single work published during this period (1960-1969) claims to offer that comprehensive philosophy, and no claim is made that the investigations, taken together, constitute it, for Ricoeur doubts that it could be elaborated by a single thinker.

How does *Interpretation Theory* stand in regard to this search? It occupies a distinct place, for works such as *Freud and Philosophy* (1965) and *The Conflict of Interpretations* (1969) are mainly investigations of the diverse uses to which language as discourse is put, while *Interpretation Theory* offers an account of the unity of human language in view of this diversity of function. In his *Interpretation Theory* we have Paul Ricoeur's philosophy of integral language.

As a result of the initial lecture presentation, a workshop on the interpretation of texts and a symposium on language were held at Texas Christian University in 1975. Professor Ricoeur returned to TCU for these events and developed his theory by offering critiques of the papers presented by TCU faculty and graduate students from widely diverse disciplines. These events indicate the power of this theory of interpretation and philosophy of language. It is our intention to make it available now to a much wider audience through this publication of the

expanded version of Paul Ricoeur's Centennial Lectures at
TCU.

This University sought the best in contemporary scholarship to help celebrate its centennial and thus properly honored Professor Ricoeur by the invitation. In turn, he offered
his best scholarship and thus honored the University and
helped to celebrate its centennial fittingly. We are grateful.

Ted Klein
Chairman, Department of Philosophy
Texas Christian University
Fort Worth, Texas

CONTENTS

INTRODUCTION

THE FOUR ESSAYS that make up this volume are based upon and expand the lectures I delivered at Texas Christian University, 27-30 November 1973, as their Centennial Lectures. They may be read as separate essays, but they may also be read as step by step approximations of a solution to a single problem, that of understanding language at the level of such productions as poems, narratives, and essays, whether literary or philosophical. In other words, the central problem at stake in these four essays is that of works; in particular, that of language as *a work*.

A complete grasp of this problem is not achieved until the fourth essay, which deals with the two apparently conflicting attitudes that we may assume when dealing with language as a work; I mean the apparent conflict between explanation and understanding. I believe, however, that this conflict is only an apparent one and that it may be overcome if these two attitudes can be shown to be dialectically related to each other. Hence it is this dialectic which constituted the horizon of my lectures.

If the dialectic between explanation and understanding may be said to provide the ultimate reference of my remarks, the first step taken in its direction must be a decisive one: we must cross the threshold beyond which language stands as *discourse*. Accordingly, the topic of the first essay is that of language as discourse. But, to the extent that only written language fully displays the criteria of discourse, a second investigation concerns the amplitude of the changes that affect discourse when it is no longer spoken, but written. Hence the title of my second essay, "Speaking and Writing."

The theory of the text, which emerges from this discussion, is advanced a step further with the question of the *plurivocity* belonging not only to words (polysemy), or even to sentences (ambiguity), but to full works of discourse such as poems, narratives, and essays. This problem of plurivocity, discussed in the third essay, provides the decisive transition to the problem of interpretation ruled by the dialectic of explanation and understanding, which I have indicated is the horizon of this whole set of essays.

I wish to express my gratitude and thanks to the people of Texas Christian University for the opportunity they extended me of delivering the lectures that form the basis of this work and also for their gracious hospitality during my stay there. I was pleased to be able to contribute to their centennial celebration.

1.

LANGUAGE AS DISCOURSE

THE TERMS IN WHICH THE PROBLEM of language as discourse will be discussed in this essay are modern in the sense that they could not have been adequately formulated without the tremendous progress of modern linguistics. Yet if the terms are modern, the problem itself is not a new one. It has always been known. In the *Cratylus*, Plato had already shown that the problem of the "truth" of isolated words or names must remain undecided because naming does not exhaust the power or the function of speaking. The *logos* of language requires at least a name and a verb, and it is the intertwining of these two words which constitutes the first unit of language and thought. Even this unit only raises a claim to truth; the question must still be decided in each instance.

The same problem recurs in the more mature works of Plato such as the *Theaetetus* and the *Sophist*. There the question is to understand how error is possible, i.e., how it is possible to say what is not the case, if to speak always means to say something. Plato is again compelled to conclude that a word by itself is neither true nor false, although a combination of words may mean something yet grasp nothing. The bearer of this paradox, once again, is the sentence, not the word.

Such is the first context within which the concept of discourse was discovered: error and truth are "affections" of discourse, and discourse requires two basic signs — a noun and a verb — which are connected in a synthesis which goes beyond the words. Aristotle says the same thing in his treatise *On Interpretation*. A noun has a meaning and a verb has, in

1

addition to its meaning, an indication of time. Only their conjunction brings forth a predicative link, which can be called *logos*, discourse. It is this synthetic unit which carries the double act of assertion and denial. An assertion may be contradicted by another assertion, and it may be true or false.

This short summary of the archaic stage of our problem is intended to remind us of both the antiquity and the continuity of the problem of language as discourse. However, the terms within which we shall now discuss it are quite new because they take into account the methodology and discoveries of modern linguistics.

In terms of this linguistics, the problem of discourse has become a genuine problem because discourse now can be opposed to a contrary term, which was not recognized or was taken for granted by the ancient philosophers. This opposite term today is the autonomous object of scientific investigation. It is the linguistic code which gives a specific structure to each of the linguistic systems, which we know as the various languages spoken by different linguistic communities. Language here then means something other than the general capacity to speak or the common competence of speaking. It designates the particular structure of the particular linguistic system.

With the words "structure" and "system" a new problematic emerges which tends, at least initially, to postpone, if not cancel, the problem of discourse, which is condemned to recede from the forefront of concern and become a residual problem. If discourse remains problematic for us today, it is because the main achievements of linguistics concern language as structure and system and not as used. Our task therefore will be to rescue discourse from its marginal and precarious exile.

Langue and *Parole:* The Structural Model

The withdrawal of the problem of discourse in the contemporary study of language is the price we must pay for the tremendous achievements brought about by the famous *Cours de linguistique général* of the Swiss linguist Ferdinand de Saussure.[1] His work relies on a fundamental distinction between language as *langue* and as *parole*, which has strongly shaped modern linguistics. (Note that Saussure did not speak of "discourse," but of "*parole*." Later we shall understand why.) *Langue* is the code—or the set of codes—on the basis of which a particular speaker produces *parole* as a particular message.

To this main dichotomy are connected several subsidiary distinctions. A message is individual, its code is collective. (Strongly influenced by Durkheim, Saussure considered linguistics to be a branch of sociology.) The message and the code do not belong to time in the same way. A message is a temporal event in the succession of events which constitute the diachronic dimension of time, while the code is in time as a set of contemporaneous elements, i.e., as a synchronic system. A message is intentional; it is meant by someone. The code is anonymous and not intended. In this sense it is unconscious, not in the sense that drives and impulses are unconscious according to Freudian metapsychology, but in the sense of a nonlibidinal structural and cultural unconscious.

More than anything else, a message is arbitrary and contingent, while a code is systematic and compulsory for a given speaking community. This last opposition is reflected in the affinity of a code for scientific investigation; particularly in a sense of the word science which emphasizes the quasi-algebraic level of the combinatory capacities implied by such finite sets of discrete entities as phonological, lexical, and syntactical systems. Even if *parole* can be scientifically described, it falls under many sciences including acoustics, physiology, sociology, and the history of semantic changes, whereas *langue* is the object of a single science, the description of the *synchronic systems* of language.

This rapid survey of the main dichotomies established by Saussure is sufficient to show why linguistics could make progress under the condition of bracketing the message for the sake of the code, the event for the sake of the system, the intention for the sake of the structure, and the arbitrariness of the act for the systematicity of combinations within synchronic systems.

3

The eclipse of discourse was further encouraged by the tentative extension of the structural model beyond its birth place in linguistics properly speaking, and by the systematic awareness of the theoretical requirements implied by the linguistic model as a structural model.

Extension of the structural model concerns us directly insofar as the structural model was applied to the same categories of texts that are the object of our interpretation theory. Originally the model concerned units smaller than the sentence, the signs of the lexical systems and the discrete units of the phonological systems from which the significant units of lexical systems are compounded. A decisive extension occurred, however, with the application of the structural model to linguistic entities larger than the sentence and also to non-linguistic entities similar to the texts of linguistic communication.

As concerns the first type of application, the treatment of folktales by the Russian formalists such as V. Propp[2] marks a decisive turn in the theory of literature, especially as regards the narrative structure of literary works. The application of the structural model to myths by Claude Lévi-Strauss constitutes a second example of a structural approach to long strings of discourse; an approach similar to, yet independent of the formal treatment of folklore proposed by the Russian formalists.

As concerns the extension of the structural model to non-linguistic entities, the application may be less spectacular — including as it does, road signals, cultural codes such as table manners, costume, building and dwelling codes, decorative patterns, etc.—but it is theoretically interesting in that it gives an empirical content to the concept of semiology or general semantics, which was developed independently by Saussure and Charles S. Pierce. Linguistics here becomes one province of the general theory of signs, albeit a province that has the privilege of being both one species and the paradigmatic example of a sign-system.

This last extension of the structural model already implies a theoretical apprehension of the postulates that govern semiology in general and structural linguistics in particular.

4

Taken together, these postulates define and describe the structural model as a model.

First, a synchronic approach must precede any diachronic approach because systems are more intelligible than changes. At best, a change is a partial or a global change in a state of a system. Therefore the history of changes must come after the theory that describes the synchronic states of the system. This first postulate expresses the emergence of a new type of intelligibility directly opposed to the historicism of the nineteenth century.

Second, the paradigmatic case for a structural approach is that of a finite set of discrete entities. At first glance, phonological systems may seem to satisfy this second postulate more directly than do lexical systems where the criterion of finiteness is more difficult to apply concretely. However, the idea of an infinite lexicon remains absurd in principle. This theoretical advantage of phonological systems — only a few dozen distinctive signs characterize any given linguistic system — explains why phonology moved to the forefront of linguistic studies following Saussure's work, even though for the founder of structural linguistics, phonology was taken to be an auxiliary science to the core of linguistics: semantics. The paradigmatic position of systems constituted of finite sets of discrete entities lies in the combinatory capacity and the quasi-algebraic possibilities pertaining to such sets. These capacities and possibilities add to the type of intelligibility instituted by the first postulate, that of synchronicity.

Third, in such a system no entity belonging to the structure of the system has a meaning of its own; the meaning of a word, for example, results from its opposition to the other lexical units of the same system. As Saussure said, in a system of signs there are only differences, but no substantial existence. This postulate defines the formal properties of linguistic entities, formal here being opposed to substantial in the sense of an autonomous positive existence of the entities at stake in linguistics and, in general, in semiotics.

Fourth, in such finite systems, all the relations are immanent to the system. In this sense semiotic systems are "closed," i.e., without relations to external, non-semiotic reality. The definition of the sign given by Saussure already implied this postulate: instead of being defined by the external relation between a sign and a thing, a relation that would make linguistics dependent upon a theory of extra-linguistic entities, the sign is defined by an opposition between two aspects, which both fall within the circumspection of a unique science, that of signs. These two aspects are the signifier—for example, a sound, a written pattern, a gesture, or any physical medium — and the signified — the differential value in the lexical system. The fact that the signifier and the signified allow for two different kinds of analysis—phonological in the first case, semantical in the second—but only together constitute the sign, not only provides the criterion for linguistic signs, but also, by extension, that of the entities of every semiotic system, which may be defined on the condition of "weakening" this criterion.

The last postulate alone suffices to characterize structuralism as a global mode of thought, beyond all the technicalities of its methodology. Language no longer appears as a mediation between minds and things. It constitutes a world of its own, within which each item only refers to other items of the same system, thanks to the interplay of oppositions and differences constitutive of the system. In a word, language is no longer treated as a "form of life," as Wittgenstein would call it, but as a self-sufficient system of inner relationships.

At this extreme point language as discourse has disappeared.

Semantics versus Semiotics: The Sentence

To this unidimensional approach to language, for which signs are the only basic entities, I want to oppose a two dimensional approach for which language relies on two irreducible entities, signs and sentences.

This duality does not coincide with that of *langue* and *parole* as defined in Saussure's *Cours de linguistique générale*, or even as that duality was later reformulated as the opposition between code and message. In the terminology of *langue* and

6

parole, only *langue* is an homogeneous object for a unique science, thanks to the structural properties of the synchronic systems. *Parole*, as we said, is heterogeneous, besides being individual, diachronic, and contingent. But *parole* also presents a structure that is irreducible in a specific sense to that of the combinatory possibilities opened up by the oppositions between discrete entities. This structure is the synthetic construction of the sentence itself as distinct from any analytic combination of discrete entities. My substitution of the term "discourse" for that of *"parole"* (which expresses only the residual aspect of a science of *"langue"*) is intended not only to emphasize the specificity of this new unit on which all discourse relies, but also to legitimate the distinction between semiotics and semantics as the two sciences which correspond to the two kinds of units characteristic of language, the sign and the sentence.

Moreover, these two sciences are not just distinct, but also reflect a hierarchical order. The object of semiotics — the sign — is merely virtual. Only the sentence is actual as the very event of speaking. This is why there is no way of passing from the word as a lexical sign to the sentence by mere extension of the same methodology to a more complex entity. The sentence is not a larger or more complex word, it is a new entity. It may be decomposed into words, but the words are something other than short sentences. A sentence is a whole irreducible to the sum of its parts. It is made up of words, but it is not a derivative function of its words. A sentence is made up of signs, but is not itself a sign.

There is therefore no linear progression from the phoneme to the lexeme and then on to the sentence and to linguistic wholes larger than the sentence. (Each stage requires new structures and a new description.) The relation between the two kinds of entities may be expressed in the following way, following the French Sanskritist Emile Benveniste: language relies on the possibility of two kinds of operations, integration into larger wholes, and dissociation into constitutive parts. The sense proceeds from the first operation, the form from the second.

7

The distinction between two kinds of linguistics — semiotics and semantics — reflects this network of relations. Semiotics, the science of signs, is formal to the extent that it relies on the dissociation of language into constitutive parts. Semantics, the science of the sentence, is immediately concerned with the concept of sense (which at this stage can be taken as synonymous with meaning, before the forthcoming distinction between sense and reference is introduced), to the extent that semantics is fundamentally defined by the integrative procedures of language.

For me, the distinction between semantics and semiotics is the key to the whole problem of language, and my four essays are based upon this initial methodological decision. As I said in my introductory remarks, this distinction is simply a reassessment of the argument of Plato in the *Cratylus* and the *Theaetetus* according to which the *logos* relies on the intertwining of at least two different entities, the noun and the verb. But, in another sense, this distinction today requires more sophistication because of the existence of semiotics as the modern counterpart of semantics.

The Dialectic of Event and Meaning

The next part of this essay will be devoted to the search for adequate criteria to differentiate semantics and semiotics. I shall construct my arguments from the convergence of several approaches, which have to do for different reasons with the specificity of language as discourse. Those approaches are the linguistics of the sentence that provide the general title semantics; the phenomenology of meaning proceeding from the first *Logical Investigation* of Husserl;[3] and the kind of "linguistic analysis" that characterizes the Anglo-American philosophical description of "ordinary language." All these partial achievements will be gathered under a common title, the dialectic of event and meaning in discourse, for which I shall first describe the event pole, then the meaning pole as the abstract components of this concrete polarity.

Discourse as Event

Starting from the Saussurean distinction between *langue* and *parole*, we may say, at least in an introductory way, that discourse is *the* event of language. For a linguistics applied to the structure of systems, the temporal dimension of this event expresses the epistemological weakness of a linguistics of *parole*. Events vanish while systems remain. Therefore the first move of a semantics of discourse must be to rectify this epistemological weakness of *parole* proceeding from the fleeting character of the event as opposed to the stability of the system by relating it to the ontological priority of discourse resulting from the actuality of the event as opposed to the mere virtuality of the system.

If it is true that only the message has a temporal existence, an existence in duration and succession, the synchronistic aspect of the code putting the system outside of successive time, then this temporal existence of the message testifies to its actuality. The system in fact does not exist. It only has a virtual existence. Only the message gives actuality to language, and discourse grounds the very existence of language since only the discrete and each time unique acts of discourse actualize the code.

But this first criterion alone would be more misleading than illuminating if the "instance of discourse," as Benveniste calls it, were merely this vanishing event. Then science would be justified in discarding it, and the ontological priority of discourse would be insignificant and without consequence. An act of discourse is not merely transitory and vanishing, however. It may be identified and reidentified as the same so that we may say it again or in other words. We may even say it in another language or translate it from one language into another. Through all these transformations it preserves an identity of its own which can be called the propositional content, the "said as such."

We therefore have to reformulate our first criterion — discourse as event—in a more dialectical way in order to take into account the relation which constitutes discourse as such, the relation between event and meaning. But before being able to

9

grasp this dialectic as a whole, let us consider the "objective" side of the speech event.

Discourse as Predication

Considered from the point of view of the propositional content, the sentence may be characterized by a single distinctive trait: it has a predicate. As Benveniste observes, even the grammatical subject may be lacking, but not the predicate. What is more, this new unit is not defined by its opposition to other units, as a phoneme to another phoneme or a lexeme to another lexeme within the same system. There are not several kinds of predicates; at the level of categoremes (*categorema*, in Greek = *praedicatum*, in Latin), there is just one kind of linguistic utterance, the proposition, which constitutes just one class of distinctive units. Consequently, there is no unit of a higher order that could provide a generic class for the sentence conceived as a species. It is possible to connect propositions according to an order of concatenation, but not to integrate them.

This linguistic criterion may be related to descriptions established by the theorists of ordinary language. The predicate, which Benveniste says is the only indispensable factor of the sentence, makes sense in those paradigmatic cases where its "functions" may be connected to and opposed to the "function" of the logical subject. Then an important feature of the predicate comes to the forefront on the basis of the antithesis between predicate and subject. Whereas the genuinely logical subject is the bearer of a singular identification, what the predicate says about the subject can always be treated as a "universal" feature of the subject. Subject and predicate do not do the same job in the proposition. The subject picks out something singular — Peter, London, this table, the fall of Rome, the first man who climbed Mt. Everest, etc.—by means of several grammatical devices which serve this logical function: proper names, pronouns, demonstratives (this and that, now and then, here and there, tenses of the verb as related to the present), and "definite descriptions" (the so and so). What they all have in common is that they all identify one and only one item. The predicate, in contrast, designates a kind of quality, a class of things, a type of relation, or a type of action.

This fundamental polarity between singular identification and universal predication gives a specific content to the notion of the proposition conceived of as the object of the speech event. It shows that discourse is not merely a vanishing event, and as such an irrational entity, as the simple opposition between *parole* and *langue* might suggest. Discourse has a structure of its own but it is not a structure in the analytical sense of structuralism, i.e., as a combinatory power based on the previous oppositions of discrete units. Rather, it is a structure in the synthetic sense, i.e., as the intertwining and interplay of the functions of identification and predication in one and the same sentence.

The Dialectic of Event and Meaning

Discourse considered as either an event or a proposition, that is, as a predicative function combined with an identification, is an abstraction, which depends upon the concrete whole that is the dialectical unity of the event and meaning in the sentence.

This dialectical constitution of discourse might be overlooked by a psychological or an existential approach which would concentrate on the interplay of functions, the polarity of singular identification and universal predication. It is the task of a concrete theory of discourse to take this dialectic as its guideline. Any emphasis on the abstract concept of a speech event is justified only as a way of protesting against an earlier, more abstract reduction of language, the reduction to the structural aspects of language as *langue*, for the notion of speech as an event provides the key to the transition from a linguistics of the code to a linguistics of the message. It reminds us that discourse is realized temporally and in a present moment, whereas the language system is virtual and outside of time. But this trait appears only in the movement of actualization from language to discourse. Every apology for speech as an event, therefore, is significant if, and only if, it makes visible the relation of actualization, thanks to which our linguistic competence actualizes itself in performance.

11

But this same apology becomes abusive itself as soon as the event character is extended from the problematic of actualization, where it is valid, to another problematic, that of understanding. *If all discourse is actualized as an event, all discourse is understood as meaning.* By meaning or sense I here designate the propositional content, which I have just described, as the synthesis of two functions: the identification and the predication. It is not the event insofar as it is transient that we want to understand, but its meaning — the intertwining of noun and verb, to speak like Plato — insofar as it endures.

In saying this I am not taking a step backward from the linguistics of speech (or discourse) to the linguistics of language (as *langue*). It is in the linguistics of discourse that the event and the meaning are articulated. The supressing and the surpassing of the event in the meaning is a characteristic of discourse itself. It attests to the intentionality of language, the relation of noesis and noema in it. If language is a *meinen*, an intending, it is so precisely due to this *Aufhebung* through which the event is cancelled as something merely transient and retained as the *same* meaning.

Before drawing the main consequence of this dialectical interpretation of the notion of speech event for our hermeneutical enterprise, let us elaborate more completely and more concretely the dialectic itself on the basis of some important corollaries of our axiom: that if all discourse is actualized as an event, it is understood as meaning.

Utterer's Meaning and Utterance Meaning

The Self-Reference of Discourse

The concept of meaning allows two interpretations which reflect the main dialectic between event and meaning. To mean is both what the speaker means, i.e., what he intends to say, and what the sentence means, i.e., what the conjunction between the identification function and the predicative function yields. Meaning, in other words, is both noetic and noematic. We may connect the reference of discourse to its speaker with the event side of the dialectic. The event is somebody speaking. In this sense, the system or code is

12

anonymous to the extent that it is merely virtual. Languages do not speak, people do. But the propositional side of the self-reference of discourse must not be overlooked if the utterer's meaning, to use a term of Paul Grice's, is not to be reduced to a mere psychological intention. The mental meaning can be found nowhere else than in discourse itself. The utterer's meaning has its mark in the utterance meaning. How?

The linguistics of discourse, which we are calling semantics to distinguish it from semiotics, provides the answer. The inner structure of the sentence refers back to its speaker through grammatical procedures, which linguists call "shifters." The personal pronouns, for example, have no objective meaning. "I" is not a concept. It is impossible to substitute a universal expression for it such as "the one who is now speaking." Its only function is to refer the whole sentence to the subject of the speech event. It has a new meaning each time it is used and each time it refers to a singular subject. "I" is the one who in speaking applies to himself the word "I" which appears in the sentence as a logical subject. There are other shifters, other grammatical bearers of the reference of the discourse to its speaker as well. They include the tenses of the verb to the extent that they are centered around the present and therefore refer to the "now" of the speech event and of the speaker. The same thing is true of the adverbs of time and space and the demonstratives, which may be considered as egocentric particulars. Discourse therefore has many substitutable ways of referring back to its speaker.

By paying attention to these grammatical devices of the self-reference of discourse we obtain two advantages. On the one hand, we get a new criterion of the difference between discourse and linguistic codes. On the other hand, we are able to give a nonpsychological, because purely semantic, definition of the utterer's meaning. No mental entity need be hypothesized or hypostasized. The utterance meaning points back towards the utterer's meaning thanks to the self-reference of discourse to itself as an event.

This semantic approach is reinforced by two other contributions to the same dialectic of the event and the proposition.

13

Locutionary and Illocutionary Acts.

The first one is the well known linguistic analysis (in the Anglo-American sense of this term) of the "speech-act." J. L. Austin was the first to notice that "performatives"—such as promises—imply a specific commitment by the speaker who *does* what he says in saying it. By saying, "I promise," he actually promises, i.e., puts himself under the obligation of doing what he says he will do. This "doing" of the saying may be assimilated to the event pole on the dialectic of event and meaning. But this "doing" also follows semantic rules which are exhibited by the structure of the sentence: the verb must be that of the first person indicative. Here, too, a specific "grammar" supports the performative force of the discourse. The performatives are only particular cases of a general feature exhibited by every class of speech act, whether they be commands, wishes, questions, warnings, or assertions. All of them, besides saying something (the locutionary act), do something in saying (the illocutionary act), and yield effects *by* saying (the perlocutionary act).

The illocutionary act is what distinguishes a promise from an order, a wish, or an assertion. And the "force" of the illocutionary act presents the same dialectic of event and meaning. In each case a specific "grammar" corresponds to a certain intention for which the illocutionary act expresses the distinctive "force." What can be expressed in psychological terms such as believing, wanting, or desiring, is invested with a semantic existence thanks to the correlation between these grammatical devices and the illocutionary act.

The Interlocutionary Act

The other contribution to the dialectic of the event and the propositional content is given by what could be called the interlocutionary act or the allocutionary act, to preserve the symmetry with the illocutionary aspect of the speech act.

One important aspect of discourse is that it is addressed to someone. There is another speaker who is the addressee of the discourse. The presence of the pair, speaker and hearer, constitutes language as communication. The study of language from the point of view of communication does not begin with the sociology of communication, however. As Plato says, dialogue is an essential structure of discourse. Questioning and answering sustain the movement and the dynamic of speaking, and in one sense they do not constitute one mode of discourse among others. Each illocutionary act is a kind of question. To assert something is to expect agreement, just as to give an order is to expect obedience. Even soliloquy — solitary discourse — is dialogue with oneself, or, to cite Plato once more, *dianoia* is the dialogue of the soul with itself.

Some linguists have attempted to reformulate all the functions of language as variables within an all encompassing model for which communication is the key. Roman Jakobson, for example, starts from the threefold relation between speaker, hearer, and message, then adds three other complementary factors which enrich his model. These are code, contact, and context. On the basis of this six factor system he establishes a six function schema. To the speaker corresponds the emotive function, to the hearer the conative, to the message the poetic function. The code designates the metalinguistic function, while the contact and the context are the bearers of the phatic and the referential functions.

This model is interesting in that it (1) describes discourse directly and not as a residue of language; (2) describes a structure of discourse and not only an irrational event; and (3) it subordinates the code function to the connecting operation of communication.

But in turn this model calls for a philosophical investigation, which may be provided by the dialectic of event and meaning. For the linguist, communication is a fact, even a most obvious fact. People do actually speak to one another. But for an existential investigation communication is an enigma, even a wonder. Why? Because being-together, as the existential condition for the possibility of any dialogical structure of discourse, appears as a way of trespassing or overcoming the fundamental solitude of each human being. By solitude I do not mean that fact that we often feel isolated as in a crowd, or that we live and die alone, but, in a more radical sense, that what is experienced by one person cannot be transferred whole as such and such experience to someone

15

else. My experience cannot directly become your experience. An event belonging to one stream of consciousness cannot be transferred as such into another stream of consciousness. Yet, nevertheless, something passes from me to you. Something is transferred from one sphere of life to another. This something is not the experience as experienced, but its meaning. Here is the miracle. The experience as experienced, as lived, remains private, but its sense, its meaning, becomes public. Communication in this way is the overcoming of the radical non-communicability of the lived experience as lived.

This new aspect of the dialectic of event and meaning deserves attention. The event is not only the experience as expressed and communicated, but also the intersubjective exchange itself, the happening of dialogue. The instance of discourse is the instance of dialogue. Dialogue is an event which connects two events, that of speaking and that of hearing. It is to this dialogical event that understanding as meaning is homogeneous. Hence the question: what aspects of discourse itself are meaningfully communicated in the event of dialogue?

A first answer is obvious. What can be communicated is first of all the propositional content of discourse, and we are led back to our main criterion—discourse as event plus sense. Because the sense of a sentence is, so to speak, "external" to the sentence it can be transferred; this exteriority of discourse to itself — which is synonymous with the self-transcendence of the event in its meaning—*opens* discourse to the other. The message has the ground of its communicability in the structure of its meaning. This implies that we communicate the synthesis of both the identification function (of which the logical subject is the bearer) and the predicative function (which is potentially universal). By speaking to somebody we point towards the unique thing that we mean, thanks to the public devices of proper names, demonstratives, and definite descriptions. I help the other to identify the same item that I myself am pointing to, thanks to the grammatical devices which provide a singular experience with a public dimension.

The same is true for the universal dimension of the predicate communicated by the generic dimension of the lexical entities.

Of course, this first level of mutual understanding does not go without some misunderstanding. Most of our words are polysemic; they have more than one meaning. But it is the contextual function of discourse to screen, so to speak, the polysemy of our words and to reduce the plurality of possible interpretations, the ambiguity of discourse resulting from the unscreened polysemy of the words. And it is the function of dialogue to initiate this screening function of the context. The contextual is the dialogical. It is in this precise sense that the contextual role of dialogue reduces the field of misunderstanding concerning the propositional content and partially succeeds in overcoming the non-communicability of experience.

The propositional content is only the correlate of the locutionary act, however. What about the communicability of the other aspects of the speech act, especially the illocutionary act? It is here that the dialectic of the act and the structure, the event and the meaning, is the most complex. How can the character of discourse, which is to be either constative or performative, either an act of stating something or of ordering, wishing, promising, or warning, be communicated and understood? More radically, can we communicate the speech act as an illocutionary act?

There is no doubt that it is easier to mistake one illocutionary act for another illocutionary act than it is to misunderstand a propositional act. The main reason is that nonlinguistic facts are intertwined with the linguistic marks, and these factors—which include physiognomy, gesture, and intonation of the voice — are more difficult to interpret because they do not rely on discrete units, their codes being more unstable and their message easier to conceal or fake. Nevertheless the illocutionary act is not without linguistic marks. They include the use of grammatical moods such as the indicative, subjunctive, imperative, and optative, as well as the tenses and codified adverbial terms or other equivalent

17

periphrastic devices. Writing not only preserves these linguistic marks of oral speech, it also adds supplementary distinctive signs such as quotation marks, exclamation marks, and question marks to indicate the physiognomic and gestural expressions, which disappear when the speaker becomes a writer. In many ways therefore illocutionary acts can be communicated to the extent that their "grammar" provides the event with a public structure.

I am inclined to say that the perlocutionary act—what we do by speaking — frighten, seduce, convince, etc. — is the least communicable aspect of the speech act, inasmuch as the non-linguistic has priority over the linguistic in such acts. The perlocutionary function is also the least communicable because it is less an intentional act, calling for an intention of recognition on the part of the hearer, than a kind of "stimulus" generating a "response" in a behavioral sense. The perlocutionary function helps us rather to identify the boundary between the act character and the reflex character of language.

The locutionary and illocutionary acts are acts — and therefore events — to the extent that their intention implies the intention of being recognized for what they are: a singular identification, universal predication, statement, order, wish, promise, etc.[4] This role of recognition allows us to say that the intention of saying is itself communicable to a certain extent. The intention does have a psychological aspect which is experienced as such only by the speaker. In the promise, for example, there is a commitment; in an assertion, a belief; in a wish, a want; etc., which constitute the psychological condition of the speech act, if we follow John Searle's analysis.[5] But these "mental acts" (Peter Geach) are not radically incommunicable. Their intention implies the intention of being recognized, therefore the intention of the other's intention. This intention of being identified, acknowledged, and recognized as such by the other is part of the intention itself. In the vocabulary of Husserl, we could say that it is the noetic in the psychic.

The criterion of the noetic is the intention of communicability, the expectation of recognition in the intentional act itself. The noetic is the soul of discourse as dialogue. The difference between the illocutionary and the perlocutionary, therefore, is nothing else than the presence in the former and the absence in the latter of the intention to produce in the listener a certain mental act by means of which he will recognize my intention.

This reciprocity of intentions is the event of dialogue. The bearer of this event is the "grammar" of recognition included in the intended meaning.

To conclude this discussion of the dialectic of event and meaning, we may say that language is itself the process by which private experience is made public. Language is the exteriorization thanks to which an impression is transcended and becomes an ex-pression, or, in other words, the transformation of the psychic into the noetic. Exteriorization and communicability are one and the same thing for they are nothing other than this elevation of a part of our life into the *logos* of discourse. There the solitude of life is for a moment, anyway, illuminated by the common light of discourse.

Meaning as "Sense" and "Reference"

In the two preceding sections the dialectic of event and meaning has been developed as an inner dialectic of the meaning of discourse. To mean is what the speaker does. But it is also what the sentence does. The utterance meaning — in the sense of the propositional content — is the "objective" side of this meaning. The utterer's meaning — in the threefold sense of the self-reference of the sentence, the illocutionary dimension of the speech act, and the intention of recognition by the hearer — is the "subjective" side of the meaning.

This subjective-objective dialectic does not exhaust the meaning of meaning and therefore does not exhaust the structure of discourse. The "objective" side of discourse itself may be taken in two different ways. We may mean the "what" of discourse or the "about what" of discourse. The "what" of discourse is its "sense," the "about what" is its "reference." This distinction between sense and reference was introduced into modern philosophy by Gottlob Frege in his famous article *"Ueber Sinn und Bedeutung,"* which has been translated into English as "On Sense and Reference."[6] It is a distinction which can be directly connected with our initial distinction between semiotics and semantics. Only the sentence level allows us to distinguish what is said and about what it is said. In the system of language, say as a lexicon, there is no problem of reference; signs only refer to other signs within the system. With the sentence, however, language is directed beyond itself. Whereas the sense is immanent to the discourse, and objective in the sense of ideal, the reference expresses the movement in which language transcends itself. In other words, the sense correlates the identification function and the predicative function within the sentence, and the reference relates language to the world. It is another name for discourse's claim to be true.

The decisive fact here is that language has a reference only when it is used. As Strawson has shown in his famous response to Russell's article, "On Denoting," the same sentence, i.e., the same sense, may or may not refer depending on the circumstances or situation of an act of discourse.[7] No inner mark, independent of the use of a sentence, constitutes a reliable criterion of denotation. Consequently, the dialectic of sense and reference is not unrelated to the previous dialectic of event and meaning. To refer is what the sentence does in a certain situation and according to a certain use. It is also what the speaker does when he applies his words to reality. That someone refers to something at a certain time is an event, a speech event. But this event receives its structure from the meaning as sense. The speaker refers to something on the basis of, or through, the ideal structure of the sense. The sense, so to speak, is traversed by the referring intention of the speaker. In this way the dialectic of event and meaning receives a new development from the dialectic of sense and reference.

But the dialectic of sense and reference is so original that it can be taken as an independent guideline. Only this dialectic says something about the relation between language and the ontological condition of being in the world. Language is not a world of its own. It is not even a world. But because we are in the world, because we are affected by situations, and because we orient ourselves comprehensively in those situations, we have something to say, we have experience to bring to language.

This notion of bringing experience to language is the ontological condition of reference, an ontological condition reflected within language as a postulate which has not immanent justification; the postulate according to which we presuppose the existence of singular things which we identify. We presuppose that something must be in order that something may be identified. This postulation of existence as the ground of identification is what Frege ultimately meant when he said that we are not satisfied by the sense alone, but we presuppose a reference.[8] And this postulation is so necessary that we must add a specific prescription if we want to refer to fictional entities such as characters in a novel or a play. This additional rule of suspension confirms that the function of singular identification raises in an originary way a legitimate question of existence.

But this intentional pointing toward the extra-linguistic would rely on a mere postulate and would remain a questionable leap beyond language if this exteriorization were not the counterpart of a previous and more originary move starting from the experience of being in the world and proceeding from this ontological condition towards its expression in language. It is because there is first something to say, because we have an experience to bring to language, that conversely, language is not only directed towards ideal meanings but also refers to what is.

As I said, this dialectic is so fundamental and so originary that it could rule the whole theory of language as discourse and even provide a reformulation of the nuclear dialectic of event and meaning. If language were not fundamentally referential, would or could it be meaningful? How could we know that a sign stands for something, if it did not receive its direction towards something for which it stands from its use in discourse? Finally, semiotics appears as a mere abstraction of semantics. And the semiotic definition of the sign as an inner difference between signifier and signified presupposes its semantic definition as reference to the thing for which it stands. The most concrete definition of semantics, then, is the

21

theory that relates the inner or immanent constitution of the sense to the outer or transcendent intention of the reference.

This universal signification of the problem of reference is so broad that even the utterer's meaning has to be expressed in the language of reference as the self-reference of discourse, i.e., as the designation of its speaker by the structure of discourse. Discourse refers back to its speaker at the same time that it refers to the world. This correlation is not fortuitious, since it is ultimately the speaker who refers to the world in speaking. Discourse in action and in use refers backwards and forwards, to a speaker and a world.

Such is the ultimate criterion of language as discourse.

Some Hermeneutical Implications

It is possible, even at this early stage of our inquiry, to anticipate some of the implications of the preceding analysis for our interpretation theory.

They mainly concern the use and abuse of the concept of speech event in the Romanticist tradition of hermeneutics. Hermeneutics as issuing from Schleiermacher and Dilthey tended to identify interpretation with the category of "understanding," and to define understanding as the recognition of an author's intention from the point of view of the primitive addressees in the original situation of discourse. This priority given to the author's intention and to the original audience tended, in turn, to make dialogue the model of every situation of understanding, thereby imposing the framework of inter-subjectivity on hermeneutics. Understanding a text, then, is only a particular case of the dialogical situation in which someone responds to someone else.

This psychologizing conception of hermeneutics has had a great influence on Christian theology. It nourished the theologies of the Word-Event for which the event par excellence is a speech event, and this speech event is the Kerygma, the preaching of the Gospel. The meaning of the original event testifies to itself in the present event by which we apply it to ourselves in the act of faith.

My attempt here is to call into question the assumptions of this hermeneutic from the point of view of a philosophy of discourse in order to release hermeneutics from its psychologizing and existential prejudices. But my purpose is not to oppose to this hermeneutic based on the category of the speech event a hermeneutic which would merely be its opposite, as would be a structural analysis of the propositional content of texts. Such a hermeneutic would suffer from the same non-dialogical onesidedness. The assumptions of a psychologizing hermeneutic — like those of its contrary hermeneutic — stem from a double misunderstanding of the dialectic of event and meaning in discourse and the dialectic of sense and reference in meaning itself. This twofold misunderstanding in turn leads to assigning an erroneous task to interpretion, a task which is well expressed in the famous slogan, "to understand an author better than he understood himself." Therefore what is at stake in this discussion is the correct definition of the hermeneutical task.

I do not claim that the present essay suffices by itself to eliminate all misunderstanding. Without a specific investigation of writing, a theory of discourse is not yet a theory of the text. But if we succeed in showing that a written text is a form of discourse, discourse under the condition of inscription, then the conditions of the possibility of discourse are also those of the text. As our discussion of these conditions has shown, the notion of the speech event is not cancelled, rather it is submitted to a series of dialectical polarities summarized under the double title of event and meaning and sense and reference. These dialectical polarities allow us to anticipate that the concepts of intention and dialogue are not to be excluded from hermeneutics, but instead are to be released from the onesidedness of a non-dialectical concept of discourse.

It is in this way that the present essay is, if not the kernel of the whole series, truly the *initial* essay in the strong sense of the word.

2.

SPEAKING AND WRITING

To the extent that hermeneutics is text-oriented interpretation, and inasmuch as texts are, among other things, instances of written language, no interpretation theory is possible that does not come to grips with the problem of writing. The purpose of this essay therefore is twofold. I want first to show that the transition from speaking to writing has its conditions of possibility in the theory of discourse described in the first essay, especially in the dialectic of event and meaning considered there. My second purpose is to connect the kind of intentional exteriorization that writing exhibits with a central problem of hermeneutics, that of distanciation. This same concept of exteriority, which in the first part of this essay will be more used than criticized, will become problematic in the second part. Plato's critique of writing as a kind of alienation will provide the turning point from the descriptive to the critical treatment of the exteriorization of discourse proper to writing.

From Speaking to Writing

What happens in writing is the full manifestation of something that is in a virtual state, something nascent and inchoate, in living speech, namely the detachment of meaning from the event. But this detachment is not such as to cancel the fundamental structure of discourse discussed in my first essay. The semantic autonomy of the text which now appears is still governed by the dialectic of event and meaning. Moreover, it may be said that this dialectic is made obvious and explicit by writing. Writing is the full manifestation of discourse. To hold, as Jacques Derrida does,[1] that writing has a root distinct from speech and that this foundation has been misunderstood due to our having paid excessive attention to speech, its voice, and its *logos*, is to overlook the grounding of both modes of the actualization of discourse in the dialectical constitution of discourse.

I propose instead that we begin from the schema of communication described by Roman Jakobson in his famous article, "Linguistics and Poetics."[2] To the six main "factors" of communicative discourse — the speaker, hearer, medium or channel, code, situation, and message—he relates six correlative "functions": the emotive, conative, phatic, metalinguistic, referential, and poetic functions. Taking this schema as a starting point, we may inquire into what alterations, transformations, or deformations affect the interplay of facts and functions when discourse is inscribed in writing.

Message and Medium: Fixation

The most obvious change from speaking to writing concerns the relation between the message and its medium or channel. At first glance, it concerns only this relation, but upon closer examination, the first alteration irradiates in every direction, affecting in a decisive manner all the factors and functions. Our task, therefore, will be to proceed from this central change toward its various peripheral effects.

As a simple change in the nature of the medium of communication, the problem of writing is identical to that of the fixation of discourse in some exterior bearer, whether it be stone, papyrus, or paper, which is other than the human voice. This inscription, substituted for the immediate vocal, physiognomic, or gestural expression, is in itself a tremendous cultural achievement. The human fact disappears. Now material "marks" convey the message. This cultural achievement concerns the event character of discourse first and subsequently the meaning as well. It is because discourse only exists in a temporal and present instance of discourse that it may flee as speech or be fixed as writing. Because the event appears and disappears, there is a problem of fixation, of inscription. What we want to fix is discourse, not language as *langue*. It is only by extension that we fix by inscription the alphabet, the lexicon, and the grammar, all of which serve that which alone is to be fixed: discourse. The atemporal system of language neither appears or disappears, it simply does not happen. Only discourse is to be fixed, because discourse as event disappears.

But this nondialectical description of the phenomenon of fixation does not reach the core of the process of inscription. Writing may rescue the instance of discourse because what writing actually does fix is not the event of speaking but the "said" of speaking, i.e., the intentional exteriorization constitutive of the couple "event-meaning." What we write, what we inscribe is the noema of the act of speaking, the meaning of the speech event, not the event as event. This inscription, in spite of the perils that we shall later evoke following Plato in the second part of this essay, is discourse's destination. Only when the *sagen* — the "saying" — has become *Aus-sage*, e-nunciation, only then, is discourse accomplished as discourse in the full expression of its nuclear dialectic.

It is not necessary here that we consider at length the notion of the speech event in terms of its complete description as a speech act, i.e., as a locutionary, illocutionary, and perlocutionary act. As I have shown in my first essay, each of these acts gives way to the dialectic of event and meaning. Thanks to the grammatical marks which express it in an exterior and public way, the intentional exteriorization of discourse concerns the whole hierarchy of partial speech acts. The locutionary act exteriorizes itself in the sentence, the inner structure of which may be identified and re-identified as being the same, and which, therefore, may be inscribed and preserved. To the extent that the illocutionary act can be exteriorized thanks to grammatical paradigms and procedures expressive of its "force," it too can be inscribed. But to the extent that in spoken discourse the illocutionary force depends upon mimicry and gesture, and upon the nonarticulated aspects of discourse, which we call prosody, it must be acknowledged that the illocutionary force is less inscribable than the propositional meaning. Finally, the perlocutionary act is the least inscribable aspect of discourse for the reasons

27

given in the previous essay. It characterizes spoken language more than it does written language.

In all cases it is the intentional exteriorization proper to the different layers of the speech act that makes inscription in writing possible, so that in the final analysis the extension of the problematics of fixation is equal to that of the intentional exteriorization of the speech act with its multidimensional structure.

Now, does the problematics of fixation and inscription exhaust the problem of writing?

In other words, is writing only a question of a change of medium, where the human voice, face, and gesture are replaced by material marks other than the speaker's own body?

When we consider the range of social and political changes which can be related to the invention of writing, we may surmise that writing is much more than mere material fixation. We need only remind ourselves of some of these tremendous achievements. To the possibility of transferring orders over long distances without serious distortions may be connected the birth of political rule exercised by a distant state. This political implication of writing is just one of its consequences. To the fixation of rules for reckoning may be referred the birth of market relationships, therefore the birth of economics. To the constitution of archives, history. To the fixation of law as a standard of decisions, independent from the opinion of the concrete judge, the birth of the justice and juridical codes, etc. Such an immense range of effects suggests that human discourse is not merely preserved from destruction by being fixed in writing, but that it is deeply affected in its communicative function.

A second consideration may encourage us to pursue this new thought. Writing raises a specific problem as soon as it is not merely the fixation of a previous oral discourse, the inscription of spoken language, but is human thought directly brought to writing without the intermediary stage of spoken language. Then writing takes the place of speaking. A kind of short-cut occurs between the meaning of discourse and the material medium. Then we have to do with literature in the original sense of the word. The fate of discourse is delivered over to *littera*, not to *vox*.

The best way to measure the extent of this substitution is to look at the range of changes which occur among the other components of the communication process.

Message and Speaker

The first connection to be altered is that of the message to the speaker. This change indeed is itself one of two symmetrical changes, which affect the interlocutionary situation as a whole. The relation between message and speaker at one end of the communication chain and the relation between message and hearer at the other are together deeply transformed when the face-to-face relation is replaced by the more complex relation of reading to writing, resulting from the direct inscription of discourse in *littera*. The dialogical situation has been exploded. The relation writing-reading is no longer a particular case of the relation speaking-hearing.

If we consider these changes in more detail we see that the reference of the discourse back to its speaker is affected in the following way. In discourse, we said, the sentence designates its speaker by diverse indicators of subjectivity and personality. But in spoken discourse this ability of discourse to refer back to the speaking subject presents a character of immediacy because the speaker belongs to the situation of interlocution. He is there, in the genuine sense of being-there, of *Da-sein*. Consequently the subjective intention of the speaker and the discourse's meaning overlap each other in such a way that it is the same thing to understand what the speaker means and what his discourse means. The ambiguity of the German *meinen* and the English "to mean" — which we examined in the preceding essay—attests to this overlapping in the dialogical situation. With written discourse, however, the author's intention and the meaning of the text cease to coincide. This dissociation of the verbal meaning of the text and the mental intention of the author gives to the concept of inscription its decisive significance, beyond the mere fixation of previous oral discourse. Inscription becomes synonymous with the semantic autonomy of the text, which results from the discon-

29

nection of the mental intention of the author from the verbal meaning of the text, of what the author meant and what the text means. The text's career escapes the finite horizon lived by its author. What the text means now matters more than what the author meant when he wrote it.

This concept of semantic autonomy is of tremendous importance for hermeneutics. Exegesis begins with it, i.e., it unfolds its procedures within the circumscription of a set of meanings that have broken their moorings to the psychology of the author. But this de-psychologizing of interpretation does not imply that the notion of authorial meaning has lost all significance. Here again a non-dialectical conception of the relation between event and meaning would tend to oppose one alternative to the other. On the one hand, we would have what W. K. Wimsatt calls the intentional fallacy, which holds the author's intention as the criterion for any valid interpretation of the text, and, on the other hand, what I would call in a symmetrical fashion the fallacy of the absolute text: the fallacy of hypostasizing the text as an authorless entity. If the intentional fallacy overlooks the semantic autonomy of the text, the opposite fallacy forgets that a text remains a discourse told by somebody, said by someone to someone else about something. It is impossible to cancel out this main characteristic of discourse without reducing texts to natural objects, i.e., to things which are not man-made, but which, like pebbles, are found in the sand.

The semantic autonomy of the text makes the relation of event and meaning more complex and in this sense reveals it as a dialectical relation. The authorial meaning becomes properly a dimension of the text to the extent that the author is not available for questioning. When the text no longer answers, then it has an author and no longer a speaker. The authorial meaning is the dialectical counterpart of the verbal meaning, and they have to be construed in terms of each other. These concepts of author and authorial meaning raise a hermeneutical problem contemporaneous with that of semantic autonomy.

Message and Hearer

At the opposite end of the communication chain the relation of the textual message to the reader is no less complex than is the relation to the author. Whereas spoken discourse is addressed to someone who is determined in advanced by the dialogical situation—it is addressed to you, the second person — a written text is addressed to an unknown reader and potentially to whoever knows how to read. This universaliziaton of the audience is one of the more striking effects of writing and may be expressed in terms of a paradox. Because discourse is now linked to a material support, it becomes more spiritual in the sense that it is liberated from the narrowness of the face-to-face situation.

Of course this universality is only potential. In fact, a book is addressed to only a section of the public and reaches its appropriate readers through media that are themselves submitted to social rules of exclusion and admission. In other words, reading is a social phenomenon, which obeys certain patterns and therefore suffers from specific limitations. Nevertheless, the proposition which says that a text is potentially addressed to whoever knows how to read must be retained as a limit on any sociology of reading. A work also creates its public. In this way it enlarges the circle of communication and properly initates new modes of communication. To that extent, the recognition of the work by the audience created by the work is an unpredictable event.

Once again the dialectic of meaning and event is exhibited in its fullness by writing. Discourse is revealed as discourse by the dialectic of the address, which is both universal and contingent. On the one hand, it is the semantic autonomy of the text which opens up the range of potential readers and, so to speak, creates the audience of the text. On the other hand, it is the response of the audience which makes the text important and therefore significant. This is why authors who do not worry about their readers and despise their present public keep speaking of their readers as a secret community, sometimes projected into a cloudy future. It is part of the meaning of a text to be open to an indefinite number of readers and,

31

therefore, of interpretations. This opportunity for multiple readings is the dialectical counterpart of the semantic autonomy of the text.

It follows that the problem of the appropriation of the meaning of the text becomes as paradoxical as that of the authorship. The right of the reader and the right of the text converge in an important struggle that generates the whole dynamic of interpretation. Hermeneutics begins where dialogue ends.

Message and Code

The relation between message and code is made more complex by writing in a somewhat indirect way. What I have in mind here concerns the function of literary genres in the production of discourse as such and such a mode of discourse, whether poem, narrative, or essay. This function undoubtedly concerns the relation between message and code since genres are generative devices to produce discourse as. . . . Before being classificatory devices used by literary critics to orient themselves in the profusion of literary works, therefore before being artifacts of criticism, they are to discourse what generative grammar is to the grammaticality of individual sentences. In this sense, these discursive codes may be joined those phonological, lexical, and syntactical codes which rule the units of discourse, sentences. Now the question is to what extent literary genres are genuinely codes of writing? Only in an indirect, but nevertheless decisive way.

Literary genres display some conditions which theoretically could be described without considering writing. The function of these generative devices is to produce new entities of language longer than the sentence, organic wholes irreducible to a mere addition of sentences. A poem, narrative, or essay relies on laws of composition which in principle are indifferent to the opposition between speaking and writing. They proceed from the application of dynamic forms to sets of sentences for which the difference between oral and written language is unessential. Instead, the specificity of these dynamic forms seems to proceed from another dichotomy than that of speaking and hearing, from the application to discourse of categories borrowed from another field, that of

32

practice and work. Language is submitted to the rules of a kind of craftsmanship, which allows us to speak of production and of works of art, and, by extension of works of discourse. Poems, narratives, and essays are such works of discourse. The generative devices, which we call literary genres, are the technical rules presiding over their production. And the style of a work is nothing else than the individual configuration of a singular product or work. The author here is not only the speaker, but also the maker of this work, which is his work.

But, if the dichotomy between theory and practice is irreducible to the pair speaking-writing, writing plays a decisive role precisely in the application of the categories of practice, technique, and work to discourse. There is production when a form is applied to some matter in order to shape it. When discourse is transferred to the field of production it is also treated as a stuff to be shaped. It is here that writing interferes. Inscription as a material support, the semantic autonomy of the text as regards both the speaker and the hearer, and all the related traits of exteriority characteristic of writing help to make language the matter of a specific craftsmanship. Thanks to writing, the works of language become as self-contained as sculptures. It is not by chance that "literature" designates both the status of language as written (*littera*) and as embodied in works according to literary genres. With literature the problems of inscription and production tend to overlap. The same may be said for the concept of text, which combines the condition of inscription with the texture proper to the works generated by the productive rules of literary composition. Text means discourse both as inscribed and wrought.

Such is the specific affinity that reigns between writing and the specific codes which generate the works of discourse. This affinity is so close that we might be tempted to say that even oral expressions of poetic or narrative compositions rely on processes equivalent to writing. The memorization of epic poems, lyrical songs, parables and proverbs, and their ritual recitation tend to fix and even to freeze the form of the work in such a way that memory appears as the support of an inscription similar to that provided by external marks. In this extended sense of inscription, writing and the production of works of discourse according to the rules of literary composition tend to coincide without being identical processes.

Message and Reference

I have postponed considering the most complex changes that occur in the functioning of discourse, which may be ascribed to writing, until the end of this inquiry. They concern the referential function of discourse in the schema of communication proposed by Roman Jakobson, and they are the most complex effects for two reasons. On the one hand, the distinction between sense and reference introduces in discourse a more complex dialectic than that of event and meaning, which provides us with the model of exteriorization that makes writing possible. It is, so to speak, a dialectic of the second order where the meaning itself, as immanent "sense," is externalized as transcendent reference, in the sense that thought is directed through the sense towards different kinds of extralinguistic entities such as objects, states of affairs, things, facts, etc. On the other hand, most of the alterations of reference which will be considered are not to be ascribed to writing as such but to writing as the ordinary mediation of the modes of discourse which constitute literature. Some of these alterations are even directly produced by the strategy proper to specific literary genres such as poetry. Inscription, then, is only indirectly responsible for the new fate of reference.

Yet despite these reservations, the following may be said: in spoken discourse the ultimate criterion for the referential scope of what we say is the possibility of showing the thing referred to as a member of the situation common to both speaker and hearer. This situation surrounds the dialogue, and its landmarks can all be shown by a gesture or by pointing a finger. Or it can be designated in an ostensive manner by the discourse itself through the oblique reference of those indicators which include the demonstratives, the adverbs of time and place, and the tenses of the verb. Finally they can be described in such a definite way that one, and only one, thing may be identified within the common framework of reference. Indeed, the ostensive indicators and, still more, the

34

definite descriptions work in the same way in both oral and written discourse. They provide singular identifications, and singular identifications need not rely on showing in the sense of a gestural indication of the thing referred to. Nevertheless singular identifications ultimately refer to the here and now determined by the interlocutionary situation. There is no identification which does not relate that about which we speak to a unique position in the spatio-temporal network, and there is no network of places in time and space without a final reference to the situational here and now. In this ultimate sense, all references of oral language rely on monstrations, which depend on the situation perceived as common by the members of the dialogue. All references in the dialogical situation consequently are situational.

It is this grounding of reference in the dialogical situation that is shattered by writing. Ostensive indicators and definite descriptions continue to identify singular entities, but a gap appears between identification and monstration. The absence of a common situation generated by the spatial and temporal distance between writer and reader; the cancellation of the absolute here and now by the substitution of material external marks for the voice, face, and body of the speaker as the absolute origin of all the places in space and time; and the semantic autonomy of the text, which severs it from the present of the writer and opens it to an indefinite range of potential readers in an indeterminate time—all these alterations of the temporal constitution of discourse are reflected in parallel alterations of the ostensive character of the reference.

Some texts merely restructure for their readers the conditions of ostensive reference. Letters, travel reports, geographical descriptions, diaries, historical monographs, and in general all descriptive accounts of reality may provide the reader with an equivalent of ostensive reference in the mode of "as if" ("as if you were there"), thanks to the ordinary procedures of singular identification. The heres and theres of the text may be tacitly referred to the absolute here and there of the reader, thanks to the unique spatio-temporal network to which both writer and reader ultimately belong and which they both acknowledge.

This first extension of the scope of reference beyond the narrow boundaries of the dialogical situation is of tremendous consequence. Thanks to writing, man and only man has a world and not just a situation. This extension is one more example of the spiritual implications of the substitution of material marks for the bodily support of oral discourse. In the same manner that the text frees its meaning from the tutelage of the mental intention, it frees its reference from the limits of situational reference. For us, the world is the ensemble of references opened up by the texts, or, at least for the moment, by descriptive texts. It is in this way that we may speak of the Greek "world," which is not to imagine anymore what were the situations for those who lived there, but to designate the nonsituational references displayed by the descriptive accounts of reality.

A second extension of the scope of reference is much more difficult to interpret. It proceeds less from writing as such as from the open or covert strategy of certain modes of discourse. Therefore it concerns literature more than writing, or writing as the channel of literature. In the construction of his schema of communication, Roman Jakobson relates the poetic function — which is to be understood in a broader sense than just poetry — to the emphasis of the message for its own sake at the expense of the reference. We have already anticipated this eclipsing of the reference by comparing poetic discourse to a self-contained sculptural work. The gap between situational and non-situational reference, implied in the "as if" reference of descriptive accounts, is now unbridgeable. This can be seen in fictional narratives, i.e., in narratives that are not descriptive reports where a narrative time, expressed by specific tenses of the verbs, is displayed by and within the narrative without any connection to the unique space-time network common to ostensive and non-ostensive discription.

Does this mean that this eclipse of reference, in either the ostensive or descriptive sense, amounts to a sheer abolition of all reference? No. My contention is that discourse cannot fail to be about something. In saying this, I am denying the ideology of absolute texts. Only a few sophisticated texts, along the line of Mallarmé's poetry, satisfy this ideal of a text without reference. But this modern kind of literature stands as a limiting case and an exception. It cannot give the key to all other texts, even poetic texts, in Jakobson's sense, which include all fictional literature whether lyrical or narrative. In one manner or another, poetic texts speak about the world. But not in a descriptive way. As Jakobson himself suggests, the reference here is not abolished, but divided or split. The effacement of the ostensive and descriptive reference liberates a power of reference to aspects of our being in the world that cannot be said in a direct descriptive way, but only alluded to, thanks to the referential values of metaphoric and, in general, symbolic expressions.

We ought to enlarge our concept of the world, therefore, not only to allow for non-ostensive but still descriptive references, but also non-ostensive and non-descriptive references, those of poetic diction. The term "world" then has the meaning that we all understand when we say of a new born child that he has come into the world. For me, the world is the ensemble of references opened up by every kind of text, descriptive or poetic, that I have read, understood, and loved. And to understand a text is to interpolate among the predicates of our situation all the significations that make a *Welt* out of our *Umwelt*. It is this enlarging of our horizon of existence that permits us to speak of the references opened up by the text or of the world opened up by the referential claims of most texts.

In this sense, Heidegger rightly says, in his analysis of *Verstehen* in *Being and Time*,[3] that what we understand first in a discourse is not another person, but a "pro-ject," that is, the outline of a new way of being in the world. Only writing — given the two reservations made at the beginning of this section—in freeing itself, not only from its author and from its originary audience, but from the narrowness of the dialogical situation, reveals this destination of discourse as projecting a world.

A Plea for Writing

The preceding analysis has reached its goal. It has shown the full manifestation of the nuclear dialectic of event and meaning, and of the intentional exteriorization already at work in oral discourse, although in an inchoative way. But by pushing it to the forefront it has made problematic what could be taken for granted as long as it remained implicit. Is not this intentional exteriorization delivered over to material marks a kind of alienation?

This question is so radical that it requires that we assume in the most positive way the condition of exteriority, not only as a cultural accident, as a contingent condition for discourse and thought, but as a necessary condition of the hermeneutical process. Only a hermeneutic using distanciation in a productive way may solve the paradox of the intentional exteriorization of discourse.

Against Writing

The attack against writing comes from afar. It is linked to a certain model of knowledge, science, and wisdom used by Plato to condemn exteriority as being contrary to genuine reminiscence.[4] He presents it in the form of a myth because philosophy here has to do with the coming to being of an institution, a skill, and a power, lost in the dark past of culture and connected with Egypt, the cradle of religious wisdom. The king of Thebes receives in his city the god Theuth, who has invented numbers, geometry, astronomy, games of chance, and *grammata* or written characters. Questioned about the powers and possible benefits of his invention, Theuth claims that the knowledge of written characters would make Egyptians wiser and more capable of preserving the memory of things. No, replies the king, souls will become more forgetful once they have put their confidence in external marks instead of relying on themselves from within. This "remedy" (*pharmakon*) is not reminiscence, but sheer re-memoration. As to instruction, what this invention brings is not the reality, but the resemblance of it; not wisdom, but its appearance.

The commentary of Socrates is no less interesting. Writing is like painting which generates non-living being, which in turn remains silent when asked to answer. Writings, too, if one questions them in order to learn from them, "signify a unique thing always the same." Besides this sterile sameness, writings are indifferent to their addressees. Wandering here and there, they are heedless of whom they reach. And if a dispute arises, or if they are injustly despised, they still need the help of their father. By themselves they are unable to rescue themselves.

According to this harsh critique, as the apology for true reminiscence, the principle and soul of right and genuine discourse, discourse accompanied with wisdom (or science), is written in the soul of the one who knows, the one who is able to defend himself, and keep silent or talk as required by the soul of the person addressed.

This Platonic attack against writing is not an isolated example in the history of our culture. Rousseau and Bergson, for example, for different reasons link the main evils that plague civilization to writing. For Rousseau, as long as language relied only on the voice, it preserved the presence of oneself to oneself and to others. Language was still the expression of passion. It was eloquence, not yet exegesis. With writing began separation, tyranny, and inequality. Writing ignores its addressee just as it conceals its author. It separates men just as property separates owners. The tyranny of the lexicon and of grammar is equal to that of the laws of exchange, crystallized in money. Instead of the Word of God, we have the rule of the learned and the domination of the priesthood. The break-up of the speaking community, the partition of the soil, the analycity of thought, and the reign of dogmaticism were all born with writing.

An echo of Platonic reminiscence may, therefore, still be heard in this apology for the voice as the bearer of one's presence to oneself and as the inner link of a community without distance.

Bergson directly questions the principle of exteriority, which witnesses to the infiltration of space into the temporality of sound and its continuity. The genuine word emerges

39

from the "intellectual effort" to fulfill a previous intention of saying, in the search for the appropriate expression. The written word, as the deposit of this search, has severed its ties with the feeling, effort, and dynamism of thought. The breath, song, and rhythm are over and the figure takes their place. It captures and fascinates. It scatters and isolates. This is why the authentic creators such as Socrates and Jesus have left no writings, and why the genuine mystics renounce statements and articulated thought.

Once more the interiority of the phonic effort is opposed to the exteriority of dead imprints which are unable to "rescue" themselves.

Writing and Iconicity

The rejoinder to such critiques must be as radical as the challenge. It is no longer possible to rely on just a description of the movement from speaking to writing. The critique summons us to legitimate what has been hitherto simply taken for granted.

A remark made in passing in the *Phaedrus* provides us with an important clue. Writing is compared to painting, the images of which are said to be weaker and less real than living beings. The question here is whether the theory of the *eikon*, which is held to be a mere shadow of reality, is not the presupposition of every critique addressed to any mediation through exterior marks..

If it could be shown that painting is not this shadowy reduplication of reality, then it would be possible to return to the problem of writing as a chapter in a general theory of iconicity, such as François Dagognet elaborates in his book, *Ecriture et Iconographie*.[5]

Far from yielding less than the original, pictorial activity may be characterized in terms of an "iconic augmentation," where the strategy of painting, for example, is to reconstruct reality on the basis of a limited optic alphabet. This strategy of contraction and miniaturization yields more by handling less. In this way, the main effect of painting is to resist the entropic tendency of ordinary vision — the shadow image of Plato —

and to increase the meaning of the universe by capturing it in the network of its abbreviated signs. This effect of saturation and culmination, within the tiny space of the frame and on the surface of a two-dimensional canvas, in opposition to the optical erosion proper to ordinary vision, is what is meant by iconic augmentation. Whereas in ordinary vision qualities tend to neutralize one another, to blur their edges, and to shade off their contrasts, painting, at least since the invention of oil painting by Dutch artists, enhances the contrasts, gives colors back their resonance, and lets appear the luminoisity within which things shine. The history of the techniques of painting teaches us that these meaningful effects followed upon the material invention of pigments made active by being mixed with oil. This selection of what I just called the optic alphabet of the painter allowed him to preserve the colors from diluting and tarnishing and to incorporate into his pictures the deep refraction of light beneath the mere reflective effect of surface luminosity.

Because the painter could master a new alphabetic material — because he was a chemist, distillator, varnisher, and glazer — he was able to write a new text of reality. Painting for the Dutch masters was neither the reproduction nor the production of the universe, but its metamorphosis.

In this respect, the techniques of engraving and etching are equally instructive. Whereas photography—at least unskilled photography — grasps everything but holds nothing, the magic of engraving, celebrated by Baudelaire, may exhibit the essential. This is because engraving, as with painting, although with other means, relies on the invention of an alphabet, i.e., a set of minimal signs, consisting of syncope points, strokes, and white patches, which enhance the trait and surround it with absence.

Impressionism and abstract art, as well, proceed more and more boldly to the abolition of natural forms for the sake of a merely constructed range of elementary signs whose combinatory forms will rival ordinary vision. With abstract art, painting is close to science in that it challenges perceptual forms by relating them to non-perceptual structures. The graphic capture of the universe, here too, is served by a radical

41

denial of the immediate. Painting seems only to "produce," no longer to "reproduce." But it catches up with reality at the level of its elements, as does the God of the *Timaeus*. Constructivism is only the boundary case of a process of augmentation where the apparent denial of reality is the condition for the glorification of the non-figurative essence of things. Iconicity, then, means the revelation of a real more real than ordinary reality.

This theory of iconicity — as aesthetic augmentation of reality — gives us the key to a decisive answer to Plato's critique of writing. Iconicity is the re-writing of reality. Writing, in the limited sense of the word, is a particular case of iconicity. The inscription of discourse is the transcription of the world, and transcription is not reduplication, but metamorphosis.

This positive value of the material mediation by written signs may be ascribed, in writing as in painting, to the invention of notational systems presenting analytical properties: discreteness, finite number, combinatory power. The triumph of the phonetic alphabet in Western cultures and the apparent subordination of writing to speaking stemming from the dependence of letters on sounds, however, must not let us forget the other possibilities of inscription expressed by pictograms, hieroglyphs, and above all, by ideograms, which represent a direct inscription of thought meanings and which can be read differently in different idioms. These other kinds of inscription exhibit a universal character of writing, equally present in phonetic writing, but which the dependence on sounds there tends to dissimulate: the space-structure not only of the bearer, but of the marks, themselves, of their form, position, mutual distance, order, and linear disposition. The transfer from hearing to reading is fundamentally linked to this transfer from the temporal properties of the voice to the spatial properties of the inscribed marks. This general spatialization of language is complete with the appearance of printing. The visualization of culture begins with the dispossession of the power of the voice in the proximity of mutual presence. Printed texts reach man in solitude, far from the ceremonies that gather the community. Abstract relations, telecommunications in the proper sense of the word, connect the scattered members of an invisible public.

Such are the material instruments of the iconicity of writing and the transcription of reality through the external inscription of discourse.

Inscription and Productive Distanciation

We are now prepared for a final step. It will lead us to find in the process of interpretation itself the ultimate justification of the exteriorization of discourse.

The problem of writing becomes a hermeneutical problem when it is referred to its complementary pole, which is reading. A new dialectic then emerges, that of distanciation and appropriation. By appropriation I mean the counterpart of the semantic autonomy, which detached the text from its writer. To appropriate is to make "one's own" what was "alien." Because there is a general need for making our own what is foreign to us, there is a general problem of distanciation. Distance, then, is not simply a fact, a given, just the actual spatial and temporal gap between us and the appearance of such and such work of art or discourse. It is a dialectical trait, the principle of a struggle between the otherness that transforms all spatial and temporal distance into cultural estrangement and the ownness by which all understanding aims at the extension of self-understanding. Distanciation is not a quantitative phenomenon; it is the dynamic counterpart of our need, our interest, and our effort to overcome cultural estrangement. Writing and reading take place in this cultural struggle. Reading is the *pharmakon*, the "remedy," by which the meaning of the text is "rescued" from the estrangement of distanciation and put in a new proximity, a proximity which suppresses and preserves the cultural distance and includes the otherness within the ownness.

This general problematic is deeply rooted both in the history of thought and in our ontological situation.

Historically speaking, the problem which I am elaborating is the reformulation of a problem to which the eighteenth

43

century Enlightenment gave its first modern formulation for the sake of classical philology: how to make once more present the culture of antiquity in spite of the intervening cultural distance? German Romanticism gave a dramatic turn to this problem by asking how we can become contemporaneous with past geniuses? More generally, how is one to use the expressions of life fixed by writing in order to transfer oneself into a foreign psychic life? The problem returned again after the collapse of the Hegelian claim to overcome historicism by the logic of the Absolute Spirit. If there is no recapitulation of past cultural heritages in an all encompassing whole delivered from the onesidedness of its partial components, then the historicity of the transmission and reception of these heritages cannot be overcome. Then the dialectic of distanciation and appropriation is the last word in the absence of absolute knowledge.

This dialectic may also be expressed as that of the tradition as such, understood as the reception of historically transmitted cultural heritages. A tradition raises no philosophical problem as long as we live and dwell within it in the naiveté of the first certainty. Tradition only becomes problematic when this first naiveté is lost. Then we have to retrieve its meaning through and beyond estrangement. Henceforth the appropriation of the past proceeds along an endless struggle with distanciation. Interpretation, philosophically understood, is nothing else than an attempt to make estrangement and distanciation productive.[6]

Placed against the background of the dialectic of distanciation and appropriation, the relation between writing and reading accedes to its most fundamental meaning. At the same time, the partial dialectical processes, separately described in the opening section of this essay, following Jakobson's model of communication, make sense as a whole.

It will be the task of a discussion applied to the controversial concepts of explanation and understanding to grasp as a whole the paradoxes of authorial meaning and semantic autonomy, the personal addressee and the universal audience, the singular message and the typical literary codes, and the immanent structure and the world displayed by the text; a discussion I shall undertake in my fourth essay.

3.

METAPHOR AND SYMBOL
Translated by David Pellauer

This third essay is intercalated between the closing words of the preceding essay and the decisive discussion of the concepts of explanation and understanding in the following one for two specific reasons, both of which concern the extension of the field of the theory of interpretation.

The first reason concerns the functioning of the signification in works of literature as opposed to scientific works, whose significations are to be taken literally. The question here is whether the surplus of meaning characteristic of literary works is a part of their signification or if it must be understood as an external factor, which is noncognitive and simply emotional. I will consider metaphor as the touchstone of the cognitive value of literary works in the remarks which follow. If we can incorporate the surplus of meaning of metaphors into the domain of semantics, then we will be able to give the theory of verbal signification its greatest possible extension.

But is the verbal signification the whole signification? Is there not a surplus of meaning which goes beyond the linguistic sign? In my earlier writings, especially *The Symbolism of Evil* and *Freud and Philosophy*,[1] I directly defined hermeneutics by an object which seemed to be both as broad and as precise as possible, I mean the symbol. As regards the symbol, I defined it in turn by its semantic structure of having a double-meaning. Today I am less certain that one can attack the problem so directly without first having taken linguistics into account. Within the symbol, it now seems to me, there is something non-semantic as well as something semantic, and I will attempt to justify this assertion at the beginning of the second part of this essay. But assuming for the moment that I am correct, it follows that a better hypothesis would be to approach the symbol in terms of a structure of double-meaning, which is not a purely semantic structure, which, as we shall see, is the case with metaphor. But if the theory of metaphor can serve as a preparatory analysis leading up to the theory of the symbol, in return the theory of the symbol will allow us to extend our theory of signification by allowing us to include within it, not only verbal double-meaning, but non-verbal double-meaning as well. Thus metaphor and symbol will serve to mark out the field of extension for the theory of interpretation to be discussed in my concluding essay.

The Theory of Metaphor

Metaphor, says Monroe Beardsley, is "a poem in minia-ture."[2] Hence the relation between the literal meaning and the figurative meaning in a metaphor is like an abridged version within a single sentence of the complex interplay of significa-tions that characterize the literary work as a whole. Here by a literary work I mean a work of discourse distinguished from every other work of discourse, especially scientific discourse, in that it brings an explicit and an implicit meaning into relation.

The first question to be considered deals with the cognitive status of these two meanings. Within the tradition of logical positivism this distinction between explicit and implicit meaning was treated as the distinction between cognitive and emotive language. And a good part of literary criticism influ-enced by this positivist tradition transposed the distinction between cognitive and emotive language into the vocabulary of denotation and connotation. For such a position only the denotation is cognitive and, as such, is of a semantic order. A connotation is extra-semantic because it consists of the weav-ing together of emotive evocations, which lack cognitive value. The figurative sense of a text, therefore, must be seen as being bereft of any cognitive significance. But is this limita-tion of cognitive significance to just the denotative aspects of a sentence correct?

46

Such is the problem for which metaphor may function as a test case. If we can show that the relation between the literal and figurative meaning in a metaphor is a relation internal to the overall signification of the metaphor, we will thereby obtain a model for a purely semantic definition of literature, which will be applicable to each of its three essential classes: poetry, essays, and prose fiction. We can then say that what a poem states is related to what it suggests just as its primary signification is related to its secondary signification where both significations fall within the semantic field. And literature is that use of discourse where several things are specified at the same time and where the reader is not required to choose among them. It is the positive and productive use of ambiguity.

If we abstract for the moment from the world of the work revealed by this interplay of meanings, we may concentrate our analysis on the verbal design, i.e., the work of discourse, which generates the semantic ambiguity that characterizes a literary work. It is this work of discourse that can be seen in miniature in metaphor.

The theory of metaphor comes down to us from the ancient rhetoricians, but this theory will not fulfill the role we expect of it without one important revision. This revision, briefly stated, shifts the problem of metaphor from the semantics of the word to the semantics of the sentence.

In traditional rhetoric metaphor is classed as a trope, i.e., as one of the figures which classify the variations in meaning in the use of words and, more precisely, in the process of denomination. Metaphor belongs to the language game which governs naming. Thus we read in Aristotle's *Poetics* that a metaphor is "the application to a thing of a name that belongs to something else, the transference taking place from genus to species, from species to genus, from species to species, or proportionally."[3] His *Rhetoric* takes this definition for granted, simply adding a marginal note concerning the use of comparative images, which are characterized as a special form of the proportional metaphor in which the comparison is explicitly marked by a comparative term such as "is like . . ." Comparison, in other words, is an expanded form of

47

metaphor. Cicero and Quintilian later inverted this model and said that a metaphor is simply an abridged comparison.

Now what presuppositions are implicit in this rhetorical treatment of metaphor? It is first admitted that words are to be taken in isolation from one another, each one having within itself a signification, which Aristotle calls its "current" meaning. By this he means that it is common to a certain population and fixed by the norms operative in that speaking community. Rhetoric begins, then, where the lexical code ends. It treats the figurative significations of a word, those significations which may subsequently become part of ordinary usage. The underlying question here is to account for these variations in significations. Why do these deviations from the ordinary, these figures of style, occur? The ancient rhetoricians generally replied that it was the purpose of a figure either to fill a semantic lacuna in the lexical code or to ornament discourse and make it more pleasing. Because we have more ideas than we have words to express them, we have to stretch the significations of those we do have beyond their ordinary use. Or, in those cases where a suitable word is already available, we might choose to use a figurative word in order to please or perhaps to seduce our audience. This second strategy of rhetorical figures reflects one of the central aspects of the general function of rhetoric, namely, persuasion. That is, rhetoric is a means of influencing an audience through the use of means of discourse which are not those of proof or violence. It aims at making the probable more attractive.

Metaphor is one of these rhetorical figures, the one where resemblance serves as the reason for substituting a figurative word for a missing or an absent literal word. It must be distinguished from the other figures of style, such as metonymy, for example, where contiguity takes the place that resemblance occupies in metaphor.

This is a very schematic summary of the long history of rhetoric, which begins with the Greek sophists and is continued by Aristotle, Cicero, and Quintilian, until it dies away in the nineteenth century. What remains constant in this tradition, however, can be schematized in the following six propositions.

48

(1) Metaphor is a trope, a figure of discourse that concerns denomination.

(2) It represents the extension of the meaning of a name through deviation from the literal meaning of words.

(3) The reason for this deviation is resemblance.

(4) The function of resemblance is to ground the substitution of the figurative meaning of a word in place of the literal meaning, which could have been used in the same place.

(5) Hence the substituted signification does not represent any semantic innovation. We can translate a metaphor, i.e., replace the literal meaning for which the figurative word is a substitute. In effect, substitution plus restitution equals zero.

(6) Since it does not represent a semantic innovation, a metaphor does not furnish any new information about reality. This is why it can be counted as one of the emotive functions of discourse.

These are the presuppositions of classical rhetoric which a modern semantic treatment of metaphor calls into question. This new semantics finds its best expression in the works of authors such as I.A. Richards, Max Black, Monroe Beardsley, Colin Turbayne, and Philip Wheelwright, among others.[4] And among these authors, it is the work of Richards that is truly pioneering because it marks the overthrow of the traditional problematic.

If Richards could reject the last two implications of the classical model — that a metaphor does not involve any new information and that therefore its function is purely decorative—it was because he broke away from the initial presuppositions.

The first presupposition to be rejected is that a metaphor is simply an accident of denomination, a displacement in the signification of words. With this presupposition classical rhetoric limited itself to the description of an effect of meaning that is really the result of the impact on the word of a production of meaning that takes place at the level of a complete utterance or sentence. This is the first discovery of a semantic approach to metaphor. Metaphor has to do with semantics of the sentence before it concerns the semantics of a word. And since a metaphor only makes sense in an utterance, it is a phenomenon of predication, not denomination. When the poet speaks of a "blue angelus," or a "mantle of sorrow," he puts two terms, which, following Richards, we may call the tenor and the vehicle, in tension. And only the ensemble constitutes the metaphor. So we should not really speak of the metaphorical use of a word, but rather of the metaphorical utterance. The metaphor is the result of the tension between two terms in a metaphorical utterance.

This first thesis implies a second. If a metaphor only concerns words because it is first produced at the level of a complete sentence, then the first phenomenon to consider is not any deviation from the literal meaning of the words, but the very functioning of the operation of predication at the level of the sentence. What we have just called the tension in a metaphorical utterance is really not something that occurs between two terms in the utterance, but rather between two opposed interpretations of the utterance. It is the conflict between these two interpretations that sustains the metaphor. In this regard, we can even say, in a general fashion, that the strategy of discourse by means of which the metaphoric utterance obtains its result is absurdity. This absurdity is only revealed through the attempt to interpret the utterance literally. The angelus is not blue, if blue is a color; sorrow is not a mantle, if the mantle is a garment made of cloth. Thus a metaphor does not exist in itself, but in and through an interpretation. The metaphorical interpretation presupposes a literal interpretation which self-destructs in a significant contradiction. It is this process of self-destruction or transformation which imposes a sort of twist on the words, an extension of meaning thanks to which we can make sense where a literal interpretation would be literally nonsensical. Hence a metaphor appears as a kind of riposte to a certain inconsistency in the metaphorical utterance literally interpreted. With Jean Cohen, we can call this inconsistency a "semantic impertinence," or to use a more supple and inclusive expression than that, "contradiction" or "absurdity", which are used by Max Black and Monroe Beardsley.[5]

To summarize this thesis: taking into account the lexical values of the words in a metaphorical utterance, we can only make sense, i.e., we can only save the whole utterance, by submitting the words in question to a kind of work of meaning—which, following Beardsley, we have called a metaphorical twist — thanks to which the utterance begins to make sense.

It is now possible to return to the third presupposition of the classical rhetorical conception of metaphor, the role of resemblance. This has often been misunderstood. Often it has been reduced to the role of images in poetic discourse, so that for many critics, especially the older ones, studying an author's metaphors meant discussing the nomenclature of the images used to illustrate his ideas. But if metaphor does not consist in clothing an idea in an image, if it consists instead in reducing the shock engendered by two incompatible ideas, then it is in the reduction of this gap or difference that resemblance plays a role. What is at stake in a metaphorical utterance, in other words, is the appearance of kinship where ordinary vision does not perceive any relationship. The functioning of a metaphor is here close to what Gilbert Ryle has called a "category mistake." It is, in effect, a calculated error, which brings together things that do not go together and by means of this apparent misundersanding it causes a new, hitherto unnoticed, relation of meaning to spring up between the terms that previous systems of classification had ignored or not allowed.

When Shakespeare speaks of time as a beggar,[6] he teaches us to see time as . . . , to see time like a beggar. Two previously distant classes are here suddenly brought together and the work of resemblance consists precisely in this bringing together of what once was distant. Aristotle, thus, was correct in this regard when he said that to be good at inventing metaphors was to have an eye for resemblances.

From this description of the work of resemblance in metaphorical utterances, another opposition to the purely rhetorical conception of metaphor follows. For classical rhetoric, one will recall, a trope was the simple substitution of one word for another. But substitution is a sterile operation, whereas in a live metaphor the tension between the words, or, more precisely, between the two interpretations, one literal and the other metaphoric, at the level of the entire sentence, elicits a veritable creation of meaning of which classical rhetoric can only note the result. It cannot account for this creation of meaning. Within a tension theory of metaphor, however, such as we are here opposing to a substitution theory, a new signification emerges, which embraces the whole sentence. In this sense, a metaphor is an instantaneous creation, a semantic innovation which has no status in already established language and which only exists because of the attribution of an unusual or an unexpected predicate. Metaphor therefore is more like the resolution of an enigma than a simple association based on resemblance; it is constituted by the resolution of a semantic dissonance. We will not recognize the specificity of this phenomenon so long as we limit our consideration to dead metaphors, which are really no longer metaphors properly speaking. By a dead metaphor, I mean such expressions as "the foot of a chair" or "a mountain." Live metaphors are metaphors of invention within which the response to the discordance in the sentence is a new extension of meaning, although it is certainly true that such inventive metaphors tend to become dead metaphors through repetition. In such cases, the extended meaning becomes part of our lexicon and contributes to the polysemy of the words in question whose everyday meanings are thereby augmented. There are no live metaphors in a dictionary.

Two final conclusions may be drawn from this analysis, and they stand in opposition to the last two presuppositions of the classical theory. First, real metaphors are not translatable. Only metaphors of substitution are susceptible of a translation which could restore the literal signification. Tension metaphors are not translatable because they create their meaning. This is not to say that they cannot be paraphrased, just that such a paraphrase is infinite and incapable of exhausting the innovative meaning.

The second conclusion is that a metaphor is not an ornament of discourse. It has more than an emotive value because it offers new information. A metaphor, in short, tells us something new about reality.

From Metaphor to Symbol

The advantage of taking up the problem of double-meaning in terms of metaphors rather than symbols is twofold. First, metaphor has been the object of long and detailed study by rhetoricians; second, the renewal of this investigation by semantics, which takes up the structural problems left unresolved by rhetoric, is limited to those linguistic factors that give a homogeneous linguistic constitution to the phenomenon in question.

Such is not the case with symbols. The study of symbols runs into two difficulties which make any direct access to their double-meaning structure difficult. First, symbols belong to too many and too diverse fields of research. I considered three such fields in my earlier writings. Psychoanalysis, for instance, deals with dreams, other symptoms, and cultural objects akin to them as being symbolic of deep psychic conflicts. Poetics, on the other hand, if we understand this term in a broad sense, understands symbols to be the privileged images of a poem, or those images that dominate an author's works, or a school of literature, or the persistent figures within which a whole culture recognizes itself, or even the great archetypal images which humanity as a whole—ignoring cultural differences — celebrates.

At this point we are close to the third use of the word "symbol" by the history of religions. Mircea Eliade, for example, recognizes such concrete entities as trees, labyrinths, ladders, and mountains as symbols insofar as they represent symbols of space and time, or flight and transcendence, and point beyond themselves to something wholly other, which manifests itself in them. Thus the problem of symbols is dispersed among many fields of research and so divided among them that it tends to become lost in their proliferation.

The second difficulty with symbols is that the concept "symbol" brings together two dimensions, we might even say, two universes, of discourse, one linguistic and the other of a non-linguistic order. The linguistic character of symbols is attested to by the fact that it is indeed possible to construct a semantics of symbols, i.e., a theory that would account for their structure in terms of meaning or signification. Thus we can speak of the symbol as having a double meaning or a first and a second order meaning. But the non-linguistic dimension is just as obvious as the linguistic one. As the examples just cited indicate, a symbol always refers its linguistic element to something else. Thus psychoanalysis links its symbols to hidden psychic conflicts; while the literary critic refers to something like a vision of the world or a desire to transform all language into literature; and the historian of religion sees in symbols the milieu of manifestations of the Sacred, or what Eliade calls hierophanies.

It is just this external complexity of symbols which accounts for my effort to clarify them in light of the theory of metaphor.

This may be done in three steps. It is first possible to identify the semantic kernel characteristic of every symbol, however different each might be, on the basis of the structure of meaning operative in metaphorical utterances. Second, the metaphorical functioning of language will allow us to isolate the non-linguistic stratum of symbols, the principle of its dissemination, through a method of contrast. Finally, in return, this new understanding of symbols will give rise to further developments in the theory of metaphor, which would otherwise remain concealed. In this way the theory of symbols will allow us to complete that of metaphor.

I hypothesize that these developments will provide enough of the missing intermediary steps to allow us to bridge the gap between metaphors and symbols.

The Semantic Moment of a Symbol

The relation between the literal meaning and the figurative meaning of a metaphorical utterance provides an appropriate guideline which will allow us to identify the properly semantic traits of a symbol. These traits are the ones that relate every form of symbol to a language, thereby assuring the unity of symbols despite their being dispersed among the numerous places where they emerge or appear. The appearance of this semantic dimension is the result of a theoretical approach so long as we still confuse the semantic nature of symbols with their other traits which resist any transposition to language. The symbol, in effect, only gives rise to thought if it first gives rise to speech. Metaphor is the appropriate re-agent to bring to light this aspect of symbols that has an affinity for language.

Here a tension theory of metaphor is more useful than a substitution theory. The metaphorical twist, which our words must undergo in response to the semantic impertinence at the level of the entire sentence, can be taken as the model for the extension of meaning operative in every symbol. In the three areas of investigation cited above, for example, a symbol, in the most general sense, functions as a "surplus of significa-tion." Freud's treatment of little Hans' wolf signifies more than we mean when we describe a wolf. The sea in ancient Babylonian myths signifies more than the expanse of water that can be seen from the shore. And a sunrise in a poem by Wordsworth signifies more than a simple meteorological phenomenon.

As in metaphor theory, this excess of signification in a symbol can be opposed to the literal signification, but only on the condition that we also oppose two interpretations at the same time. Only for an interpretation are there two levels of signification since it is the recognition of the literal meaning that allows us to see that a symbol still contains more mean-ing. This surplus of meaning is the residue of the literal interpretation. Yet for the one who participates in the sym-bolic signification there are really not two significations, one literal and the other symbolic, but rather a single movement, which transfers him from one level to the other and which assimilates him to the second signification by means of, or through, the literal one.

Symbolic signification, therefore, is so constituted that we can only attain the secondary signification by way of the primary signification, where this primary signification is the sole means of access to the surplus of meaning. The primary signification gives the secondary signification, in effect, as the meaning of a meaning. This trait marks the difference between a symbol and an allegory. Allegory is a rhetorical procedure that can be eliminated once it has done its job. Having ascended the ladder, we can then descend it. Allegory is a didactic procedure. It facilitates learning, but can be ignored in any directly conceptual approach. In contrast, there is no symbolic knowledge except when it is impossible to directly grasp the concept and when the direction towards the concept is indirectly indicated by the secondary signification of a primary signification.

Next, the work of resemblance characteristic of symbols can also be associated with the corresponding process in metaphors. The interplay of similarity and dissimilarity presents, in effect, the conflict between some prior categorization of reality and a new one just being born. As one author has put it, metaphor is an idyll with a new partner who resists while giving in. And metaphor has long been compared to stereoscopic vision where the different concepts may be said to come together to give the appearance of solidity and depth.

In a symbol, it is true that these relations are more confused, not being as nicely articulated on a logical level. This is why we speak of assimilation rather than apprehension: the symbol assimilates rather than apprehends a resemblance. Moreover, in assimilating some things to others it assimilates us to what is thereby signified. This is precisely what makes the theory of symbols so fascinating, yet deceiving. All the boundaries are blurred — between the things as well as between the things and ourselves. Later we will be able to catch hold of one of the factors operative here when we turn to the non-linguistic stratum of symbols.

If the theory of metaphor is as clarifying as I say it is, it is because a work of language has already taken place, a work which places things at a distance from the utterance and which, within the utterance, distanciates the predicate from the subject. In fact, to speak of metaphor as a bizarre form of predication is already to invoke some principle of articulation which is lacking in the symbolic order.

Once again it is the metaphorical functioning of language that allows us to justice to another trait of symbols, which is obstinately emphasized by their defenders, yet for which they lack the key. We readily concede that a symbol cannot be exhaustively treated by conceptual language, that there is more in a symbol than in any of its conceptual equivalents; a trait which is eagerly embraced by the opponents of conceptual thinking. For them, one must choose: either the symbol or the concept. But metaphor theory leads us to a different conclusion. It shows how new possibilities for articulating and conceptualizing reality can arise through an assimilation of hitherto separated semantic fields. Far from being a part of conceptual thinking, such semantic innovation marks the emergence of such thought. This is why the theory of symbols is led into the neighborhood of the Kantian theory of the schematism and conceptual synthesis by the theory of metaphor. There is no need to deny the concept in order to admit that symbols give rise to an endless exegesis. If no concept can exhaust the requirement of further thinking borne by symbols, this idea signifies only that no given categorization can embrace all the semantic possibilities of a symbol. But it is the work of the concept alone that can testify to this surplus of meaning.

The Non-Semantic Moment of a Symbol

It now is possible to identify the non-semantic side of symbols, if we continue our method of contrasts, and if we agree to call semantic those traits of symbols which (1) lend themselves to linguistic and logical analysis in terms of signification and interpretation, and (2) overlap the corresponding traits of metaphors. For something in a symbol does not correspond to a metaphor and, because of this fact, resists any linguistic, semantic, or logical transcription.

This opacity of a symbol is related to the rootedness of symbols in areas of our experience that are open to different methods of investigation. That psychoanalysis should consider dreams as the paradigm for substituted and disguised representations, for example, presupposes that one first takes sleep into consideration as the context for oneiric activity. Poetic images are no less bound to a global form of behavior which in German is called *dichten* (to compose or write poetry; literally "to poeticize"). And would we have religious symbols if man had not given himself over to very complex, yet specific forms of behavior designed to invoke, implore, or repulse the supernatural forces, which dwell in the depths of human existence, transcending and dominating it?

Thus in a variety of ways symbolic activity lacks autonomy. It is a bound activity, and it is the task of many disciplines to reveal the lines that attach the symbolic function to this or that non-symbolic or pre-linguistic activity.

The case of psychoanalysis is especially illuminating, although I will not dwell at length upon it here since I have dealt with it in detail elsewhere. I will only say that in psychoanalysis symbolic activity is a boundary phenomenon linked to the boundary between desire and culture, which is itself a boundary between impulses and their delegated or affective representatives. This is the boundary between primary repression — which affects the first witnesses of our impulses — and secondary repression, which is repression properly speaking — that repression which occurs after the fact and which only allows derivative offshoots, indefinite substitute signs, or signs of signs to appear. This position of the psychoanalytic sign on the boundary between a conflict of impulses and an interplay of signifiers means that psychoanalysis must develop a mixed language, which connects the vocabulary of the dynamics or energetics — we might even speak of a hydraulics — of impulses with that of a textural exegesis. And many psychoanalytical terms bear the mark of this double origin. *The Interpretation of Dreams*, for instance, introduces the concept of censorship, which expresses the repressive action of a force at the level of the production of a text, albeit a text which is first revealed as erased or disfigured.

Similarly, we might point to those diverse procedures Freud placed under the generic title of the "dream work." As work, these procedures operate mechanically as displacements, condensation, decomposition, etc., procedures that Freud sums up under the general heading *Entstellung*, which has been translated as "distortion" or "deformation". At the same time, however, this interplay of forces can be read in the text of the dream account understood as a kind of palimpsest, riddle,

58

or hieroglyph. Psychoanalysis must, therefore, assume the mixed epistemological status which these hybrid concepts impose upon it insofar as these deep conflicts resist any reduction to linguistic processes, yet cannot be read anywhere else than in the dream or symbolic text. Such a mixed conceptualization does not betray some fault in the conceptualization of psychoanalysis, but on the contrary the exact recognition of the place where its discourse occurs: in the intermingling of force and meaning, impulse and discourse, energetics and semantics.

This brief discussion of psychoanalysis allows us to grasp one reason why the symbol does not pass over into metaphor. Metaphor occurs in the already purified universe of the *logos*, while the symbol hesistates on the dividing line between *bios* and *logos*. It testifies to the primordial rootedness of Discourse in Life. It is born where force and form coincide.

It is more difficult to say what makes poetic language a "bound" language. As a first approximation, in fact, it is an unbound or liberated language that is freed from certain lexical, syntactical, and stylistic constraints. It is freed, above all, from the intended references of both ordinary and scientific language, which, we may say by way of contrast, are bound by the facts, empirical objects, and logical constraints of our established ways of thinking. But may we also not say, again by way of contrast, that the poetic world is just as hypothetical a space as is the mathematical order in relation to any given world? The poet, in short, operates through language in a hypothetical realm. In an extreme form we might even say that the poetic project is one of destroying the world as we ordinarily take it for granted, just as Husserl made the destruction of our world the basis of the phenomenological reduction. Or without going quite so far, we could say, following Northrop Frye, that as the inversion of ordinary language, poetic language is not directed outwards, but inwards towards an interior, which is nothing other than the mood structured and expressed by a poem. Here a poem is like a work of music in that its mood is exactly coextensive with the internal order of symbols articulated by its language.

59

It is in this sense that poetry is liberated from the world. But if it is liberated in this sense, in another sense it is bound, and it is bound precisely to the extent that it is also liberated. What has just been said about the mood, which is coextensive with the symbolic order of a poem, shows that a poem is not some gratuitous form of verbal word play. Rather, the poem is bound by what it creates, if the suspension of ordinary discourse and its didactic intention assumes an urgent character for the poet, this is just because the reduction of the referential values of ordinary discourse is the negative condition that allows new configurations expressing the meaning of reality to be brought to language. Through those new configurations new ways of being in the world, of living there, and of projecting our innermost possibilities onto it are also brought to language. Therefore to limit ourselves to saying that a poem structures and expresses a mood is not to say much, for what is a mood if it is not a specific manner of being in the world and relating oneself to it, of understanding it and interpreting it? What binds poetic discourse, then, is the need to bring to language modes of being that ordinary vision obscures or even represses. And in this sense, no one is more free than the poet. We might even say that the poet's speech is freed from the ordinary vision of the world only because he makes himself free for the new being which he has to bring to language.

Finally, the symbolism of the Sacred as it has been studied, for example, by Mircea Eliade is particularly appropriate for our meditation on the rootedness of discourse in a nonsemantic order. Even before Eliade, Rudolf Otto, in his book, *The Idea of the Holy*, strongly emphasized the appearance of the Sacred as power, strength, efficacity. Whatever objections we might raise about his description of the Sacred, it is valuable in that it helps us to be on guard against all attempts to reduce mythology linguistically. We are warned from the very beginning that we are here crossing the threshold of an experience that does not allow itself to be completely inscribed within the categories of *logos* or proclamation and its transmission or interpretation. The numinous element is not first a question of language, if it ever really becomes one, for to speak of power is to speak of something other than speech even if it implies the power of speaking. This power as efficacity *par excellence* is what does not pass over completely into the articulation of meaning.

It is true that the notion of hierophany, which Eliade substitutes for the too massive notion of the numinous, does imply that manifestations of the Sacred have a form or structure, but even then no special privilege is bestowed upon speech. The Sacred may equally well manifest itself in stones or trees as bearers of efficacity.

The preverbal character of such an experience is attested to by the very modulations of space and time as sacred space and sacred time, which result and which are inscribed beneath language at the aesthetic level of experience, in the Kantian sense of this expression.

The bond between myth and ritual attests in another way to this non-linguistic dimension of the Sacred. It functions as a logic of correspondences, which characterize the sacred universe and indicate the specificity of *homo religiosus's* vision of the world. Such ties occur at the level of the very elements of the natural world such as the sky, earth, air, and water. And the same uranian symbolism makes the diverse epiphanies communicate among themselves, while at the same time they also refer to the divine immanent in the hierophanies of life. Thus to divine transcendence there is opposed a proximate sacred as attested to by the fertility of the soil, vegetative exuberance, the flourishing of the flocks, and the fecundity of the maternal womb.

Within the sacred universe there are not living creatures here and there, but life is everywhere as a sacrality, which permeates everything and which is seen in the movement of the stars, the return to life of vegetation each year, and the alternation of birth and death. It is in this sense that symbols are bound within the sacred universe: the symbols only come to language to the extent that the elements of the world themselves become transparent.

This bound character of symbols makes all the difference between a symbol and a metaphor. The latter is a free invention of discourse; the former is bound to the cosmos. Here we touch an irreducible element, an element more irreducible than the one that poetic experience uncovers. In the sacred universe the capacity to speak is founded upon the capacity of the cosmos to signify. The logic of meaning, therefore, follows from the very structure of the sacred universe. Its law is the law of correspondences, correspondences between creation *in illo tempore* and the present order of natural appearances and human activities. This is why, for example, a temple always conforms to some celestial model. And why the hierogamy of earth and sky corresponds to the union between male and female as a correspondence between the macrocosm and the microcosm. Similarly there is a correspondence between the tillable soil and the feminine organ, between the fecundity of the earth and the maternal womb, between the sun and our eyes, semen and seeds, burial and the sowing of grain, birth and the return of spring.

There is a triple correspondence between the body, houses, and the cosmos, which makes the pillars of a temple and our spinal columns symbolic of one another, just as there are correspondences between a roof and the skull, breath and wind, etc. This triple correspondence is also the reason why thresholds, doors, bridges, and narrow pathways outlined by the very act of inhabiting space and dwelling in it correspond to the homologous kinds of passage which rites of initiation help us to cross over in the critical moments of our pilgrimage through life: moments such as birth, puberty, marriage, and death.

Such is the logic of correspondences, which binds discourse in the universe of the Sacred. We might even say that it is always by means of discourse that this logic manifests itself for if no myth narrated how things came to be or if there were no rituals which re-enacted this process, the Sacred would remain unmanifested. As regards ritual, which as such is one modality of making or doing—a doing of something marked by power, it would lack the power to organize space and time without an instituting word, without a discourse which tells how one should act in response to the manifestation of power. And as regards the symbolism that circulates among the elements of the world, this too brings into play a whole work of language. Even more, symbolism only works when its structure is interpreted. In this sense a minimal hermeneutic is required for the functioning of any symbolism. But this linguistic articulation does not suppress what I have called the adherence to symbolism characteristic of the sacred universe, rather it presupposes it. Interpretation of a symbolism cannot even get under way if its work of mediation were not legitimated by an immediate liaison between the appearance and the meaning in the hierophany under consideration. The sacredness of nature reveals itself in saying itself symbolically. The revealing grounds the saying, not the reverse.

If we now bring together the preceding analyses, I am inclined to say that what asks to be brought to language in symbols, but which never passes over completely into language, is always something powerful, efficacious, forceful. Man, it seems, is here designated as a power to exist, indirectly discerned from above, below, and laterally. The power of impulses which haunt our phantasies, of imaginary modes of being which ignite the poetic word, and of the all-embracing, that most powerful something which menaces us so long as we feel unloved, in all these registers and perhaps in others as well, the dialectic of power and form takes place, which insures that language only captures the foam on the surface of life.

The Intermediate Degrees between Symbol and Metaphor

My last remarks — as adventured and adventurous as they might be — render the whole enterprise of elucidating symbols in light of the theory of metaphor vain if the description of symbols does not solicit in return some new developments in metaphor theory.

This feedback of the theory of symbols on the theory of metaphor first invites us to reflect upon the functioning of metaphors in a chain or network. In the analysis proposed above, metaphors remain dispersed events, in a way, places in discourse. The comparison of metaphor to an enigma or a riddle tends to limit the analysis to individual windfalls, and therefore to a transitory aspect of language. In fact, by calling metaphor a semantic innovation, we emphasize the fact that it

63

only exists in the moment of invention. Lacking any status in established language, a metaphor is in the strong sense of the word, an event of discourse. The result is that when a metaphor is taken up and accepted by a linguistic community it tends to become confused with an extension of the polysemy of words. It first becomes a trivial, then a dead metaphor. Symbols, in contrast, because they plunge their roots into the durable constellations of life, feeling, and the universe, and because they have such an incredible stability, lead us to think that a symbol never dies, it is only transformed. Hence if we were to hold fast to our criteria for a metaphor, symbols must be dead metaphors. If not, what makes the difference?

Metaphorical functioning would be completely inadequate as a way of expressing the different temporality of symbols, what we might call their insistence, if metaphors did not save themselves from complete evanescence by means of a whole array of intersignifications. One metaphor, in effect, calls for another and each one stays alive by conserving its power to evoke the whole network. Thus within the Hebraic tradition God is called King, Father, Husband, Lord, Shepherd, and Judge as well as Rock, Fortress, Redeemer, and Suffering Servant. The network engenders what we can call root metaphors, metaphors which, on the one hand, have the power to bring together the partial metaphors borrowed from the diverse fields of our experience and thereby to assure them a kind of equilibrium. On the other hand, they have the ability to engender a conceptual diversity, I mean, an unlimited number of potential interpretations at a conceptual level. Root metaphors assemble and scatter. They assemble subordinate images together, and they scatter concepts at a higher level. They are the dominant metaphors capable of both engendering and organizing a network that serves as a junction between the symbolic level with its slow evolution and the more volatile metaphorical level.

There is a second aspect of metaphorical functioning that also tends to bring it closer to symbols. Beyond its constituting a network, a set of metaphors presents an original hierarchical constitution, as Philip Wheelwright has strongly

64

emphasized in his works on metaphor, *The Burning Fountain*, and, especially, *Metaphor and Reality*.[8] It is possible to describe the metaphoric game at various levels of organization depending upon whether we consider the metaphors in isolated sentences, or as underlying a given poem, or as the dominant metaphors of a poet, or the typical metaphors of a particular linguistic community or a given culture, which can extend so far as to include large cultural spheres such as Christianity. Finally, certain metaphors are so radical that they seem to haunt all human discourse. These metaphors, which Wheelwright calls archetypes, become indistinguishable from the symbolic paradigms Eliade studies in his *Patterns in Comparative Religion*.[9]

So it appears as though certain fundamental human experiences make up an immediate symbolism that presides over the most primitive metaphorical order. This originary symbolism seems to adhere to the most immutable human manner of being in the world, whether it be a question of above and below, the cardinal directions, the spectacle of the heavens, terrestrial localization, houses, paths, fire, wind, stones, or water. If we add that this anthropological and cosmic symbolism is in a kind of subterranean communication with our libidinal sphere and through it with what Freud called the combat between the giants, the gigantomachy between eros and death, we will see why the metaphorical order is submitted to what we can call a request for work by this symbolic experience. Everything indicates that symbolic experience calls for a work of meaning from metaphor, a work which it partially provides through its organizational network and its hierarchical levels. Everything indicates that symbol systems constitute a reservoir of meaning whose metaphoric potential is yet to be spoken. And, in fact, the history of words and culture would seem to indicate that if language never constitutes the most superficial layer of our symbolic experience, this deep layer only becomes accessible to us to the extent that it is formed and articulated at a linguistic and literary level since the most insistent metaphors hold fast to the intertwining of the symbolic infrastructure and metaphoric superstructure.

The theory of metaphor can finally be extended in a third way in the direction of the most specific traits of symbols. Numerous authors have remarked upon the kinship between metaphors and models. This kinship plays a decisive role, for example, in the work of Max Black, which is even entitled *Models and Metaphors*.[10] And from his side, the English theologian Ian Ramsey has attempted to elucidate the function of religious language by revising Max Black's theory in an appropriate fashion.[11]

Such a rapprochement between models and metaphors allows us to develop the theory of metaphor in a direction hitherto neglected in our brief presentation of this theory, I mean its referential dimension. If we adopt the distinction introduced by Frege between sense and reference—the sense being the pure predicative relation, the reference its pretention to say something about reality, in short, its truth value—it appears as if every discourse can be investigated in terms of both its internal organization, which makes it a message, which can be identified and reidentified, and its referential intention, which is its pretention to say something about something.[12]

Now Max Black says that a model has the same structure of sense as a metaphor, but it constitutes the referential dimension of a metaphor. What is this referential value? It is a part of the heuristic function, that is, the aspect of discovery, of a metaphor and a model, of a metaphor as a model.

In scientific language, a model is essentially a heuristic procedure that serves to overthrow an inadequate interpretation and to open the way to a new and more adequate one. In Mary Hesse's terms, it is an instrument of redescription, an expression that I will use in the remainder of this analysis.[13] But it is important to understand that this term is to be taken in its strictly epistemological use.

The redescriptive power of a model can only be understood if, following Max Black, we carefully distinguish between three sorts of models: scale models, as, for example, a model boat; analogical models, which deal with structural identity, as, for example, a schematic diagram in electronics; and finally, theoretical models, which from an epistemological

point of view, are the real models and which consist of construing an imaginary object more accessible to description as a
more complex domain of reality whose properties correspond
to the properties of the object. As Max Black puts it, to describe a domain of reality in terms of an imaginary theoretical
model is a way of seeing things differently by changing our
language about the subject of our investigation. This change
of language proceeds from the construction of a heuristic
fiction and through the transposition of the characteristics of
this heuristic fiction to reality itself.

Let us apply this concept of model to metaphor. The
guideline here is the relation between the two notions of a
heuristic fiction and the redescription that occurs through the
transference of this fiction to reality. It is this double movement that we also find in metaphor, for "a memorable
metaphor has the power to bring two separate domains into
cognitive and emotional relation by using language directly
appropriate for the one as a lens for seeing the other. . . ."[14]
Thanks to this detour through the heuristic fiction we perceive new connections among things. The basis of this
transfer is the presumed isomorphism between the model and
its domain of application. It is this isomorphism that legiti-
mates the "analogical transfer of a vocabulary" and that allows
a metaphor to function like a model and "reveal new relationships."[15]

Let us carry this analysis even further in its application to
metaphor. Considered in terms of its referential bearing, poetic language has in common with scientific language that it
only reaches reality through a detour that serves to deny our
ordinary vision and the language we normally use to describe
it. In doing this both poetic and scientific language aim at a
reality more real than appearances. The theory of models thus
allows us to satisfactorily interpret the paradox of poetic language evoked earlier. This paradox, we said, following Northrop Frye and other literary critics, gives poetic discourse a
centripetal direction opposed to the centrifugal direction,
which characterizes descriptive and didactic discourse. This
is why poetry creates its own world. The suspension of the
referential function of the first degree affects ordinary lan-

guage to the benefit of a second degree reference, which is attached precisely to the fictive dimension revealed by the theory of models. In the same way that the literal sense has to be left behind so that the metaphorical sense can emerge, so the literal reference must collapse so that the heuristic fiction can work its redescription of reality.

In the case of metaphor, this redescription is guided by the interplay between differences and resemblances that gives rise to the tension at the level of the utterance. It is precisely from this tensive apprehension that a new vision of reality springs forth, which ordinary vision resists because it is attached to the ordinary use of words. The eclipse of the objective, manipulable world thus makes way for the revelation of a new dimension of reality and truth.

In speaking this way I am saying nothing more than Aristotle said when dealing with tragedy in his *Poetics*. The composition of a story or a plot—Aristotle speaks here of a *mythos*—is the shortest path to mimesis, which is the central ideal of all poetry. In other words, poetry only imitates reality by recreating it on a mythical level of discourse. Here fiction and redescription go hand in hand.

Must we not conclude then that metaphor implies a tensive use of language in order to uphold a tensive concept of reality? By this I mean that the tension is not simply between words, but within the very copula of the metaphorical utterance. "Nature is a temple where living pillars . . ." Here "is" signifies both is and is not. The literal "is" is overturned by the absurdity and surmounted by a metaphorical "is" equivalent to "is like . . ." Thus poetic language does not tell how things literally are, but what they are like. Can we not then call insistent metaphors—those metaphors that are closest to the symbolic depths of our existence—metaphors that owe their privilege of revealing what things are like to their organization into networks and hierarchical levels?

To conclude, I will say that we must accept two contrary propositions concerning the relationship between metaphors and symbols. On one side, there is more in the metaphor than in the symbol; on the other side, there is more in the symbol than in the metaphor.

There is more in the metaphor than in the symbol in the sense that it brings to language the implicit semantics of the symbol. What remains confused in the symbol—the assimilation of one thing to another, and of us to things; the endless correspondence between the elements — is clarified in the tension of the metaphorical utterance.

But there is more in the symbol than in the metaphor. Metaphor is just the linguistic procedure—that bizarre form of predication — within which the symbolic power is deposited. The symbol remains a two-dimensional phenomenon to the extent that the semantic face refers back to the non-semantic one. The symbol is bound in a way that the metaphor is not. Symbols have roots. Symbols plunge us into the shadowy experience of power. Metaphors are just the linguistic surface of symbols, and they owe their power to relate the semantic surface to the presemantic surface in the depths of human experience to the two-dimensional structure of the symbol.

4.

EXPLANATION AND UNDERSTANDING

The final problem to be dealt with in this series of essays concerns the range of attitudes that a reader may entertain when confronted with a text. In the previous essays the emphasis was on the speaker, writer, or author and the questions dealt with were: What is meant when somebody speaks? When somebody writes? When somebody means more than what he actually says? Now we ask what is it to understand a discourse when that discourse is a text or a literary work? How do we make sense of written discourse?

Beyond Romanticist Hermeneutics

With the dialectic of explanation and understanding, I hope to provide my interpretation theory with an analysis of writing, which will be the counterpart of that of the text as a work of discourse. To the extent that the act of reading is the counterpart of the act of writing, the dialectic of event and meaning, so essential to the structure of discourse, as we saw in the first essay, generates a correlative dialectic in reading between understanding or comprehension (the *verstehen* of the German hermeneutical tradition) and explanation (the *erklären* of that same tradition). Without imposing too mechanical a correspondence between the inner structure of the text as the discourse of the writer and the process of interpretation as the discourse of the reader on our discussion, it may be said, at least in an introductory fashion, that understanding is to reading what the event of discourse is to the utterance of discourse and that explanation is to reading what the verbal and textual autonomy is to the objective meaning of dis-

71

course. A dialectical structure of reading therefore corresponds to the dialectical structure of discourse. This correspondence confirms my statement in my prefatory remarks that the theory of discourse presented in the first essay governs all the subsequent developments of my interpetation theory.

Just as the dialectic of event and meaning remains implicit and difficult to recognize in oral discourse, that of explanation and understanding is quite impossible to identify in the dialogical situation that we call conversation. We explain something to someone else in order that he can understand. And what he has understood, he can in turn explain to a third party. Thus understanding and explanation tend to overlap and to pass over into each other. I will surmise, however, that in explanation we ex-plicate or unfold the range of propositions and meanings, whereas in understanding we comprehend or grasp as a whole the chain of partial meanings in one act of synthesis.

This nascent, inchoative polarity between explanation and understanding as it is dimly perceived in the communication process of conversation becomes a clearly contrasting duality in Romanticist hermeneutics. Each term of the pair there represents a distinct and irreducible mode of intelligibility.

Explanation finds its paradigmatic field of application in the natural sciences. When there are external facts to observe, hypotheses to be submitted to empirical verification, general laws for covering such facts, theories to encompass the scattered laws in a systematic whole, and subordination of empirical generalizations to hypothetic-deductive procedures, then we may say that we "explain." And the appropriate correlate of explanation is nature understood as the common horizon of facts, laws and theories, hypotheses, verifications, and deductions.

Understanding, in contrast, finds its originary field of application in the human sciences (the German *Geisteswissenschaften*), where science has to do with the experience of other subjects or other minds similar to our own. It relies on the meaningfulness of such forms of expression as physiognomic, gestural, vocal, or written signs, and upon documents

72

and monuments, which share with writing the general character of inscription. The immediate types of expression are meaningful because they refer directly to the experience of the other mind which they convey. The other, less direct sources such as written signs, documents, and monuments are no less significant, except that they convey the other mind's experiences indirectly, not directly, to us. The necessity of interpreting these signs proceeds precisely from the indirectness of the way in which they convey such experiences. But there would be no problem of interpretation, taken as a derivative of understanding, if the indirect sources were not indirect expressions of a psychic life, homogenous to the immediate expressions of a foreign psychic life. This continuity between direct and indirect signs explains why "empathy" as the transference of ourselves into another's psychic life is the principle common to every kind of understanding, whether direct or indirect.

The dichotomy between understanding and explanation in Romanticist hermeneutics is both epistemological and ontological. It opposes two methodologies and two spheres of reality, nature and mind. Interpretation is not a third term, nor, as I shall attempt to demonstrate, the name of the dialectic between explanation and understanding. Interpretation is a particular case of understanding. It is understanding applied to the written expressions of life. In a theory of signs that de-emphasizes the difference between speaking and writing, and above all that does not stress the dialectic of event and meaning, it can be expected that interpretation only appears as one province within the empire of comprehension or understanding.

A different distribution of the concepts of understanding, explanation, and interpretation is suggested, however, by the maxim derived from my analysis in the first essay that if discourse is produced as an event, it is understood as meaning. Here mutual understanding relies on sharing in the same sphere of meaning. Already in oral conversation, for example, the transfer into a foreign psychic life finds support in the sameness of the shared sphere of meaning. The dialectic of

73

explanation and understanding has already begun. To understand the utterer's meaning and to understand the utterance meaning constitute a circular process. The development of explanation as an autonomous process proceeds from the exteriorization of the event in the meaning, which is made complete by writing and the generative codes of literature. Then understanding, which is more directed towards the intentional unity of discourse, and explanation, which is more directed towards the analytic structure of the text, tend to become the distinct poles of a developed dichotomy. But this dichotomy does not go so far as to destroy the initial dialectic of the utter's and the utterance meaning. As we saw in the second and third essays, this dialectic is mediated by more and more intermediary terms, but never canceled. In the same way the polarity between explanation and understanding in reading must not be treated in dualistic terms, but as a complex and highly mediated dialectic. Then the term interpretation may be applied, not to a particular case of understanding, that of the written expressions of life, but to the whole process that encompasses explanation and understanding. Interpretation as the dialectic of explanation and understanding or comprehension may then be traced back to the initial stages of interpretative behavior already at work in conversation. And while it is true that only writing and literary composition provide a full development of this dialectic, interpretation must not be referred to as a province of understanding. It is not defined by a kind of object — "inscribed" signs in the most general sense of the term — but by a kind of process: the dynamic of interpretative reading.

For the sake of a didactic exposition of the dialectic of explanation and understanding, as phases of a unique process, I propose to describe this dialectic first as a move from understanding to explaining and then as a move from explanation to comprehension. The first time, understanding will be a naive grasping of the meaning of the text as a whole. The second time, comprehension will be a sophisticated mode of understanding, supported by explanatory procedures. In the beginning, understanding is a guess. At the end, it satisfies the concept of appropriation, which was described in the third essay as the rejoinder to the kind of distanciation linked to the full objectification of the text. Explanation, then, will appear as the mediation between two stages of understanding. If isolated from this concrete process, it is a mere abstraction, an artifact of methodology.

From Guess to Validation

Why must the first act of understanding take the form of a guess? And what has to be guessed in a text?

The necessity of guessing the meaning of a text may be related to the kind of semantic autonomy that I ascribed to the textual meaning in my second essay. With writing, the verbal meaning of the text no longer coincides with the mental meaning or intention of the text. This intention is both fulfilled and abolished by the text, which is no longer the voice of someone present. The text is mute. An asymmetric relation obtains between text and reader, in which only one of the partners speaks for the two. The text is like a musical score and the reader like the orchestra conductor who obeys the instructions of the notation. Consequently, to understand is not merely to repeat the speech event in a similar event, it is to generate a new event beginning from the text in which the intial event has been objectified.

In other words, we have to guess the meaning of the text because the author's intention is beyond our reach. Here perhaps my opposition to Romanticist hermeneutics is most forceful. We all know the maxim—which indeed antedates the Romantics, since Kant knows and cites it[1]—to understand an author better than he understood himself. Now even if this maxim may receive different interpretations, even if it may be retained with proper qualifications (as I shall attempt to show below), it led hermeneutics astray inasmuch as it expressed the ideal of "congeniality" or a communion from "genius" to "genius" in interpretation. The Romanticist forms of hermeneutics overlooked the specific situation created by the disjunction of the verbal meaning of the text from the mental intention of the author. The fact is that the author can no longer "rescue" his work, to recall Plato's image, which I

75

discussed in the second essay. His intention is often unknown to us, sometimes redundant, sometimes useless, and sometimes even harmful as regards the interpretation of the verbal meaning of his work. In even the better cases it has to be taken into account in light of the text itself.

In conclusion, then, there is a problem of interpretation not so much because of the incommunicability of the psychic experience of the author, but because of the very nature of the verbal intention of the text. The surpassing of the intention by the meaning signifies precisely that understanding takes place in a nonpsychological and properly semantical space, which the text has carved out by severing itself from the mental intention of its author.

The dialectic of *erklären* and *verstehen* begins here. If the objective meaning is something other than the subjective intention of the author, it may be construed in various ways. Misunderstanding is possible and even unavoidable. The problem of the correct understanding can no longer be solved by a simple return to the alleged situation of the author. The concept of guess has no other origin. To construe the meaning as the verbal meaning of the text is to make a guess.

But, as well shall see below, if there are no rules for making good guesses, there are methods for validating those guesses we do make.[2] In this new dialectic both terms are required. Guessing corresponds to what Schleiermacher called the "divinatory," validation to what he called the "grammatical." Both are necessary to the process of reading a text.

The transition from guessing to explaining is secured by an investigation of the specific object of guessing. We have answered our first question, why do we have to guess in order to understand? We still have to say what is to be guessed by understanding.

First, to construe the verbal meaning of a text is to construe it as a whole. Here we rely more on the analysis of discourse as work than on the analysis of discourse as written. A work of discourse is more than a linear sequence of sentences. It is a cumulative, holistic process.

Since this specific structure of the work cannot be derived from that of the single sentences, the text as such has a kind of plurivocity, which is other than the polysemy of individual words, and other than the ambiguity of individual sentences. This textual plurivocity is typical of complex works of discourse and opens them to a plurality of constructions. The relation between whole and parts — as in a work of art or an animal — requires a specific kind of "judgment" for which Kant has given the theory in the *Critique of Judgment*. Concretely, the whole appears as a hierarchy of topics, of primary and subordinate topics that are not, so to speak, at the same altitude, so as to give the text a stereoscopic structure. The reconstruction of the text's architecture, therefore, takes the form of a circular process, in the sense that the presupposition of a certain kind of whole is implied in the recognition of the parts. And reciprocally, it is in construing the details that we construe the whole. There is no necessity, no evidence, concerning what is important and what is unimportant. The judgment of importance is itself a guess.

Second, to construe a text is to construe it as an individual. As we saw in the second essay, if a work is produced according to generic (and genetic) rules, it is also produced as a singular being. Only *technê* generates individuals, says Aristotle, whereas *epistêmê* grasps species. Kant, from another point of view, confirms this statement: the judgment of taste is only about individuals. Concretely, the work of discourse, as this unique work, can only be reached by a process of narrowing down the scope of generic concepts, which include the literary genre, the class of texts to which this text belongs, and the types of codes and structures that intersect in this text. This localization and individualization of the unique text is also a guess.

The text as a whole and as a singular whole may be compared to an object, which may be viewed from several sides, but never from all sides at once. Therefore the reconstruction of the whole has a perspectival aspect similar to that of a perceived object. It is always possible to relate the same

77

sentence in different ways to this or that other sentence considered as the cornerstone of the text. A specific kind of
onesidedness is implied in the act of reading. This onesidedness grounds the guess character of interpretation.

Third, the literary texts involve potential horizons of meaning, which may be actualized in different ways. This trait is
more directly related to the role of the secondary metaphoric
and symbolic meanings described in the third essay than to
the theory of writing developed in the second one. A few years
ago I used to link the task of hermeneutics primarily to the
deciphering of the several layers of meaning in metaphoric
and symbolic language. I think today, however, that
metaphoric and symbolic language is not paradigmatic for a
general theory of hermeneutics. This theory must cover the
whole problem of discourse, including writing and literary
composition. But, even here, the theory of metaphor and of
symbolic expressions may be said to provide a decisive extension to the field of meaningful expressions, by adding the
problematic of multiple meaning to that of meaning in general. Literature is affected by this extension to the degree that it
can be defined in semantic terms by the relation between
primary and secondary meanings in it. The secondary meanings, as in the case of the horizon, which surrounds perceived
objects, open the work to several readings. It may even be said
that these readings are ruled by the prescriptions of meaning
belonging to the margins of potential meaning surrounding
the semantic nucleus of the work. But these prescriptions too
have to be guessed before they can rule the work of interpretation.

As concerns the procedures for validation by which we test
our guesses, I agree with E. D. Hirsch that they are closer to a
logic of probability than to a logic of empirical verification. To
show that an interpretation is more probable in the light of
what we know is something other than showing that a conclusion is true. So in the relevant sense, validation is not verification. It is an argumentative discipline comparable to the juridical procedures used in legal interpretation, a logic of uncertainty and of qualitative probability. It follows from this
understanding of validation that we may give an acceptable

sense to the opposition between the *Naturwissenschaften* and the *Geisteswissenschaften* without conceding anything to the alleged Romanticist dogma of the ineffability of the individual. The method of converging indices, which characterizes the logic of subjective probability, provides a firm basis for a science of the individual, which may rightly be called a science. And since a text is a quasi-individual, the validation of an interpretation applied to it may be said to give a scientific knowledge of the text.

Such is the balance between the genius of guessing and the scientific character of validation, which constitutes a modern presentation of the dialectic between *verstehen* and *erlären*.

At the same time, we are also enabled to give an acceptable meaning to the famous concept of the hermeneutical circle. Guess and validation are in a sense circularly related as subjective and objective approaches to the text. But this circle is not a vicious one. That would be the case if we were unable to escape the kind of "self-confirmability" which, according to Hirsch,[3] threatens the relation between guess and validation. But to the procedures of validation there also belong procedures of invalidation similar to the criteria of falsifiability proposed by Karl Popper in his *Logic of Discovery*.[4] Here the role of falsification is played by the conflict between competing interpretations. An interpretation must not only be probable, but more probable than another interpretation. There are criteria of relative superiority for resolving this conflict, which can easily be derived from the logic of subjective probability.

To conclude this section, if it is true that there is always more than one way of construing a text, it is not true that all interpretations are equal. The text presents a limited field of possible constructions. The logic of validation allows us to move between the two limits of dogmatism and scepticism. It is always possible to argue for or against an interpretation, to confront interpretations, to arbitrate between them and to seek agreement, even if this agreement remains beyond our immediate reach.[5]

79

From Explanation to Comprehension

The preceding description of the dialectic between understanding as guessing and explanation as validation was roughly the counterpart of the dialectic between event and meaning. The following presentation of the same dialectic, but in the reverse order, may be related to another polarity in the structure of discourse, that of sense and reference. As I said in the first essay, this new dialectic can be considered from one point of view as an extension of the first one. The reference expresses the full exteriorization of discourse to the extent that the meaning is not only the ideal object intended by the utterer, but the actual reality aimed at by the utterance. But, from another point of view, the polarity of sense and reference is so specific that it deserves a distinct treatment, which reveals its fate in writing and, above all, in some literary uses of discourse. The same points will hold for the counterparts of the theory of the text in the theory of reading.

We have seen that the referential function of written texts is deeply affected by the lack of a situation common to both writer and reader. It exceeds the mere ostensive designation of the horizon of reality surrounding the dialogical situation. Of course, written sentences keep using ostensive devices, but these ostensive terms can no longer hold for ways of showing what is referred to. This alteration of the ostensive designation has positive and negative implications. On the one hand, it implies an extension of the referred to reality. Language has a world now and not just a situation. But, to the extent that this world, for most of its parts, has not been shown, but merely designated, a complete abstraction of the surrounding reality becomes possible. This is what happens with some works of discourse, in fact with most literary works, in which the referential intention is suspended, or at least those in which the reference to the familiar objects of ordinary discourse is suspended, to say nothing for the time being of another kind of reference to some of the more deeply rooted aspects or dimensions of our being in the world.

The new dialectic between explanation and comprehension is the counterpart of these adventures of the referential function of the text in the theory of reading. The abstraction from the surrounding world made possible by writing and actualized by literature gives rise to two opposed attitudes. As readers, we may either remain in a kind of state of suspense as regards any kind of referred to reality, or we may imaginatively actualize the potential non-ostensive references of the text in a new situation, that of the reader. In the first case, we treat the text as a worldless entity. In the second, we create a new ostensive reference thanks to the kind of "execution" that the act of reading implies. These two possibilities are equally entailed by the act of reading conceived of as their dialectical interplay.

The first way of reading is exemplified today by the various structural schools of literary criticism. Their approach is not only possible, but legitimate. It proceeds from the acknowledgement of what I have called the suspension or suppression of the ostensive reference. The text intercepts the "worldly" dimension of the discourse — the relation to a world which could be shown — in the same way as it disrupts the connection of the discourse to the subjective intention of the author. To read, in this way, means to prolong the suspension of the ostensive reference and to transfer oneself into the "place" where the text stands, within the "enclosure" of this worldless place. According to this choice, the text no longer has an exterior, it only has an interior. To repeat, the very constitution of the text as a text and of the system of texts as literature justifies this conversion of the literary object into a closed system of signs, analogous to the kind of closed system that phonology discovered underlying all discourse, and which Saussure called *langue*. Literature, according to this working hypothesis, becomes an analogon of *langue*.

On the basis of this abstraction, a new kind of explanatory attitude may be extended towards the literary object. This new attitude is not borrowed from an area of knowledge alien to language, but it comes from the same field, the semiological field. It is henceforth possible to treat texts according to the explanatory rules that linguistics successfully applied to the elementary systems of signs which underlie the use of language. We have learned from the Geneva school, the Prague

81

school, and the Danish school of linguistics that it is always possible to abstract systems from processes and to relate these systems, whether they be phonological, lexical, or syntactical, to units which are already defined through opposition to other units of the same system. This interplay of distinctive entities within finite sets of such units, as we have seen in the first essay, defines the notion of structure in modern linguistics.

It is this structural model that is now applied to texts, i.e., to sequences of signs longer than the sentence, which is the last kind of unit that linguistics takes into account.

This extension of the structural model to texts is a daring endeavor. Is not a text more on the side of *parole*—of speech— than on the side of *langue*? Is it not a succession of utterances, and therefore, in the final analysis, a succession of sentences? Did we not show in our first essay the opposition between spoken and written language, as contained in the concept of discourse which we opposed to *langue*? Such questions indicate at least that the extension of the structural model to texts does not exhaust the field of possible attitudes in regard to text. We must therefore limit this extension of the linguistic model to being just one of the possible approaches to the notion of interpreting texts. Let us, however, first consider an example of such an approach in some detail before moving on to consider a second possible conception of interpretation.

In his essay "The Structural Study of Myth," Claude Lévi-Strauss formulates the working hypothesis of structural analysis in regard to one category of texts, that of myths.[6] He says, "Myth, like the rest of language, is made up of constituent units. These constituent units presuppose the constituent units present in language when analyzed on other levels—namely phonemes, morphemes, and sememes—but they, nevertheless, differ from the latter in the same way as the latter differ among themselves; they belong to a higher and more complex order. For this reason, we shall call them *gross constituent units*."[7]

Using this hypothesis, the large units, which are at least the same size as the sentence and which, when put together, form the narrative proper to the myth, will be able to be treated

82

according to the same rules that apply to the smallest units know to linguistics. It is to insist on this likeness that Lévi-Strauss calls them mythemes, just as we speak of phonemes, morphemes, and sememes. But in order to remain within the limits of the analogy between mythemes and the lower level units, the analysis of texts will have to perform the same sort of abstraction as that practiced by the phonologist. For the latter, the phoneme is not a concrete sound, in an absolute sense, with its acoustic quality. It is not a substance, to speak like Saussure, but a form, that is to say, an interplay of relations. Similarly, a mytheme is not one of the sentences of a myth, but an oppositive value attached to several individual sentences, which form "a bundle of relations." It "is only as bundles that these relations can be put to use and combined so as to produce a meaning."[8] What is here called a meaning is not at all what the myth means, in the sense of its philosophical or existential content or intuition, but rather the arrangement or disposition of the mythemes themselves; in short, the structure of the myth.

I would like to briefly recall here the analysis that Lévi-Strauss offers of the Oedipus myth following this method. He first separates the sentences of the myth into four columns. In the first column he places all those sentences which speak of an over-esteemed kinship relation: for example, Oedipus weds Jocasta, his mother; Antigone buries Polyneices, her brother, in spite of the order not to do so. In the second column are the same relations, but inverted as an under-esteemed kinship relation: Oedipus kills his father, Laios; Eteocles kills his brother, Polyneices. The third column is concerned with monsters and their destruction. The fourth groups together all the proper names whose meanings suggest a difficulty in walking upright: lame, clumsy, swollen foot.

Comparison of the four columns reveals a correlation. Between numbers one and two, we have kinship relationships in turn over-esteemed and under-esteemed. Between three and four, there is an affirmation and then a negation of man's autochthony. "It follows that column four is to column three as column one is to column two. . . . By a correlation of this type, the overrating of blood relations is to the underrating of blood relations as the attempt to escape autochthony is to the impossibility to succeed in it."[9]

The myth thus appears as a sort of logical instrument which draws together contradictions in order to overcome them. "The inability to connect two kinds of relationships is overcome (or rather replaced) by the assertion that contradictory relationships are identical inasmuch as they are both self-contradictory in a similar way."[10]

We can indeed say that we have explained the myth, but not that we have interpreted it. We have, by means of structural analysis, brought out the logic of the operations that relate the four bundles of relationships among themselves. This logic constitutes "the structural law of the myth" under consideration.[11] It will not go unnoticed that this law is preeminently an object of reading and not at all of speaking, in the sense of a reciting where the power of myth would be re-enacted in a particular situation. Here the text is only a text, and reading inhabits it only as a text, thanks to the suspension of its meaning for us and the postponement of all actualization through contemporary discourse.

I have just cited an example from the field of myths. I could cite another from a neighboring field, that of folklore narratives. This field has been explored by the Russian formalists of the school of Propp and by the French specialists of the structural analysis of narratives, Roland Barthes and A. J. Greimas. The postulates used by Lévi-Strauss are also used by these authors. The units above the sentence have the same composition as those below it. The meaning of an element is its ability to enter into relation with other elements and with the whole work. These postulates define the closure of the narrative. The task of structural analysis therefore consists in performing a segmentation (the horizontal aspect) and then establishing various levels of integration of parts in the whole (the hierarchical aspect). But the units of action, which are segmented and organized in this way, have nothing to do with psychological traits susceptible of being lived or with behavioral segments susceptible of falling under a behaviorist psychology. The extremities of these sequences are only switching

84

points in the narrative, such that if one element is changed, all the rest is different, too. We here recognize a transposition of the commutative method from the phonological level to the level of the narrative units. The logic of action then consists in linking together action kernels, which together constitute the narrative's structural continuity. The application of this technique results in a "dechronologizing" of the narrative, so as to make apparent the narrative logic underlying the narrative time. Ultimately, the narrative is reduced to a combination of a few dramatic units such as promising, betraying, hindering, aiding, etc., which would thus be the paradigms of action. A sequence is a succession of action kernels, each one closing off an alternative opened up by the preceding one. The elementary units, in their turn, fit in with larger units. For example, the encounter embraces such elementary actions as approaching, summoning, greeting, etc. To explain a narrative is to get hold of this symphonic structure of segmental actions.

To the chain of actions correspond similar relations between the "actors" in the narrative. By this one does not mean psychological subjects, but formalized roles correlative to the formalized actions. The actors are defined only by the predicates of action, by the semantic axes of the sentence and the narrative: the one who does the acts, to whom the acts are done, with whom the acts are done, etc. It is the one who promises, who receives the promise, the giver, the receiver, etc. Structural analysis thus brings out a hierarchy of actors correlative to the hierarchy of actions.

The next step is to assemble together the parts of the narrative to form a whole and put it back into narrative communication. It is then a discourse addressed by the narrator to a receiver. But, for structural analysis, the two interlocutors must be looked for nowhere else than in the text. The narrator is designated by the narrative signs, which themselves belong to the very constitution of the narrative. There is nothing beyond the three levels of actions, actors, and narration that falls within the semiological approach. Beyond the last level there is left only the world of the users of the narrative, which itself falls under other semiological disciplines that deal with social, economic, or ideological systems.

This transposition of a linguistic model to the theory of narrative perfectly corroborates my initial remark regarding the contemporary understanding of explanation. Today the concept of explanation is no longer borrowed from the natural sciences and transferred into a different field, that of written documents. It proceeds from the common sphere of language thanks to the analogical transference from the small units of language (phonemes and lexemes) to the large units beyond the sentence, including narrative, folklore, and myth.

This is what the structural schools mean by explanation in the rigorous sense of the term.

I now want to show in what way explanation (*erklären*) requires understanding (*verstehen*) and how understanding brings forth in a new way the inner dialectic, which constitutes interpretation as a whole.

As a matter of fact, nobody stops with a conception of myths and narratives as formal as this algebra of constitutive units. This can be shown in a number of ways. First, even in the most formalized presentation of myths by Lévi-Strauss, the units, which he calls mythemes, are still expressed as sentences, which bear meaning and reference. Can anyone say that their meaning as such is neutralized when they enter into the bundle of relations, which alone is taken into account by the logic of the myth? Even this bundle of relations must be written in the form of a sentence. In the case of the Oedipus myth, the alternation between over-evaluated and under-evaluated kinship relationships means something that has deep existential bearings. Finally, the kind of language game that the whole system of oppositions and combinations embodies would lack any kind of significance if the oppositions themselves, which Lévi-Strauss tends to mediate in his presentation of the myth, were not meaningful oppositions concerning birth and death, blindness and lucidity, sexuality and truth. Without these existential conflicts there would be no contradictions to overcome, no logical function of the myth as an attempt to solve these contradictions.[12]

Structural analysis does not exclude, but presupposes, the opposite hypothesis concerning myth, i.e., that it has meaning as a narrative of origins. Structural analysis merely represses this function. But it cannot suppress it. The myth would not even function as a logical operator if the propositions that it combines did not point towards boundary situations. Structural analysis, far from getting rid of this radical questioning, restores it at a higher level of radicality.

If this is true, could we not then say that the function of structural analysis is to lead us from a surface semantics, that of the narrated myth, to a depth semantics, that of the boundary situations, which constitute the ultimate "referent" of the myth?

I believe that if this were not the case, structural analysis would be reduced to a sterile game, a divisive algebra, and even the myth itself would be bereaved of the function Lévi-Strauss himself assigns it, that of making men aware of certain oppositions and of tending towards their progressive mediation. To eliminate this reference to the aporias of existence around which mythic thought gravitates would be to reduce the theory of myth to the necrology of the meaningless discourses of mankind.

If, on the contrary, we consider structural analysis as one stage — albeit a necessary one — between a naive interpretation and a critical one, between a surface interpretation and a depth interpretation, then it would be possible to locate explanation and understanding at two different stages of a unique hermeneutical arc.

Taking the notion of depth semantics as our guideline, we can now return to our initial problem of the reference of the text. We can now give a name to this non-ostensive reference. It is the kind of world opened up by the depth semantics of the text, a discovery, which has immense consequences regarding what is usually called the sense of the text.

The sense of a text is not behind the text, but in front of it. It is not something hidden, but something disclosed. What has to be understood is not the initial situation of discourse, but what points towards a possible world, thanks to the non-ostensive reference of the text. Understanding has less than ever to do with the author and his situation. It seeks to grasp the world-propositions opened up by the reference of the text. To understand a text is to follow its movement from sense to

87

reference: from what it says, to what it talks about. In this process the mediating role played by structural analysis constitutes both the justification of the objective approach and the rectification of the subjective approach to the text. We are definitely enjoined from identifying understanding with some kind of intuitive grasping of the intention underlying the text. What we have said about the depth semantics that structural analysis yields rather invites us to think of the sense of the text as an injunction coming from the text, as a new way of looking at things, as an injunction to think in a certain manner.

This is the reference borne by the depth semantics. The text speaks of a possible world and of a possible way of orientating oneself within it. The dimensions of this world are properly opened up by and disclosed by the text. Discourse is the equivalent for written language of ostensive reference for spoken language. It goes beyond the mere function of pointing out and showing what already exists and, in this sense, transcends the function of the ostensive reference linked to spoken language. Here showing is at the same time creating a new mode of being.

CONCLUSION

To conclude the last essay and the whole series of essays, I want now to return to the problem raised at the end of the second essay about the dialectic of distanciation and appropriation. This dialectic has an existential overtone. Distanciation meant above all estrangement, and appropriation was intended as the "remedy" which could "rescue" cultural heritages of the past from the alienation of distance. This exchange between distance and proximity defined the historicity of interpretation in the absence of any Hegelian absolute knowledge. But at the same time I made a plea for a concept of productive distanciation, according to which the predicament of cultural distance would be transformed into an epistemological instrument. But how can distance be made productive?

The dialectic of explanation and understanding may provide an answer to the extent that it constitutes the epistemological dimension of the existential dialectic. On the basis of this dialectic, productive distance means methodological distanciation.

This active methodological distanciation finds an appropriate expression in the general trend of literary criticism and biblical criticism insofar as it yields to the anti-historicist reaction influenced by Frege and Husserl — at least the Husserl of the *Logical Investigations*. What has been labeled "historicism" is the epistemological presupposition that the content of literary works and in general of cultural documents receives its intelligibility from its connection to the social conditions of the community that produced it or to which it was destined. To explain a text then means primarily to consider it as the expression of certain socio-cultural needs and as a response to certain perplexities well localized in space and time.

The "logicist" rejoinder to such "historicism" proceeded from a rational refutation of the epistemological presupposition of historicism. For Frege and Husserl a "meaning" (and they had in mind not the meaning of a text, but that of a sentence) is not an idea that somebody has in his mind. It is not a psychic content, but an ideal object which can be identified and reidentified by different individuals at different times as being one and the same. By ideality they meant that the meaning of a proposition is neither a physical nor a psychic reality. In Frege's terms, *Sinn* is not *Vorstellung*, if we call *Vorstellung* (idea, representation) the mental event linked to the actualization of the sense by a given speaker in a given situation. The sameness of the sense in the infinite series of its mental actualizations constitutes the ideal dimension of the proposition.

In a similar manner, Husserl described the content of all intentional acts as noematic objects, irreducible to the psychic side of the acts themselves. The notion of an ideal *Sinn* borrowed from Frege was extended in that way by Husserl to all psychic achievements, not only to logical acts, but also to perceptual, volitional, and emotional acts. For an objective phenomenology, every intentional act without exception must be described from its noematic sides as the correlate of a corresponding noetic act.

This reversal in the theory of propositional acts has important implications for hermeneutics, inasmuch as this discipline is understood as the theory of the fixation of life-expressions by writing. After 1900, Dilthey himself made the utmost effort to introduce into his theory of meaning the kind of ideality that he found in Husserl's *Logical Investigations*. In Dilthey's late works, the inner connection (*Zusammenhang*), which gives a text or a work of art or a document its capacity to be understood by another person and to be fixed by writing, is something similar to the ideality that Frege and Husserl recognized as the meaning of a proposition. If this comparison holds, then the act of *verstehen* is less *geschichtlich* and more *logisch* than the famous article of 1900, *"Die Entstehung der Hermeneutik"* had claimed it was.[13] The whole theory of the *Geisteswissenschaften* was affected by this important shift.

Corresponding to this reversal from historicity to logicity in the general explanation of cultural expressions we may point to a similar move in the field of literary criticism, both in America and on the Continent. A wave of "anti-historicism" followed the previous excesses of psychological and sociological explanations. For this new explanatory attitude, a text is not primarily a message addressed to a specific range of readers and, in that sense, not a segment in a historical chain; inasmuch as it is a text, it is a kind of atemporal object, which has, so to speak, cut its ties from all historical development. The access to writing implies this overcoming of the historical process, the transfer of discourse to a sphere of ideality that allows an indefinite widening of the sphere of communication.

I must admit that I take this anti-historicist trend into account in my own efforts and that I agree with its main presupposition concerning the objectivity of meaning in general.

First, it is in agreement with the main concepts of this study: the semantic autonomy of written discourse and the self-contained existence of the literary work are ultimately grounded in the objectivity of meaning of oral discourse itself. Second, this anti-historicism is the implicit presupposition of the "explanatory" procedures applied by literary criticism and biblical criticism more or less under the influence of structuralism. Placed against the background of the dialectic between explanation and understanding or comprehension, the existential concept of distanciation receives an epistemological development. The text — objectified and dehistoricized — becomes the necessary mediation between writer and reader.

The existential concept of appropriation is no less enriched by the dialectic between explanation and understanding. Indeed, it must lose nothing of its existential force. To "make one's own" what was previously "foreign" remains the ultimate aim of all hermeneutics. Interpretation in its last stage wants to equalize, to render contemporaneous, to assimilate in the sense of making similar. This goal is achieved insofar as interpretation actualizes the meaning of the text for the present reader.

Appropriation remains the concept for the actualization of the meaning as addressed to somebody. Potentially a text is addressed to anyone who can read. Actually it is addressed to me, *hic et nunc*. Interpretation is completed as appropriation when reading yields something like an event, an event of discourse, which is an event in the present moment. As appropriation, interpretation becomes an event.

But the concept of appropriation is in need of a critical counterpart, which the concept of comprehension alone can bring forth. Without this epistemological complement, appropriation is in danger of being misconceived. This may happen in several ways.

According to the first misconception, appropriation appears as a return to the Romanticist claim to a "congenial" coincidence with the "genius" of the author. A return to the central analysis of the present essay is sufficient to prevent our accepting this hermeneutical prejudice. What is indeed to be understood — and consequently appropriated — in a text?

Not the intention of the author, which is supposed to be hidden behind the text; not the historical situation common to the author and his original readers; not the expectations or feelings of these original readers; not even their understanding of themselves as historical and cultural phenomena. What has to be appropriated is the meaning of the text itself, conceived in a dynamic way as the direction of thought opened up by the text. In other words, what has to be appropriated is nothing other than the power of disclosing a world that constitutes the reference of the text. In this way we are as far as possible from the Romanticist ideal of coinciding with a foreign psyche. If we may be said to coincide with anything, it is not the inner life of another ego, but the disclosure of a possible way of looking at things, which is the genuine referential power of the text.

92

This link between disclosure and appropriation is, to my mind, the cornerstone of a hermeneutic which would claim both to overcome the shortcomings of historicism and to remain faithful to the original intention of Schleiermacher's hermeneutics.

To understand an author better than he could understand himself is to display the power of disclosure implied in his discourse beyond the limited horizon of his own existential situation. The process of distanciation, of atemporalization, to which I connected the phase of *erklärung*, is the fundamental presupposition for this enlarging of the horizon of the text.

In this sense, appropriation has nothing to do with any kind of person to person appeal. It is instead close to what Hans-Georg Gadamer calls a fusion of horizons (*Horizonverschmelzung*): the world horizon of the reader is fused with the world horizon of the writer. And the ideality of the text is the mediating link in this process of horizon fusing.

According to a second misconception, the hermeneutical task would be ruled by the understanding of the original addressee of the text. This task as Gadamer has convincingly demonstrated is completely misconceived. The letters of Paul are no less addressed to me than to the Romans, the Galatians, the Corinthians, and the Ephesians. Only the dialogue has a "thou" whose identification precedes discourse. The meaning of a text is open to anyone who can read. The omnitemporality of the meaning is what opens it to unknown readers. Hence the historicity of reading is the counterpart of this specific omnitemporality; since the text has escaped its author and his situation, it has also escaped its original addressee. Henceforth it may provide itself with new readers. This widening of the range of readers is the consequence of the initial transgression of the first event into the universality of sense. In this sense, writing is the paradigmatic mediation between two word-events: a word-event engenders a new word-event under the condition of the overcoming of the event in the universality of the sense; this universality alone may generate new speech events.

According to a third misconception, the appropriation of the meaning of a text by an actual reader would place the interpretation under the empire of the finite capacities of understanding of this reader. This objection has often been raised against all brands of "existential" hermeneutics. It has been opposed to the Heideggerian concept of *Vorverständnis* and to the restatement of the "hermeneutical circle" by Bultmann. If we must "believe" in order to "understand," then there is no difference between pre-understanding and mere projection of our prejudices.

The English (and French) translation of *Aneignung* by appropriation reinforces this mistrust: Are we not putting the meaning of the text under the power of the subject who interprets it? This objection may be removed if we keep in mind that what is "made one's own" is not something mental, not the intention of another subject, presumably hidden behind the text, but the project of a world, the pro-position of a mode of being in the world that the text opens up in front of itself by means of its non-ostensive references. Far from saying that a subject already mastering his own way of being in the world projects the *a priori* of his self-understanding on the text and reads it into the text, I say that interpretation is the process by which disclosure of new modes of being — or if you prefer Wittgenstein to Heidegger, of new forms of life — gives to the subject a new capacity for knowing himself. If the reference of the text is the project of a world, then it is not the reader who primarily projects himself. The reader rather is enlarged in his capacity of self-projection by receiving a new mode of being from the text itself.

Appropriation, in this way, ceases to appear as a kind of possession, as a way of taking hold of things; instead it implies a moment of dispossession of the egoistic and narcissistic ego. This process of dispossessing is the work of the kind of universality and atemporality emphasized in explanatory procedures. And this universality in its turn is linked to the disclosing power of the text as distinct from any kind of ostensive reference. Only the interpretation that complies with the injunction of the text, that follows the "arrow" of the sense and that tries to think accordingly, initiates a new self-understanding. In this self-understanding, I would oppose the self, which proceeds from the understanding of the text, to the ego, which claims to precede it. It is the text, with its universal power of world disclosure, which gives a self to the ego.

REFERENCE NOTES

ESSAY I

[1] Ferdinand de Saussure, *Cours de linguistique générale* (Paris: Payot, 1971); English trans., by Wade Baskin, *Course in General Linguistics* (New York: McGraw-Hill, 1966).

[2] V. Propp, *Morphology of the Folktale* (Bloomington, Indiana: Indiana University Press, 1958).

[3] Edmund Husserl, *Logical Investigations*, trans. J. N. Findlay (London: Routledge & Kegan Paul, 1970), 2 vols.

[4] This point has been made forcefully and convincingly by Paul Grice. See his "Meaning," *Philosophical Review*, 66 (1957): 377-88; "Utterer's Meaning, Sentence-Meaning, and World-Meaning," *Foundations of Language*, 4 (August 1968): 225-45; "Utterer's Meaning and Intentions," *Philosophical Review*, 78 (1969): 147-77.

[5] John Searle, *Speech Acts: An Essay in the Philosophy of Language* (New York: Cambridge University Press, 1969).

[6] G. Frege, "On Sense and Reference," trans. Max Black, in *Translations from the Philosophical Writings of Gottlob Frege*, Peter Geach and Max Black (eds.) (Oxford: Basil Blackwell, 1970), pp. 56-78.

[7] P. F. Strawson, "On Referring," *Mind*, 59 (1950); 320-44. See also Bertrand Russell, "On Denoting," *Mind*, 14 (1905): 479-93; reprinted in *Logic and Knowledge: Essays 1901-1950* (London: George Allen & Unwin, 1956), pp. 39-56.

[8] Frege, op. cit., p. 61; see also p. 63.

ESSAY II

[1] Jacques Derrida, *La voix et le phénoméne* (Paris: Presses Universitaires de France, 1967); *L'écriture et la différence* (Paris: Seuil, 1967); *De la grammatologie* (Paris: Les Editions de Minuit, 1967); "La Mythologie blanche," *Rhétorique et philosophie*, *Poétique*, 5 (1955); reprinted in *Marges de la philosophie* (Paris: Les Editions de Minuit, 1972), pp. 247-324.

[2] In T. A. Sebeok (ed.), *Style in Language* (Cambridge: Massachusetts Institute of Technology Press, 1960), pp. 350-377.

³Martin Heidegger, *Being and Time*, trans. John Macquarrie & Edward Robinson (New York: Harper & Brothers, 1962).

⁴*Phaedrus*, 274e-277a.

⁵François Dagognet, *Ecriture et iconographie* (Paris: Vrin, 1973).

⁶For a discussion of this concept of distanciation in contemporary hermeneutics, see my article, "The Hermeneutical Function of Distanciation," *Philosophy Today*, 17:2 (Summer 1973): 129-41.

ESSAY III

¹*The Symbolism of Evil*, trans. Emerson Buchanan (New York: Harper & Row, 1967); *Freud and Philosophy: An Essay on Interpretation*, trans. Denis Savage (New Haven: Yale University Press, 1970).

²Monroe Beardsley, *Aesthetics* (New York: Harcourt, Brace and World, 1958), p. 134.

³*Poetics*, XXI, 4.

⁴See I. A. Richards, *The Philosophy of Rhetoric* (Oxford: Oxford University Press, 1936); Max Black, *Models and Metaphors* (Ithaca, New York: Cornell University Press, 1962); Monroe Beardsley, op. cit.; Idem., "Metaphor," *Encyclopedia of Philosophy*, Paul Edwards (ed.) (New York: Macmillan, 1967), vol. 5, pp. 284-89; Idem., "The Metaphorical Twist," *Philosophy and Phenomenological Research*, 22 (1962): 293-307; Colin Turbayne, *The Myth of Metaphor* (Columbia, South Carolina: University of South Carolina Press, 1970), rev. ed.; Philip Wheelwright, *The Burning Fountain* (Bloomington, Indiana: Indiana University Press, 1968), rev. ed.

⁵Jean Cohen, *Structure du langage poétique* (Paris: Flammarion, 1966).

⁶Time hath, my lord, a wallet at his back
Wherein he puts alms for oblivion,
A great-sized monster of ingratitude.
Those scraps are good deeds past, which are devoured
As fast as they are made, forgot as soon
As done.

"Troilus and Cressida," III, 3, 11. 145-50. Cited in Marcus B. Hester, *The Meaning of Poetic Metaphor* (The Hague: Mouton, 1967), p. 164.

[7]Rudolf Otto, *The Idea of the Holy: An Inquiry into the Non-Rational Factor in the Idea of the Divine and its Relation to the Rational*, trans. John W. Harvey (New York: Oxford University Press, 1958).

[8]Philip Wheelwright, op. cit.; *Metaphor and Reality* (Bloomington, Indiana: Indiana University Press, 1962).

[9]Mircea Eliade, *Patterns in Comparative Religion*, trans. Rosemary Sheed (Cleveland and New York: The World Publishing Company, 1958).

[10]Max Black, op. cit.

[11]Ian Ramsey, *Models and Mystery* (New York: Oxford University Press, 1964); *Models for Divine Activity* (London: S.C.M. Press, 1973); *Religious Language* (London: S.C.M. Press, 1957).

[12]See Essay I, note 6.

[13]Mary B. Hesse, *Models and Analogies in Science* (Notre Dame, Indiana: University of Notre Dame Press, 1966).

[14]Max Black, op. cit., p. 236.

[15]Ibid., p. 238.

ESSAY IV

[1]*Critique of Pure Reason*, trans. N. K. Smith (New York: St. Martin's Press, 1965), A314, B370, p. 310.

[2]E. D. Hirsch says very convincingly, "The act of understanding is at first a genial (or a mistaken) guess and there are no methods for making guesses, no rules for generating insights. The methodological activity of interpretation commences when we begin to test and criticize our guesses." *Validity in Interpretation* (New Haven: Yale University Press, 1967), p. 203.

[3]Ibid., pp. 164-207.

[4]Karp Popper, *The Logic of Scientific Discovery* (New York: Harper & Row, 1968).

[5]In this part of my essay I have largely drawn on materials borrowed from E. D. Hirsch. I am sufficiently indebted to his

point of view to say where I disagree with him. In spite of his insistance on the mute character of the text, he maintains that the aim of the interpretation is to recognize what the author meant. "All valid interpretation, of every sort, is founded on the re-cognition of what an author meant." (p. 126) In fact, however, the intention of the author is lost as a psychical event. Moreover, the intention of writing has no other expression than the verbal meaning of the text itself. Hence all information concerning the biography and the psychology of the author constitutes only a part of the total information which the logic of validation has to take into account. This information, as distinct from the text interpretation, is in no way normative as regards the task of interpretation.

[6]In *Structural Anthropology*, trans. Claire Jacobson and Brooke Grundfest Schoepf (Garden City, New York: Anchor Books, 1967) pp. 208-28.

[7]Ibid., pp. 206-7.

[8]Ibid., p. 207.

[9]Ibid., p. 212.

[10]Ibid.

[11]Ibid., p. 214.

[12]Lévi-Strauss seems to admit this, in spite of himself, when he writes, "If we keep in mind that mythical thought always progresses from the awareness of oppositions toward their resolution, the reason for these choices becomes clearer." (Ibid., p. 221.) And again, "the myth provides a kind of logical tool." (Ibid., p. 212.) In the background of the myth there is a question which is a highly meaningful one: "Is one born from one or from two?" Even formalized in this way, "Is the same born from the same or from the other?", the question expresses anxiety and agony regarding our origin.

[13]*Gesammelte Schriften*, vol. 5., pp. 317-38.

INDEX

Prepared by Larry Bouchard

tion; meaning, utterer's; speaking

Speaking, 16, 18 *passim*; *see also* discourse, spoken

Speech act, 14, 17, 18-19, 27; *see also* illocutionary act, locutionary act, perlocutionary act

Speech event, 10-13, 20, 22-23, 27, 93

Strawson, P. F., 20, 97 n. 7

Structural analysis, 82-88

Structuralism, 6; *see also* linguistics, structural model of; structural analysis

Subject, 10, *see also* predication

Symbol and symbolism, 45-46, 53-69, 78; and history of religions, 53-54; and poetics, *see* poetry; and psychoanalysis, 53-54, 57-59; linguistic and nonlinguistic, 53-54; nonsemantic moment of, 57-63; religious, 57-58; semantic moment of, 54-57

Text, 23, 25, 31-33, 35, 75-79, 91, 94-95; and appropriation, 92-93; and reference, 80-81, 87-88; fallacy of absolute text, 30; literary, 78, 81; semantic autonomy of, 25, 29-31, 33, 35, 43, 71, 75, 91; sense of, 87; *see also* discourse, written

Trope, 47, 79, 51

Truth, 20, 66, 28; and falsity, 1-2; in Plato, 1-2

Turbayne, Colin, 49, 98 n.4

Understanding, 22, 37, 71-88; as guess, 74, 75-79; 80, 86, 99 n.6; *see also* explanation and understanding, dialectic of

Validation, 76, 78-80, 99-100 n.5

Voice, 39, 42

Wheelwright, Phillip, 49, 64-65, 98 n.4, 99 n.8

Wimsatt, W. K., 30

Wisdom, in Plato, 38-39

Wittgenstein, Ludwig, 6, 94

Word, 48-50; and meaning, 5; and sentence, 7; in Plato and Aristotle, 1; lexical value of, 50-51; word-event, 22, 93

Wordsworth, William, 55

Work and practice, 33; *see also* discourse as work, literary work

World, 20, 22, 36-37, 80, 88, 92; *see also* being in the world

Writer, 35; horizon of, 93; *see also* writing

Writing, 23, 25-44, 72-75; *see also* discourse, written; language, written

THIS BOOK WAS DESIGNED BY
JUDITH M. OELFKE
SET IN TEN-POINT PALATINO
BY FORT WORTH LINOTYPING COMPANY
AND PRINTED ON WARREN'S OLDE STYLE WOVE
BY MOTHERAL PRINTING COMPANY